SGML

*An Author's Guide to
the Standard Generalized
Markup Language*

SGML

An Author's Guide to the Standard Generalized Markup Language

Martin Bryan

Quorum Technical Services Ltd

Addison-Wesley Publishing Company

Wokingham, England · Reading, Massachusetts
Menlo Park, California · New York · Don Mills,
Ontario · Amsterdam · Bonn · Sydney · Singapore
Tokyo · Madrid · San Juan

The examples in this book have been included for their instructional value. They have been tested with care but are not guaranteed for any particular purpose. The publisher does not offer any warranties or representations, nor does it accept any liabilities with respect to the examples.

Many of the designations used by manufacturers and sellers to distinguish their products are claimed as trademarks. Addison-Wesley has made every attempt to supply trademark information about manufacturers and their products mentioned in this book. A list of the trademark designations and their owners appears on p. xviii.

Cover designed by Crayon Design of Henley-on-Thames and printed by the Riverside Printing Co. (Reading) Ltd.
Typeset by Quorum Technical Services Ltd, Cheltenham, UK.
Printed and bound in Great Britain by MacKays of Chatham PLC, Chatham, Kent.

First printed 1988.

British Library Cataloguing in Publication Data
Bryan, Martin
    SGML: an author's guide to the Standard Generalized Markup Language
    1. Publishing. Applications of computer systems
    I. Title
    070.5'028'5

ISBN 0–201–17535–5

Library of Congress Cataloging in Publication Data
Bryan, Martin.
    SGML: an author's guide to the standard generalized markup language.

    Bibliography: p.
    Includes index.
    1. SGML (Computer program language)   I. Title.
QA76.73.S44B79   1988   005   88–24193
ISBN 0–201–17535–5 (pbk.)

Foreword

The ability to use words freely and effectively is one of the most important assets our society has to offer. Nowadays it is a truism that the Gutenberg revolution set in hand the trends that led to the industrial revolution and to the development of democratic organizations, so that the past 500 years can be accurately designated as the Print Age.

It is also widely recognized that we are now in the grip of a new revolution – the release from the drudgery of calculating data and of searching for the right information – brought about by electronics, and the whole new accessibility of information and the spur to thinking that results. We are now on the verge of obtaining a large part of the information we need in our lives from different forms of electronic access.

Electronic information may not replace books, newspapers and periodicals, and other forms of 'conventional' information, as the traditional media have valuable qualities to offer as well. But it does mean that the information and ideas in the conventional media will also need to be available in many other forms. If this is to happen in a way that provides maximum possible access, a degree of ordering of information and the acceptance of conventions as to how it is identified and described are essential.

SGML – Standard Generalized Markup Language – is one of the most important of those conventions. It is the internationally recognized standard for identifying text, enabling the different parts of the text's structure to be identified and described so that each part can be handled and accessed as appropriate. As such, it is a development of major significance in information management. As with all such developments, the work that has gone into it is colossal and complex, but the demands on the user are relatively simple and straightforward.

This book sets out those structures and rules in a way that is designed for the professional people – authors, publishers and other handlers of text – who need to use it. It is an invaluable guide to what is now an indispensible part of publishing technique.

Clive Bradley
Chief Executive
The Publishers Association
July 1988

Preface

Information is the key to success in our fiercely competitive world: without it, most businesses and governments would collapse. As the pace of life increases, the ability to communicate information speedily is becoming an increasingly important part of the success or failure of most organizations.

The past few decades have seen an explosion in the field of data communication. Satellites now make it possible to receive television pictures, radio broadcasts or telephone calls from almost anywhere on the planet without noticeable delay. What is happening now on the Tokyo Stock Market will affect the London Stock Market in a few minutes; Washington's assessment of an international situation will be known in the Kremlin faster than it will be known in Philadelphia. The very survival of our planet depends on the ability of governments to communicate with each other.

Yet, one area of information transfer has so far been little affected by these new communication techniques. For bulk dissemination of information, the printed page still provides the fastest and most cost-effective means of communication. Millions of printed pages are produced every day, many destined to be briefly scanned by no more than one person.

While the printed page is still the best way to communicate bulk information, it takes time to prepare and, more importantly, to move from its source to its destination. If we are to speed up the communication of printed material we need to reduce both the time taken to prepare the printed page and the time required to transfer it to its destination.

Early in the 1980s the International Standards Organization (ISO) took the bold step of undertaking the preparation and publication of a suite of standards designed to facilitate the speedy and efficient transfer of a wide range of documents between computer-based systems. One of the first products of the working groups set up to implement this policy was a new international standard for the markup of electronically prepared documents. Called the Standard Generalized Markup Language (SGML), this standard was designed to formalize the way in which documents are prepared. It does this not by laying down a set of rules saying 'this is how you should code documents', but by formalizing a set of rules that can be used by document originators to say 'this is how I have coded my document'.

Defining the structure of a document is not, however, the sole purpose of SGML. It also tackles the problem of how to transfer documents from computer to computer. It does this by providing an internationally agreed reference point that may be used as a starting point by document originators when telling the document's recipients about the coding techniques used in the preparation of the document. The techniques provided in the standard allow computers with different character sets and coding schemes to communicate in an internationally agreed way. Once this is possible, the barriers between computer systems can be removed and information can, at last, flow freely around the world.

The importance of SGML can be seen from two, related, facts. First, and perhaps more importantly, SGML was being used by both the United States Department of Defense and the Office of Official Publications of the European Communities, amongst others, *before* the standard was formally approved by the ISO. Secondly, within two months of the standard's publication, ISO announced that it was the fastest selling standard they had ever produced, having already outsold the ten-year-old specification for the FORTRAN programming language.

Perhaps the best illustration of the role of SGML in international communications is the story of the production of the final printed proof of the standard. Only hours after making the final editorial changes to the SGML-coded standard at his home in California, the standard's editor, Charles Goldfarb, boarded a plane bound for Geneva. On checking in at his hotel a few hours later, he was handed a package containing printed copies of the standard which had, during his journey, been transmitted, courtesy of IBM and CERN, to ISO's Geneva headquarters. By the end of the century such occurrences will be commonplace as SGML permits the rapid dissemination of printed information among users.

Structure and contents

Those of us who were first introduced to SGML by looking at the official standard soon became aware that this is not the ideal way to learn the language. By their very nature, standards are extremely formal and tend to be rather terse. The SGML standard was slightly better than most standards in this respect in that it did contain a number of annexes that tried to explain how the SGML could be used, but these were, in themselves, only a taster of the real power of SGML and, like the rest of the standard, presumed a certain amount of background knowledge on the part of the reader.

In writing this book I have tried, as far as possible, to avoid any need for previous knowledge on the part of readers, though I do presume that they have had some experience of the process of writing reports or books. I have also had to presume some familiarity with the role of word processors for preparing text electronically, though I have kept this to a minimum. In the first chapter I have, therefore, attempted to set the scene by explaining how electronically prepared text has been coded in the past, and how SGML differs from these traditional approaches to the problems of marking up text.

Rather than start by launching straight into the rules for using SGML, I have chosen to look in Chapter 2 at how authors can analyse the structure of documents, and to show how similar logical elements occur in many different types of document.

I have chosen a rather controversial starting point for my detailed description of SGML in Chapter 3, in that I have elected to give an overview of what is known in SGML parlance as the reference concrete syntax. Don't let this rather technical chapter put you off – it is simply setting the scene by explaining some of the facilities that are available in SGML. Do not expect to understand everything in this chapter straight away – a fuller explanation appears in Chapters 10 and 11. For new readers I suggest a quick skim of this chapter to get a flavour of how SGML works, and then down to the essence of SGML, which is covered in Chapters 4 to 6.

In Chapter 4, I describe how SGML entities are created and used. For many authors this will be the only part of SGML they will have to declare for themselves, as the rest will be done by their publishers, or someone who has had more time to study SGML. But even if you do not intend to go too deeply into the whys and wherefores of SGML I suggest you read Chapters 5 and 6 as well to get a feel for how elements and their attributes can be declared and used.

The later chapters of the book are more for the specialist, or someone using a fully featured parser, as they describe optional features and the way in which SGML systems can be configured or optimized. Chapter 7 discusses the ways in which the amount of markup that needs to be added to the file can be reduced by letting the program infer the presence of the relevant markup tag from the information it has been given about the structure of the document, while Chapter 8 looks at some advanced techniques that are available with some SGML-based products.

Chapter 9 will be of particular interest to people who are likely to use the same piece of information in a number of ways, for example as an article in a journal and a book, or in a reference book and a computer database, as it describes how different document structures can be marked up concurrently, with the various structures being linked together automatically when required. Like Chapters 10 and 11, which show how individual SGML systems can be configured using the SGML declaration, this chapter will be easier to read if you have some previous knowledge of how computers work. For a more detailed description of how an SGML-coded document is processed you should read Chapter 12, which again is somewhat technical, but should be understandable by laymen as well as computing specialists.

The three appendices to the main text should not be overlooked. In the first, I have attempted to show how the techniques described in the body of the book can be combined in such a way as to facilitate the setting of multilingual books, while Appendix B shows how characters not normally available on a computer keyboard can be requested within an SGML-coded document. In the final appendix, I have illustrated how SGML can be used to prepare a fairly complex textbook. To do this I have provided a complete document type declaration for this book, and a brief description of how each of the declared elements should be used.

Typographic conventions

To help you find your way around the terminology associated with SGML, a number of typographical conventions have been adopted throughout this book.

As each new term is introduced it is printed in a **bold typeface** so that its importance is clear. Where a particular term is explained in more than one chapter, and the term is indexed to both chapters, it is printed in bold in both chapters. Certain SGML abbreviations are also printed in this face for emphasis.

Computer printout examples, and tags entered within the text, have been printed in a special fixed width face (e.g. `<tag>`) for clarity. Within the text, such characters normally represent the codes entered by users.

Because of the complexity of SGML, it has sometimes been necessary to adopt the convention of mentioning side issues in the form of notes to the main text.

NOTE: As in ISO 8879, notes are distinguished from the main text by typographic conventions, as shown here.

Acknowledgements

This book would not have been written without the patience of many members of Working Group 8 of the International Standards Organization's Technical Subcommittee for Text and Office Systems (TC97/SC18). When I first joined this working group they had already published a draft international standard, and were busy updating this to reflect the comments they had received. Despite this at times harrowing experience, they were patient enough to re-iterate some of their earlier discussions so that the 'newcomer' could understand the basic concepts behind the formal constructs that define SGML.

In particular, I must acknowledge my debt to Charles Goldfarb, the standard's editor and chief guru, who spent many hours overcoming my initial misunderstandings and answering 'that goddamned Limey's' many detailed questions. Without Charles there would be no SGML, and this book could never have been written.

My introduction to SGML was through Joan Smith, Britain's ambassador for SGML. As well as explaining the politics of international standards work to me, Joan has spent many hours introducing me to people who are active in the SGML field. Many of the examples presented in this book have been culled, perhaps subconsciously, from these contacts and her experience.

My thanks also go to Robert Stutely of HMSO, David Barron of Southampton University and Lynne Price of Hewlett-Packard for reviewing my text and contributing so many useful suggestions for its improvement.

In preparing the example DTD for Appendix C, it was of invaluable assistance to be able to run the DTD through the two SGML parsers currently on the market. My thanks go to Jean-Pierre Gaspart of SOBEMAP in Brussels and Jeff Graubart-Cervone of Datalogics in Chicago for making this possible.

I am also grateful to Taylor & Francis, and Professor Margoninski, for permission to use part of a paper from *Contemporary Physics* (volume 27, issue 3) for Figure 2.5, to the Folio Society for permission to reproduce the title page of their 1972 edition of *Robinson Crusoe* by Daniel Defoe (available to members only) as Figure 2.11, and to Linotype Ltd for allowing me to reproduce extracts from their *Photosetting Terminology* booklet in Figure 2.13.

Lastly, my thanks must go to my patient family, who have seen little of me these last few months. Gill's welcome cups of black coffee, coupled with David's supply of biscuits, kept me going through many hours of absorbing writing.

Martin Bryan
Cheltenham
June 1988

Contents

Background to SGML

The spread of word processors and other computer-assisted text preparation devices has led to an increased awareness of the advantages of being able to transfer documents from one user to another in electronic form. Although there are a number of ways the text of a document can be transferred from machine to machine, few of the currently available techniques allow information about the way the document is to be presented on the page to be transferred with the text. Sometimes such presentation details cannot be transferred because they are coded in a machine-specific manner; sometimes the information cannot be transferred because it is too closely linked to the physical appearance of the document. Whatever the reason, the absence of such vital clues to the 'structure' of a document can lead to a degeneration of the transmitted message.

It is the structure of a document that controls the roles assigned to the various elements of the text. For example, a simple document may consist of a series of headings, each followed by one or more paragraphs of text, while a more complicated document may have a number of different levels of heading, and contain different types of text, including such elements as indented quotations, lists, figures, notes, and so on.

Normally the structure of information is indicated by differences in the appearance, or the positioning, of the various elements that make up the document. But it is important to realize that it is not appearance itself that conveys structural information. The role of a heading in a typed report is no different from that in a printed one, though it may be printed in the same typeface as the main text while the printed version may be in a different, possibly larger, typeface. Irrespective of appearance, the role of a heading is the same in any document – to help the user to identify the following text.

If inter-machine communication of electronically prepared information is to be possible on a world-wide basis, it is essential that a standard method of defining document structures be adopted by authors. A single, standardized structure is not, however, practicable as this would place unacceptable restrictions on authors. At the same time, readers do not always want to receive information in the same form. For example, some readers find it easier to read larger type sizes while others may wish to adopt a smaller format so that they can carry the document around in a pocket. Similarly, some readers may only need to see part of the text, such as an abstract of the contents, while others need access to the whole document. Any technique that meets the requirements of both authors and readers must, therefore, define a document's structure in a way that allows the author's intentions to be conveyed to the reader while also allowing the reader to retain control over the use to which the information is put.

It was in an attempt to overcome such problems that the Text and Office Systems Subcommittee of the International Standards Organization (ISO) prepared ISO 8879: *Information processing – Text and office systems – Standard Generalized Markup Language (SGML)*. Designed to allow structural information to be added to a document by embedding user-defined sequences of text characters within the text stream, SGML allows information providers to pass details of a document's structure from machine to machine in a controlled manner.

1.1   The publishing cycle

As Figure 1.1 illustrates, a number of stages are involved in the preparation of any report, paper or book. Often the author will sketch out ideas first, in the form of a set of notes or a provisional list of contents. Then, where dictation of copy to an assistant is not practicable, the author must write or type a first draft of the text.

Normally this first draft will need to be revised before it can be sent for publication. Until recently, revision involved the retyping of large parts of the document. With the advent of word processors, however, the copy correction cycle has been greatly speeded up because alterations can be made to the text without rekeying unaltered sections.

When the text has been completed to the author's satisfaction it may be submitted to a specialist publisher for publication. The publisher will normally send the manuscript to referees for comment. One or more of

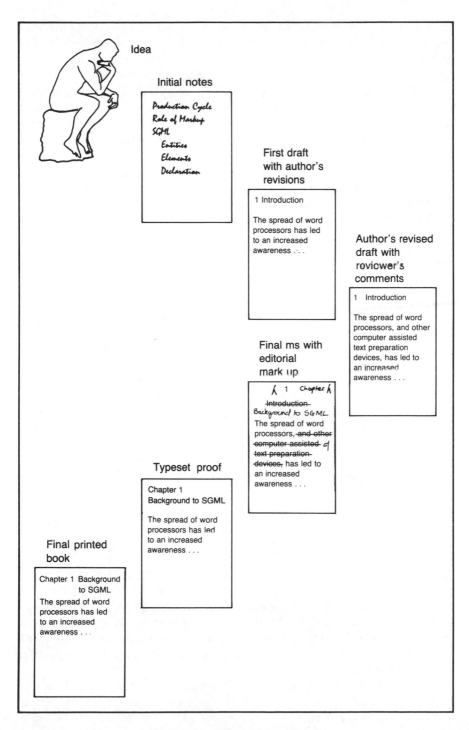

Figure 1.1   The publishing cycle.

these review stages may be necessary, with further changes being made to the text at each, before the document can be accepted for publication. The manuscript is then released to a copy editor who prepares the text for the typesetter by marking corrections to the style and detail.

Defining the appearance (format) of a published document is often the role of another specialist, called a typographic designer. In consultation with the editor, the designer sketches out a basic design and the manuscript is *marked up* with details of what typefaces and sizes should be used for the printed text, headings and other features. The designer will also supply guidelines for how the text should be made up into pages, detailing such features as the dimensions of the text area and the position and contents of the running heads and feet, as well as specifying how illustrations should be positioned on the page, and where colour may be used in text or illustrations.

When the manuscript has been marked up with corrections and design information, it is ready to be sent to a specialist typesetter for production in a high-quality typeset form. Traditionally, text has been retyped yet again at this stage, the typesetter adding the instructions that allow the appropriate typefaces and layout to appear on the typeset pages. The text then passes through various proof stages and when the final corrections have been completed to the editor's satisfaction it is given to a printer who prepares the final printed document.

As rekeying text is both time consuming and prone to error, there are many advantages in cutting down the number of times a document needs to be rekeyed during its production. One way of doing this is to pass the text between users in electronic form. This is not, however, always as straightforward as it might at first seem.

Many users of word processors do not have facilities for transmitting text via a telephone line and, unfortunately, the disks used to store data on word processors come in a variety of shapes and sizes. Even when the same type of disk is used by two machines, the way the data is stored by one program will probably differ from that used by another, so preventing the programs from reading each other's data.

Solving the problems of getting data from machine to machine is not the whole answer, however. Even where transmission of text from one word processor to another is possible, problems can occur because the instructions used to lay out (format) the document on the word processor at one end of the link differ from those being used by the program at the other end. This is especially likely to be true if the machines are used with different types of output device, for example, an advanced laser typesetter rather than a line printer.

The SGML standard (ISO 8879) provides a standardized way of coding structural information that is independent of the input and output device being used. Designed to be embedded within the document's text, SGML-coded structural information can remain with the text through all the stages of the publication cycle, reducing the need to recode the text at each production stage.

1.2   *The role of markup*

Markup is the term used to describe codes added to electronically prepared text to define the structure of the text or the format in which it is to appear. (Markup is spelt as one word when applied to electronically prepared copy to distinguish it from the traditional form of editorial or design mark up, which is handwritten onto the copy.) Any device that stores text for later recall and output uses some form of markup, though this may not be apparent to the user. Sometimes the points at which markup has been added to a document can only be identified by a change of typeface, or by the addition of a special marker to the text. Wherever a change of features is found on a printed or displayed document it can be presumed that some form of markup has been used.

Markup can take many forms. It can be visible or hidden, machine-specific or generic (of general application). It can take the form of special symbols or normal text, or be a combination of both. It can be entered on a special command line, as a separate line within the text or simply as a string of characters within the body of the text.

In many cases some form of delimiter will be used to identify the start and, optionally, end of a markup instruction. Where instructions are entered in special command lines the delimiters may not be apparent, but they will need to be present in the stored text if the program is to be able to identify instructions when the text is recalled after storage.

From the author's point of view it is an unfortunate fact of life that each word processor seems to have its own set of markup instructions. This means that authors wanting to switch to more up-to-date programs may have to undertake the costly and time consuming exercise of learning a new set of markup instructions before they can use the new program. The changeover may also require the recoding of existing text before it can be used with the new program.

Markup may also need to be changed when a new output device is added to existing equipment. If the markup instructions used by the software are machine-specific, text coded for use with one type of output device (e.g. a line printer) can only be output on a different type of device (e.g. a laser printer) if that device can accept the same codes. Normally this will mean that only a limited set of instructions can be used on the more complex device. If, however, general-purpose (generic) markup is used to code text, it becomes a relatively simple task to change the output coding associated with each type of text identified by the generic coding to make full use of the new facilities.

1.3   Types of markup ————————————————————————

There are two basic types of electronic markup instructions currently in common use:

(1)   specific markup instructions, and
(2)   generalized markup instructions.

Specific markup instructions describe the format of a document by use of instructions that are specific to the programs used to generate or output the text. Such instructions normally have immediate effect on the appearance of the text. They can either affect the appearance of the characters (e.g. by selecting bold or italic text) or the position of characters or lines (e.g. by adjusting indent, margin or spacing values).

Generalized markup instructions identify the purpose of the following text rather than its physical appearance. They indicate the basic structure of the document by marking where the various components making up the text begin and end. Typically generalized markup instructions identify such features as headings, highlighted words, quoted text, etc. When the text is output the relevant program can then decide how it should present each of these structural elements to the reader.

The differences between these two basic types of markup are explained in Sections 1.3.1 and 1.3.2. (Readers already familiar with the differences might like to jump to Section 1.4 at this point.)

1.3.1   Specific markup

Specific markup instructions can take many forms. Perhaps the best known are the Print Control Commands used by the Wordstar word processor program and its many look-alikes. Wordstar Print Control Commands consist of a special control code (displayed as ˆ) followed by a letter identifying the function required (e.g. ʙ for Bold).

There are three basic types of Wordstar Print Control Commands:

(1)   instructions that affect only the next character (e.g. ˆʜ = overprint),
(2)   instructions that affect all subsequent characters (e.g. ˆs = underline), and
(3)   instructions that affect the layout of the page (e.g. ˆo = non-break space).

Although these three basic types of markup instruction occur in most markup languages, the way in which they are used can differ from program to program. For example:

- instructions affecting only one character may appear before or after the character concerned;
- instructions that affect all subsequent characters may stay in force until the instruction is entered a second time, or may be cancelled by entry of a different instruction; and
- instructions that affect the layout of the page may have immediate effect, or may only be actioned when the next line or page is started.

Some markup instructions need to be qualified by the addition of one or more numbers or other parameters. As such instructions can be of variable length, two basic techniques are used to identify them:

(1)   placing them on a separate line, and

(2)   enclosing them within special **delimiter** characters.

Wordstar Dot Commands are an example of text formatting instructions that are placed on separate lines. A Wordstar Dot Command consists of a dot (period) followed by two letters identifying the command required and the relevant parameter(s). (The initial dot always appears in the first column on the screen.) Parameters may be variable length numbers or one of a predefined set of control words (e.g. ON or OFF).

A typical Wordstar document might start:

```
.PL 66
.MT 6
.MB 9
.LH 12
.UJ ON
^A^BChapter 1
INTRODUCTION^B
The spread of word processors ...
```

These instructions tell the program that the page length is 11 inches (.PL66 = 66 lines of the standard ⅙ inch spacing), with a top margin of 1 inch (.MT6 = 6 lines), a bottom margin of 1½ inches (.MB9 = 9 lines). Once the size of the page has been defined, the spacing between lines of text is declared by requesting a line height (.LH) of $^{12}/_{48}$ (i.e. 1½ line spacing). After switching on the microjustification facility (.UJ ON) the first of the Print Control Commands requests that the character pitch be changed to 12 characters per inch (^A = Elite) while the second (^B) requests the bold version of the typeface. This bolder face remains in force until the end of the heading, where it is switched off by a second ^B sequence.

Where delimiters are used to identify the end of instructions, more than one instruction can be entered on a line. For example, a user of the PeachText word processor would enter the equivalent markup instructions between a single pair of backslashes, in the form:

```
\PL66,TM6,BM9,SP+1,JUSTC,CPI12,BF@\@Chapter 1
INTRODUCTION@
The spread of word processors ...
```

Like most word processing packages, PeachText has its own set of mnemonics for markup instructions. While the page length and top and bottom margin instructions can be quickly associated with their Wordstar equivalents, other instructions are not so readily equated.

In PeachText, line spacing is defined in terms of the standard 1/6 inch line space rather than the 48ths of an inch used by Wordstar. In this case the requirement for half a line of extra spacing between lines is indicated by the addition of the plus sign between the SP command identifier and the number 1 indicating single line spacing.

For the microjustification request, PeachText's JUSTC instruction differs from its Wordstar equivalent (.UJ ON) in that it is switched off by entry of a different instruction (LEFT) rather than by using a different parameter for the same instruction (Wordstar's .UJ OFF).

A similar difference in basic philosophy occurs for character pitch, though in this case it is Wordstar that uses two different instructions for one PeachText instruction. In PeachText character pitch is controlled by a characters per inch (CPI) instruction that uses a numeric parameter; in contrast Wordstar provides different Print Control Commands for each change of pitch.

In the example, the last instruction within the delimited PeachText instruction set illustrates another common form of variation between word processing packages. Rather than use a special command sequence to indicate commonly used features, such as boldface and underlining, PeachText allows users to assign an otherwise little used character to the task of identifying the start and end of the section of text to be affected. In the above example the @ sign has been declared as the boldface indicator by including a special instruction (BF@) at the end of the delimited sequence. The @ is then used immediately after the instruction sequence to activate the boldface function for the next two lines.

Some word processors go even further than this and use display characteristics, such as colour or intensity, to identify text that is to be printed in a bolder face. They may also be able to display italic text as slanted characters, underlined text or reversed characters to avoid having to include specific markup instructions within the text. In all cases, however, some form of markup instruction needs to be stored with the text to inform the program that the change of format has occurred.

Another commonly used technique is for the markup instructions to be hidden from view, either temporarily or permanently. Temporarily hidden instructions can normally be redisplayed by pressing a special key or entering a specific command. Systems with permanently hidden markup instructions normally arrange for them to be displayed in a special area of the screen whenever the cursor is positioned on the first character to which they apply.

It will be seen from the above examples that interrelating the instructions used by different word processing programs is not straight-forward. To convert a file created using one package to a form that can be understood by another may require the entries to be redefined using different mnemonics in a different sequence. Sometimes the translation process involves splitting up instructions; other cases require instructions to be concatenated. The units of measurement may also change from program to program, with the consequent need for appropriate conversion facilities.

The situation becomes even more complicated when different output devices are being used. In the above examples the conversion of the page length and margin instructions is relatively straightforward as both programs define page lengths in terms of standard typewriter line spacing ($\frac{1}{6}$ inch). However, the recent availability of laser printers that can output a range of type sizes has extended the number of inter-line spacing instructions required, and made it necessary to change the units of measurement used. For instance, the popular PostScript page description language used by many laser printers allows users to define the number of parts per inch by which line and character positions should be altered. Typically values of 72 or above are used to provide high-resolution output. To make full use of such facilities a word processor should be able to use a number of different units of measurement when specifying parameters associated with type height or width.

Another complication arises when text is being sent to the very high-resolution typesetters used by printers. Traditionally, printers have used a special unit of measurement, called a **point**, to define the size of type. Unfortunately the point is not an exact fraction of an inch, though it can be thought of as approximately $\frac{1}{72}$ inch. The situation is further complicated by the fact that there are two variants of the point: a European version (the Didot point) that is slightly over $\frac{1}{72}$ inch, and an Anglo-American one which is just under $\frac{1}{72}$ inch!

Printers also use a larger unit of measurement called the **pica**, which is equal to 12 points. For the Anglo-American point the pica is nearly equivalent to the $\frac{1}{6}$ inch used for normal line spacing on a line printer or typewriter, but on mainland Europe the similarity is not so good, as the Cicero pica is 4.51 mm long, while $\frac{1}{6}$ inch is only 4.233 mm.

A typesetter might define the parameters for the simple page described above as:

```
■pl66■
■dg101■lf720■⌐
■dg108■lf1080■⌐
■nj■■p180■■sl240■■f3■Chapter 7►
INTRODUCTION►
■lf180■■p100■■sl120■■f1■The spread of word processors . . .
```

Note how, for this typesetting system, each instruction has been given its own delimiters, whereas the PeachText delimited instructions were separated by commas within one set of delimiters. Also, the measurements have been expressed in points and ⅛ of a point (e.g. LF720 = line feed of 72 points = 1 inch). In the above example the page depth has again been defined as 66 lines (of the program's initial inter-line spacing value in this case), and the text is to be justified (NJ), but major differences have taken place in the other instructions.

In the Pagitek system used for the above example, text printed in the margins at the top and bottom of the page can be altered within the job so that any running headlines or folios to be output within the margin area can be redefined as required. To allow for this flexibility, the contents of headings are stored as 'formats' by the program. Different formats are available for the top and bottom of odd and even pages, and for the text that precedes the page number and that which follows it. In the above example only two of these formats have been declared (DG101 and DG108) to simplify the comparison with Wordstar and PeachText, but in practice eight formats would be defined, some containing lines of text and others instructions.

Instead of line spacing and character spacing values being specified once at the start of the text, typeset text will normally respecify the type size and line spacing for each element of the text. For instance, the chapter title in the above example has been set in 18 point type with a line spacing of 24 points (P180, SL240) while the text has been set in 10 point type with a line spacing of 12 points (P100, SL120). Note that these instructions can appear in any order as the preceding instruction stays in force until it is superseded by the entry of the same instruction with a different parameter.

Instead of having to leave a number of blank lines wherever a gap is required in the printed text, typesetting systems allow space to be requested in any valid combination of units. In the above example, for instance, an extra 18 points of space has been added between the centred heading and the text (LF180).

Another major change of emphasis in the typesetting version of the coding is the way in which bold type is requested. In this case a special **font** of type has been requested for the heading (F3 = font 3). This font contains a complete set of bold letters, numbers and punctuation symbols, which will be used for all characters until another font is requested. To switch off bold the standard text font (font 1 in this instance) is requested immediately in front of the text.

One final point to note about the instructions used for typesetting is the inclusion of a special centring symbol (◓) at the end of the title lines. This symbol temporarily overrides the preceding justification instruction (ɴᴊ) by instructing the program to centre the contents of the current line. (On word processors the centring instruction is often placed at the start of the line.)

Many markup languages allow instructions which are specific to a particular output device to be inserted in the text. For example, the PeachText ᴏᴜᴛ instruction can be used to output any desired sequence of codes, the relevant codes being entered as a set of decimal numbers followed by commas (e.g. \ᴏᴜᴛ27,37,1\ to select the user-defined character set on an Epson printer). Such codes must be redefined before text can be output on a different device. Similarly, a new set of codes may be required if the book is to be output in a different format.

1.3.2   *Generalized markup*

To avoid having to respecify markup instructions whenever a change of format or output device is required, the concept of a generalized markup language was postulated by Goldfarb *et al.* (1970). The idea is based on two premises:

(1)   markup should describe a document's structure rather than its physical characteristics, and
(2)   markup should be rigorous so that it can be unambiguously understood by a program or a human interpreter.

The techniques postulated by Goldfarb *et al.* formed the basis of IBM's Document Composition Facility Generalized Markup Language (DCF GML), which has been extensively used for over a decade.

A typical chapter in a GML coded document might start:

```
:book.
:body.
:h1.INTRODUCTION
:p.The spread of word processors ...
```

This version differs from the earlier, specifically coded, examples in a number of important respects. Firstly, it starts with two instructions identifying the type of document being prepared (a book) and the section of the document in which the text is to be placed (the main body of the book). These instructions clearly show the structure of the document and define the role of the following text.

The next point to notice is the absence of the line containing 'Chapter 1' in the coded text. The fact that the text has not been entered by the author does not imply that it will not appear in the printed document – it merely reflects the fact that, with generic coding, the format and numbering of chapter openings (identified by the :h1. instruction) is automatically taken care of by the text formatting program. This has a number of advantages, apart from the rather obvious one of reducing the amount of keying the author needs to do. Firstly, the sequence in which chapters are output can be changed without the author having to renumber each one. Secondly, the appearance of the chapter heading (e.g. whether or not the word 'Chapter' is present, and whether numbers are to be printed using arabic or roman numerals, or simply as words) can be decided by the publisher rather than the author.

The final point to note about the GML coded version of the chapter opening is that it has not been necessary to switch off the bold effect at the end of the heading. The text formatting program knows that, when it reaches the instruction to start a paragraph of text (:p.), it should return to the standard form of text, after applying any necessary paragraph indents. As the IBM formatting program also knows where to position the first paragraph of a chapter, the author does not needed to enter any specific spacing instructions at this point either.

Another form of generic coding is that used by Xerox's Ventura Publisher text formatting program. Typically, the start of our example chapter might be stored in a Ventura text file as

```
@CHAPTER HEAD = Chapter 1<R>INTRODUCTION
The spread of word processors ...
```

In this case the associated formatting information has been stored in a separate 'style file' rather than within the document's definition. The @CHAPTER HEAD= instruction is equivalent to :h1. in the GML coded document, but here the name is more explicit. (It also consists of more than one word – a feature not allowed in many coding schemes, including SGML.) To permit the entry of more than one line of information in a heading, Ventura allows the insertion of a line break instruction (<R>) within the heading, which in this case must also contain any text that precedes the chapter title. (In Ventura the heading consists of all the text up to the next carriage return code.)

Note that no coding has been placed at the start of the first paragraph of text in the above example. This is because the Ventura program assumes that any text not preceded by a specific instruction is to be output in the standard body text size. (This technique of impliable instructions is also used in SGML.)

Another text formatting language based on the concept of generalized markup is the Scribe document specification language devised by Reid (1980) at Carnegie-Mellon University. In this case the language specification has a distinctive 'computer-flavour', many of the concepts being based on computer programming techniques. For example, a section within a chapter might start:

```
@Heading(Command Definition)
A @i[command] consists of:
@Begin(enumerate)
an initial delimiter
an identifier
one or more parameters
a closing delimiter.
@End(enumerate)
It can be seen ...
```

In this short example three different types of coding occur:

(1) gencralized coding, identifying the purpose of the following bracketed text (@Heading);

(2) typographical coding (@i) identifying the typographic appearance (italic in this case) of the text within square brackets; and

(3) programming syntax, instructing the program to number the items in the list entered between the @Begin and @End statements.

After formatting, the printed result might appear as:

Command Definition

A *command* consists of:

1) an initial delimiter

2) an identifier

3) one or more parameters

4) a closing delimiter.

It can be seen ...

Note how the items in the list have been numbered by the formatting program, which has also added space above and below the list in response to the @Begin and @End statements.

Even more computer oriented is the TeX procedural formatting language developed by Knuth at Stanford University (Knuth, 1987).

Designed specifically for the preparation of complex textbooks with a large mathematical content, the language allows complicated procedures to be built up from a set of basic building blocks. Once suitable procedures have been defined a complicated formula such as:

$$y_i^\alpha(j_k(\varphi)_0) = \frac{\partial \, ^\alpha y_i \circ \varphi}{\partial x^\alpha}(0).$$

can be entered on the author's word processor as:

```
$$y^\alpha_i(j_k(\varphi)_0)=
        {\partial\,^\alpha y_i\circ\varphi\over\partial x^\alpha}(0).$$
```

In this case $ is used to indicate the start and end of a displayed mathematical formula containing italic letters (all letters within the delimiters are set in italic), Greek characters (\alpha and \varphi), special symbols (\circ and \partial), and special procedures for building mathematical formulas (ˆ ,\, _ and \over) and delimiters ({}) for these procedures.

While such procedurally oriented languages do allow a great deal of freedom for the author, they also impose a heavy overhead – the need to learn the language in some detail before it can be used efficiently. The transference of such procedurally coded text from computer to computer is also a problem as the procedures used by both machines should be identical. Although this can be achieved by passing the underlying Pascal code between users, experience has shown that TEX programs cannot always be simply transferred between machines.

1.4   The role of SGML

Leading on from his work on GML, Dr Goldfarb (Goldfarb *et al.*, 1970) has further developed the concepts of generalized markup under the auspices of the ISO. After a number of years of work the formal definition of Standard Generalized Markup Language (SGML) was adopted as ISO Standard 8879 in October 1986.

NOTE: In July 1988 a few minor modifications were made to the standard. At the same time some paragraphs of text were added to the standard to clarify points that had not always been interpreted correctly by early users of the standard. These modifications have been incorporated into this book.

SGML differs from GML in many minor areas, and one or two major ones. In particular, it provides for the use of different types of delimiters for instructions identifying the beginning and end of an element, and allows alternative sets of delimiters to be defined. It also formalizes the information needed to format the document in such a way that it can be held with the text of the document rather than being stored in a separate style file.

SGML operates at a number of levels, depending on the features required. The standard provides facilities for defining:

- the structure of the document,

- the characters transmitted in a document,

- text that is to be used more than once in the document,

- externally created information that is to be incorporated into the text,

- special techniques used in marking up the text (tag minimization, etc.), and

- the way in which text is to be processed.

Each SGML-coded document is split into a number of clearly identifiable **elements**, each containing either text or further levels of embedded subelements. Where the element is made up of a number of levels of subelement, the lowest level in each structure always contains either text or some other form of printable information (e.g. artwork). The position and appearance of each element on the printed page is resolved as part of a process referred to as 'formatting the document'. (This process is not described in ISO 8879 as it is system dependent.) As the document is formatted, a set of procedures maps each element identifier in the text to the appropriate formatting instructions, performing any necessary paging, indexing or cross-referencing operations as each element is processed.

Defining the structure of the document is not, however, the sole purpose of SGML. Before documents can be transferred between word processors it is essential that the numeric values (codes) transmitted between machines have clearly defined meanings. ISO 8879, therefore, also defines a **reference concrete syntax** which provides a common code set for document communication. Based on the codes defined in ISO 646 (International Standards Organization, 1983), this ASCII-compatible character set defines the codes used in English for alphanumeric characters, a range of punctuation symbols and four special control characters (space, tab and the line/record start and end codes). This internationally agreed reference point can be quickly modified for use with other Latin-based languages, and for most other languages.

The SGML reference concrete syntax can be used to specify any character set required to produce a document. Once the required character set has been defined at the start of the document, users can use their normal coding scheme within the text.

The structure of an SGML-coded document, and the SGML features used in its preparation, are formally defined at the start of a document in a set of **declarations**. Normally authors will use or modify a set of SGML declarations previously defined by a *document designer*. These predefined declarations describe a set of markup instructions, known as **tags**, that can be used to identify the start or end of the logical elements used within the text. The start of each element is normally marked by a **start-tag**, an **end-tag** being used to mark the end of any element whose end cannot otherwise be determined unambiguously from the structure of the document.

NOTE: The formal definitions provided in ISO 8879 for the declaration of SGML structures and facilities are principally intended to be used by specialists known as 'document designers' or 'document analysts'. A document designer is not necessarily a designer in the visual sense of the word – he is a specialist in identifying the structure of a document. After analysing the document's structure, the document designer can prepare the declarations passed from computer to computer at the start of each SGML-coded document.

Separate sets of markup tags will normally be used for different applications, though in many cases the same basic tags will be used in each set. For instance, a paragraph of text forms a logical element of a letter, report, paper or book, and can be allocated the same markup tag in each type of document (e.g. ‹p›). By identifying such areas of commonality, document designers can reduce the number of tags that need to be remembered by authors.

Where necessary, SGML markup tags can be qualified by **attributes**. Attributes are used within SGML to identify uniquely specific tags, to cross-refer to elements identified by unique identifiers, to recall externally stored data or to indicate the role of the associated element. They can also allow users to control the way in which text is formatted.

To reduce the amount of repetitive keying within a document, SGML allows users to define **entities** (pieces of text) that are required within the text. For example, a general entity called SGML could be used to enter the phrase 'Standard Generalized Markup Language'. To prevent entities becoming confused with other text (e.g. the abbreviation SGML) references to entities are enclosed in their own delimiters, giving them the form &SGML;. The contents of each entity can either be declared within the document in which it is to be used in (local entities) or can be stored in an external file that is recalled as the document is formatted (external entities).

Because many documents consist of text written by a number of authors, SGML allows externally stored **subdocuments** to be merged with the main document. Such subdocuments can have their own set of markup tags. Like other external entities they are added to the overall document by entry of an **entity reference** at an appropriate point in the file.

Special **character references** can be used within SGML to request characters that are not included in the word processor's character set. This technique allows characters that would normally be left as blank spaces in the manuscript, for manual entry by the author, to be defined unambiguously within the body of the text, thus ensuring that they are not accidentally lost from the published book.

At a slightly more advanced level, SGML provides ways of declaring certain short cuts to document markup. Most of these short cuts are designed to reduce the amount of markup that needs to be entered in text. Markup can be reduced by:

- omitting markup tags that can be implied by the use of other tags
- using special short forms of tags, and
- using shorthand references to identify entities that contain markup tags.

These techniques make it possible to reduce the amount of markup entered at the keyboard to an absolute minimum.

Taken together, the techniques provided by SGML allow anyone keying text for publication to:

- define the structure of a document in a way that is independent of the physical appearance of the text, and
- define the characters used in preparing a document in a way that can be unambiguously understood by any person or computer receiving it.

1.5   *Using SGML* ────────────────────────────

SGML can be used at a number of levels, depending on the equipment available and the experience of the user. At the time of writing few programs are capable of providing all the facilities defined in the newly prepared SGML standard. Future SGML-based word processors will probably contain facilities that allow users to:

- automatically define the elements of a document (using either tree diagrams or a set of prompts to define the relationships between elements),

- associate text with the defined elements in a structured way,
- process the marked up text into printable documents,
- receive and interpret SGML-coded documents, and
- transmit internally stored documents in SGML-coded form.

Users may hardly notice the difference between their current word processors and such advanced SGML-based programs. Both may use the same sequences of key depressions to enter and format the text. The main difference will be in the way the text is perceived. Instead of defining a heading as a line of emboldened text it will now be identified as a special type of element (selected from a list of permissible elements). The physical format of the element will be defined, possibly at a later stage, using a special menu or form, each logical element having its own set of parameters (style sheet).

Users of advanced SGML-based programs should also be able to generate automatically (declare) a custom-built set of tags by use of a relatively simple procedure during which the program prompts for the information required. By starting at the top of a tree of elements and working down the various levels, previously defined sets of tags can be quickly modified to provide the facilities required for any new type of document.

The definition of entities will probably occur automatically in an SGML-based word processor. The techniques used will be similar to those currently used to define and save blocks of text, but instead of being able to store only a limited number of blocks of text for later recall *before the machine is switched off*, SGML-based word processors will add the defined text to the set of entity declarations at the start of the document, from where it can be recalled whenever required.

Many existing word processors can be used to prepare SGML-coded documents with the minimum of fuss. All that is required is the ability to strip out any internal coding while converting a marked up document to the ASCII format used by SGML. (Many word processing programs are supplied with this capability as a standard feature.)

Where a word processor provides facilities for converting its internal coding scheme to a different format, specific tags may not need to be entered for many of the elements in an SGML document. Provided that an internal word processor code has a unique use, it can be converted to the appropriate SGML tag before output, retaining its internal use until it is recoded for onward transmission.

Existing word processors will only be able to format SGML-coded documents if they have a program that is capable of converting SGML markup into a form that can be understood by the formatting program available on the word processor (or printer). At first sight this may seem to be a major restriction, but you will quickly find that documents with embedded SGML coding are easy to read, the coding assisting interpretation of the text so that little conversion is required before the document is proofed. Where the coding does intrude into the reading of a document it is normally a simple process to remove all markup intructions from the text before output.

Where fully formatted documents need to be produced from SGML-coded text for external review, conversion programs such as Pagikey† can be used to change SGML markup instructions to the coding used by many different types of output device. While such programs only provide a temporary solution for users of non-SGML-based word processors they do, at least, allow SGML-coded documents to be produced on many existing word processors.

References

Goldfarb, C.F., Mosher, E.J. and Peterson, T.I. (1970). 'An Online System For Integrated Text Processing', *Proceedings of the American Society for Information Science*, **7**, 147–150.

International Standards Organization (1983), *Information processing – 7-bit coded character set for information interchange* (ISO 646), Geneva: ISO.

International Standards Organization (1986), *Information Processing – Text and Office Systems – Standard Generalized Markup Language (SGML)* (ISO 8879), Geneva: ISO.

A number of other ISO Standards are mentioned at various places in the text. The issues covered in these are all discussed in ISO 8879, and all are cross-referenced in Clause 3 of that Standard.

Knuth, D.E. (1984), *The T$_E$Xbook*, Reading, Mass: Addison-Wesley.

Reid, B.K. (1980), 'Scribe: A Document Specification Language and its Compiler', PhD Thesis, Computer Science Department, Carnegie–Mellon University. (Also described in *Proceedings of the International Conference on Research and Trends in Documentation Preparation Systems,* 1981, 59–62.)

† A PC-based code conversion program supplied by Pagitek Ltd, Tewkesbury, Gloucestershire, UK.

2

SGML Documents

An SGML document is a self-contained unit that can be sent, either electronically or in printed form, to other users. There are no size constraints to SGML documents – they can range in size from a one line memo or letter to a multivolume set such as the *Encyclopaedia Britannica*.

SGML documents consist of a number of interrelated **elements**. Each element contains characters which serve a specific purpose. A particular character or word can be a member of more than one element. For instance, a word can be part of a highlighted phrase within a paragraph that forms part of a section in a chapter, and so on.

More than one set of elements can be used in a document. For example, separate element sets can be used to describe the logical and physical (layout) characteristics of the printed text. Within the layout structure, a word is part of a block of text that is to be positioned on a particular page, rather than part of a paragraph or heading.

Each SGML document starts with a **document type definition (DTD)** which defines the structure of the document in terms of the elements it contains. Within the DTD each type of element found in the document is given a name (a **generic identifier**) by which it can be recognized. When placed within special markup delimiter characters, these generic identifiers form the **tags** used to identify the start and end of each element.

To allow large documents to be generated efficiently, SGML documents can be built up from a series of **subdocuments**, each subdocument being a document in its own right. Authors can opt to process each subdocument separately, or can create a special document that links the various subdocuments together in the required order. Subdocuments can be transferred to other computers either individually or as part of the main document.

To use SGML effectively authors should, therefore, be able to recognize:

- what constitutes an SGML document
- the structure of a document, and
- how the physical appearance (format) of a document relates to its contents.

Each of these concepts will be explained in this chapter.

2.1 Types of document

From the author's point of view the most important thing about a document is that it is a unit that can be passed to another user. How big this unit is will depend on circumstances. For example, if an author has contracted to supply certain chapters of a book to his publisher on specific dates he will probably find it easiest to treat each chapter as an individual document, whereas if the contract calls for the delivery of the completed manuscript in only one batch the whole book can be considered as the document, individual parts or chapters forming subdocuments within the main document as necessary.

Another consideration in determining what constitutes a document may be the storage capacity of the word processor program being used. Many programs, for example, restrict the maximum size of individual files – often to a size that is smaller than that of individual chapters. In this case, the contents of each file may need to be considered as a subdocument of a chapter, which itself is a subdocument of a master document that combines the chapters into a book.

One word of warning, however: where SGML's advanced reference identifier facilities are being used to cross-reference figures, headings and other features automatically, care must be taken to ensure that all references fall within the same document; cross-references cannot be made between a document and its subdocuments, or between two subdocuments. Where SGML's cross-reference features are required, the computer doing the final processing must be large enough to hold the complete document (or at least that section containing the cross-references).

Parts of documents that need separate processing should be treated as separate SGML documents. For instance, complex tables may require special document type definitions, or features not used elsewhere in the document. By processing such sections separately the complexity of the DTD used for the main document can be reduced. Where preprocessed graphics are being incorporated into an SGML document by reference to external files, however, it is not necessary to create a separate subdocu ment for the processed data, as a simple external entity reference is sufficient to call in the necessary non-SGML information.

In many applications creating a document can be thought of as filling in a preprinted form. For example, a memo will normally be output on a sheet of paper that has been preprinted with the name of the company and special fields for the entry of the names of the sender and recipient, and possibly the subject and date of the memo. These preprinted fields do not, as such, constitute part of the document. *For preprinted forms the document is simply the text added to the preprinted sheet.*

This technique for reducing what needs to be typed into an SGML document can be especially useful where standard text is being used. It can be used, for instance, when generating tables with predefined headings and rules, or for preparing mailshot letters where the text is predefined but names, addresses and certain other details differ from letter to letter. By incorporating the standard text into the definition of the document's structure the amount of keyboarding required to enter an SGML document can be significantly reduced.

2.2   The structures of documents

While the structures of documents can vary in complexity from the simple format of a memo or letter to the complex format of a technical manual or a textbook, the concepts used to identify the structure of each document remain the same. One advantage of this is that the elements used to generate a simple memo or letter can also be used within a more complex document such as a textbook.

2.2.1   The structure of a memo

Figure 2.1 shows the structure of a simple memo. Each element of the structure has been ringed and allocated an identifier. In the case of the first three elements the identifier is the preprinted name of the field (from, to and date). The subject element can be considered as an optional heading to the memo. The memo, in this case, consists of a single paragraph of text, identified by the name para.

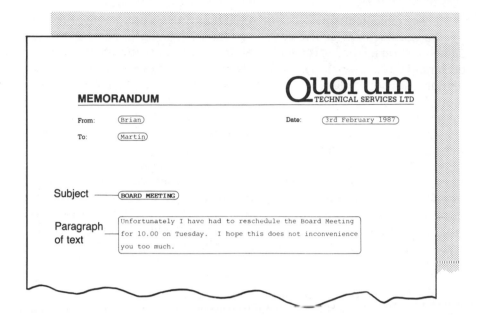

Figure 2.1   The structure of a memo.

In SGML this memo could be marked up as:

```
<!DOCTYPE memo PUBLIC "-//Quorum//DTD Memo//EN">
<memo>
<from>Brian
<to>Martin
<date>3rd February 1987
<subject>Board Meeting
<para>Unfortunately I have had to reschedule the board
meeting for 10.00 on Tuesday. I hope this does not
inconvenience you too much.
</memo>
```

The first line of the coded text contains a **document type declaration** identifying the document type definition (DTD) required for the document. In this example the definition required is one declared previously for the production of English (EN) language memos for Quorum. (A document type declaration is required at the start of each document. In many cases this declaration will be generated automatically as part of the file conversion/ transmission process to avoid the need for manual entry.)

The document type declaration (and any other declarations required for the document) is immediately followed by an SGML start-tag whose name (generic identifier) is identical to the one used for the document type declaration (e.g. ‹memo›). This compulsory **base document element** is the markup instruction that activates the document type declaration.

The elements following the ‹memo› base document element are fairly self-explanatory. The start of each element is identified by a **start-tag** consisting of the element's name entered between a pair of **delimiters** (in this case angle brackets).

Note how the date element has not been entered in the sequence that might be expected from its position on the printed memo. This illustrates one of the powers of SGML – it is based on the logical structure of the contents rather than their position or appearance. In many cases this will allow entries to be made in a more convenient sequence, with the formatting program sorting out exactly where each element should be placed.

The end of the coded memo is identified by an **end-tag** indicating that the memo has been completed. The tag consists of the name of the base document element between a pair of special end-tag delimiters (‹/ and ›). In many simple documents this final end-tag will be the only one identifying the end of an element, all other end-tags being omitted to reduce the amount of embedded coding required. (In general, end-tags may be omitted whenever no ambiguity would occur from their omission.)

2.2.2   The structure of a letter

Figure 2.2 shows the structure of a typical letter. This letter could be coded as:

```
<!DOCTYPE letter PUBLIC "-//Quorum//DTD Letter//EN">
<letter>
<ref>MB/TW/2674
<date>30th January 1987
<address>Mrs G Burton
GB Translations
29 Oldbury Road
Churchdown
Glos GL3 2PU
<dear>Gill
<p>Could you please provide us with a quote for
translating the enclosed technical manual from German.
<p>I should warn you that this manual covers a slightly
different subject from the others you have tackled for
us, and many of the examples are in French and Russian
```

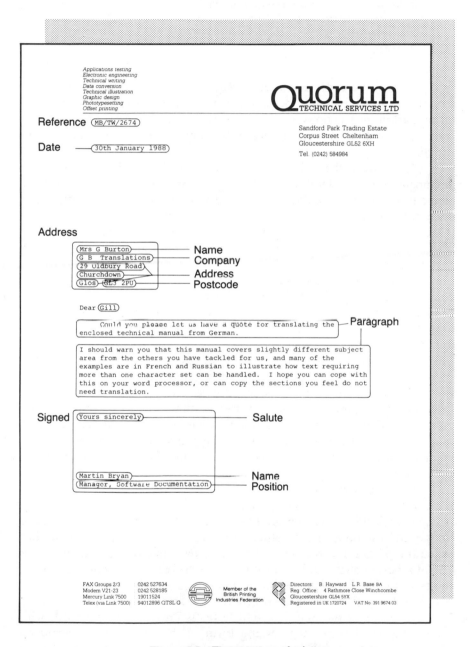

Applications testing
Electronic engineering
Technical writing
Data conversion
Technical illustration
Graphic design
Phototypesetting
Offset printing

Quorum
TECHNICAL SERVICES LTD

Reference (MB/TW/2674)

Sandford Park Trading Estate
Corpus Street Cheltenham
Gloucestershire GL52 6XH

Date ———(30th January 1988)

Tel. (0242) 584984

Address

(Mrs G Burton) ———— Name
(G B Translations) ———— Company
(29 Oldbury Road) —— Address
(Churchdown) ——— Postcode
(Glos) (GL3 2PU)

Dear (Gill)

(Could you please let us have a quote for translating the) ——Paragraph
enclosed technical manual from German.

I should warn you that this manual covers slightly different subject
area from the others you have tackled for us, and many of the
examples are in French and Russian to illustrate how text requiring
more than one character set can be handled. I hope you can cope with
this on your word processor, or can copy the sections you feel do not
need translation.

Signed (Yours sincerely) ———————— Salute

(Martin Bryan) ——————— Name
(Manager, Software Documentation) —— Position

FAX Groups 2/3   0242 527634
Modem V21-23   0242 528185   Member of the
Mercury Link 7500   19011524   British Printing
Telex (via Link 7500) 94012896 QTSL G   Industries Federation

Directors   B. Hayward   L.R. Base BA
Reg. Office   4 Rathmore Close Winchcombe
Gloucestershire GL54 5YX
Registered in UK 1720724   VAT No. 391 9674 03

Figure 2.2   The structure of a letter.

```
to illustrate how text requiring more than one character
set can be handled. I hope you can cope with this on
your word processor, or can copy the sections you feel
do not need translation.
<signed name=mtb>
</letter>
```

As is to be expected, a letter requires more elements to define its structure than a memo but, perhaps surprisingly, it does not contain many more markup instructions within the text, despite its greater length. This is made possible by the use of implied tags and short references, as will be explained shortly.

The start of the coded letter is similar to that of the memo, with a document type declaration requesting a previously declared set of element and entity definitions, followed immediately by the initial base document element, in this case ‹letter›, that activates the declared set. (Once again this element is the only one requiring an explicit end-tag.) The next two elements contain the document's unique reference number and its date.

Figure 2.2 suggests that the address element is altogether more complicated. Each address consists of a number of lines, each of which can have a specific purpose. It is here that some care needs to be taken in identifying clearly the true structure of the document, rather than its apparent structure.

The apparent structure of an address is that it starts with the recipient's name, possibly followed by a company name. This is then followed by one or more lines of address information, which may be followed by a postcode. But beware: if the markup is simply being entered to produce a printed letter there is nothing to be gained, and much to be lost, by treating the name, company and postcode as separate elements of the document where this information is not used elsewhere in the document.

In the coded example above, the various elements of the address have not been identified individually. To reduce the amount of markup needed, the address has simply been declared as comprising a series of lines of information, with no other structure. (The document designer has asked the program to recognize the end of each line of the address as the end of a nested element, but this fact is not visible to the typist.) By using the power of SGML the amount of markup required to code the address is reduced to a single start-tag preceding the first line.

The rest of the SGML-coded letter is fairly straightforward, with ‹dear› being used as the tag for the form of the recipient's name to be placed after the word 'Dear' at the top of the letter and, in this case, ‹p› being used to identify the start of each paragraph of the text.

As is the case in Figure 2.2, the formatting program may treat two paragraph tags differently, depending on where they occur in the document. Often the first paragraph of a letter will be indented while other paragraphs will be set full out with a blank line of space identifying the paragraph break. Whereas most current word processing programs would expect the typist to remember to indent the first paragraph manually, such features can be taken care of automatically by SGML's text formatting procedures. All the operator needs to do is to identify the start of the logical element called a paragraph so that the program can apply the relevant house rules to produce the final letter.

Where a special key has been assigned to the end of paragraph function, the typist may not need to enter a special tag at the start of each paragraph because the program will be able to use the code generated by this key to recognize where new paragraphs start. In such cases, entry of SGML-coded letters can be similar to typing them on a typewriter, until you come to the signature at the end of the letter.

The `<signed>` tag in the coded letter illustrates another SGML feature – the use of **attributes** to qualify a tag. In this case, entry of the writer's initials is all that is needed to tell the program:

- the form of address to be used ('Yours sincerely'),
- the space to be left for the signature (which could be added automatically by a laser printer),
- the printed version of the writer's name, and
- any supplementary details to be added to the name (such as the author's position).

To change to a less formal style of address, another attribute could be attached to the tag so that it reads `<signed type=informal name=mtb>`. This could produce an ending of the form:

```
Thanks



Martin
```

As will be seen in following chapters, attributes can be extremely powerful. They are especially useful wherever a choice exists as they can provide users of SGML with the equivalent of a whole series of nested `IF...THEN...ELSE...` programming statements, reducing the need to declare special procedures for each situation.

2.2.3 The structure of a report

Figure 2.3 shows the start of a typical report, each element of the structure once again being ringed for clarity. The report could be marked up in SGML form as:

```
<!DOCTYPE report PUBLIC "-//Quorum//DTD Report//EN">
<report>
<title>The Advantages of SGML
<author>Martin Bryan
<p>SGML provides a standardized technique for marking up
electronically prepared copy that does not presume any
typographic knowledge on the part of users. It can be
applied by almost any author/editor to code virtually
any type of book.
<p>SGML defines<li number=alpha>
<it>the structure of the document
<it>the characters to be used in the document
<it>text entities that are to be used more than once in
the document
<it>externally stored information that is to be
incorporated into the text
<it>special techniques used to markup text
<it>the way text is to be processed.</li>
<h1>The Structure of a Document
<p>The <hp1>structure</hp1> of a document can be thought
of in terms of a series of nested <ix>elements</ix>, the
start and end of each element being at some clearly
definable point in the text.
<h2>The Structure of a Memo
<p>The memo shown in Figure 2.1 of <cit>SGML:
An Author's Guide to the Standard Generalized Markup Language</cit>
shows how the structure of a memo can be
thought of as<li>
<it>a "From" line
<it>one or more "To" lines
<it>a "Date" line
<it>an optional subject line
<it>one or more paragraphs of text.</li>
```

The first two elements of the report (title and author) have been given fairly self-explanatory identifiers, as is normally the case for little-used tags that might not otherwise be remembered. Because the other tags tend to be used more than once in the document, they have all been reduced to mnemonic form, the mnemonics ranging in size from 1–3 characters, depending on the frequency with which they are likely to be used. For

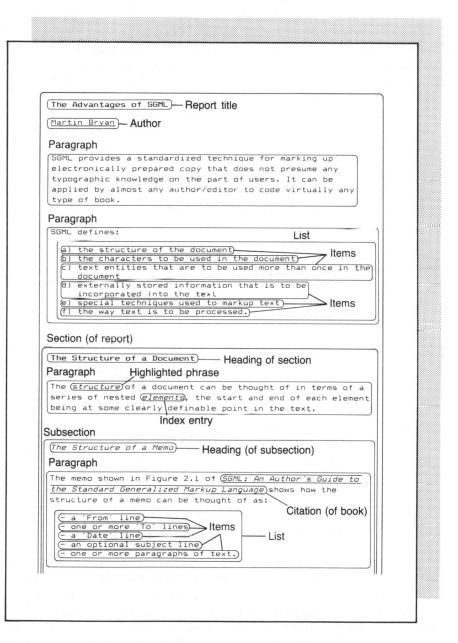

The Advantages of SGML — Report title

Martin Bryan — Author

Paragraph

SGML provides a standardized technique for marking up
electronically prepared copy that does not presume any
typographic knowledge on the part of users. It can be
applied by almost any author/editor to code virtually any
type of book.

Paragraph

SGML defines: List
a) the structure of the document
b) the characters to be used in the document   Items
c) text entities that are to be used more than once in the
   document
d) externally stored information that is to be
   incorporated into the text
e) special techniques used to markup text   Items
f) the way text is to be processed.

Section (of report)

The Structure of a Document — Heading of section
Paragraph   Highlighted phrase

The *structure* of a document can be thought of in terms of a
series of nested *elements*, the start and end of each element
being at some clearly definable point in the text.
                 Index entry
Subsection

The Structure of a Memo — Heading (of subsection)
Paragraph

The memo shown in Figure 2.1 of *SGML: An Author's Guide to
the Standard Generalized Markup Language* shows how the
structure of a memo can be thought of as:
                                Citation (of book)
- a 'From' line
- one or more 'To' lines   Items
- a 'Date' line   List
- an optional subject line
- one or more paragraphs of text.

Figure 2.3 The structure of a report.

example, the mnemonic it has been adopted, in this example, as a shorthand form of the word 'item'.

As in the previous example, the start of each paragraph of text is identified by ‹p›. (This time, though, the format of the first paragraph of text is the same as that of subsequent paragraphs.) For a report, however, the paragraph element can also contain a number of embedded elements (identifying lists, highlighted phrases, index entries, etc.), making the overall structure of the document much more complex.

Another structuring method that is used within reports is that of sections (divisions) of text. Such sections are normally readily identifiable because they have headings explaining their purpose. More than one level of such heading may apply, as illustrated in the example. The number of different types of headings and the use to which they are put varies according to the purpose of the report. A very complex report, like a book, could be split into a number of parts, each containing one or more chapters (main sections) which are further subdivided into other headed sections.

In Figure 2.3 two types of text division are shown, identified by bold and italic headings, respectively. These can be thought of as section and subsection headings. As the headings are a sufficient marker to the start of these divisions, their presence is indicated in the coded text by the tags, beginning with the letter h, identifying the start of each heading.

Rather than spell out the purpose of each division in its tag's name, a special SGML concept can be used to divide the text – the concept of levels (referred to in SGML parlance as **rank**). When this optional SGML concept is used, a number is added to the end of a tag to identify the level at which it is applied. In the example, ‹h1› indicates the first level of text division while ‹h2› is used for the second level.

NOTE: Numbers do not necessarily identify the use of the rank feature. They can be used in any generic identifier (except as the first character) as an indication of level, even where the rank feature is not being used. Often, however, their use in such identifiers has the same purpose as the rank number of a ranked element, so users of tag sets defined by document designers can normally take a number suffix on a tag as an indication of nesting level.

In the coded version of the report shown above, only one tag appears at the start of each new level, though Figure 2.3 indicates that two elements start at this point. This illustrates another SGML feature – the ability to omit tags whose presence can be implied by the program. If this feature was not used, two tags would need to be entered before each heading, one to identify the start of a new division within the text (e.g. ‹d1›), and another to flag the heading of the division (e.g. ‹h1›). However, because the presence of a *compulsory* heading can be *inferred* at the start of a new division, only the first of the tags is needed in practice. (One problem of using this feature is that it is not easy to associate a text division identification tag such as ‹d1› with a heading, so in practice the two elements will normally be renamed as ‹h1› and ‹h1t› so that the visible tag can have the form that is easiest for the end user to associate with the more visible implied element.)

Where the optional rank feature of SGML has been switched on, ranked elements can been used in ranked groups. Within each group, embedded ranked elements are considered to be at the current rank level unless specifically defined as having a different level. This means that once the rank level has been established for one of the grouped elements (typically the heading, e.g. ‹h2›), nested elements from the same group will be allocated the same suffix. This facility can be used to make a ‹p› tag into a ‹p2› tag after a second level heading.

Because SGML programs can distinguish between the paragraphs at the start of the sample report (which can be thought of as at rank level 0) and those under level 1 and 2 headings, however, any special formatting requirements, such as indented paragraphs or initial letters, can be added automatically as the text is formatted for output, even if the rank feature has not been used.

Another point to note about the SGML coding used for the text in Figure 2.3 is the fact that each of the four elements of the document printed in italics has been coded differently. The advantages of separate coding for the heading, which could end up being set in a different typeface or size, are fairly clear, but the reason for coding the other three italicized phrases differently may not immediately be obvious.

If you look at the wording of text, you can see that the roles of these italicized words differ. The first italicized word is simply a **highlighted phrase** (tagged by ‹hp1› and ‹/hp1›), which in this case happens to have been printed in italic. (The designer could equally well have asked for such words to appear in small capital letters or another typeface.) The second italicized word appears, at first sight, to have exactly the same function as its predecessor but there is one important difference – this word also has to be included in the index. To indicate this, the word has been flagged by tags identifying the start and end of an **index entry** (‹ix› and ‹/ix›) rather than those identifying a particular style of highlighted phrase.

The last item of embedded italicized text identifies a book that has been cited in the text. As the publisher may request that such **citations** be expanded to form a bibliography (which may result in their being replaced by cross-references to the bibliography) yet another pair of tags has been used to identify the italicized phrase as a citation (‹cit› and ‹/cit›).

It is important to notice that end-tags have been entered for each of these embedded elements. End-tags are compulsory wherever the end of an element occurs at a point which is not immediately followed by the start-tag of another element. An end-tag has the same name (generic identifier) as the start-tag used to identify the beginning of the embedded element, but in this case the delimiter used to identify the end-tag differs from that used for the start-tag. (In many cases, as here, the end-tag will be distinguished from the associated start-tag by the addition of a slash (/) immediately in front of the name.)

Another form of embedded element shown in Figure 2.3 is a **list**. The start of the list is identified by the ‹li› start-tag, which also marks the point where the program is to output the colon required by the publisher to indicate the start of a list. As with the other embedded items, an end-tag is used to identify the end of a list. Actually, in this example, the ‹/li› end-tag is not really necessary because end-tags are only compulsory for lists that occur in the middle of other elements; that is, where the list is immediately followed by more of the current paragraph's text or where one list is embedded within another.

Each list is made up of a number of **items**. Each item can, if required, be numbered or otherwise identified on output. In Figure 2.3 the items in the first list have been identified by individual letters, while those in the second list are simply preceded by dashes. This is achieved by the addition of a number=alpha attribute to the first list tag to specify that items in the list are to be 'numbered' alphabetically, whereas the second ‹li› tag contains no attributes, invoking the default style for the item identifier at the start of its embedded items. (The styles applied depend on how the SGML program has been set up. There are no predefined styles associated with SGML.)

Looking carefully at the coded text will show that the letters used to identify each item have not been specified by the author – they have been added by the program as the text has been formatted for output. Besides reducing the amount of keying required, this also means that a new item can be added to the list without having to renumber all the entries.

Where items in a list are referred to elsewhere in the document, renumbering of individual items can prove to be a trap for the unwary. Fortunately, SGML has provided a neat solution to this problem. Any element can be assigned an attribute that provides a unique identifier to specific occurrences of that element. If a list item is given such an attribute, reference can be made to the item by entry of a tag containing a special cross-reference attribute at the appropriate point in the text. For example, if the tag for the fourth item in the first list shown in Figure 2.3 is entered as ‹it id="external"› it could be cross-referred to within the coded text as:

    ... as shown in ‹itref refid="external"›, the ...

The program would check the page and number of the item being referred to, which it could then output in the form:

    ... as shown in item d) on page 24, the ...

If the list is extended or repositioned on another page, the program will automatically adjust the reference when it reaches the cross-reference point.

The first three entries of the second list contain another type of embedded element, a piece of text within quotes. Such quoted text needs to be specially identified as a separate element within an SGML document so that high-quality output devices, such as typesetters, can use different symbols for opening and closing quotations. (Word processors normally use the same symbol at both ends of the quoted text.)

One problem that can occur with quoted text is that some publishers prefer to use double quotes for speech or quoted text, while others prefer to use single quotes. Fortunately, one of the strengths of SGML is its ability to leave decisions such as the preferred form of quotation until just before the document is output, but to do this the quoted text must be appropriately tagged.

While tags such as ‹q› and ‹/q› could be specifically entered by the typist, this can be time consuming and the tags can detract from the readability of the text. To reduce the need for such explicit coding, the SGML **short reference** option described in Chapter 4 can be used to identify quoted text.

The SGML short reference facility associates entities, and through them element tags, with specific characters or strings of characters in the text. For example, the first quotation symbol in each list item in Figure 2.3 can be associated with an entity whose contents are the start-tag for a quotation (‹q›); and the second with the equivalent end-tag (‹/q›).

Authors who prefer to use single quotes rather than double quotes to identify quoted text can, however, run into problems if an apostrophe is also required within the quoted text. To overcome this problem, SGML allows users to declare a **short reference map** which can define a different set of short reference characters for use within the quoted text. This facility allows an apostrophe within a paragraph of text to be associated with the start of a quotation if it is immediately preceded by a space, bracket or markup tag, while within the quotation the apostrophe is only recognized as the end-tag for a quotation if it is immediately followed by a space, bracket or punctuation symbol.

NOTE: A fuller explanation of this powerful facility is given in Appendix A.

2.2.4 The structure of scientific papers

Figure 2.4 illustrates the structure of a simple scientific paper. As with the report in Figure 2.3, the basic text consists of a title element, an author element, introductory paragraphs of text and two levels of heading, each with associated text paragraphs. The fact that the title and author

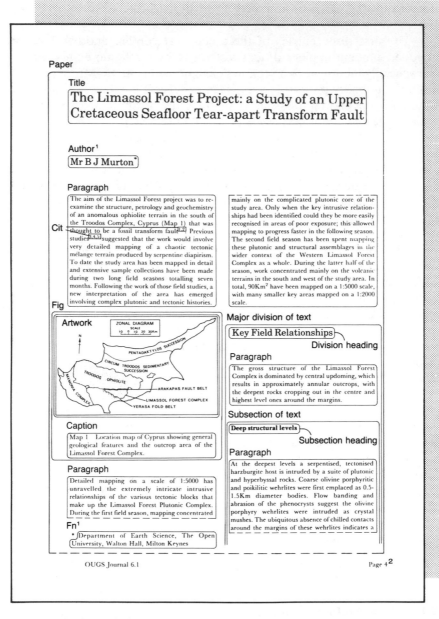

Paper

Title

The Limassol Forest Project: a Study of an Upper Cretaceous Seafloor Tear-apart Transform Fault

Author[1]

Mr B J Murton[*]

Paragraph

Cit — The aim of the Limassol Forest project was to re-examine the structure, petrology and geochemistry of an anomalous ophiolite terrain in the south of the Troodos Complex, Cyprus (Map 1) that was thought to be a fossil transform fault[1,2]. Previous studies[3,4,5] suggested that the work would involve very detailed mapping of a chaotic tectonic mélange terrain produced by serpentine diapirism. To date the study area has been mapped in detail and extensive sample collections have been made during two long field seasons totalling seven months. Following the work of those field studies, a new interpretation of the area has emerged involving complex plutonic and tectonic histories.

mainly on the complicated plutonic core of the study area. Only when the key intrusive relation-ships had been identified could they be more easily recognised in areas of poor exposure; this allowed mapping to progress faster in the following season. The second field season has been spent mapping these plutonic and structural assemblages in the wider context of the Western Limassol Forest Complex as a whole. During the latter half of the season, work concentrated mainly on the volcanic terrains in the south and west of the study area. In total, $90Km^2$ have been mapped on a 1:5000 scale, with many smaller key areas mapped on a 1:2000 scale.

Fig

Artwork

ZONAL DIAGRAM
SCALE
10 0 10 20 30Km
N
PENTADAKTYLOS SUCCESSION
CIRCUM TROODOS SEDIMENTARY SUCCESSION
TROODOS OPHIOLITE
MAMONIA COMPLEX
ARAKAPAS FAULT BELT
LIMASSOL FOREST COMPLEX
YERASA FOLD BELT

Caption

Map 1 Location map of Cyprus showing general geological features and the outcrop area of the Limassol Forest Complex.

Paragraph

Detailed mapping on a scale of 1:5000 has unravelled the extremely intricate intrusive relationships of the various tectonic blocks that make up the Limassol Forest Plutonic Complex. During the first field season, mapping concentrated

Major division of text

Key Field Relationships
Division heading

Paragraph

The gross structure of the Limassol Forest Complex is dominated by central updoming, which results in approximately annular outcrops, with the deepest rocks cropping out in the centre and highest level ones around the margins.

Subsection of text

Deep structural levels
Subsection heading

Paragraph

At the deepest levels a serpentised, tectonised harzburgite host is intruded by a suite of plutonic and hyperbyssal rocks. Coarse olivine porphyritic and poikilitic wehrlites were first emplaced as 0.5-1.5Km diameter bodies. Flow banding and abrasion of the phenocrysts suggest the olivine porphyry wehrlites were intruded as crystal mushes. The ubiquitous absence of chilled contacts around the margins of these wehrlites indicates a

Fn[1]

[*] Department of Earth Science, The Open University, Walton Hall, Milton Keynes

[1] The footnote is entered as part of the author element
[2] Folio, etc., added by text formatter, not as part of text

Figure 2.4 The structure of a simple scientific paper.

elements extend across both columns of the formatted page does not affect the way in which the text is coded. As far as the author is concerned, the main structure of the text is exactly the same as for a report, so having mastered entry of reports the author is immediately ready for more complex structures.

Of course, a few additional elements are required for scientific papers, such as those used to reserve space for figures and to number and output footnotes. Because the position of such elements can vary according to the page layout and the position at which they occur in the text, these elements are sometimes referred to as **floating elements** or **floats**. To simplify the entry of such floating elements, SGML allows them to be defined at the point at which they are initially referred to, their final position being determined by the formatting process on output. For example, the footnote shown in Figure 2.4 would be entered as:

```
<author>Mr B J Murton<fn>Department of Earth Science,
The Open University, Walton Hall, Milton Keynes</fn>
<p>The aim ...
```

On encountering this footnote element, the program will automatically try to reserve sufficient space for the element at the foot of the page (across one or two columns, according to house style) and determine which symbol or footnote number is required to link the footnote to its reference, before continuing to format the rest of the text.

A similar situation will occur with the illustration, though this time the details do not need to be entered until the end of the paragraph in which the illustration is referred to:

```
... and tectonic histories.
<fig id=map1>
<artwork sizex=85mm, sizey=52mm>
<figcap>Map 1   Location map of Cyprus showing general
geological features and the outcrop area of the Limassol
Forest Complex.
</fig>
<p>Detailed mapping ...
```

Another difference between this scientific paper and the previous report is in the treatment of citations. Though five different citations are made in the first paragraph, none of the details are shown there because, in common with most scientific papers, the citations have been moved to a separate reference bibliography at the end of the paper, where they have been numbered in the sequence in which they are referred to in the paper. However, as for footnotes, the citation details are still entered at the point of reference, even though they are formatted in a different way from the citations in the report shown in Figure 2.3. Typically the citations for Figure 2.4 would have been entered as:

```
... to be a fossil transform fault.<cit>Moores, EM and
Vine, FJ <hp1>Phil. Trans. Roy. Soc. Lond. A.</hp1> vol
268, 445&ndash;446 (1971).</cit><cit>Simonian, KO and
Gass, IG <hp1>Bull. Am. Geol. Soc.</hp1> 89, 1220&ndash;1230
(1978).</cit>. Previous studies<cit>Simonian, KO
<hp1>Open University Thesis</hp1> (unpub.
1975).</cit><cit>Bear, LM <hp1>Geol. Survey Dept.
Cyprus</hp1> Mem. 3, 180pp (1960).</cit><cit>Panayiotou,
A <hp1>Geol. Survey Dept. Cyprus</hp1> (unpublished
thesis, 1977).</cit> suggested ...
```

Note that the entered citations have not been given numbers, and no commas or spaces have been entered between them: this is all handled by the text formatter, as is the positioning of the references at the end of the main text.

NOTE: While an SGML-based program will be able to handle footnotes and citations as illustrated above, care should be taken to ensure that these facilities are available on the text formatter being used since, unlike many of the other SGML facilities, this feature is not easy to mimic on traditional text processing systems that use search and replace procedures to reformat SGML-coded text.

Another feature of scientific papers that is illustrated by Figure 2.4 is the use of mathematical symbols, such as the superior 2 used to produce the 90 Km^2 sequence at the end of the second paragraph. As far as physical appearance is concerned there is no difference between this and the 2 used in the citation at the top of the previous column, but both a reader and an SGML program recognize this symbol as a character with special significance. Except where a special superior number set is available on the keyboard, such special characters will be entered using special **entity references** of the form ² (see Chapter 4).

The structure of formal scientific papers of the type shown in Figure 2.5 differs little from that of the previous example. The most noticeable differences are that the title and author details are followed by an abstract of the contents; the first paragraph of the text under the *numbered* subsection headings contains two numbered equations; and the format of the citations differs. Typically the copy for such a paper would be coded as:

```
<!DOCTYPE paper PUBLIC "-//T+F//DTD Contemporary Physics//EN">
<paper>
<title>Photoelectron diffraction and surface science
```

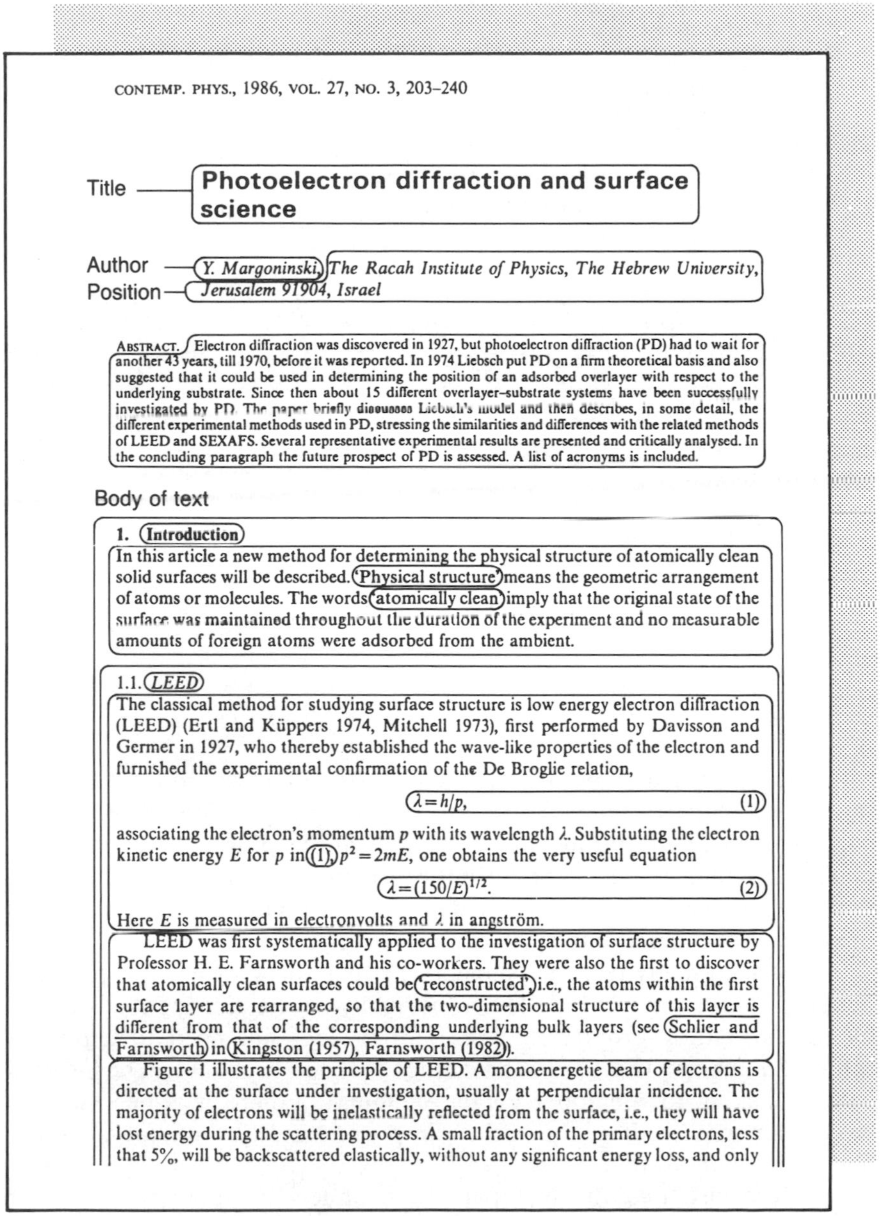

CONTEMP. PHYS., 1986, VOL. 27, NO. 3, 203–240

Title —— **Photoelectron diffraction and surface science**

Author —— Y. Margoninski, *The Racah Institute of Physics, The Hebrew University,*
Position —— *Jerusalem 91904, Israel*

ABSTRACT. Electron diffraction was discovered in 1927, but photoelectron diffraction (PD) had to wait for another 43 years, till 1970, before it was reported. In 1974 Liebsch put PD on a firm theoretical basis and also suggested that it could be used in determining the position of an adsorbed overlayer with respect to the underlying substrate. Since then about 15 different overlayer–substrate systems have been successfully investigated by PD. The paper briefly discusses Liebsch's model and then describes, in some detail, the different experimental methods used in PD, stressing the similarities and differences with the related methods of LEED and SEXAFS. Several representative experimental results are presented and critically analysed. In the concluding paragraph the future prospect of PD is assessed. A list of acronyms is included.

Body of text

1. Introduction

In this article a new method for determining the physical structure of atomically clean solid surfaces will be described. Physical structure means the geometric arrangement of atoms or molecules. The words atomically clean imply that the original state of the surface was maintained throughout the duration of the experiment and no measurable amounts of foreign atoms were adsorbed from the ambient.

1.1. LEED

The classical method for studying surface structure is low energy electron diffraction (LEED) (Ertl and Küppers 1974, Mitchell 1973), first performed by Davisson and Germer in 1927, who thereby established the wave-like properties of the electron and furnished the experimental confirmation of the De Broglie relation,

$$\lambda = h/p, \tag{1}$$

associating the electron's momentum p with its wavelength λ. Substituting the electron kinetic energy E for p in (1), $p^2 = 2mE$, one obtains the very useful equation

$$\lambda = (150/E)^{1/2}. \tag{2}$$

Here E is measured in electronvolts and λ in angström.

LEED was first systematically applied to the investigation of surface structure by Professor H. E. Farnsworth and his co-workers. They were also the first to discover that atomically clean surfaces could be reconstructed, i.e., the atoms within the first surface layer are rearranged, so that the two-dimensional structure of this layer is different from that of the corresponding underlying bulk layers (see Schlier and Farnsworth in Kingston (1957), Farnsworth (1982)).

Figure 1 illustrates the principle of LEED. A monoenergetic beam of electrons is directed at the surface under investigation, usually at perpendicular incidence. The majority of electrons will be inelastically reflected from the surface, i.e., they will have lost energy during the scattering process. A small fraction of the primary electrons, less that 5%, will be backscattered elastically, without any significant energy loss, and only

Figure 2.5 The structure of a formal scientific paper.

```
<author>Y. Margoninski
<position>The Rach Institute of Physics, The Hebrew
University, Jerusalem 91904, Israel
<abstract>Electron diffraction was discovered ...
... A list of acronyms is included.
<h1>Introduction
<p>In this article ...
... adsorbed from the ambient.
<h2 id='LEED'>
<p>The classical method for studying surface structure
is low energy electon diffraction (LEED) (<citref
refid="Ertl-K"><citref refid="Mitchell">), first
performed ...
...of the De Broglie relation,
<eqn id=Broglie>&wavelen;=&planck;<over>&momentum;</eqn>
associating the electron's momentum &momentum; with its
wavelength &wavelen;. Substituting the electron kinetic
energy &energy; for &momentum; in <eqnref refid=Broglie>,
&momentum;&sup2;=2&mass;&energy;, one obtains the very useful
equation
<eqn>&wavelen;=(150<over>&energy;)&suphalf;.</eqn>
Here &energy; is measured in electron volts and &wavelen;
in angstr&ouml;m.
<p>LEED was first ...
... underlying bulk layers (see <citref refid="Schlier"> in
<citref refid="Kingston">, <citref refid ="Farnswors">).
<p>Figure 1 ...
```

There are a number of points to be noted about the coded version of this paper. Firstly, notice how the author and position elements are concatenated in the printed text, the formatting program automatically placing a comma at the end of the author's name. Similarly the first word of the abstract element has been added by the program (so avoiding the need to worry about generating small capital letters).

As with many technical papers, the main headings of this scientific paper have been numbered. This is normally automatically taken care of by the formatting program, so the author does not need to enter the relevant numbers. This has the advantage that new sections can be inserted without having to renumber all the headings. Where it is necessary to cross-refer to a heading, the author simply allocates it a unique identifier and cross-refers to that.

Note also that the first paragraph under the subsection heading contains two equations embedded in the text. (The paragraph does not end until the word 'angström'.) The equations are automatically numbered by the text formatter – this time when it encounters the </eqn> end-tag. Each equation is divided into two major components by a short

reference entry associated with the equals symbol. Where necessary a
further division can be provided in either half by use of the ‹over› tag. This
tag identifies the point at which the numerator of a fraction ends and the
denominator begins. The formatting program can be set up to identify this
point as a place to split the relevant subelement of the equation into two
lines, separated by a horizontal rule, if they are long enough to warrant it.
In this example, however, the program has simply replaced the tag by a
slash.

The reference to the first equation in the middle section of the
paragraph has been made through a special equation reference element
(‹eqnref refid=Broglie›) to ensure that the correct number is used if the equations
are renumbered. Notice that the differences between this reference and the
one used for the item cross-reference in the report occur in the name of the
element referred to and the fact that each has its own unique identifier.

Because the citations in this paper are included in a separate section,
which is arranged alphabetically rather than in the order in which the
citations appear in the text, they have been identified in this example by the
inclusion of citation references at appropriate points. Each citation reference (‹citref›) tag contains an attribute that uniquely identifies which entry in
the bibliography the citation refers to. In this case it is presumed that the text
for each entry will be generated automatically from the citation text by the
text formatting program but, because the author has chosen to link multiple
references, the parentheses at either end of the reference have been treated
as part of the text of the document.

*NOTE: Many output systems cannot automatically generate cross-references. Even
where they can be generated the system may automatically bracket each entry
separately. (Where this is the case, the style shown in the above paper may need to be
modified.) Appendix C shows how the use of the citation reference element can be
modified to allow citations to be entered by the author where they cannot be generated
by the system.*

2.2.5   The structure of books

Figure 2.6 shows how the structure of a simple paperback novel can be
illustrated in the form of a tree diagram. By now the elements making up the
body of the text should be familiar to you. In this case, chapters are the main
division of the body of the text, their headings being flagged by the ‹h1› tag.

The major difference between novels and scientific papers concerns
the supporting material in the preliminary and final pages. In many novels
the structure of the preliminary pages is relatively simple, consisting of a
half-title page, the reverse of which may list the names of other books in
the same or related series, and a title page, on the back of which details
about copyright, publishers and printers may be printed. In certain cases

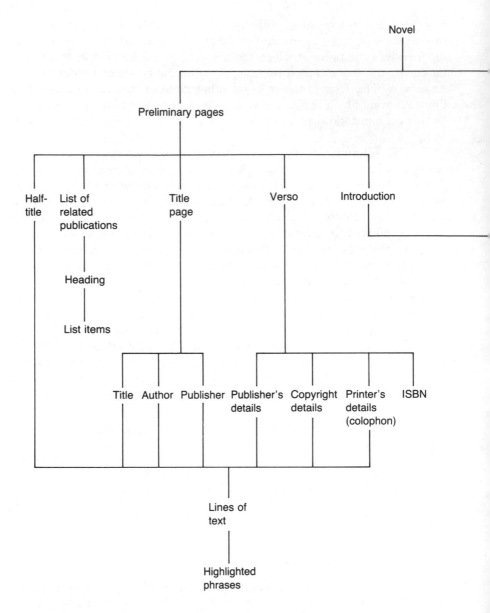

Figure 2.6   The structure of a novel.

some form of introduction, foreword, preface or author's note may also be added in front of the story.

To identify the end of the preliminary pages and the start of the main body of the text, a special tag (e.g. <body>) should be used. This will

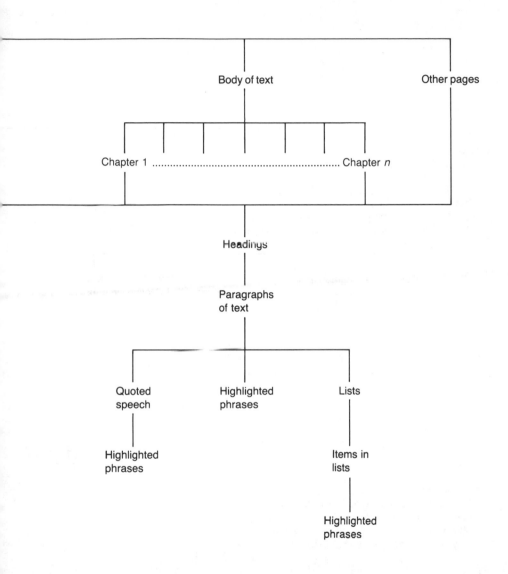

allow the formatting program to change the format of elements such as headings and paragraphs from that used in the preliminary pages to that required within the text of the story (where a difference exists).

At the end of some novels you may find that the publisher has added

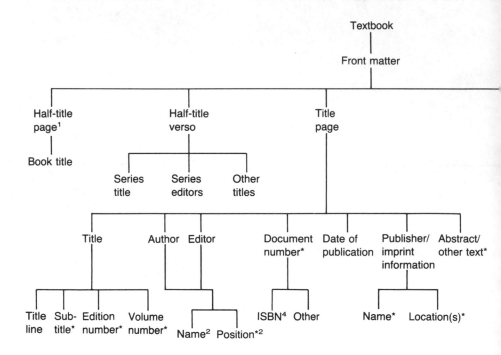

* Optional element
1 Can be generated automatically from title page
2 May be more than one author/editor and affiliation
3 May be split between title page and verso
4 May occur in more than one position

Figure 2.7   The stucture of the preliminary pages in a typical textbook.

a certain amount of advertising material to fill out the book. (You may also find some form of postscript from the author or biographical details about the author.) Such pages can normally be coded in the same way as the text, with the addition of a separate tag at the start of the section to indicate that

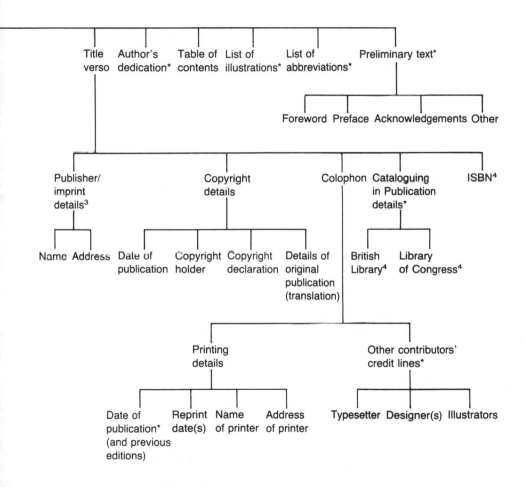

the body of the text has ended. (This may take you back to the style used for the preliminary pages.)

Hardback books, and in particular textbooks and other academic works, tend to have a slightly more complicated structure. Again they can be thought of as having three main divisions: preliminary pages, the body of the text and annexed text. Figure 2.7 suggests how the preliminary pages of a textbook could be structured.

In this example it is presumed that the initial half-title page will automatically be generated from the title entered for the title page. This means that no specific tag needs to be allocated to it, the title page being considered as the first page of the book.

NOTE: Even where series information or details of related publications are printed on the reverse of the half-title, the title page can be entered first in an SGML-coded document as positioning of elements within the book is not directly related to the sequence in which they are encountered in the coded text.

The title page should contain a title and the name of the author(s) or editor(s) of the text. It may also contain:

- a subtitle,
- the edition number,
- details of the author's position or qualifications,
- details of a translator or illustrator,
- a document identification number,
- the date of publication,
- details about the publisher(s) or imprint, and
- an abstract or other text describing the book's contents.

Other details about a publication are normally printed on the reverse of the title page (often referred to as the title-verso). Besides the standard copyright declaration, this page may include details about:

- the publisher and his or her agents,
- the printer, typesetter, designer and illustrator of the book,
- cataloguing categories specified by the British Library or Library of Congress, and
- details of any identification code allocated to the book (if not listed on the title page).

Other details related to the title page, but not necessarily falling on the first four pages of the book (i.c. the half-title and title pages and their versos), include dedications and lists of related publications.

Figures 2.8 to 2.11 illustrate the range of information that can be encountered at the start of a book. A document type definition that is capable of encoding all these pages is shown in Appendix C. (Details of how this DTD was prepared are given in the following chapters.)

INTERNATIONAL COMPUTER SCIENCE SERIES

Consulting editors   **A D McGettrick**   University of Strathclyde
                         J van Leeuwen   University of Utrecht

SELECTED TITLES IN THE SERIES:

Programming in Ada (2nd Edn.)   *J G P Barnes*

Software Engineering (2nd Edn.)   *I Sommerville*

The UNIX System   *S R Bourne*

Handbook of Algorithms and Data Structures   *G H Gonnet*

Microcomputers in Engineering and Science   *J F Craine and G R Martin*

UNIX for Super-Users   *E Foxley*

Software Specification Techniques   *N Gehani and A D McGettrick* (eds.)

Data Communications for Programmers   *M Purser*

Local Area Network Design   *A Hopper, S Temple and R C Williamson*

Prolog Programming for Artificial Intelligence   *I Bratko*

Modula-2: Discipline & Design   *A H J Sale*

Introduction to Expert Systems   *P Jackson*

Prolog   *F Giannesini, H Kanoui, R Pasero and M van Caneghem*

Programming Language Translation: A Practical Approach   *P D Terry*

System Simulation: Programming Styles and Languages   *W Kreutzer*

Data Abstraction in Programming Languages   *J M Bishop*

The UNIX System V Environment   *S R Bourne*

The Craft of Software Engineering   *A Macro and J Buxton*

An Introduction to Programming with Modula-2   *P D Terry*

Distributed Systems: Concepts and Design   *G. Coulouris and J. Dollimore*

Figure 2.8   Typical list of related publications.

LOCAL AREA NETWORK ARCHITECTURES

David Hutchison

University of Lancaster

ADDISON-WESLEY
PUBLISHING
COMPANY

Wokingham, England · Reading, Massachusetts · Menlo Park, California
New York · Don Mills, Ontario · Amsterdam · Bonn
Sydney · Singapore · Tokyo · Madrid · San Juan

Figure 2.9   Title page of typical textbook.

© 1988 Addison-Wesley Publishers Ltd.
© 1988 Addison-Wesley Publishing Company, Inc.

All rights reserved. No part of this publication may be reproduced, stored in a retrieval system, or transmitted in any form or by any means, electronic, mechanical, photocopying, recording or otherwise, without prior written permission of the publisher.

Many of the designations used by manufacturers and sellers to distinguish their products are claimed as trademarks. Addison-Wesley has made every attempt to supply trademark information about manufacturers and their products mentioned in this book. A list of the trademark designations and their owners appears on page xiv.

Cover designed by Crayon Design of Henley On Thames and printed by
The Riverside Printing Co. (Reading) Ltd.
Typeset by Quorum Technical Services Ltd, Cheltenham, UK.
Printed in Great Britain by Mackays of Chatham PLC, Chatham, Kent

First printed 1988.

British Library Cataloguing in Publication Data
Hutchison, David, *1949–*
Local area network architectures. —
(International computer science series)
1. Computer systems. Local networks. Design
I. Title II. Series
004.6'8

ISBN 0–201–14216–3

Library of Congress Cataloging in Publication Data
Hutchison, David, M. Tech
Local area network architectures/David Hutchison.
p. cm. — (International computer science series)
Bibliography: p.
Includes index.
ISBN 0–201–14216–3
1. Local area networks (Computer networks) 2. Computer network architectures. I. Title. II. Series.
TK5105.5.H88 1988
004.6'8—dc19 88-10421
CIP

Figure 2.10 Reverse of title page in typical textbook.

The Life and Strange
Surprizing Adventures of

ROBINSON CRUSOE

of York, Mariner

WHO LIVED EIGHT AND TWENTY YEARS
ALL ALONE IN AN UNINHABITED ISLAND
ON THE COAST OF AMERICA
NEAR THE MOUTH OF
THE GREAT RIVER OF OROONOQUE
HAVING BEEN CAST ON SHORE BY SHIPWRECK
WHEREIN ALL THE MEN PERISHED BUT HIMSELF
WITH AN ACCOUNT HOW HE WAS AT LAST
AS STRANGELY DELIVER'D BY PYRATES

Written by Himself

——————

Linocuts by John Lawrence

LONDON
The Folio Society
1972

Figure 2.11   Complex title page.

The following may also be found in the preliminary pages at the front of many books:

- a table of contents,
- a list of the illustrations used in the text,
- a list of abbreviations used in the text,
- one or more prefaces,
- a foreword,
- the author's acknowledgements, and
- explanatory text required to understand the main text.

The first two of these can be generated automatically by the SGML program by reference to the relevant headings or captions in the text. The program will associate the relevant printed page number with each heading/caption.

The other options in the above list can normally be treated as chapters of the book (though they might have a different format for text or headings because they fall within the preliminary pages rather than the body of the text).

The two parts of Figure 2.12 show how the text of a reasonably complicated textbook could be structured. Six basic text divisions have been specified in Figure 2.12(a): parts, chapters, sections, subsections, sub-subsections and sub-sub-subsections. Each division must be given a heading, which can optionally be followed by some text before the next lower division of text is encountered.

NOTE: In this example, which is the one used in the declaration specified in Appendix C, no allowance has been made for skipping levels of heading, other than the possibility of not using parts. In some applications a skip facility may need to be added.

Within each text section (see Figure 2.12(b)) authors can identify:

- paragraphs of text,
- notes to the main text,
- special headed topics of discussion,
- list of items, glossary definitions or other definitions of terms, and
- special elements of text, such as long quotations, paragraphs, examples, tables, etc.

Three topic elements have been allowed for in Figure 2.12(b) so that different output formats can be used to identify different types of topic.

Notice that topics are not nested one below the other – each level can be started independently of the others. It should also be noted that the optional topic headings will often be treated differently from other headings in the main text (e.g. printed in the margin when the main headings are in the text or vice versa). Such headings will not, however, normally be included in the table of contents for the book.

You may wonder why special elements of text are shown at the same level as paragraphs in Figure 2.12(b), as well as being included in the structure of paragraphs and other elements of text. This has been done to allow quotations and poems to be placed at the start of the text without a preceding ‹p› paragraph element. For example, a chapter might start:

```
<h1 id="three">Cold War: Provocation and Prevarication
<lq><hp1>Words to the heat of deeds too cold breath gives</hp1>
<l position=right>Macbeth II i 58</lq>
<n>The discovery of the Spaniards ...
```

If quotations are not allowed at the main level a ‹p› would be needed in front of the ‹lq› tag identifying the long quotation, though this may not be obvious to the author. (It is for this reason that definition of the structure of complicated documents will normally be left to specially trained document designers, whose job it is to design the element structure to fit the author's perceptions of the format of the text as exactly as possible.)

Figure 2.12 is not exhaustive, as the subelements associated with the lower levels of elements could not be added without clouding the overall structure. Many of these elements have a similar structure, consisting of text, highlighted phrases, embedded quotes, cross-references, embedded lists, etc. Fortunately SGML does not require all levels to be exhaustively declared; instead it allows you to define a group of elements as a **parameter entity**, which can then be used in a number of places within the declarations as a shorthand reference to the group.

The three types of list indicated in Figure 2.12 (and declared in the document type definition in Appendix C) are illustrated in Figure 2.13. These allow users to define:

- lists that consist simply of individual text items – which may be numbered or otherwise individually identified;

- lists, such as glossaries, where a word or phrase may be followed by one or more definitions of its meaning, or cross-references to other definitions; and

- other lists of terms (e.g. list of abbreviations, etc.) where the definition starts on the same line as the term.

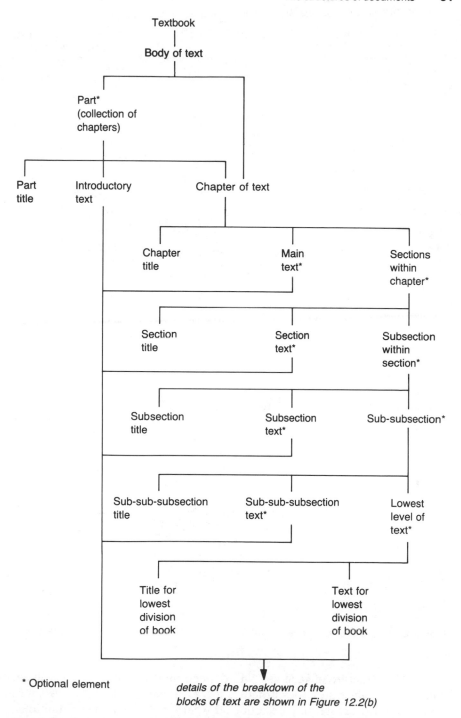

* Optional element

details of the breakdown of the blocks of text are shown in Figure 12.2(b)

Figure 2.12   The structure of the main text in a typical textbook: (a) the major divisions.

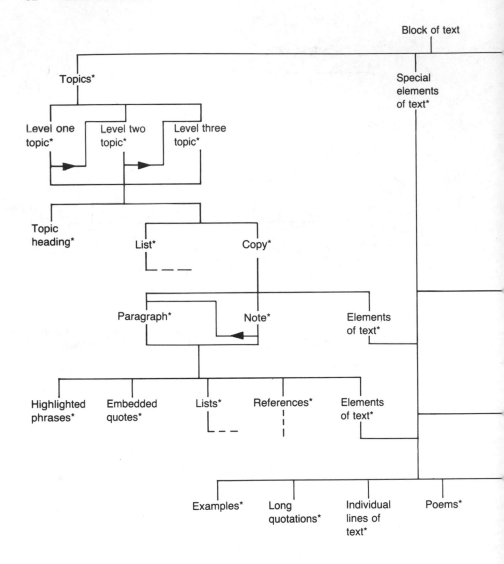

* Optional element

Figure 2.12   The structure of the main text in a typical textbook: (b) main text elements.

The structure of such lists will depend on the applications involved. Figure 2.14 illustrates the structure of a simple glossary list. A more complicated structure may be required where dictionary style definitions, including, for example, details of derivation, pronunciation and word form, are required.

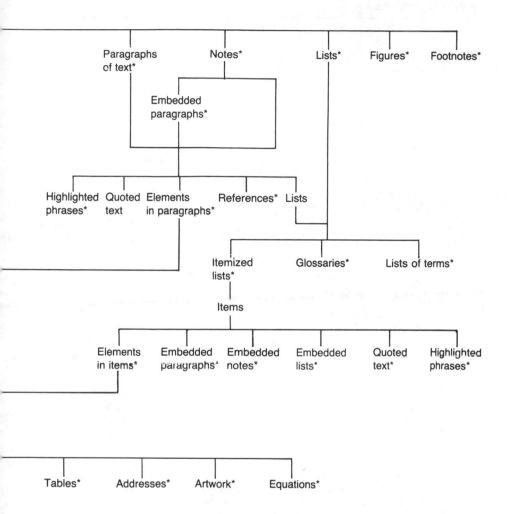

The start of a typical glossary list might be coded as:

```
<gl><hd>Typesetting Terms
<gt>accent
<gdg>A mark placed above or below a character to
```

Simple list (unnumbered)

When a marked section of text is displayed on the screen it can be:

– deleted
– copied
– moved
– underlined
– changed to uppercase or lowercase
– sorted into sequence
– totalled (numeric data only).

Glossary

DMA   E
Direct Memory Access. A type of link
between a *CPU* and its associated   **Edit**
memory.   To change or correct previously keyed
                                     files.

Dotless i
1. The lower half of a lowercase i. Used   **Ellipse**
to create í, ì, î, ï, ĩ and ī.   See *leader*.

Double Dagger   **Em**
‡. The third of the six symbols (refer-   A space whose width is equal to the
ence marks) used to refer the reader to a   current set width and whose depth is
footnote or other inclusion within the   the currently defined point size.
text. It may be combined with *, †, §, ‖   A unit of measurement equal to an em
and ¶ if more symbols are required.   space. Often incorrectly used in place
                                            of a *pica* to represent a space of 12
Dummy   *points* wide. The term 'em of set' is
A preliminary drawing, layout or other   often used in other books to distin-
representation of a finished job: a   guish the correct definition when the
scaled page layout.   term 'em' is being used for 'pica'.

Definition of terms

hf bd: half-bound   HFM: Henry Ford Museum
hfbr: high flux beam reactor   hgt: height
hfc: high-frequency current   HGTB: Haiti Government Tourist
HFC: Household Finance Corporation   Bureau
HFCC: Henry Ford Community Col-   HGW: Herbert George Wells
  lege   Hgy: Highway
hf cf: half-calf   hh: half-hard; handhole; heavy hydro-
hf cl: half-cloth (binding)   gen
hfdf: high-frequency direction finder *hh: hojas* (Spanish–leaves)
HFFF: Hungarian Freedom Fighters   h to h: heel-to-heel
  Federation   hH: heavy hydrogen
HFGA: Hall of Fame for Great Ameri- HH: Harry Hansen; Helen Hunt Jack-
  cans   son; Her (His) Highness; His Holi-
hfh: half-hard (steel)   ness; Howard Hanson; Huntington
HFIA: Heat and Frost Insulators and   Hartford
  Asbestos Workers Union   HH: Herren (German–gentlemen)
hfm: hold for money   H/H: Havre-Hamburg (range of ports)

Figure 2.13 Types of list.

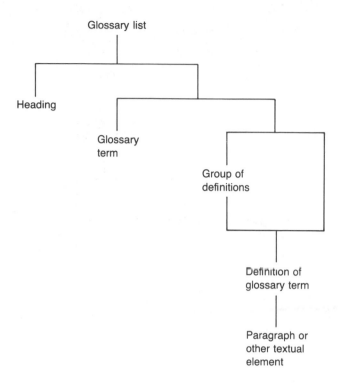

Figure 2.14   The structure of a typical glossary list.

```
change its sound or emphasis
<gd>A mark placed within a word to indicate the stress
to be applied
<gt>alphabet length
<gd>The combined length of all the <hp1>lowercase</hp1>
alphabetic letters (a-z) &ndash; expressed in points
<gt>...
```

NOTE: For further details of the use of the glossary list tag and its associated sub-elements refer to Appendix C.

Figure 2.15 illustrates a structure that might be suitable for the annexed text of a book. In this case the appendices are considered as a separate section of the back matter that can be grouped into a number of parts if required. Otherwise appendices, glossaries, bibliographies and other sections of text incorporated into the back matter are treated in exactly the same way as chapters of text (see Figure 2.12).

Where the facility is supported by the formatting program, indexes

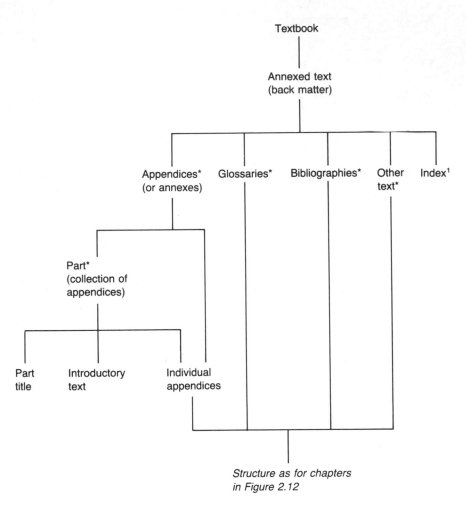

* Optional element
1 Automatically generated from entries in text (or other parts of book)

Figure 2.15   The structure of annexed text in a typical textbook.

can be generated automatically from index entries flagged in the text. The program will automatically place these at the point indicated by the ⟨index⟩ tag, which should be entered at an appropriate point at the back of the book.

It can be seen from the above analyses of the structure of documents that different structures are required for different types of documents, and for similar types of documents with different levels of complexity. Normally, however, authors will not be expected to analyse their work in this amount of detail. They will be provided with a previously specified document structure, which may need to be modified slightly to meet the particular requirements. The techniques used to declare the changes required are described in the following chapters.

2.3   Formatting structured documents

Before going into detail about the use of SGML, a word should be said about how the structure of documents is related to the appearance (format) of the final document.

A formatting program needs to know the format required for each element defined in the structure of a document. The techniques employed for this will depend on the type of text formatter being used and the level to which it has been integrated with SGML.

At the simplest level, formatting will simply involve a replacement of each SGML element tag with a set of markup codes relevant to the output device being used. In such cases a replacement string will need to be defined for each tagged element and for each attribute or combination of attributes that can be used to qualify the element. (Entity references will also need to be expanded or otherwise translated to local coding.)

At a slightly higher level, the formatting program may be given the names of one or more procedures (computer program modules) to be carried out when an element or attribute is encountered. These procedures may range in complexity from those that position the element at the required point to procedures for extracting and numbering index or contents list entries.

A fully featured SGML system may format a document for output by generating a second structure, called a **layout structure**, that is coded by the addition of further tags to the coded document. The generic identifiers for these added tags start with a bracketed name identifying the structure to which they belong (e.g. ⟨(layout)block⟩ or ⟨(layout)p⟩). More than one **concurrent document** may be present at the same time. For example, one structure may define how the formatted document should be displayed on a screen, while another defines the format to be used when outputting to a printer. The process of associating document structures is carried out by use of SGML **link type declarations**. These allow elements and attributes in the base document set or one of its subdocuments to be *linked* to other elements or attributes in a concurrent document type. (This process is described in more detail in Chapter 9.)

SGML also allows special, application-specific, **processing instructions** to be added to the text to control the output format, and allows
process-specific data content **notations** to be used for entering specially
coded data. Such techniques allow pictorial data to be incorporated with
the text and provide access to other special facilities that might be available
on the output device.

3

The Reference Concrete Syntax

If documents are to be successfully transmitted from one user to another it is important that both parties associate each transmitted code with a particular character or function. In addition, the meanings of any special groups of codes used for marking up the document need to be agreed so that markup can be correctly distinguished from the text.

The rules defining the meanings of codes and reserved names used by a particular language are referred to as the **syntax** of the language. Two distinct types of syntax have been defined for SGML: an **abstract syntax** that is used to specify how SGML declarations and document type declarations should be constructed; and a more concrete set of rules for defining how specific documents have been coded. This latter set of rules is referred to as the **concrete syntax**.

One particular concrete syntax, called the **reference concrete syntax**, has been formally defined within ISO 8879 to provide a reference against which alternative concrete syntaxes can be compared. Any system claiming to conform to the standard published in ISO 8879 must be able to accept documents coded in this reference concrete syntax. If such a conforming system is able to pass documents to other machines, it must also be able to output them using the reference concrete syntax as well as any local coding scheme.

Because the reference concrete syntax is central to the functioning of SGML, it is advisable, though not essential, that potential users have a grasp of its structure and purpose. This chapter shows how the reference concrete syntax has been defined, and explains the purpose of each of the default options. Details of how to change these default options are given in Chapters 10 and 11.

3.1   *The role of the SGML declaration*

Each SGML document transferred to another system must start with a declaration, called the **SGML declaration**, which defines the coding scheme (syntax) used in its preparation. (While stored within a system the SGML declaration does not need to be present.) Most SGML-based programs will automatically add the SGML declaration to the document as it is transferred to another system, but documents prepared by programs that are not SGML-based will need to have formal SGML declarations added to the start of the document before transmission.

Figure 3.1 shows an SGML declaration suitable for a document prepared using SGML's reference concrete syntax. (Such documents are referred to as **basic SGML documents**.) The SGML declaration starts with a **markup declaration open** (**mdo**) sequence consisting of the ISO 646 (ASCII) codes ‹! (decimal 60 followed by decimal 33). These codes are compulsory because SGML declarations must be entered using SGML's reference concrete syntax. (The declaration is closed by a matching **markup declaration close** (**mdc**) angle bracket (›, decimal 62) at the end of the declaration.)

The rest of the first line of the SGML declaration consists of the ISO 646 letters SGML followed by a delimited string containing the number and date of the ISO standard in which SGML is defined ("ISO 8879-1986"). This statement indicates which version of the standard was used to prepare the following declarations.

The second line of the SGML declaration contains some text bracketed by pairs of hyphens. Any text entered in an SGML markup declaration between pairs of hyphens is treated as a comment. In this case the comment acts as a heading explaining the purpose of the following entries.

The names of the six main clauses that make up an SGML declaration are shown in the first column of the definitions that follow the comment. They identify:

- document character set details (CHARSET),
- capacity set details (CAPACITY),
- the scope of the following concrete syntax (SCOPE),
- the concrete syntax to be used within the document (SYNTAX),

```
<!SGML "ISO 8879-1986"
        -- Declaration for typical Basic SGML Document --
   CHARSET   BASESET   "ISO 646-1983//CHARSET International
                       Reference Version (IRV)//ESC 2/5 4/0"
             DESCSET   0   9  UNUSED
                       9   2  9
                       11  2  UNUSED
                       13  1  13
                       14  18 UNUSED
                       32  95 32
                       127 1  UNUSED
   CAPACITY  PUBLIC    "ISO 8879-1986//CAPACITY Reference//EN"
   SCOPE     DOCUMENT
   SYNTAX    SHUNCHAR  CONTROLS 0 1 2 3 4 5 6 7 8 9 10 11 12 13
                                14 15 16 17 18 19 20 21 22 23 24 25 26
                                27 28 29 30 31 127 255
             BASESET   "ISO 646-1983//CHARSET International
                       Reference Version (IRV)//ESC 2/5 4/0"
             DESCSET   0 128 0
             FUNCTION  RE        13
                       RS        10
                       SPACE     32
                       TAB SEPCHAR 9
             NAMING    LCNMSTRT  ""
                       UCNMSTRT  ""
                       LCNMCHAR  "-."
                       UCNMCHAR  "-."
                       NAMECASE  GENERAL YES
                                 ENTITY  NO
             DELIM     GENERAL   SGMLREF
                       SHORTREF  SGMLREF
             NAMES     SGMLREF
             QUANTITY  SGMLREF
   FEATURES  MINIMIZE  DATATAG NO  OMITTAG YES  RANK    NO  SHORTTAG YES
             LINK      SIMPLE  NO  IMPLICIT NO  EXPLICIT NO
             OTHER     CONCUR  NO  SUBDOC  NO   FORMAL  NO
   APPINFO   NONE
   >
```

Figure 3.1   SGML declaration for a basic SGML document.

- special SGML features used within the document (FEATURES), and
- application-specific information entered within the declaration (APPINFO).

   The key item in this list is the SYNTAX clause, as it is this that controls the codes that can be used for document markup. In Figure 3.1 the syntax has been defined by use of the reference concrete syntax definition provided in Figure 7 of ISO 8879. (The reference concrete syntax could equally well have been requested by entering SYNTAX PUBLIC "ISO 8879-1986//SYNTAX Reference//EN", the formal public declaration for the reference concrete syntax, as used in Figure 8 of ISO 8879.)

3.2 The reference concrete syntax

The declaration for SGML's reference concrete syntax given in the SYNTAX clause shown in Figure 3.1 contains eight major sections, each identified by a keyword in the second column. These sections define:

- the numbers of any codes which the program is to ignore because they are control or other non-SGML characters (SHUNCHAR) rather than data characters;
- the syntax's character set, consisting of a base character set (BASESET) declaration followed by a description of how these characters are to be used within the concrete syntax (DESCSET);
- which codes represent functions required by the syntax (FUNCTION);
- the rules to be applied when defining tag and entity names (NAMING);
- the markup delimiters to be used in the document (DELIM);
- naming conventions to be used within markup declarations (NAMES); and
- the quantity set required for the document (QUANTITY).

The **base character set** used for the reference concrete syntax is that defined in international standard ISO 646. This 7-bit character set, known as the International Reference Version (IRV), is used as a starting point for all international standards that define character sets (e.g. ISO 4873 and ISO 6937). It also matches, in all major respects, the American Standard Code for Information Interchange (ASCII) used by many computer systems. (ISO 646 does allocate different names to some of the control characters but these names do not affect the way the codes are normally used.) The following **described character set portion** of the character set description shows that all 128 characters defined in ISO 646, starting from position 0 in the list, are mapped to identical positions in the reference concrete syntax.

Table 3.1 shows the codes defined in ISO 646. It will be seen that codes with values less than 32, and that with a value of 127, have been allocated to control functions, while codes with values between 32 and 126 are associated with printable (data) characters. (Characters outside this range can be added to the document's character set using techniques described here, and in Chapter 11, or can be accessed by use of entity or character references – see Chapter 4).

Table 3.1   The ISO 646 character set.

Value		ISO (16-bit)	ISO name/	
Decimal	Octal	representation	character	Purpose
0	0	0/0	NUL	Null code
1	1	0/1	TC1/SOH	Transmission code 1/
				Start of header
2	2	0/2	TC2/STX	Transmission code 2/
				Start of text
3	3	0/3	TC3/ETX	Transmission code 3/
				End of text
4	4	0/4	TC4/EOT	Transmission code 4/
				End of transmission
5	5	0/5	TC5/ENQ	Transmission code 5/Enquire
6	6	0/6	TC6/ACK	Transmission code 6/
				Acknowledge
7	7	0/7	BEL	Bell
8	10	0/8	FE0/BS	Format effector 0/Backspace
9	11	0/9	FE1/HT	Format effector 1/
				Horizontal tab
10	12	0/10	FE2/LF	Format effector 2/Line feed
11	13	0/11	FE3/VT	Format effector 3/
				Vertical tab
12	14	0/12	FE4/FF	Format effector 4/Form feed
13	15	0/13	FE5/CR	Format effector 5/
				Carriage return
14	16	0/14	SO	Shift out
15	17	0/15	SI	Shift in
16	20	1/0	TC7/DLE	Transmission code 7/
				Data link escape
17	21	1/1	DC1	Device control character 1
18	22	1/2	DC2	Device control character 2
19	23	1/3	DC3	Device control character 3
20	24	1/4	DC4	Device control character 4
21	25	1/5	TC8/NAK	Transmission code 8/
				Negative acknowledge
22	26	1/6	TC9/SYN	Transmission code 9/
				Synchronize
23	27	1/7	TC10/ETB	Transmission code 10/
				End of text block
24	30	1/8	CAN	Cancel
25	31	1/9	EM	End of media
26	32	1/10	SUB	Substitute character
27	33	1/11	ESC	Escape
28	34	1/12	FS/DT/IS4	Frame separator/ISO 6937
				document terminator
29	35	1/13	GS/PT/IS3	Group separator/ISO 6937
				page terminator

Table 3.1   (cont.)

Value		ISO (16-bit)	ISO name/	
Decimal	**Octal**	**representation**	**character**	**Purpose**
30	36	1/14	RS/IS2	Record separator
31	37	1/15	US/IS1	Unit separator
32	40	2/0		Space
33	41	2/1	!	Exclamation mark
34	42	2/2	"	Quotation mark
35	43	2/3	#	Number sign
36	44	2/4	¤	General currency sign
37	45	2/5	%	Percent
38	46	2/6	&	Ampersand
39	47	2/7	'	Apostrophe
40	50	2/8	(	Left parenthesis
41	51	2/9	)	Right parenthesis
42	52	2/10	*	Asterisk
43	53	2/11	+	Plus sign
44	54	2/12	,	Comma
45	55	2/13	-	Hyphen
46	56	2/14	.	Full stop
47	57	2/15	/	Solidus
48	60	3/0	0	
49	61	3/1	1	
50	62	3/2	2	
51	63	3/3	3	
52	64	3/4	4	
53	65	3/5	5	
54	66	3/6	6	
55	67	3/7	7	
56	70	3/8	8	
57	71	3/9	9	
58	72	3/10	:	Colon
59	73	3/11	;	Semicolon
60	74	3/12	<	Less-than sign
61	75	3/13	=	Equals sign
62	76	3/14	>	Greater-than sign
63	77	3/15	?	Question mark
64	100	4/0	@	Commercial at
65	101	4/1	A	
66	102	4/2	B	
67	103	4/3	C	
68	104	4/4	D	
69	105	4/5	E	
70	106	4/6	F	
71	107	4/7	G	
72	110	4/8	H	
73	111	4/9	I	

Table 3.1   (cont.)

| Value | | ISO (16-bit) | ISO name/ | |
Decimal	Octal	representation	character	Purpose
74	112	4/10	J	
75	113	4/11	K	
76	114	4/12	L	
77	115	4/13	M	
78	116	4/14	N	
79	117	4/15	O	
80	120	5/0	P	
81	121	5/1	Q	
82	122	5/2	R	
83	123	5/3	S	
84	124	5/4	T	
85	125	5/5	U	
86	126	5/6	V	
87	127	5/7	W	
88	130	5/8	X	
89	131	5/9	Y	
90	132	5/10	Z	
91	133	5/11	[	Left square bracket
92	134	5/12	\	Reverse solidus
93	135	5/13	]	Right square bracket
94	136	5/14	^	Circumflex accent
95	137	5/15	_	Low line
96	140	6/0	`	Grave accent
97	141	6/1	a	
98	142	6/2	b	
99	143	6/3	c	
100	144	6/4	d	
101	145	6/5	e	
102	146	6/6	f	
103	147	6/7	g	
104	150	6/8	h	
105	151	6/9	i	
106	152	6/10	j	
107	153	6/11	k	
108	154	6/12	l	
109	155	6/13	m	
110	156	6/14	n	
111	157	6/15	o	
112	160	7/0	p	
113	161	7/1	q	
114	162	7/2	r	
115	163	7/3	s	
116	164	7/4	t	
117	165	7/5	u	

Table 3.1 (cont.)

Value		ISO (16-bit)	ISO name/	
Decimal	**Octal**	**representation**	**character**	**Purpose**
118	166	7/6	v	
119	167	7/7	w	
120	170	7/8	x	
121	171	7/9	y	
122	172	7/10	z	
123	173	7/11	{	Left curly bracket
124	174	7/12	|	Vertical line
125	175	7/13	}	Right curly bracket
126	176	7/14	˜	Tilde
127	177	7/15	DEL	Delete

If the character numbers entered in the SHUNCHAR section of the SYNTAX clause are compared with the list shown in Table 3.1, it will be clear that the characters to be shunned when the reference concrete syntax is being used are those defined as control codes within ISO 646. These characters do not form part of the markup in an SGML file, so they are generally ignored while the structure of the SGML file is being checked (a process referred to as *document parsing*).

There are, however, certain control codes that are significant within an SGML document, not as characters but as codes which serve particular functions. These codes are identified in the FUNCTION section of the syntax definition. In the case of the reference concrete syntax, four special functions are recognized:

(1)   Record End (RE),

(2)   Record Start (RS),

(3)   the space character (SPACE), and

(4)   the horizontal tab code (TAB).

The carriage return code (0/13) is used as the record end code for the reference concrete syntax, with the line feed code (0/10) being used for the record start. (Some word processors may use these two codes the other way round. Such programs will need to define a variant concrete syntax using the techniques defined in Chapter 10.)

The space character (2/0) is also treated as a function character because it has a special function as a *separator* within SGML markup declarations. In certain cases the Tab code (0/9) may also be used as a separator but, since it does not have exactly the same role as the space, it is placed into a special group of **separator characters** identified by the SEPCHAR control word.

In the reference concrete syntax, all 128 characters within the basic character set have their standard meanings, as defined in ISO 646, so no further description of the purpose of the characters has been given in the DESCSET section of the syntax definition. Where changes are made to the purpose of specific codes, however, this section can be used to describe the altered meanings of the codes (for further details see Chapter 10).

NOTE: It should be noted that, in the DESCSET clause used to define the document's character set in the CHARSET definition at the start of the SGML declaration, control codes that have not been allocated specific SGML functions are defined as UNUSED.

The NAMING section of the syntax definition defines the characters that can be used in tag or entity names, and in SGML identifiers that act as names. By default, SGML presumes that names can only start with alphabetic characters, in either upper or lower-case, with subsequent characters being alphanumeric. The LCNMSTRT and UCNMSTRT lines allow other, non-alphanumeric, characters to be defined as upper- and lower-case name start characters, while the LCNMCHAR and UCNMCHAR lines define which non-alphanumeric characters may be used within names.

In the reference concrete syntax, only alphabetic characters may be used as name start characters (in either shift), but within names the standard English language alphanumeric characters (a–z, A–Z and 0–9) may be supplemented by full stops and hyphens (which can be used in either shift).

NOTE: The use of digits as name start characters is specifically forbidden in the standard, to allow SGML parsers to distinguish between names (and name tokens) and numbers (and number tokens).

The NAMECASE entries in the NAMING section of the SYNTAX clause show that, within the reference concrete syntax, upper-case substitution of lower-case characters is generally allowed, but for entity names such substitution is not permitted. General substitution (GENERAL YES) allows tag names and tag identifiers to be entered in any shift, thereby reducing the likelihood of misinterpretation of the document structure. To ensure that entity names are not unnecessarily restricted, however, the program is asked to distinguish between lower-case and upper-case characters within entity references and declarations. This allows different definitions to be declared for, say, ISO, iso and Iso.

NOTE: As will be seen in Chapter 10, the need to be able to associate upper- and lower-case characters has an effect on the way the LCNMSTRT, UCNMSTRT, LCNMCHAR and LCNMCHAR entries are defined.

The GENERAL SGMLREF entry in the DELIM section of the syntax definition shows that the general default set of SGML delimiters is to apply in the reference

Table 3.2   Reference concrete syntax delimiter set.

Code(s)	Name	Purpose
&	ERO	Entity reference open *or*
&	AND	And connector (within declaration group)
&#	CRO	Character reference open
%	PERO	Parameter entity reference open
;	REF	Entity reference close
<	STAGO	Start-tag open
</	ETAGO	End-tag open
<!	MDO	Markup declaration open
<?	PIO	Processing instruction open
>	TAGC	Tag close *or*
>	MDC	Markup declaration close *or*
>	PIC	Processing instruction close
(	GRPO	Group open (within declaration)
)	GRPC	Group close (within declaration)
[	DSO	Declaration subset open *or*
[	DTGO	Data tag group open
]	DSC	Declaration subset close *or*
]	DTGC	Data tag group close
]]	MSC	Marked section close
"	LIT	Start or end of literal string
'	LITA	Alternative start or end of literal string
=	VI	Value indicator (within attributes)
--	COM	Start and end of comment
-	MINUS	Exclusion set identifier
+	PLUS	Inclusion set identifier *or*
+	PLUS	Required and repeatable occurrence indicator
*	REP	Optional and repeatable occurrence indicator
?	OPT	Optional occurrence indicator
|	OR	Or connector (within declaration group)
,	SEQ	Sequence connector (within declaration group)
/	NET	Null end-tag
#	RNI	Reserved name indicator

concrete syntax. Table 3.2 lists these default delimiters. (The use of each of the general delimiters will be explained in the following chapters.) The SHORTREF SGMLREF entry shows that the standard set of SGML short reference characters, illustrated in Table 3.3, can be used with the reference concrete syntax. (If other characters are to be used as short references to entities they must be added to this list by use of the techniques described in Chapter 4.)

In the concrete reference syntax most punctuation characters can be used as short reference delimiters, though tag delimiters (&, <, /, !, ? and >) and certain other significant symbols (e.g. apostrophe, backslash, full stop

Table 3.3 Reference concrete syntax short reference delimiters.

Code(s)	Value(s)	Purpose
&#TAB;	9	Horizontal tab
&#RS;	10	Record start (line feed)
&#RE;	13	Record end (carriage return)
&#SPACE;	32	Space
"	34	Quotation mark
#	35	Number sign
%	37	Percent
'	39	Apostrophe
(	40	Left parenthesis
)	41	Right parenthesis
*	42	Asterisk
+	43	Plus sign
,	44	Comma
-	45	Hyphen
:	58	Colon
;	59	Semicolon
=	61	Equals sign
@	64	Commercial at
[	91	Left square bracket
]	93	Right square bracket
^	94	Circumflex accent
	95	Low line
{	123	Left curly bracket
		124	Vertical line
}	125	Right curly bracket
~	126	Tilde
--	45,45	Two hyphens
BB	66,66	Two or more blanks (spaces or tabs)
B&#RE;	66,13	Trailing blank(s) followed by record end
&#RS;B	10,66	Record start followed by leading blanks
&#RS;B&#RE;	10,66,13	Blank records (one or more blanks)
&#RS;&#RE;	10,13	Empty record

and the general currency sign) are excluded, as are the basic alphanumeric characters. Six special code sequences are also defined in the reference concrete syntax short reference set. These allow common word processor coding conventions to be used as short references to entities or tags (e.g. two hyphens to identify a long dash, or two or more spaces or tabs to indicate an indent or column break).

The last two entries in the SYNTAX clause also use the SGMLREF option, this time to select the default values for reserved names and for quantities. The default set of reserved names are the English names used within the SGML declarations in this book (e.g. DOCTYPE, SGML, ENTITY, ELEMENT, etc.). These default names, which are listed in Table 10.2, can be changed for other languages by the addition of a statement associating one of the reference syntax names with a new name in the NAMES entry in the SYNTAX clause (e.g. NAMES SGMLREF ENTITY DING).

A list of the default quantity set values is given in Figure 10.3. For authors the significant entries in the default quantity set are:

- NAMELEN, which restricts the maximum length of entity and tag names used with the reference concrete syntax to eight characters; and

- TAGLVL, which restricts the number of nested (open) tags to 24.

The purpose of the other quantity entries will be explained in Chapter 10.

3.3 Other clauses in the SGML declaration

The BASESET and DESCSET clauses in the document character set description that starts the SGML declaration can be used to extend the document's character set beyond the code set used to markup the document, as defined in the SYNTAX clause. (For full details of this technique refer to Chapter 11.) For example, the 94 character supplementary set of graphic characters for text communication defined in ISO Standard 6937/2 could be added to the document's character set by placing the following entries underneath the existing DESCSET entry in the CHARSET clause at the start of the SGML declaration:

```
BASESET  "ISO 6937-1983//CHARSET Latin alphabetic and
          non-alphabetic graphic characters//ESC 2/9 6/12"
DESCSET  128 33 UNUSED -- Control character positions --
         161 94 161    -- 94 characters in set --
         255  1 UNUSED -- 255 is shunned character --
```

The extra characters would be accessed by codes with values between 161 and 254, other codes greater than 128 being ignored.

The described character set portion of the document character set description shown in Figure 3.1 defines the purpose of the characters in ISO 646 more clearly than the matching entry in the SYNTAX clause. It can be interpreted as:

- the nine control codes starting from 0 (e.g. 0–8), the two control codes starting from position 11 (11 and 12), the 18 control codes starting from position 14 (14–31) and the control code in position 127 are not used within the document (they are, therefore, considered to be non-SGML characters);

- the two control codes starting at position 9 (e.g. Tab and Record Start) and the one in position 13 (Record End) have special significance within the document (i.e. they are function codes); and
- there are 95 data characters, starting from position 32 (the position of the space, which is also one of the special function characters).

The capacity set used with the reference concrete syntax is the one defined in Figure 5 of ISO 8879 (reproduced as Table 11.2 in Chapter 11). This **reference capacity set** restricts the total number of characters within SGML declarations and derived attributes to 35 000 characters. (This value may need to be altered by document designers specifying very complex documents. The rules for altering the CAPACITY section of an SGML declaration will be given in Chapter 11.)

By default the scope of the SYNTAX clause of an SGML declaration is the whole document (i.e. the syntax is used in both declarations and text). If, however, the character set defined in the syntax section is only used in the text (i.e. all declarations have been coded using the reference concrete syntax) the default SCOPE DOCUMENT entry of the declaration would be changed to read SCOPE INSTANCE. (The special rules that apply in this case will be explained in Chapter 11.)

The FEATURES clause of the SGML declaration shows which of SGML's optional features are required in the document. The optional features available in SGML are:

- using data within a document as tags (DATATAG),
- omitting tags whose presence can be unambiguously implied (OMITTAG),
- using a rank number to define the level of an element (RANK),
- shortening tags by leaving out names that can be implied (SHORTTAG),
- linking document structures using either simple, implicit or explicit links (SIMPLE, IMPLICIT or EXPLICIT),
- defining more than one concurrent structure within a document (CONCUR),
- incorporating subdocuments with different element structures (or entity sets) within a document (SUBDOC), and
- checking public identifiers to ensure that the entered details provide a formal description of the relevant external entity (FORMAL).

In a basic SGML document, however, only the OMITTAG and SHORTTAG options are available, all other options being set to NO.

The last clause in the SGML declaration can be used to transmit any application-specific information (APPINFO) needed to understand the following document. The format of such data must be agreed by parties using the document. In the concrete reference syntax no application-specific information is used.

3.4 *Alternative concrete syntaxes*

ISO 8879 also identifies some special sets of alternative concrete syntaxes. The most important of these are:

- the core concrete syntax,
- basic and core multicode concrete syntaxes, and
- national variant concrete syntaxes.

The **core concrete syntax** is exactly the same as the reference concrete syntax except that the SHORTREF entry in the DELIM section is followed by NONE rather than SGMLREF. Documents that do not use the SHORTREF feature can be prepared using this alternative concrete syntax so that they can be processed by systems that do not support the short reference feature. (A document prepared using the core concrete syntax is referred to as a **minimal SGML document**.)

Where the code extension techniques defined in ISO 2022 are being used to extend the character set beyond the 95 characters available in the reference concrete syntax, the **multicode basic concrete syntax** defined in Annex D of ISO 8879 can be used (see Chapter 10). If the short reference facility is not required the equivalent **multicode core concrete syntax** can be used.

Because the character sets used by many languages do not conform exactly to the reference version defined in ISO 646, variants of the reference concrete syntax will be needed for documents prepared in languages other than English. For most languages a variant concrete syntax will be defined by the standards authority for the relevant country. This syntax will take into account any special accented characters needed for the language and define local versions of reserved names. Each such variant concrete syntax will be publicly declared as a **public concrete syntax** and will be given a **public identifier** that can be used to call it from within another SGML declaration. For example, the German variant concrete syntax might be identified as:

```
SYNTAX PUBLIC "ISO 8879-1986//SYNTAX Deutscher Hinweis//DE"
```

3.5 *The advantages of using publicly declared concrete syntaxes*

In theory each document prepared using SGML could define its own variant for the concrete syntax. If this happened, however, any system receiving an SGML document would have to work out how to convert the incoming document to its own syntax. While such a conversion could be carried out automatically by a clever program, this is not how SGML is intended to be used in practice.

The SGML declaration uses an internationally agreed coding scheme so that it can be read by humans as well as computers. The declaration is placed at the start of a transmitted document so that it can be quickly identified and decoded. In many cases the information in it will be used by a human operator to set up the conversion tables needed to change the incoming syntax to that preferred by the receiving system.

This possibility of human intervention raises the probability of human error, which in turn points out two advantages of using publicly declared concrete syntaxes rather than tailor-made ones:

- their conversion tables are less likely to contain errors, and
- conversion tables prepared for publicly declared concrete syntaxes are likely to have been tested on other documents.

Document transfer will be faster if authors stick to previously declared syntaxes, preferably using the reference concrete syntax or the variant appropriate to their language.

Entity Declaration and Use

An **entity** is defined in ISO 8879 as 'a collection of characters that can be referenced as a unit'. Because SGML places no constraints on the maximum size of an entity (other than those required to fit into the available computer memory) a complete SGML document, or any subsection of the document, can be treated as an entity.

An entity that contains a complete SGML document is known as an **SGML document entity**. SGML document entities have three main sections:

(1)   an **SGML declaration** defining the syntax and character set used within the document,

(2)   declarations defining the structure of the document (the **document type definition**), and

(3)   the text of the document.

SGML document entities can contain references to other types of entities. **SGML subdocument entities** are used to incorporate SGML-coded text which has been stored as a separate document into the main document. Such text may have been prepared using a different set of markup tags from that used in the main document (see Chapter 9). Text that conforms to the declarations defined for the base document type of the main document can be incorporated in the form of an external **SGML text entity**, while graphics or other data containing a mixture of SGML and non-SGML codes can be incorporated into the document in the form of a **non-SGML data entity**. Each of these types of **external entity** can be requested by the author at the required point in the text by entry of an appropriate **external entity reference**.

Within an SGML document, two further types of **embedded entity** are available: **general entities** and **parameter entities**. General entities contain characters that are to form part of the text of a document. Parameter entities are sets of characters required as part of one or more SGML declarations.

Embedded entities are the key to understanding SGML. (In many cases they will be the only feature of SGML that authors will need to declare for themselves.) Each embedded entity has two components: an **entity declaration** and **entity references**. The entity declaration defines the contents of the entity; the entity references indicate where those contents are to appear within the document.

Entity declarations form part of the document type definition entered at the start of each SGML document or subdocument. Each entity declaration consists of an **entity name** followed by details of the text or markup coding to be output whenever a reference to that name is encountered in the text (see Section 4.2). Declarations can either be entered manually by the author/typist or be generated by the text processor as part of an editing function.

Entity references are used within the document to identify the points at which the contents previously declared for the entity are to be output. Entity references consist of an entity name entered between a special pair of delimiter characters. When the parsing program identifies the end of a valid entity reference, it replaces the entire reference with the replacement text associated with the entered entity name in the entity declaration with the same entity name.

Closely associated with SGML entities are **character references** and **short references**. Character references allow authors to enter characters that are not available on the keyboard by reference to a character number or a function name. Short references allow single characters or specially defined groups of characters to act as a shorthand reference to an entity.

4.1   Types of entity

The two main types of entities are **general entities** and **parameter entities**. These can be further subdivided into entities that are declared and referenced in the same document and those whose contents or declarations are stored externally to the document being processed.

4.1.1   General entities

General entity references are used to output previously defined text and/or markup instructions within a document. They can be used wherever parsable text can be entered (i.e. whenever markup recognition is not suppressed – see Chapter 8).

A general entity reference consists of:

- an entity reference open (**ero**) delimiter,
- an entity name, and
- a reference end sequence.

When the reference concrete syntax is being used the entity reference open delimiter is & and the entity name must be a name of not more than eight characters identifying a previously declared entity. The name must start with a valid (alphabetic) **name start character**, which may be followed by up to seven other **name characters**, which can be alphabetic, numeric or either a hyphen or a full stop. The reference end sequence is either:

- a semicolon (the default **refc** reference close delimiter),
- a Record End (RE) code, or
- a character, such as a space, which is not part of a valid entity name.

A typical general entity reference will, therefore, take the form &name;, or just &name if immediately followed by a space or Record End code.

While the fact that entities can be terminated by any character, such as a space, which cannot form part of a valid entity name, can be a useful way of reducing keying, this form of termination should be used with caution. One problem is that some word processors replace spaces with a single Record End code when they fall at the end of a line of text. However, if the SGML program sees a Record End code at the end of a reference it will treat it as a reference end symbol rather than part of the text record containing the entity reference. In this case the space immediately after the entity reference may be lost when replacement takes place. For this reason it is safer always to use a semicolon as the terminator of an entity reference.

If a special entity, known as the **default entity**, is declared in a document type definition, its contents will be output whenever an otherwise undeclared name is encountered within an entity reference. Normally the default entity will contain a special message showing that an unrecognized entity name has been encountered. This message will often be treated as a separate paragraph to ensure that it stands out in the processed document, for example:

```
**** Undeclared entity reference found ****
```

Where more than one concurrent document type has been allowed in a variant concrete syntax, entity names may be qualified by the name of a previously declared document type (for example &(version1)ISO; – see Chapter 9 for further details).

External entities

External entities are general entities whose contents are stored in files other than the one containing the document currently being processed. As well as normal text such files may contain:

- a subdocument to be incorporated within the main document,
- data containing codes not recognized in SGML (non-SGML data), or
- system-specific information that only applies on certain machines.

As with other general entities, external entities are called by use of an entity reference of the form &name;, but in this case the contents of the entity are taken from a separate file, or some other source known to the SGML program, which is identified as a separate source within the associated entity declaration (see Section 4.3).

4.1.2   Parameter entities

Parameter entity references form a special group of entity references that are only used within SGML markup declarations. Typically they will form a reference to a group of element names that are commonly used together within an element declaration. (For full details of their use in element declarations refer to Chapter 5.)

A distinction is made between general entities and parameter entities to avoid the possibility of an author accidentally trying to declare an entity whose name has already been used by a document designer as part of a, possibly hidden, document declaration. By distinguishing between the uses to which the two types of entity are put, it is possible to use the same name for a parameter entity and a general entity.

Parameter entities can also be used within document type declarations to recall externally stored declarations for use within a document type definition. Such recalled data can take the form of 'publicly declared' sets of declarations that are intended to be used for more than one document, or system-specific declarations that have been stored as a separate file for convenience.

A parameter entity reference consists of:

- a parameter entity reference open (**pero**) delimiter,

- an entity name, and
- a reference end sequence.

When the reference concrete syntax is being used the parameter entity reference open delimiter is % and the entity name must be a name of not more than seven characters identifying a previously declared parameter entity. (The seven character restriction applies because, in this case, the % is treated as part of the entity name as well as being the delimiter for the entity.) As with general entity references, the reference end sequence is either:

- a semicolon (the default **refc** reference close delimiter),
- a Record End (RE) code, or
- a character, such as a space, which is not part of a valid entity name.

A typical parameter entity reference will, therefore, have the form %name;.

4.2   Entity declarations

4.2.1   Position

Entity declarations form part of a **document type declaration** defined at the start of an SGML document or subdocument. The document type declaration must immediately follow the SGML declaration. When the reference concrete syntax is being used document type declarations start:

```
<!DOCTYPE docname
```

where docname is a unique **document type name** used to identify the logical structure used for the document/subdocument.

Where an externally stored document type definition is being used as part (or all) of the document type declaration, the relevant external identifier can be entered immediately after the document type name (by use of the options detailed in Section 4.3.3) to give the DOCTYPE declaration the form:

```
<!DOCTYPE docname optional-external-identifier ... >
```

The start of the locally defined set of entity and element declarations (referred to as the **document type declaration subset**) is identified by a **declaration subset open (dso)** delimiter entered immediately after the document's name or external identifier. A matching **declaration subset close (dsc)** delimiter is used to identify the end of the document type declaration subset; this must immediately precede the markup declaration close (**mdc**) code that terminates the DOCTYPE declaration. In the reference concrete syntax the left square bracket ([) is used for **dso**, the right square bracket (]) is used for **dsc** and the **mdc** code is the greater than sign (>), giving the document type declaration the overall form:

```
<!DOCTYPE docname optional-external-identifier
[--local declarations--] >
```

4.2.2 Structure

Within the document type declaration subset, each individual entity declaration is entered between its own set of markup declaration delimiters. (From Chapter 3 you should remember that, in the reference concrete syntax, <! is used for the markup declaration open (**mdo**) delimiter while > is used for the markup declaration close delimiter.) The reserved name ENTITY (or its previously declared replacement) follows the **mdo** to identify the declaration as an entity declaration. The rest of the declaration consists of the **entity name** followed by the replacement **entity text** to give an entity declaration the general form:

```
<!ENTITY name "replacement entity text">
```

In its basic form the entity text will consist of a string of characters delimited by a matched pair of either quotation marks (") or apostrophes ('). A typical entity declaration might be entered as:

```
<!ENTITY aw "Addison-Wesley">
```

Such an entity would be called by entering the entity reference &aw; in the text.

The replacement string can include markup codes, such as element tags, entity references, character references, short references and data tags, which will be interpreted as the entity text is added to the document. For example, a general entity declaration might take the form:

```
<!ENTITY rev "<hp1>Revision Subject&dagger;</hp1>" >
```

When this entity is called, by entering &rev; in the text, the program will recognize the embedded text as a highlighted phrase bracketed by a <hp1> start-tag and a </hp1> end-tag. Before outputting this highlighted phrase in the appropriate font the program will expand the reference to the entity called dagger to obtain the system-specific code needed to generate a dagger symbol.

One word of warning, however: do not put the entity name within the replacement text, otherwise you will form a recursive loop, which will cause the program to exceed the maximum permitted number of entity levels as soon as it encounters the first reference to the entity. It also pays to make sure that the replacement string does not contain any characters that might be treated as short references which should be mapped to the entity being defined.

It should be noted that while any number of spaces and tab codes can be used to separate the entity name from the preceding reserved name and the following replacement text, any such codes entered within the delimited entity text will be retained as part of the definition. Once the closing delimiter has been entered for the entity text, however, any number of spaces, tab codes and comments can precede the markup declaration close code identifying the end of the entity declaration.

Parameter entities

A parameter entity declaration is distinguished from a general entity declaration by having a parameter entity reference open delimiter (for example %) and a space immediately in front of the required name to give it the form:

```
<!ENTITY % name "replacement text" >
```

Typically the replacement text for a parameter entity will consist of a series of element names separated by the relevant SGML group connectors (see Table 5.1), for example:

```
<!ENTITY % heading "h0|h1|h2|h3|h4">
```

(Other examples of the use of parameter entities are given in Chapter 5.)

One word of warning is required here – it is important to remember that parameter entities must be declared before the entity is referred to within the document type definition. (This restriction is particularly important when using parameter entities to define large sets of attribute default values, as the natural reaction here is to recognize the need for a parameter entity to store the relevant values, then to put a reference to the entity in the attribute definition before entering the associated entity declaration!)

The inclusion of comments

The purpose of an entity can be explained by incorporating **comments** within the definition. When the reference concrete syntax is being used, the start and end of each comment must be indicated by entering a pair of (consecutive) hyphens. Like the replacement entity text, comments can take up more than one line, for example:

```
<!ENTITY disclaim "Users should note that all International
Standards undergo revision from time to time and that
any reference made herein to any other International
Standard implies its latest edition, unless otherwise
stated." -- Must appear in the Foreword of each ISO
            standard -- >
```

4.2.3   *Alternative forms of entity declaration*

For general entities, variations to the basic declaration allow users to specify:

- a default entity,
- entities containing only start- and end-tags for elements,
- entities that are to be treated as marked sections, processing instructions or other forms of markup declaration,
- entities consisting entirely of character data, and
- entities containing system-specific replacement text.

A special default entity can be declared by using the reserved word #DEFAULT in place of an entity name, for example:

```
<!ENTITY #DEFAULT
  "&RE;&RS;*** Undeclared entity reference found ***&RE;">
```

The replacement text for this default entity will be used whenever a general entity reference is encountered whose name is not recognized as one of the currently declared entities.

Where entities, such as those that are to be associated with short references (see Section 4.5), consist solely of an element start-tag or end-tag, the role of the entity can be unambiguously defined by preceding the *undelimited* element name, and any associated attributes, with a STARTTAG or ENDTAG keyword. For example, the declaration:

```
<!ENTITY formula STARTTAG "eqn type=TEX" >
```

will cause the program to replace &formula; with <eqn type=TEX>, while:

```
<!ENTITY ef ENDTAG "eqn" --end of formula-- >
```

will cause it to replace &ef; with </eqn>.

Alternatively, the two entities could have been defined as:

```
<!ENTITY formula "<eqn type=TEX>" >
<!ENTITY ef      "</eqn>"          >
```

but in this case the program would not know that the replacement text contained an element tag which needed further processing until it had added the replacement text to the main text stream. By specifically declaring that the replacement text consists of an element tag, the process of element recognition can be speeded up and the tag becomes independent of the delimiter set being used.

Other keywords that can be used to identify embedded SGML markup instructions before output are:

- MS to identify the text as a marked section (bracketed by <![and]]> – see Chapter 8),

- MD to identify the text as a markup declaration (bracketed by <! and >), and

- PI to identify the text as a processing instruction (bracketed by <? and > – see Chapter 8).

Typically, these keywords will be used in entity declarations such as:

```
<!ENTITY nomap MD "USEMAP #EMPTY">
```

This declaration allows the entity reference &nomap; to be used to generate the commonly used <!USEMAP #EMPTY> markup declaration. (The role of this markup declaration will be explained in Section 4.5.2.)

Where a document, such as this one, contains text that may be mistakenly interpreted as a markup tag, it may be necessary to declare special entities that can be used to output SGML delimiter characters. The characters most likely to need treating in this way are the markup declaration open code (normally <) and the entity reference open code (normally &). The following declarations can be used to set up entities with suitable, ISO standard, entity names:

```
<!ENTITY lt   "<" >
<!ENTITY amp  "&" >
```

If, for example, the paragraph start-tag <p> was to be output as part of the text of a document in which it was also being used as a tag, it could be entered as <p>. (This would not be recognized as a valid start-tag because tags and entity references are only recognized if they are

contained within the same entity.) Similarly, the general entity reference
&SGML; could be entered as &SGML; to ensure that it is not replaced by the
declared replacement text for the SGML entity (or the default entity).

It should be noted that the semicolon is a compulsory element of
both the last two entity references because they are followed by a name
character. If the semicolon had been left out of the first example, the
program would have tried to find an entity whose declared name was ltp. In
the case of the second example, the program would look for an entity
called ampSGML. If entities with these names had not previously been declared,
and no default entity had been defined, the parser should flag the entity as
invalid.

Where SGML's SHORTTAG feature is being used (see Chapter 7) the
solidus (/) may need to be output in a position in which it could be
interpreted as an end-tag for an element. In such a case a simple entity
reference of the form:

```
<!ENTITY sol   "/" --solidus = shilling stroke-->
```

would not suffice as the program would, after replacing the / entity
reference, recognize the replacement character as a valid markup character
(because it occurred within a single entity). To avoid this possibility the
reserved name CDATA can be placed immediately in front of the replacement
string to give the entity declaration the form:

```
<!ENTITY sol   CDATA      "/">
```

The inclusion of the CDATA keyword tells the program that the
replacement text is to be treated purely as character data. This means that
any characters within the string that could possibly be interpreted as
markup codes will be ignored. This feature may also be used with longer
strings. For example, the declaration:

```
<!ENTITY para CDATA "<p>">
```

could be used to set up the ¶ entity so that it outputs the characters <p>
rather than the start-tag for a paragraph (which would be output if the CDATA
reserved name was not used).

It is sometimes necessary to use system-specific information in the
replacement text for entities. To allow receiving programs to identify
expansions that they might not handle in exactly the same way on each
system, the reserved word SDATA can be used to identify entity declarations
containing system-specific replacement text. For example, the entity
declaration used to identify the Æ ligature might be:

```
<!ENTITY AElig SDATA "[AElig]"--=capital AE dipthong (ligature)-->
```

In this case the program will expand Æ to give [AElig], which the text formatter will recognize as the coding that generates the character Æ. When this entity declaration is sent to another system, however, the SDATA reserved word can be recognized and the receiving program can ask its operator to provide the coding needed to generate the relevant replacement character(s).

It should be noted, however, that while characters defined as valid in the document's character set but as invalid in the document's concrete syntax can be included in SDATA entities, non-SGML characters that have been declared as unused in the document's character set cannot be specified in an SDATA entity declaration.

4.3   External entities

Two main types of external entity are recognized by SGML:

(1)   entities that are specific to the system preparing/transmitting the document, and

(2)   publicly declared entities whose purpose is known to more than one system.

Each of these main types can be further subdivided into:

- SGML subdocument entities,
- SGML text entities, and
- data entities containing text or non-SGML data not marked up using SGML tags.

External entities are identified by means of an **external identifier** which indicates the type of entity being defined (publicly declared or system-specific) and, optionally, the source of the data to be added to the document.

4.3.1   System-specific external entities

The simplest way of declaring a **system-specific external entity** (i.e. an entity whose meaning is known only to the systems it is used on) is to use the reserved name SYSTEM in place of the replacement text in the entity declaration, giving the declaration the form:

```
<!ENTITY file.doc SYSTEM>
```

where file.doc is a valid entity name that is also recognized by the system as a reference to a file that it should add to the text.

More typically, however, the entity declaration will be qualified by a **system identifier** that uniquely identifies the source of the required entity. In many instances the system identifier will consist of a file name, optionally qualified by a pathname, for example:

```
<!ENTITY ch4 SYSTEM "c:\SGML\manual\chapter4.doc">
```

When the program identifies a reference to the declared entity name (&ch4;) within the text, it will call up the file identified by the system identifier and output its contents in place of the entity reference.

Alternative markup notations

When a system-specific external entity contains data that has been coded using a form of markup that differs from that used in the main document the system identifier can be qualified by an **entity type** statement. (If the entity type statement is not present the entity is presumed to be a parsable SGML text entity.) Four variant entity types are recognized:

(1) subdocuments that are coded in SGML using an alternative docu-ment type definition,

(2) character data (CDATA) entities that contain only valid SGML char-acters but which are coded using a special notation,

(3) non-SGML data (NDATA) entities that contain codes outside the set declared to be valid SGML characters for the document, and

(4) specific character data (SDATA) entities that contain characters whose role is specific to the local system.

Where the retrieved entity contains data that is not coded in SGML (i.e. consists of non-SGML characters, non-parsable character data or system-specific information), the entity must be declared as a **data entity**. This is indicated by placing the appropriate reserved word (CDATA, NDATA or SDATA) immediately after the system identifier (or the word SYSTEM if no identifier is present) followed by a compulsory **notation name** identifying the type of coding used within the data entity.

The following examples illustrate two ways in which non-SGML data entities containing illustrations can be declared:

```
<!ENTITY pie12 SYSTEM "pie12.img" NDATA piechart>
<!ENTITY fig1-3 SYSTEM NDATA halftone>
```

When using the SYSTEM keyword either the system identifier (for example pie12.img) or the entity name (for example fig1-3) must be sufficient to allow the program to identify uniquely the file required, while the notation name must be one that is declared, within the same document type declaration, as a valid notation for the document. The **notation declaration** used for this purpose has the general form:

```
<!NOTATION name identifier>
```

where name is the notation name used after NDATA in the entity declaration and identifier is a valid **notation identifier**, which is either system-specific or publicly declared. If the notation identifier is system-specific, it will consist of the reserved word SYSTEM followed by a system identifier which will be recognized by systems processing the text, for example:

```
<!NOTATION piechart SYSTEM "pie chart graphics program">
```

To see how the above declarations would be used in practice, consider what happens when a reference to the &pie12; entity defined above is encountered within text. Once the program has identified the end of the entity reference, it will ask the system to send it the contents of the file known as pie12.img. The system will process the data stored in the requested file using the rules specified in the system's pie chart graphics program. When the stored data has been converted into a form suitable for output within the document, it is sent to the SGML program, which will use it as the replacement text for the entered entity reference.

When the system has finished sending the decoded data to the document it will transmit a special, system-dependent, signal, known as an **entity end** signal, to the SGML parser. This signal is output by the system at the end of each entity to tell the parser that it can continue processing the rest of the text now that the entity reference has been satisfied.

NOTE: The entity end signal is not a control code and need not be one of the codes declared within the document's character set. It can be any signal or group of signals recognized by the SGML program as an indication that the end of an entity's replacement text has been received.

Where an external entity contains character data or other system-specific information, its declaration must also be qualified by a suitable notation name, for example:

```
<!ENTITY file1   SYSTEM CDATA "TEX-file" >
<!ENTITY special SYSTEM "b:logotype.174" SDATA "logo" >
```

where the associated notation declarations could take the form:

```
<!NOTATION TEX-file SYSTEM "TEX formatter" >
<!NOTATION logo     SYSTEM "Logo generation subsystem" >
```

NOTE: Notation declarations can have associated data attributes. Where attributes have been declared for a notation the required attribute values can be entered immediately after the notation name to form a qualified external entity declaration (see Chapter 6).

Locally stored subdocuments

If a system-specific entity contains a complete SGML-coded document, including the appropriate document type definition, it can be declared as a system-specific **SGML subdocument entity** by placing the reserved word SUBDOC after the entity's system identifier, for example:

```
<!ENTITY annex SYSTEM "sgmlfile.doc" SUBDOC>
```

NOTE: This feature can only be used if the SGML declaration has a FEATURES clause containing a SUBDOC YES entry. Unless otherwise declared, the FEATURES clause defaults to SUBDOC NO.

When an SGML program that has received the above entity declaration encounters the entity reference &annex; within the text, it will ask the system to send it the contents of sgmlfile.doc. While it is processing this subdocument it will use the document type declaration provided at the start of the recalled file, rather than the one currently in use. When the subdocument has been incorporated into the main document, the original document type declaration will be restored.

4.3.2 *Publicly declared external entities*

Publicly declared external entities are external entities that contain declarations, text or other data designed to be used on more than one SGML system.

Many publicly declared entities consist solely of a predefined set of markup declarations which can be used to extend declaration subsets defined within the document. When the relevant parameter entity reference is encountered in the document type declaration, the program will add the declarations it has previously stored as a publicly declared entity to the end of the local declarations.

The advantage of using publicly declared entities is that, because such entities are presumed to be known by any receiving system, their full declarations do not need to be transmitted between systems. Instead, all the user needs to do is add the necessary public entity declarations, with the associated references, to the document to tell receiving systems which of the prestored sets of declarations are required.

Publicly declared external entities are said to be 'publicly declared' because the relevant declarations are presumed to be common knowledge to systems using them, but the declarations can be 'private' in the sense that they do not need to be known to everyone. Where necessary, the relevant declarations can be restricted to the systems which have agreed to use them, so allowing these systems to call document type definitions or standard text required for a number of different documents.

There are, however, certain publicly declared entities that may truly be called 'publicly declared'. These contain sets of declarations that have been defined by one of the organizations authorized by the International Standards Organization (ISO) to keep registers of declarations used in more than one document. Once a declaration set has been registered in this way it will have a unique name by which it can be recognized by all systems using it.

In addition, ISO have declared certain sets of entities as internationally recognized entities that may be used to identify characters or other constructs defined in international standards. Such sets are identified by special **ISO owner identifiers**. Normally, ISO owner identifiers consist of the letters ISO followed by the number of the standard referred to. This identifier is further qualified by entry of the publication date of the standard to provide a unique reference to a particular version of the standard containing the required declarations, for example "ISO 8879-1986". (For character sets a special type of registration number can also be used. In such cases the relevant registration number is preceded by the words ISO Registration Number.)

Before requesting any publicly declared entity it is important to check that the relevant declarations will be available to any system receiving the marked-up SGML document. *The fact that an entity has been publicly declared does NOT mean that it will be known to all SGML systems*, it simply means that its definition does not need to be transmitted between systems that already know the definition.

Requesting publicly declared external entities

Publicly declared external entities which just contain text can be requested by entering a declaration of the form:

```
<!ENTITY name PUBLIC "public identifier" >
```

This entity can be recalled at any point in the text by entering a general entity reference of the form &name;.

If the entity contains SGML markup declarations that are to be added to the document type definition, it must be declared by entering a parameter entity declaration of the form:

```
<!ENTITY % name PUBLIC "public identifier">
```

the entity then being recalled by entering the relevant parameter entity reference (for example `%name;`) at some point between the entity declaration and the declaration subset close character (`]`) marking the end of the document type declaration subset.

The `public identifier` used in the entity declaration of the above external entities is either a formal public identifier or a name agreed between users.

NOTE: If the FEATURES clause of the current SGML declaration contains the entry FORMAL YES the public identifier must be a formal public identifier (see below).

ISO 8879 restricts the characters that may be used in agreed names to a special set of **minimum data characters** consisting of the upper- and lower-case alphabetic letters, spaces (or record start and end codes), numbers and a set of characters declared to be part of a special character class. These special characters are:

```
' ( ) + , . - / : = ?
```

NOTE: This list of special characters cannot be extended or otherwise altered in the SGML declaration. If you wish to use an agreed name to identify a set of declarations you must make sure your name consists only of characters mapped in the current document character set to these special characters or one of the standard ASCII/ISO 646 alphanumeric characters.

Formal public identifiers

Formal public identifiers fall into one of three categories:

- those defined by the ISO,
- those allocated to registered declaration sets, or
- unregistered declarations.

A typical ISO registered entity set will be identified within the document type definition of the document using the set by a declaration of the form:

```
<!ENTITY % ISOpub PUBLIC
 "ISO 8879-1986//ENTITIES Publishing//EN">
```

This declaration must then be invoked by incorporating the parameter entity `%ISOpub;` into the document type declaration before the closing square bracket, for example:

```
<!DOCTYPE docname [
 <!ENTITY % ISOpub PUBLIC
  "ISO 8879-1986//ENTITIES Publishing//EN">
```

```
.
.      -- other required declarations --
.
%ISOpub; ]>
```

It will be seen from the above example that, in this case, the formal public identifier has three components, separated from each other by a pair of solidus strokes. The three components are:

(1)   an **ISO owner identifier** which shows the number and date of the standard being referred to;

(2)   a **public text class** (for example ENTITIES – see below) and an associated **public text description** (for example Publishing); and

(3)   a **public text language** code (for example EN for English).

Entity sets registered by bodies other than ISO will use a **registered owner identifier** in place of the ISO owner identifier. The registered name is preceded by +// to identify the following identifier as one applying to a registered set. A typical declaration might be:

```
<!ENTITY % IBMchars PUBLIC
 "+//IBM//ENTITIES IBM PC Character Set//EN">
```

One registered owner identifier that is of special interest to book publishers is that assigned to the International Standard Book Numbering Agency. This special identifier allows publishers to be identified by reference to the group and publisher identifiers that form the first part of the ISBNs assigned to their books. For example, a set of entity declarations for use in Addison-Wesley publications could be assigned an identifier of the form:

```
<!ENTITY % AWacc PUBLIC "+//ISBN/0 201/Addison-Wesley
                 //ENTITIES Accented Characters//EN"
```

Here the registered owner identifier is made up of three parts, separated by single slashes:

(1)   the letters ISBN that identify the identifier as one assigned by the International Standard Book Numbering Agency or one of its agents;

(2)   the unique number assigned to the publisher; and consisting of a group identifier followed, after a space, by a publisher identifier; and

(3)   the name of the publisher.

Where the declarations have not been formally registered, an **unregistered owner identifier** must be used as the owner identifier. This has the same form as a registered owner identifier, except that a hyphen is used in place of the initial plus. The name used to identify the owner must consist of one of the minimum data characters (alphanumeric or special) allowed in public identifiers. A typical declaration might take the form:

```
<!ENTITY % AWacc PUBLIC
   "-//Addison-Wesley//ENTITIES Accented Characters//EN">
```

NOTE: This entity set is defined in Appendix B and used in the document type declaration shown in Appendix C.

The **public text class keyword** that follows the owner identifier indicates the type of declarations defined in the external entity. The keyword may have one of the following forms:

- ENTITIES where the external entity contains only entity declarations;
- ELEMENTS where the external entity contains element, attribute or notation declarations, with their associated parameter entities, comments, processing instructions and marked sections;
- DTD where the external entity contains a document type declaration subset containing declarations defining the document's structure and entities;
- SUBDOC where the external entity contains the document type declaration and the text for a subdocument to be used within the current document (see Chapter 9);
- DOCUMENT where the external entity starts with an SGML declaration defining the required concrete syntax, etc., followed by a document type declaration for the base document and, where applicable, the relevant text;
- TEXT where the only text of the document (including any element tags and entity references) is to be called from the external entity;
- NONSGML where the retrieved data consists of preprocessed data containing non-SGML characters;
- SHORTREF where the external entity contains only the short reference, entity and map use declarations making up a short reference set (see Section 4.5);
- SYNTAX where the external entity only contains details of the concrete syntax to be used in the document;
- CHARSET where the external entity only contains details of the base character set to be used within a document type declaration;
- NOTATION where the external entity contains only details of the notation to be used for processing non-SGML data;

- LPD   where the external entity contains only the link set, attribute and entity declarations making up a link type declaration subset (see Chapter 9); or
- CAPACITY   where the external entity contains only capacity set declarations (see Chapter 11).

NOTE: All public text class keywords must be entered using capital letters only.

Only one keyword may appear in any formal identifier, though most of the keywords can be used more than once in a document. (Only one syntax or capacity declaration may be made in any document.)

Where the TEXT, NONSGML or SUBDOCUMENT public text class keywords are used in a public identifier within an entity declaration the entity must be defined as a general entity. With the exception of the NOTATION keyword described below, all other keywords may only be used in parameter entity declarations because they contain markup declarations that need to be added to any local declarations.

The NOTATION option differs slightly from the other public text class keywords in that it is only used to qualify notation declarations. It is typically used in the form:

```
<!NOTATION tex PUBLIC "-//local//NOTATION TEX Formula//EN">
```

This declaration defines a notation called tex as a locally recognized notation that will be used to process English, T_EX-format formulae.

Each public text class keyword is qualified by a **public text description** explaining the purpose of the publicly declared entity. (This description is restricted to the alphanumeric and special minimum data characters used for public identifiers.) Where the entity consists of declarations that are not generally available to the public, the public text description should be preceded by an **unavailable text indicator** (-//) to give the identifier the form:

```
<!ENTITY % name PUBLIC
         "-//owner//class -//description//language" >
```

The **public text language** parameter that normally ends a formal public identifier must be one of the two character codes for identifying languages defined in ISO 639. (The single letter alternatives defined in ISO 639 may not be used in SGML.) This language code tells the system which language the public text has been prepared in. The currently defined codes include those shown in Table 4.1.

Codes have also been defined for most European languages, including 'dead' languages, such as Latin, and for international languages, such as Esperanto, Interlingua and Interlingue.

Table 4.1 Languages codes as defined in ISO 639.

Code	Language	Code	Language
EN	English	AR	Arabic
FR	French	HE	Hebrew
DE	German	RU	Russian
GR	Greek	CH	Chinese
IT	Italian	JA	Japanese
NL	Dutch	HI	Hindi
ES	Spanish	UR	Urdu
PT	Portuguese	SA	Sanskrit

Note that the language codes are all defined as a pair of capital letters. These codes cannot be replaced by the equivalent lower-case letters within the formal public identifier, even if the name case rules in the SGML declaration permit general substitution of tag characters, because the standard specifically states that the upper-case form must be used for all public text language values.

Where the public text class keyword is CHARSET the public text language code should be replaced by a **public text designating sequence**. This sequence of codes uniquely identifies the selected character set by using techniques defined in ISO 2022. Each sequence starts with an Escape code (1/11, hexadecimal 1B) followed by a number indicating the type of code set being described. This number is further qualified by one or more numbers identifying the required set of characters.

The types of code that can be indicated by the first code after the Escape code include:

- 2/1 to identify the set as defining a C0 standard control code set (32 characters, starting at 0/0),
- 2/2 to identify the set as defining a C1 supplementary control code set (32 characters, starting at 8/0),
- 2/4 to identify the set as a multiple-byte 94 character code set,
- 2/5 to identify the set as one not defined by ISO 2022,
- 2/8 to identify the set as a standard 94 character G0 set (starting at position 2/1),
- 2/9 to identify the set as a 94 character G1 supplementary character code set (starting at 10/1),
- 2/10 to identify the set as a G2 alternative 94 character supplementary code set (overlaying G1 at 10/1),

- 2/11 to identify the set as a G3 alternative 94 character supplementary code set (overlaying G1 at 10/1),

- 2/13 to identify the set as a 96 character G1 supplementary character code set (starting at 10/0),

- 2/14 to identify the set as a G2 alternative 96 character supplementary code set (overlaying G1 at 10/0), and

- 2/15 to identify the set as a G3 alternative 96 character supplementary code set (overlaying G1 at 10/0).

A typical declaration for a publicly declared entity that defines a document's character set might be:

```
<!ENTITY % ISO646 PUBLIC "ISO 646-1983//CHARSET
   International Reference Version (IRV)//ESC 2/5 4/0">
```

This declaration identifies the publicly declared external entity known as ISO 646 as the one containing the definitions required to define part or all of the character set to be used in the document. The character set required is that specified in the 1983 version of ISO standard 646, which defines an international reference version character set that has been allocated the default public text designating sequence ESC 2/5 4/0.

NOTE: ESC 2/5 4/0 *is a special sequence used to return to the basic* G0 *character set from a character set defined outside ISO 2022.*

Where a publicly declared entity consists of entity declarations which contain system-specific data (i.e. use the SDATA option) the associated formal public identifier can be further qualified by the addition of a **public text display version** description. This description identifies which types of device the defined entities will be recognized by.

A typical extended entry might take the form:

```
<!ENTITY % Quorum PUBLIC
      "-//Quorum Technical Services Ltd//ENTITIES
         Special Characters//EN//APL100"          >
```

This declaration identifies a publicly declared set of entities that Quorum Technical Services use to identify the special characters available on their APL100 typesetting terminals.

The public text display version can also be used to qualify NONSGML entities to identify how they might be displayed, but it cannot be used when the class name is CAPACITY, CHARSET, NOTATION or SYNTAX. (These declarations occur only in the SGML declaration, which are always displayed using the reference concrete syntax.)

When creating a formal public identifier it is important not to split the literal string immediately after one of the slashes (solidii) used to identify the start of a new component within the public identifier. This is because the start of a new line in the delimited string will be treated as if a space had been entered, and spaces are not permitted immediately after a slash. As the above example shows, however, the public identifier literal string can be split immediately after the public text keyword or after any other word in the string. (It can also be put in a line of its own if this removes the need for a line break within the literal string.)

4.3.3   Using publicly declared document type declarations

External identifiers can also be used to add externally stored declarations to a document type declaration. In this case the SYSTEM or PUBLIC keyword immediately follows the document type name at the start of the document type declaration. The relevant keyword is followed by a space and the required identifier to produce the DOCTYPE's optional-external-identifier (see Section 4.2.1).

Typically, the optional-external-identifier will identify an external entity containing the element and parameter entity declarations required for the document type declaration subset, together with any associated declarations for short references, notations, etc. A typical example might be:

```
<!DOCTYPE text book PUBLIC
    "-//Addison-Wesley//DTD SGML: An Author's Guide to the Standard Generalized Markup Language//EN"
    [ -- local declarations -- ]>
```

The recalled declarations will be added to any declarations specified in the local document type declaration subset. Though defined at the start of the document type declaration, these declarations will, in fact, be added to the *end* of any declarations in the subset. Because SGML only recognizes the first definition of an entity it receives, the fact that the recalled declarations are added to the end of the subset ensures that any declarations entered in the local document type declaration subset will override a definition with the same name in the recalled declarations. For example, if the document type declaration subset contains the definition:

```
<ENTITY p CDATA "<p>">
```

while the recalled document type definition contains the entity:

```
<ENTITY p STARTTAG p>
```

the local definition would be used within the document, causing all &p; entity references (or short references calling this entity) to be output as the character string ‹p›, rather than being recognized as a paragraph element tag.

Only one external identifier can be associated with each document type declaration (normally, but not necessarily, that of a document type declaration subset). Where more than one set of externally stored or publicly declared declarations is required in a document, the other entities will have to be declared and called within the local document declaration subset. For example, a document type declaration might start:

```
<!DOCTYPE   textbook PUBLIC
     "-//Addison-Wesley//DTD SGML: An Author's Guide to the Standard Generalized Markup
     Language//EN"
[ <!ENTITY % AWacc  PUBLIC
     "-//Addison-Wesley//ENTITIES Accented Characters//EN"    >
  <!ENTITY copyrite PUBLIC
     "-//Addison-Wesley//TEXT Copyright + Disclaimer//EN"    >
  <!ENTITY annex    SYSTEM "sgmlfile.doc" SUBDOC            >
  <!NOTATION setm   PUBLIC "+//BSI//NOTATION SETM coding//EN" >
     .
        -- other local declarations --
     .
  %AWacc; ]>
```

Note that only the first of the three entity declarations has been entered as a parameter entity and that this entity has been called by entry of a reference within the same document type declaration subset. The copyrite and annex entities, on the other hand, contain text that is to be added to the document at the place the relevent entity references are entered by the author. To allow them to be called from within the document they have been declared as general entities. (It should be noted, however, that the optional-external-identifier preceding the document type declaration subset cannot be entered as a parameter entity reference as it must be specified before any entities are defined.)

Where required, public identifiers can be further qualified by system identifiers showing where the relevant details can be found on the system. For example, if the required declarations were stored in a file called elements.def a document type declaration might start:

```
<!DOCTYPE manual PUBLIC
   "-//Quorum//ELEMENTS A4 manual//EN" "elements.def"
   [ ... ]>
```

Note that, for publicly declared entities, the word SYSTEM does not precede the system identifier.

4.4 Character references

Some input keyboards cannot access all the characters available on the printer, or other output device, being used to output SGML documents. Characters that cannot be entered by use of a dedicated keystroke can be entered either as a character reference or as a reference to a previously declared system-specific (SDATA) entity, or by using a combination of both techniques.

A **character reference** is a special reference entered within the text that specifies the required character either by entry of its decimal value or by reference to the function name it has been allocated in the currently defined concrete syntax (for example RE, RS, TAB or SPACE).

A special **character reference open** (**cro**) delimiter is used to identify character references. In the reference concrete syntax **cro** is defined as &#, giving a typical character reference the form:

    {

or

    &#TAB;

Character references can be used within the replacement text of an entity declaration. For example, the entity declaration:

    <!ENTITY microns "ém">

could be defined to allow &microns; to be entered to generate the characters µm.

Character references are often used when a double quote is required in the replacement text of an entity. For example, to define a piece of quoted text within an entity it could be declared as:

    <!ENTITY ISO
      ""International Standards Organization"">

Alternatively the entity could be defined within single quotes as:

    <!ENTITY ISO
      '"International Standards Organization "'>

but in this event the quoted text can only contain apostrophes entered as character references of the form ' if the replacement text is not to be prematurely ended.

Character references can be used to incorporate non-SGML characters into the text of a document, without needing to declare a special non-SGML external entity to hold the characters. As such they are suitable for short insertions of non-SGML data, but will not normally be convenient for entering large amounts of data coded using non-SGML characters.

Because numeric character references are always remembered in that form, rather than being replaced by the equivalent internal code, they can be used to output function codes that might otherwise be recognized as a delimiter by the SGML program. For example,  will always be output as a carriage return, whereas &#RE; might be interpreted as the the end of an entity reference rather than a code to be sent to the printer.

One point to remember about character references is that the numbers used may need to be altered if the document's character set is changed or if the document is passed to a system using a different character set. For this reason special characters should, wherever possible, be defined within a document's character set.

4.5   Short references

Short references are characters, or strings of characters, that provide a shorthand reference to an entity within the main text of a document.

In the reference concrete syntax most non-alphanumeric characters not used as markup delimiters are defined as valid short reference delimiters. The reference concrete syntax also defines six strings of characters that are commonly used when preparing text on a word processor as possible short references. (A full list of the default set of short reference delimiters was given in Table 3.3.)

Other characters declared in the document's character set can be added to this set by entering them as part of the DELIM section of the document's syntax definition (see Chapter 10). Each additional short reference string required is declared, between literal delimiters ("), at the end of the SHORTREF entry in the SGML declaration. Typically the extended entry will take the form:

```
DELIM GENERAL  SGMLREF
        SHORTREF SGMLREF "??" "!!" "=/" "+-" "-+"
```

In the above example five new short reference sequences have been added to the default set shown in Table 3.3. These sequences could be used, for example, to access special characters such as the upside-down versions of the question mark and exclamation mark, and commonly used mathematical symbols such as not equals and the two variants of the plus and minus sign.

It should be noted, however, that character sequences used as general SGML markup delimiters should not be used as short reference delimiter strings since their use here would prevent their use as markup (for a more detailed explanation of this restriction see Chapters 10 and 12).

Short references are mapped to entities in **short reference mapping declarations**. More than one mapping declaration can be defined in a document but only one map will be in force at any one time.

The current short reference map is determined by use of **short reference use declarations**. Normally these will be declared in the document type definition so that they are activated automatically whenever a particular element or group of elements is used. Alternatively, map use can be explicitly requested from within the text (see Section 4.5.2).

4.5.1   Short reference mapping declarations

Short reference mapping declarations are identified by an initial keyword of SHORTREF (or its declared replacement) immediately after the markup declaration open sequence, for example <!SHORTREF. This is followed by a unique **map name** that is used to identify the mapping declaration in associated short reference use declarations.

The map name is followed by definitions linking the short reference delimiters to be used while the map is in force to one of the entities defined in the current document type definition. The relevant short reference characters, which must be taken from the strings defined in the current SGML declaration, are entered as parameter literals (i.e. between pairs of quotation marks or pairs of apostrophes). This string is followed by a space and the name of the entity containing the replacement text for the specified short reference character(s).

A typical short reference mapping declaration might take the form:

```
<!SHORTREF tablemap "("  row
                    "¦"  column
                    ")"  endrow   >
```

In this example three short reference characters are being used to identify the rows and columns in a table. The associated entity references might be:

```
<!ENTITY row    STARTTAG "r" >
<!ENTITY column STARTTAG "c" >
<!ENTITY endrow ENDTAG   "r" >
```

Whenever the tablemap short reference map is in force the string (A¦B¦C¦D) will be expanded to <r>A<c>B<c>C<c>D</r>.

A short reference delimiter character (or string) can be used only once in any particular mapping declaration. If the entered short reference delimiter is not one of those defined in the SGML declaration currently in force the mapping will not take place and the short reference will be treated as part of the text. (At least one valid short reference string must be specified in each short reference mapping declaration.)

4.5.2   Short reference use declarations

There are two ways in which a short reference map can be activated – automatically or manually. Automatic mapping of short references is achieved by entering short reference use declarations within a document type definition. Manual mapping occurs when a short reference use declaration is entered as part of the markup within the text.

An automatically actioned short reference use declaration has the general form:

```
<!USEMAP map-name element-list>
```

where `map-name` identifies a map defined in an associated short reference mapping declaration and `element-list` contains the names of the elements that are to activate the map.

The map declared above would, typically, be invoked by the declaration:

```
<!USEMAP tablemap table>
```

This declaration tells the program that the map declared with the name of `tablemap` is to be used whenever an element called `table` is being processed. This map will stay in force until the end-tag for the table element (`</table>`) is encountered or implied, unless it is overridden by another map that has been set up to apply to a valid subelement of the table element.

If more than one element is to activate a particular map, the element names must be entered as a **name group**. Name groups are bracketed by **group open (grpo)** and **group close (grpc)** codes, each name within the group being separated by a **sequence connector (seq)**, an **and connector (and)** or an **or connector (or)** – but never a combination of connectors. When the reference concrete syntax is being used a typical declaration will take the form:

```
<!USEMAP quotes (p,n,xmp,l,poem)>
```

If any of the listed elements is started by entry of an appropriate start-tag, the `quote` map will automatically become the current map, overriding any existing map until the associated end-tag is identified. Once the end-tag for the element that first invoked the map has been recognized, the parser will remove the map, restoring any previously active map if appropriate. For example, if an example (‹xmp›) was nested within a paragraph (‹p›), the map would be activated by both start-tags but it would remain in force until the end of paragraph element as the end-tag for the example (‹/xmp›) would simply return the parser to using the map associated with the original paragraph tag. (The role of the quotes map will be explained more fully shortly.)

Maps may be activated from within the text of a document by entry of a declaration of the form:

    ‹!USEMAP map-name›

In this case no element name is stated, the map remaining in force while the current element (i.e. the last one to be specified or implied) is in force. As with automatically actioned maps, the requested map will be used for any embedded subelements for which separate maps have not been specified; but if an embedded subelement is associated with another map, that map will override the previous map *until such time as the end-tag for the subelement is encountered*.

A special variant of the short reference use declaration can be used to declare an **empty map** that temporarily disables any maps currently in force. The empty map is specified by replacing the map name with the reserved word #EMPTY to give a declaration of the form:

    ‹!USEMAP #EMPTY›

for a short reference use declaration within the text, or:

    ‹!USEMAP #EMPTY element-list›

for a map declared within the document type definition.

A typical use of this latter facility is to disable short references generally within figures by adding a declaration such as:

    ‹USEMAP #EMPTY fig›

to the document type definition. This declaration tells the program that, while the ‹fig› element is in force, no short references are to be recognized, any character strings declared as short references automatically being treated as text. As soon as the figure has been completed though, the map previously being used will be restored.

Within text the ‹!USEMAP #EMPTY› option will often be called by means of an entity reference, such as &nomap;, which will typically be defined as:

    ‹!ENTITY nomap MD "USEMAP #EMPTY" ›

If desired, this entity can be called through one of the short reference strings in a short reference map.

4.5.3 Using short references

A typical use of a short reference is to identify automatically the start and end of a quotation by looking for quotation marks in the text. Typically, two – almost identical – short reference mapping declarations will be defined:

```
<!SHORTREF quotes    '"'   start-qt  >
<!SHORTREF endquote  '"'   end-qte   >
```

The associated entity declarations would be:

```
<!ENTITY  start-qt  STARTTAG "q">
<!ENTITY  end-qte   ENDTAG   "q">
```

The first of the above short references needs to be active whenever quoted text might be encountered in the text. This would typically be achieved by use of a `<!USEMAP quotes ...` declaration of the type shown above. The second map will be activated, within the quoted text, by entry of a declaration reading:

```
<!USEMAP endquote q >
```

Within a paragraph of text (or a note, example, poem or single line of text, etc.), the first quotation mark encountered will be identified by the `quote` map as a call to the `start-qt` entity, which will be expanded to produce a `<q>` tag identifying the start of the quoted text. When the expanded tag is processed by the program, it will activate the `endquote` map so that the next quotation mark will be identified as a call to the `end-qte` entity, which in turn will be expanded to give `</q>`. Having closed down the embedded quote element the program will restore the original `quote` map so that the next quotation mark will be identified as the start of a new piece of quoted text.

Although this technique provides a very useful method of reducing the number of tags that need to be entered by a typist, a word of caution is required for new users. *When choosing suitable short reference delimiters you must make sure they are unique.* For instance, if you choose the apostrophe as the delimiter used to start and end quoted text, how will quote delimiters be distinguished from other apostrophes within the text? It might be possible to declare short reference delimiters consisting of a space and an apostrophe that could be used to identify the start of a quote. A matching short reference delimiter consisting of an apostrophe followed

by a space could be used to generate the end-tag for the quote, but this
sequence would not recognize the end of quoted text where the quotation
mark is followed by other punctuation symbols, and might be identified
erroneously if the text contained any embedded plural possessive words,
such as those found in the phrase "the bosses' toilet". While further short
reference delimiters can be defined to cover most situations, this can lead
to fairly complicated maps which could be avoided by careful choice of
short reference delimiters. (This situation is explored further in Appendix
A, which shows how multiple levels of quoted matter can be catered for in
multilingual text.)

A similar problem can occur if two short reference strings start with
the same sequence of characters. For example, if the SGML declaration
contained the entry:

```
SHORTREF SGMLREF "##"
```

both a single hash and a double hash would be valid short reference
delimiters. If the map currently being used only contained a mapping for
the single hash variant, for example:

```
<!SHORTREF newmap "#" hash >
```

a string of three hashes (###) would be interpreted as ##&hash;. In this case
the first two hashes have been recognized as a valid SGML short
reference string which is currently unmapped, so the characters have been
passed through as they are, while the final hash has been recognized as
the single hash short reference which is to be mapped to the entity whose
name is hash.

Before leaving the subject of short references it should be noted that
short reference strings are not recognized within delimited markup.

4.6   Entity sets

An **entity set** is a set of entity declarations that are commonly used in the
same document. As such they are often stored together as a separate file
that can be used as a publicly declared external entity.

Entity sets are typically used to declare:

- names allocated to graphic characters not directly accessible on the
  system,

- how special characters should be displayed on a specific system, and

- text to be used in a number of documents.

Entity sets may also contain:

- parameter entity declarations,
- comment declarations (see Chapter 5),
- processing instructions (see Chapter 8), and
- marked section declarations (see Chapter 8),

which complement the entity declarations within the set.

As with all external entities, there are two basic types of entity set:

(1)   publicly declared entity sets, and
(2)   system-specific private entity sets.

4.6.1   Publicly declared entity sets

Publicly declared entity sets are typically used to define sets of characters which are not part of the main ASCII character set or the document's character set. These agreed entity names can be converted by any receiving system to the local equivalent by use of appropriate system-specific (SDATA) replacement text.

Appendix B shows a number of entity sets that could be used to prepare textbooks. Special character sets are suggested for:

- accented characters,
- stand-alone accents,
- Greek characters,
- standard graphics and fractions,
- standard publishing characters, and
- mathematical symbols.

(Many of these entity sets are based on the ISO registered entity sets defined in Annex D of ISO 8879. The standard also defines sets for non-Western accented characters, alternative Greek characters, Cyrillic characters, rule drawing and an extended set of entities for mathematical setting.)

Each of the entity sets in Appendix B has an associated set of entity declarations which provide access to the characters on a particular system. A typical entry might be:

```
<!ENTITY sup2 SDATA "[sup2]" -- Superscript 2 -- >
```

This declaration shows that the entity reference ² is to be replaced by the system-specific string [sup2] to generate a superscript 2 on the printed page.

Wherever possible, entity set declarations should start with a comment declaration indicating the purpose of the set and how it should be invoked. For example, the declarations for the set of accented characters defined in Appendix B should start:

```
<!-- Addison-Wesley Accented Character Entities:
   To invoke this publicly declared set of entities in
   your document, include the following entity declaration
   and parameter entity reference in your document type
   declaration subset:
      <!ENTITY % AWacc PUBLIC
      "-//Addison-Wesley//ENTITIES Accented Characters//EN">
      %AWacc;
-->
```

To invoke this entity set on a system that has the relevant entity declaration file users need only add the declaration and parameter entity reference specified in the comment.

4.6.2   Private entity sets

Private entity sets are typically used to define text entities that are to be used in a number of locally produced documents. On some systems they may also be used to define the way entities should be used to generate special characters.

Each entity set should be prepared as a separate file. As with publicly declared entity sets, the entity declarations making up the entity set may be preceded by a comment declaration indicating the purpose of the set and how it should be invoked.

Private entity sets require the addition of a single entity declaration to the document type declaration subset, to identify the system-specific external file containing the predefined declarations. Where the entity contains text that will be called by entry of an entity reference in the main document, the entity set will be invoked by entry of a general entity declaration of the form:

```
<!ENTITY verso SYSTEM "verso.txt" -- Text to go on back of title page -- >
```

Entities containing markup declarations will need to be defined as parameter entities within the document type definition by entry of a parameter entity declaration of the form:

```
<!ENTITY % name SYSTEM "filename" >
```

In this case the accompanying parameter entity reference (`%name;`) must also be entered within the associated document type declaration subset to invoke the external entity.

A document type definition can call any number of different entity sets, and contain its own entity declarations. The sequence in which the sets are called may be important. Normally, entity sets will be called after the document's entity declarations to ensure that any locally declared entities having the same name as one of the entities in an entity set will retain their local declarations. (Remember, the first declaration read is the one used by the system.) If, for some reason, the same entity name is used in two or more of the requested entity sets, the declaration used will be the one in the set whose parameter entity reference was encountered first.

Externally stored entity sets can also be used to define the entities required by short reference mapping declarations. By combining these two powerful facilities, authors can significantly reduce the amount of keying needed to produce a finished SGML document.

5

Declaring and Using SGML Elements

5.1   Types of element
5.2   Declaring elements
5.3   Element sets
5.4   Generating new element sets
5.5   Using elements

Because most SGML documents are coded using predefined sets of elements, authors will not normally need to prepare element declarations for the tags they intend to use in their documents. Instead they will call one or more sets of element declarations from an external source as part of the document type definition.

Predefined sets of element declarations should be accompanied by a description showing how each of the tags declared by the document designer is intended to be used. (A typical example is shown in Appendix C, which defines a set of tags suitable for coding an Addison-Wesley textbook.) In many cases the tag descriptions will be accompanied by a diagram showing how the various elements are interrelated. This diagram will often take the form of a tree diagram similar to those used in Chapter 2 to explain the structure of textbooks.

While well prepared descriptions and diagrams can provide a reasonable understanding of the structure of an SGML document, they rarely tell the whole story. The full structure of an SGML document often only becomes apparent when you look at the formal definitions of the elements in the document type declaration associated with the text. To understand this structure authors need to be able to interpret element declarations within the document type declaration subset they are using. (This does not mean they need to be able to generate element declarations – it simply means that they need to know how to 'read' element declarations.)

5.1   Types of element ⸻⸻⸻⸻⸻⸻⸻

The following types of element are found in SGML documents:

- base document elements,
- embedded elements,
- qualified elements,
- ranked elements, and
- minimized elements.

The first element specified in any SGML document is the **base document element**. This element must be formally *declared*, within the document type declaration, by entry of an element declaration whose name is the same as that of the initial document type declaration. Typically, the name chosen will identify the general class of documents the tag set is designed to be used for (for example ‹textbook›).

Normally the last tag entered within an SGML document will be an end-tag whose name matches that used for the first tag (for example ‹/textbook›). This tag ensures that the end of the document is correctly identified by the SGML program.

Further elements can be *embedded* between the two tags identifying the limits of the base document element, up to the level specified by the current **tag level quantity**. (In the reference concrete syntax this value is 24, i.e. up to 24 levels of embedded elements can be used within each base document element.)

Where necessary, elements can be *qualified* by **attributes**. As will be explained further in Chapter 6, an attribute is a value that is used during the processing of the element's content to control such things as the format, content or structure of the document. (In computer programming terms, attributes are equivalent to the parameters used to qualify commands sent to a computer.) In the reference concrete syntax, up to 40 different attributes may be associated with any element, provided that the total length of the attribute names and values does not exceed 960 characters.

Elements can optionally be *ranked* so that specific groups of elements are used at the same **rank level**. Rank level is specified by adding a number to the end of the element's generic identifier (name). When the rank feature is being used, the current rank level can be implied from that of preceding elements.

Minimized elements are elements whose presence or name can be implied by the parser. Provided the relevant features have been allowed in the current SGML declaration, a number of different types of element minimization can be used within a document, including:

- omitted tags,

- empty start-tags,
- empty end-tags,
- unclosed start-tags,
- unclosed end-tags,
- null end-tags (NET), and
- NET-enabling start-tags.

In addition, **data tags** can be used to tag elements automatically by reference to predefined character strings, using techniques similar to those used for short references. A full description of the various techniques for element minimization is given in Chapter 7.

5.2   Declaring elements

As with entity declarations, **element declarations** form part of the document type declaration subset that follows the document type name and any optional-external-identifier in the DOCTYPE declaration. Each element is declared within its own set of markup delimiters, the reserved name ELEMENT (or its previously declared replacement) being used to identify the declaration as an element declaration.

In its shortest form an element declaration takes the form:

```
<!ELEMENT name contents>
```

where name is a **generic identifier** that uniquely identifies an element of the document and contents is either a formal declaration of the type of data that may be entered within the element, or a **content model** showing which subelements can be embedded within the element.

More than one element name can be associated with a declared set of contents by use of a **name group** in place of the generic identifier. Like the name group used in the short reference use declaration described in Chapter 4, the group consists of a set of connected element names bracketed by group open and group close sequences. The required element names are typically connected by an **or** connector (| in the reference concrete syntax) to give an entry of the form:

```
<!ELEMENT (name-1|name-2|...|name-n) contents>
```

Unless otherwise specified for the current concrete syntax, the maximum length of an element name, like that of an entity name, must not exceed eight characters. The first character must be alphabetic or one of the additional **name start characters** added to the currently defined concrete syntax (see Chapters 3 and 10). Subsequent characters may be alphanumeric characters or one of the currently defined additional **name characters** (for example a full stop or hyphen in the reference concrete syntax).

When the OMITTAG entry in the FEATURES section of the current SGML declaration reads OMITTAG YES (as it does in the reference concrete syntax), two extra characters *must* be entered between the name and content of the element declaration to define the type of **omitted tag minimization** to be applied to the element. These extra characters define whether or not a tag can be omitted if its presence can be unambiguously implied from the model of the element it is embedded within. The first of the additional characters is O (the letter O, not the number zero) if the start-tag for the element can be omitted, or - (the hyphen symbol) if it cannot. The second character is set to O if the end-tag can be omitted: otherwise it is -. The two characters must be separated from each other and from the adjacent name and content entries by one or more spaces to give the entry the form:

```
<!ELEMENT name  S E   contents>
```

where s indicates whether or not the start-tag can be omitted and ε indicates whether or not the end-tag can be omitted. An element whose end-tag may be omitted might be declared as:

```
<!ELEMENT artwork   - O   EMPTY>
```

This element declaration defines an **empty element**, ⟨artwork⟩, which has no embedded content. The element is simply a tag that marks the point at which space is to be left for insertion of an illustration; no text characters need to be entered within this empty element. The ⟨artwork⟩ start-tag cannot be omitted but, as the element contains no text, the end-tag must be omitted as it serves no purpose. (We will explain how the size of a piece of artwork can be specified by use of attributes of the artwork element in Chapter 6.)

5.2.1 Model groups

When an element declaration's contents consist of a **content model** defining which subelements can be embedded within the element, the various subelements *must* be defined as a **model group**. Like name groups, model groups consist of one or more connected element names bracketed by group open and group close delimiter sequences, for example:

```
<!ELEMENT novel   - O   (prelims, body, other) >
```

Table 5.1   SGML group connectors.

Default character	Delimiter name	Meaning
,	seq	All must occur, in the order specified
&	and	All must occur, in any order
|	or	One *and only one* must occur

In this case, a novel is said to be made up of three nested subelements – prelims, body and other – each of which contains further nested model groups.

For model groups, unlike other name groups, the type of **connector** used is significant. Three types of connector are used in model groups to define the logical sequence in which elements are to appear (see Table 5.1).

The **sequence connector** (a comma – , in the reference concrete syntax) connects elements which must occur in the indicated sequence. Where the sequence in which the elements are used is not fixed, subelement names should be connected with an **and connector** (&) rather than the sequence connector. If more than one element could be applicable at a given point, the relevant element names can be connected by an **or connector** (|). The following pages will show how each of these connectors is used.

The use of each embedded subelement can be further qualified by the addition of an **occurrence indicator**. Three types of occurrence indicator are defined in SGML:

(1)   plus for repeatable elements that must occur at least once at the current level,

(2)   opt for optional elements that can occur at most once at the current level, and

(3)   rep for optional elements that may be repeated more than once at the current level.

In the reference concrete syntax the symbols used to represent these occurrence indicators are +, ? and *, respectively.

When determining the effect of occurrence indicators and connectors it is important to realize that occurrence indicators have a higher precedence than connectors. For this reason a model group such as (p|note)+ differs from one defined as (p+|note+) because the first model permits any sequence of text paragraphs and notes to be entered, whereas the second model only permits a set of paragraphs *or* a set of notes to be entered within the relevant element.

Model groups can be nested within each other up to the level indicated by SGML's GRPLVL quantity value. (The reference concrete syntax allows up to 16 levels of nested model groups.) Each nested model group can, if necessary, have its elements linked by a different connector and the whole group can be qualified by an occurrence indicator.

Parameter entities (see Chapter 4) can be used to define the contents of model groups, but here a word of warning is required: *you cannot associate an occurrence indicator with a parameter entity*. To see the implications of this restriction, consider the following three entity declarations:

```
<!ENTITY % copy1 "(plnote|%element;)+"  >
<!ENTITY % copy2 "plnote|%element;"     >
<!ENTITY % copy3 "(plnote|%element;)"   >
```

In the first declaration the parameter entity consists of a bracketed model group *plus* an associated occurrence indicator which shows that at least one of the (repeatable) elements must be present. This entity can be used on its own to define the model group of the following declaration:

```
<!ELEMENT abstract %copy1; >
```

Alternatively, the second parameter entity could be used to declare the element in a declaration of the form:

```
<!ELEMENT abstract (%copy2;)+ >
```

In this case the model group's brackets and occurrence indicator have both been entered within the element declaration rather than the entity declaration.

The third of the parameter entities cannot, however, be associated with an occurrence indicator. If the abstract element was declared as:

```
<!ELEMENT abstract %copy3;+ >
```

it would be rejected as invalid by an SGML parser. The reasons for the rejection are, unfortunately, somewhat obscure. To make element (and other) declarations more readable, ISO 8879 prohibits the use of parameter entities that do not contain complete SGML tokens, including any surrounding separators (for example spaces) and connectors. The definition for a model group does not, therefore, permit the occurrence indicator to be preceded by anything other than a group close delimiter, so both the delimiter and the occurrence indicator must occur in the same SGML entity – in this case either in the parameter entity or in the element declaration.

NOTE: Further examples of the use of occurrence indicators and nested model groups, and the other options mentioned in this section, are provided in Section 5.3.1.

When using parameter entities to define part or all of a model group it is important to remember that the associated entity declaration must precede the entity reference. The safest way to ensure this is to place all parameter entity declarations at the start of the document type declaration.

Model groups can also be qualified by the addition of lists of **exceptions**. There are two types of exceptions:

(1)   **inclusions** defining elements that can be included at any point in the model group (i.e. within the current element or any element embedded in it); and

(2)   **exclusions** identifying embedded elements that cannot be used while the current element remains unclosed.

Exceptions are specified by entry of additional bracketed name groups immediately after the model group defining the permitted contents of the element. The name group is preceded by a plus sign if the names identify inclusions or a hyphen (minus sign) if they represent exclusions. Both sets may be present at the same time, provided they are separated from each other and the preceding model group by one or more spaces (or other valid SGML separators such as comments and parameter entity references) and that exclusions are specified before any inclusions.

Although inclusions can be used in almost any situation, exclusions that prohibit the use of embedded elements required as part of a model group are not permitted. (The effect of this restriction is explained more fully in Section 5.3.3.)

Inclusions are typically used at the start of a document to allow commonly occurring items, such as footnotes, figures and index entries, to occur anywhere in the text. For example, the definition given for the base document element in Appendix C is:

```
<!ELEMENT textbook  - 0  (front|body|back?)  +(%floats;|ix) >
```

where %floats; is defined as:

```
<!ENTITY % floats "fig|fn" >
```

A typical declaration using an exclusion is:

```
<!ELEMENT xmp  - 0  (#PCDATA|%copy;|%lists;)*  -(xmp) >
```

This declaration indicates that, while entering an example (<xmp>) within text, a second example cannot be opened within any of its embedded elements.

A variant of the basic content model allows the word ANY to replace an element declaration's model group (including its brackets). This tells the program that any element defined within the same document type declaration can be used as an embedded element. (Because this option can lead to complicated document type definitions, it is normally only used when declaring the base document element for a document which is essentially unstructured, or while creating temporary document type declarations.)

5.2.2 Text elements

A special form of model group **content token** is used to indicate points in a model at which the element can contain text. Called a **primitive content token**, it consists of a **reserved name indicator** (# in the reference concrete syntax) followed by the reserved name PCDATA, which stands for **parsed character data**. The #PCDATA keyword indicates that, at that point, the element can contain text which has been checked by the SGML parser before being output to ensure that any embedded tags or entity references have been resolved.

A special feature of the #PCDATA keyword is that it is automatically presumed to have a repeatable occurrence indicator. This rule allows inclusion elements, short reference use declarations (see Chapter 4) and link set use declarations (see Chapter 9) to be embedded within text without being specifically declared in the model.

Where nested subelements cannot occur within an element, its contents can be declared to consist of one of the following types of **declared content**:

- **replaceable character data** (RCDATA) containing text, character references and/or general entity references that resolve to character data;

- **character data** (CDATA) containing only valid SGML characters that do not need further processing; or

- EMPTY, that is having contents that are either implied or otherwise automatically generated by the program.

Here the reserved name completely replaces the model group, including its brackets. Because, unlike PCDATA, these reserved names cannot be confused with similarly named elements in a model group, they do not need to be preceded by the reserved name indicator, so a typical entry has the form:

```
<!ELEMENT ISBN - - CDATA >
```

It should be noted that, in the case of elements defined using the replaceable character data and character data options, the program will ignore any requests to start a new element until such time as it encounters a valid end-tag open delimiter, i.e. </ followed by a valid name start character. (Further details of the consequence of these rules, and the use of the CDATA and RCDATA reserved names, will be found in Section 5.3.4.)

5.2.3   Comments within element declarations

Comments may be used at any point where spaces are permitted within an element declaration, to enter notes on the use of the declaration. (Comments cannot, however, be entered within name or model groups.) Comments can run over more than one line if necessary. They must be preceded and followed by two adjacent hyphens, for example:

```
<!ELEMENT position - 0 (#PCDATA|l+)  -- one or more lines of text
                                        describing position(s) held
                                        or qualifications --    >
```

5.3   Element sets ⎯⎯⎯⎯⎯⎯⎯⎯⎯⎯⎯⎯⎯

Element sets are sets of interlinked declarations that define the structure of a document or part of a document. Element sets can contain:

- element declarations,
- attribute definition list declarations (see Chapter 6),
- notation declarations (see Chapter 4),
- parameter entity declarations (see Chapter 4),
- comment declarations,
- processing instructions (see Chapter 8), and
- marked section declarations (see Chapter 8).

Many elements sets start with one or more **comment declarations**. Comment declarations are declarations which contain only comments. The markup declaration start sequence is immediately followed by the two hyphens identifying the start of a comment (or by whatever alternative comment start and end delimiter has been defined in the current concrete syntax). The closing delimiter for the comment is *immediately* followed by the markup declaration close symbol to give a declaration of the form:

```
<!-- Elements used in a typical textbook -->
```

NOTE: Make sure you do not fall into the trap that I fell into the first time I tried to use comment declarations. Unlike comments embedded within element and entity declarations, comment declarations cannot have spaces on either side as spaces are not permitted between the initial markup declaration open sequence (<!) and the opening comment delimiter. The following declaration is, therefore, illegal:

```
<! -- Elements used in a typical textbook -- >
```

as it should have been entered as:

```
<!-- Elements used in a typical textbook -->
```

Note, however, that a space is permitted after the second of the comment delimiters.

Comment declarations are normally used to provide headings for element or entity sets. As the following example shows, comment declarations can be particularly useful for entering headings for the columns that make up a set of element declarations:

```
                 <!-- Headed Sections-->
      <!--Elements    NAME(S)  MIN    CONTENT (EXCEPTIONS) --
        --Attributes ELEMENT(S) NAME   VALUE        DEFAULT -->
```

Note that more than one comment can be included in a single comment declaration, if required. In the above case, the extra hyphens have been added to balance the heading.

A special short form of comment declaration consisting of a markup declaration open delimiter immediately followed by a markup declaration close delimiter (for example <!>) can be used where the comment declaration is simply being inserted to provide a blank space between markup declarations. (This form of dummy line should be used wherever a blank line is required between element declarations in an element set to indicate that the line has deliberately been left blank.)

The structure of the rest of the element set will depend on the preferences of the document designer who prepared it. Some sets, such as the one defined in Annex E of ISO 8879, consist of a series of element declarations followed by a second set of declarations defining the attributes associated with the elements. Other sets, such as the one declared in Appendix C of this book, have mixed sets of element and attribute definition list declarations, the attributes for a particular element normally being defined immediately below the relevant element declaration.

The order in which the elements are defined will also vary from set to set. Normally the definitions will be grouped so that, to some extent, they represent the tree structure used as a basis for the content model; but this order will often be modified by the fact that a single declaration may suffice for more than one element. The use of parameter entity references within the set will also affect the order in which elements are declared (see Section 5.3.1).

5.3.1   *Analysing a typical element set*

To show how an element set can be analysed we will take a look at some of
the elements defined for a textbook in the document type declaration in
Appendix C.

The base document element, whose name matches that of the document type declaration, provides the starting point for the analysis of any
element set. The declaration for this element allows the contents of the next
level in the document's structure to be identified. In our example, the base
document element is the ‹textbook› element, which has been declared as:

```
<!ELEMENT textbook - 0 (front, body, back?) +(%floats;lix) >
```

This shows that the second level structure of a textbook consists of three
subelements:

(1)   ‹front›, containing the front matter of the text (for example the title
       and preliminary pages);
(2)   ‹body›, containing the body of the text; and
(3)   ‹back›, containing the back matter of the text (for example the
       appendices and indexes).

Each of these subelements must be used in the sequence indicated in the
declaration because the element names in the model group are connected
by the comma used in the reference concrete syntax as the sequence
connector.

The declaration for the textbook base document element also shows:

●   that the ‹textbook› start-tag is compulsory but that the ‹/textbook› end-tag
     may optionally be omitted at the end of the textbook (-0);
●   that back matter is an optional part of the textbook (though it will
     normally be present); and
●   that the elements defined in the parameter entity called %floats;,
     together with the ‹ix› index entry element, may be included at any
     point in the text.

The parameter entity declaration used for the floats entity is defined
as:

```
<!ENTITY % floats "figlfn" --items positioned relative to a page-->
```

When this reference is resolved by the SGML parser the inclusion
statement becomes:

```
+(figlfnlix)
```

to indicate that figures, footnotes and index entries can be 'included' at any point within the textbook.

Further levels of embedded element can be identified from this initial sublevel by looking at the declarations associated with the appropriate elements. For example, the ‹body› element is declared in Appendix C as part of a combined entry for the body and appendix elements of the form:

```
<!ELEMENT (body|appendix) - O (h0|h1)+  -- body of text & appendices -->
```

Note that, in this case, a single element declaration is being used at two different levels within the document's structure, the ‹appendix› element being a subelement of the ‹back› element, which is at the same level in the structure as the ‹body› element. This is acceptable because the SGML program can use the entered content model twice, once at the first sublevel and again at the second sublevel.

The start-tag of a ‹body› or ‹appendix› element must be present but its end-tag may be omitted if its presence can be implied by entry of another element which has been declared at the same level (for example the ‹back› element that normally follows the body of the text). The minimization details of the declaration consist, therefore, of a hyphen followed, after a space, by a capital O.

The content model defined for the ‹body› element also contains elements that appear at two different levels in the document's structure. The first level contains the ‹h0› part subelement. Alternatively, the body of the text may be divided directly into chapters (represented by the ‹h1› heading tag), without intervening part titles or associated introductory text. As chapters are subelements of a part, they represent a further level within the structure, as illustrated in Figure 2.12(a).

The names allocated to parts and chapters are not quite so obvious as those used for the previous level of elements. Although it would be possible to declare these elements with names such as ‹part› and ‹chapter›, this concept would not have been so useful at lower levels in the document's structure, since the default limit of eight characters to a name prevents names, such as subsection or sub-subsection, being used with the reference concrete syntax. To overcome this potential problem, a general heading name (h) has been adopted, the name being qualified by numbers indicating the appropriate level. This has two advantages:

(1)   it keeps the tags used to identify headings short, and

(2)   it allows the level at which text is being entered to be easily identified, even when the headings are not numbered.

Because the most commonly used headings are those for chapters, sections and subsections, these have been allocated ‹h1›, ‹h2› and ‹h3› respectively. Parts, which are at a higher level than chapters, are identified by entry of a ‹h0› tag.

The plus sign following the bracketed content model for the ‹body› element is an SGML occurrence indicator. For the ‹body› element the plus sign indicates that at least one part or chapter must occur within the body of the text. The **or** connector (|) linking the two element names shows that either of these elements can be embedded within the body of the text, and that they can be used in any order. This permits structures that have an opening chapter followed by one or more parts, as well as those made up of a number of parts or chapters.

In Appendix C the part (‹h0›) element is declared as:

```
<!-- Highest division of body - for example Part -->
<!ELEMENT h0      - 0   (h0t, (%text;)*, h1+) >
```

This declaration shows that parts consist of:

- a part title (the ‹h0t› element),
- some optional text, and
- one or more chapters.

The fact that the h0t entry is followed immediately by the sequence connector, without an intervening occurrence indicator, shows that:

- a part title element (‹h0t›) *must* precede all other elements within each ‹h0› element, and
- only one heading can be entered for each part declared within the body of the text.

One interesting consequence of this is that the presence of the ‹h0t› start-tag can be inferred from the presence of the ‹h0› tag as they must, implicitly at least, always occur together.

The text parameter entity has been declared elsewhere in the current document type declaration as:

```
<!ENTITY % text "%topics;|%copy;|%lists;" >
```

When the parameter entity reference is resolved by the SGML program, the content model for a part becomes:

```
(h0t, (%topics;|%copy;|%lists;)*, h1+)
```

The SGML program will need to resolve the parameter references in the nested model group before it can determine the full structure of any text associated with the part title. In Appendix C the relevant parameter entities have been declared as:

```
<!ENTITY % topics    "top1|top2|top3"              >
<!ENTITY % copy      "p|note|%element;"            >
<!ENTITY % lists     "li|glossli|terms"            >
```

where the embedded %element; parameter entity has been defined as:

```
<!ENTITY % element   "xmp|lq|l|poem|table|adr|artwork|eqn" >
```

This means that text associated with a part heading can consist of:

- different levels of headed topic (<top1>, <top2> or <top3>),
- paragraphs of text (<p>) or notes (<note>),
- examples (<xmp>),
- indented long quotations (<lq>),
- poems (<poem>) or individual lines of text (<l>),
- tables (<table>),
- addresses (<adr>),
- previously prepared artwork (<artwork>),
- equations (<eqn>),
- lists (<li>),
- lists of glossary definitions (<glossli>), and
- lists of terms (<terms>),

the tags being entered in any sequence (for example with a quotation, poem or illustration before the first paragraph of text if required).

It should be noted that the **or** connector used within the nested group differs from that used in the main model group, which uses the **seq** connector. As no further levels of nesting are associated with the nested parameter entities (which do not contain any brackets), all four parameter entities must have the same connector, the **or** connector in this case. (If different types of connector were used in the entities, the program would report an error when analysing the model group since connectors cannot be mixed within a single pair of group delimiters.)

The optional and repeatable occurrence indicator (*) associated with the group close delimiter of the nested subgroup indicates that the whole group is optional (i.e. the part title need not be followed by text) so, if text elements are present, any such element may be used, repeatedly if necessary, in conjunction with any of the other defined elements.

Once any text elements required to qualify the part title have been entered, the sequence connector (,) following the bracketed subgroup indicates that a ‹h1› chapter start-tag must be entered next. The plus occurrence indicator associated with the ‹h1› element indicates that this element is both required and repeatable.

The structure of part titles is further defined within a declaration that covers all section titles in a textbook:

```
<!ELEMENT (%titles;)  0 0  (#PCDATA|q|%phrases;)* >
```

Here a parameter entity called %titles; has been used in place of the element name. The parameter entity reference has been placed within brackets to ensure that the program recognizes that a name group has been used in place of a single element name. The declaration for the %titles; parameter entity is:

```
<!ENTITY % titles "h0t|h1t|h2t|h3t|h4t|h5t" >
```

When the bracketed parameter entity reference is expanded it forms a group identifying the six different levels of heading defined for textbooks.

Both start- and end-tags can be omitted from section titles. In fact, title tags never need to be entered in the document as the program can always infer the start-tag from the preceding heading tag (for example ‹h0t› is automatically implied whenever ‹h0› is entered). Similarly the end-tag can always be omitted because the SGML program can infer its use from the presence of either an embedded text element or a lower level of heading.

The content model used for the heading declaration in Appendix C contains three entries:

(1)   #PCDATA to indicate that the element may contain character data when its contents have been parsed (checked) by the program,

(2)   q to indicate that quoted text can be entered as part of a title, and

(3)   %phrases; to indicate that the data can include embedded highlighted phrases (or cited book titles).

Because the model group is followed by the **rep** occurrence indicator (*) the embedded subelements can be used repeatedly in any sequence or can be ignored if a blank, though possibly numbered, heading is required.

The phrases parameter entity is defined as:

```
<!ENTITY % phrases "hp0|hp1|hp2|hp3|cit" >
```

This parameter entity is used within a number of element declarations to allow the nesting of up to four types of highlighted phrase and cited book or paper titles within textual elements. When it is used in the declaration for titles, the expanded content model becomes:

```
(#PCDATAlqlhp0lhp1lhp2lhp3lcit)*
```

to indicate that part, chapter and section titles can consist of multiple sequences of characters and highlighted phrases.

The declaration given for phrase subelements in Appendix C is:

```
<!ELEMENT (%phrases;) - - (#PCDATAlql%phrases;)+ >
```

This definition shows that, as well as text, phrases and citations can contain quoted text or other, nested, forms of highlighted phrase. Note, however, that in this case both the start- and end-tag are compulsory for each level of phrase used and that some form of text must be present within the element (as indicated by the + **plus** occurrence indicator).

5.3.2   Ranked elements

The highlighted phrases defined in Appendix C could, alternatively, be defined by use of SGML's **ranked element** feature if the FEATURES clause of the current SGML declaration contained the entry RANK YES. (Rank is not available when the reference concrete syntax is being used. For this reason highlighted phrases have not been defined as ranked elements in Appendix C.)

For ranked elements, the element name is split into two parts – a **rank stem** and a **rank suffix**. The rank stem normally consists of the letters in the element names (e.g. hp) while the rank suffix represents the number (e.g. 0–9) placed at the end of the name to identify the relevant level. Within the element declaration, a space is placed between these two parts to indicate that they are being used separately. (The space must not be entered within a start- or end-tag.) Highlighted phrases could, therefore, be declared as:

```
<!ELEMENT hp 0    - -   (#PCDATAlql%phrases;)* >
<!ELEMENT hp 1    - -   (#PCDATAlql%phrases;)* >
<!ELEMENT hp 2    - -   (#PCDATAlql%phrases;)* >
<!ELEMENT hp 3    - -   (#PCDATAlql%phrases;)* >
```

These declarations define a set of elements whose names consist of the letters hp followed, optionally, by a number. Both the start- and end-tags of highlighted phrases are, in this case, compulsory and the phrases may contain quoted text or further nested phrases as well as parsed character data. Where a number is not entered as part of the tag, the last used rank suffix will be added to the rank stem by the parser. For example, if the last phrase to be used was entered using the tag ‹hp2› the program will interpret a start-tag just consisting of the rank stem (for example ‹hp›) as a request to repeat highlighting level 2 for the following text.

Ranked elements can be grouped into a **ranked group** if they share a common content model. In ranked groups a single rank suffix is applied to all elements in the group. This has some very interesting consequences. For example, if the element declaration entered in a document type declaration was:

```
<!ELEMENT (h|p|note) 1   - 0  (#PCDATA|q|%phrases;)* >
<!ELEMENT (h|p|note) 2   - 0  (#PCDATA|q|%phrases;)* >
<!ELEMENT (h|p|note) 3   - 0  (#PCDATA|q|%phrases;)* >
```

heading, paragraph and note levels could be interlinked. To see how this works, consider the following example of coded text:

```
<h1>SGML Declarations
<p>All SGML declarations start with the markup
declaration open delimiter sequence (&lt;!) followed by
a reserved name identifying the type of declaration
being made (for example ENTITY or ELEMENT).
<note>Reserved names can be modified in the NAMES
section of the document's syntax declaration.
<h2>Entity Declarations
<p>Entity declarations link entity names with suitable
strings of replacement text.
<note>Entity names must start with a letter and may not
be more than eight characters long.
<h>Element Declarations
<p>Element declarations .....
```

Within a ranked group SGML uses the current rank suffix for any elements from the same group which have not been given a specific rank suffix. This means that the first of the ‹p› tags in the above example will be treated as ‹p1› tag by the program, the following ‹note› tag being treated as ‹note1›.

When a tag with a different rank suffix is entered, however, the new rank suffix becomes the current rank level for all elements in the group. This means that the ‹p› immediately after the ‹h2› entry is treated by the SGML parser as a ‹p2› entry, the following ‹note› being seen as ‹note2›. Similarly, the unnumbered heading tagged by the ‹h› start-tag will be allocated a rank suffix of 2 to generate a second ‹h2› start-tag.

Use of this very powerful feature can help to reduce the amount of coding that needs to be entered in a document and can make keying simpler, but users need to be aware of its implications. In particular, it should be noted that some SGML parsers may not support this facility.

Because of this the rank feature cannot be used in basic SGML documents, where the FEATURES section of the SGML declaration defaults to RANK NO.

5.3.3   Exceptions

Two types of exceptions can be used to qualify a model group entered within an element declaration – inclusions and exclusions.

It was shown earlier how figures, footnotes and index elements could be added to the declaration of the base document element so that their tags could be included at any point in a document. In general, any element declared in the inclusion group of an element which has been defined at a higher level in the document structure than that currently in force can be used as an *optional* subelement of an embedded element. Such subelements may be repeated any number of times within the group and may be embedded within themselves if not otherwise excluded.

The role of exclusions can be much more difficult to interpret than that of inclusions. Consider the following definitions for three levels of headed topic within text:

```
<!ELEMENT top1 - 0 (th, (%text;)+) -(top1) >
<!ELEMENT top2 - 0 (th, (%text;)+) -(top2) >
<!ELEMENT top3 - 0 (th, (%text;)+) -(top3) >
```

The exclusion specified for topic level 1 stops any further level 1 topics being opened until the current topic is completed. Because the %text; parameter entity includes an embedded %topics; parameter entity, however, level 2 and level 3 topics can be embedded within level 1.

Similarly, once a level 2 topic has been opened, no further level 2 topics can be embedded within it, though level 3 topics can be requested. But care must be taken. Unless the level 2 topic is embedded within a level 1 topic, there is nothing to stop a level 1 topic from being started within the second level. The effect of this on the way the document is output will depend on how the various levels of topics are being used.

It should not be thought that the above declarations are invalid. There may be special reasons for allowing higher level topics to be embedded within topics. Where the format of each level of topic is sufficiently different for them to be distinguished, there can be a case for allowing a first level of topic to be embedded within a second level. But beware – such reasons can lead to problems.

Consider what would happen if, under a topic heading, you wanted to quote some text that itself contained topic headings of the same level/type. This would be impossible with the above declarations because, once the exception has been declared, it remains in force for all embedded elements. To allow for quoted topics, the above declarations would need to be modified by removal of the exclusions, to a form similar to that used in Appendix C:

```
<!ELEMENT top1 - 0 (th, (%copy;|%lists;|top2)+ >
<!ELEMENT top2 - 0 (th, (%copy;|%lists;|top3)+ >
<!ELEMENT top3 - 0 (th, (%copy;|%lists;)+)        >
```

In this case, once a topic has been started, lower level topics such as levels 2 and 3 can only be called in the proper sequence since the %copy; parameter entity does not permit directly embedded topics.

If, however, a long quotation is started within a topic, further nested topic levels can be requested since the declaration for the <lq> element is:

```
<!ELEMENT lq - - (#PCDATA|%text;|h2|h3|h4|h5)+ -(fn) >
```

The %text; entity in this declaration permits further topic elements to be entered while the long quotation element is still open, but, once it has been closed, further topics can only be requested at levels below the current one. Similarly, headed sections and subsections of chapters can be included within quoted text, though the model does draw the line at authors quoting complete chapters or parts of books!

By allowing elements to be used as embedded elements at levels lower than they would otherwise be permitted, it is possible to define sections of text such as:

```
<top2>Second Level Topics
<p>In this section we will show how topics can be
nested.
<top3>Nesting topics
<p>Nesting of higher level topics is permitted only if
the nested topic is entered as part of a long quotation
such as:
<lq><top1>First Level Topics
<p>Where nested topics are required users should start
by using the first topic level.
<top2>Nested Second Level Topics
<p>Nesting second level topics within second or third
level topics can only be achieved by use of embedded
long quotations.</lq>
<p>Once the quotation has been ended the previous
level of topic, for example the third level, is restored.
</top2>
```

The points to notice about this example are:

• the long quotation allows a higher level of topic to be started;

- once the embedded ⟨top1⟩ start-tag has been used within the quoted text, other topics must occur at a lower level unless another embedded long quotation is started;

- when the quotation is completed by entry of the ⟨/lq⟩ end-tag, the program returns to the level 3 topic in force when the quoted text started; and

- the final ⟨/top2⟩ end-tag closes down both the initial level 2 topic and the embedded level 3 topic, permitting any level of topic to be started next.

Whenever exclusions are used, care should be taken to ensure that there will never be a situation in which the excluded element may need to be embedded at a lower level in the document's structure. If it is suspected that this may be necessary, techniques such as those described above should be used to control the permitted levels of nesting.

One place where exceptions can be useful is where it is necessary to disable temporarily a subelement that has been declared as an inclusion for a higher level element. For example, if footnotes and figures have been declared as inclusions to the base document element they will need to be excluded from footnotes and, possibly, quoted matter. For footnotes the following declaration can be used:

```
<!ELEMENT fn - - (#PCDATA|lq|%phrases;|%refs;|%copy;)* -(%floats;) -- footnote -->
```

Here both the figure and footnote elements defined by the %floats; parameter entity reference have been excluded as embedded units of a footnote since they are inappropriate in such situations. By contrast, the declaration given above for the ⟨lq⟩ long quotation element only excluded footnotes (because their positioning would be ambiguous) while figures were still permitted.

The above examples also illustrate how the elements declared in a model group can affect which subelements can be used while a particular element is open. As footnotes have been defined using the %phrases;, %refs; and %copy; parameter entities they can only contain quotations, highlighted phrases and citations, cross-references to tables, headings, embedded paragraphs, notes or other embeddable text elements, while long quotations, which contain the %text; parameter entity reference in their declaration, can also include topics and lists. In fact, lists can also be used in footnotes, provided that they are defined as part of a paragraph or note. The difference with a long quotation is that the quoted text can consist of just a list, with no preceding paragraph element. Such subtle differences can be difficult to spot and can constitute a trap for the unwary. It is for this reason that most element sets are prepared by specially trained document designers.

5.3.4   Data within elements

We have already seen how the #PCDATA reserved name can be used within a
model group to identify elements that can contain text after any entity
references and tags have been resolved.

Where an element can contain only text consisting of characters
declared within the document's character set, without any embedded entity
or character references, the element can be declared with the word CDATA in
place of the bracketed model group, for example:

```
<!ELEMENT ISBN  - -  CDATA --ISBN (or ISSN) number-- >
```

The ISBN element can be declared as a character data element because it
should contain only the relevant International Standard Book Number, for
example 0 201 17535 5.

Note that, in this case, neither the start- nor the end-tag can be
omitted. This is one of the penalties of using the CDATA option – some form of
end-tag must be present because, while the CDATA element is in force, the
program only searches for embedded end-tag delimiters (for example </ in
the reference concrete syntax) that are followed by valid name start
characters. This need not be a disadvantage, however, if the NET (null end
tag) minimization option is being used. In such cases the ISBN can be
entered in the form <ISBN/0 201 17535 5/. (For full details of the use of this
option refer to Chapter 7.)

Where the element may also contain entity or character references
that need to be resolved before output, the element can be declared as
containing replaceable character data by use of the reserved name RCDATA to
give a declaration of the form:

```
<!ELEMENT eqn    - -  RCDATA  -- equation -- >
```

In this case, equations may contain data characters, character
references or references to entities that resolve to data characters (i.e. do
not contain non-SGML characters, processing instructions or tagged
SGML text). Once again, the end-tag is compulsory as the program only
looks for end-tag delimiters while the element is open. This means that any
markup declarations and element start-tags entered while an equation
element is open will be treated as data characters, though any entity
references and character references will be expanded when encountered.

Some elements, such as indexes, tables of contents and cross-
references, never contain any entered data as their contents are automatically generated by the program. In this case, the contents of the element
should be declared using the reserved name EMPTY to give an entry of the
form:

```
<!ELEMENT (toc|fig|list|index)   - 0  EMPTY >
```

Since empty elements never have an end-tag because they never contain data, the second of the tag omission characters must always be 0 for such elements. (The start-tag entry may also be set to 0 if the element's presence can be defined unambiguously from its use in another element's model.) Again, the reserved name does not need to be preceded by a reserved name indicator as it is not part of a model group and cannot, therefore, be mistaken for an element of the same name.

An element may also be declared as empty if it can only contain non-SGML characters that are stored as part of a separate file. In this case, an attribute must be used to identify the source of the data that is to be included in the document (see Chapter 6). Normally, however, external data will be incorporated into the document by reference to an external non-SGML data entity (see Chapter 4).

5.4   Generating new element sets

Very few SGML element sets need to be generated from scratch. Normally, existing sets can be modified or two or more existing sets can be combined to give an extended document structure.

There are cases, however, where it may be easier to create a completely new element set to declare the required document structure. Normally, this will only be necessary when special non-standard types of documents are being defined. Even in this case, many of the element declarations are likely to be copied from those used in existing sets.

5.4.1   Modifying existing sets

Before modifying an existing element set it is important that the currently declared document structure is fully understood. If the relevant tree diagrams and element descriptions are available this should not be difficult, but if all you have is an uncommented document type declaration, it may take some time to work out all the details of the existing structure.

Where the changes required to the existing structure are minor, their incorporation into the document type declaration subset is usually a simple matter. Major changes may, however, require a careful reappraisal of the parameter entities used within the document. This latter point is especially important where two or more existing element sets are being combined because both sets may contain parameter entities that have the same name but different declarations.

Before a new element is added to a document's structure, its role should be carefully assessed. As mentioned in Chapter 2, it is possible to identify elements which serve no real purpose as far as the document is concerned. For example, the apparent structure of an address is that it starts with the recipient's name, possibly followed by a company name. This is then followed by one or more lines of address information, which may be followed by a postcode. If special elements are declared for the name, company and postcode lines, the amount of coding needed within the address element of a letter would increase. A typical address might need to be entered as:

```
<address>
<name>Mrs G Burton
<company>G B Translations
<aline>29 Oldbury Road
<aline>Churchdown
<aline>Glos
<postcode>GL3 2PU
</address>
```

While there is nothing to be gained – and much to be lost – by treating the name, company and postcode as separate elements of the letter, this information may be important if the letter is to be stored as part of a database. In such circumstances, further elements could also be declared to store details of the town, area and country in which the company concerned is located, to allow entered addresses to be recovered as part of a larger subset of addresses (for example for inclusion in a mail shot).

Obviously there are certain advantages in not breaking down the address into its constituent parts – especially where the coding is being entered manually. However, where a more complex set of definitions is required to facilitate automatic data retrieval or the use of other advanced facilities, it is possible to reduce the amount of coding required by other means. For example, one way of reducing the amount of coding that needs to be entered might be to create a dummy file containing the relevant tags without their text entries. For a letter such a file might take the form:

```
<!DOCTYPE letter PUBLIC "-//Quorum//DTD Letter//EN">
<letter><ref>
<date>
<address><name>
<company>
<aline1>
<aline2>
<town>
<area>
<postcode>
<country>
</address><dear>
<p>

<signed name = mtb>
</letter>
```

Note that, in this example file, tags without contents have not been placed on separate lines but have been placed on the same line as the next tag. This is to avoid the possibility of the typist accidentally entering text for these purely structural elements. (Fields that are not required can be skipped by the operator, the formatting program automatically removing any blank address lines.)

The problems associated with analysing the structure of even such a relatively simple element as an address illustrate one of the skills that needs to be developed by an SGML document designer – the ability to define structures in terms that are immediately understandable to the document's creators. While complex data structures can provide more flexible information, they may require extra coding at the input stage. Where coding cannot be implied from the structure of the document or be otherwise automatically generated from the data (for example by use of data tags – see Chapter 7), its use should be obvious to the person keying the text. *If the start and end of each element are not obvious to the typist it is unlikely that the element will be coded correctly.*

5.4.2   Creating new element sets

When creating a completely new element set you should always start by defining the base document element. Once the elements that make up this initial element have been identified they should be declared before other embedded subelements.

Once the basic structure of the document has been defined it will normally be found that most of the declarations required for embedded textual elements are similar to those used in existing element sets. In most cases, it will be simpler to copy an existing definition from another set rather than try to redefine the element from first principles; but, if you do so, be sure to check that the definition used does do exactly what you expect it to. (For example, there is a subtle difference between the models used for the ‹body› element in Annex E of ISO 8879, (h0+|h1+), and Appendix C of this book, (h0|h1)+, which affects how chapters can be combined with parts.)

It is advisable to use existing element names wherever possible, even when the use of the element slightly changes between applications. Where elements are named consistently, users will find it easier to recognize the elements and will be less likely to enter the wrong tags. As well as reducing the likelihood of keying errors, the use of commonly recognized names will also reduce the time needed to train operators in the use of the new document structure.

Comments and comment declarations should be used liberally throughout any element set to explain the purpose of each element and to detail any restrictions that may apply. Document designers should always remember that what may seem to them to be an obvious restriction on the use of embedded elements may not be so obvious to someone new to element sets, and they should ensure that the purpose of such restrictions is clearly explained by use of appropriate comments.

Structured element sets

Another way of making element sets easier to understand is to structure the declarations so that elements declared at the same level start underneath each other. (Programmers will recognize this as an extension of the technique known as structured programming.) By applying this technique you can build up structured element sets in simple stages. For example, you could initially define a novel in the form shown in Figure 5.1.

From this structured list it is easy to see that a simple novel has three main components at its second level: preliminary pages, the body of the text and other text pages. The prelims subelement can be seen to be made up of a half-title page, an optional list of related publications, a title page and its reverse, and one or more optional introductory sections.

Once a basic structured list has been prepared, its contents can be expanded into a fully defined document type declaration subset by adding the appropriate declarations. Typically the final element set will start:

```
<!ELEMENT novel          - - (prelims, body, otherm)              >
    <!ELEMENT      prelims  - 0 (half-t,related?,title-p,verso,intro*)
                                        -- preliminary pages -->
        <!ELEMENT    half-t  0 0 (#PCDATA|%text;) -- half-title page -->
        <!ELEMENT    related - 0 (heading, pli+)
                                        -- list of related publications -- >
            <!ELEMENT heading 0 0 RCDATA        -- heading for list -- >
            <!ELEMENT pli     0 0 (#PCDATA)
                                        -- title in publication list -- >
    ...
```

While such structured sets can make the relationships of elements easier to understand, structures can be complicated by use of parameter entities. In the case of the novel detailed above only two parameter entities have been used in the main structure to simplify the relationships. (Other entities may, however, be embedded within these entities.) Where more parameter entities are used, as in Appendix C, a structured format may not be suitable.

5.4.3 Extending publicly declared element sets

A **publicly declared element set** is one whose declaration is known by both receiving and sending systems, so the relevant declarations do not need to be transmitted between the systems.

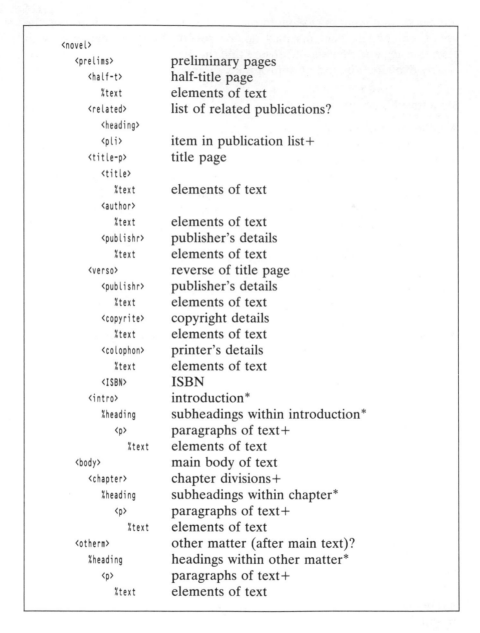

Figure 5.1 Structured element list for a novel.

Publicly declared element sets can either be recalled as part of a publicly declared document type declaration (see Section 4.3.3) or can be called as a separate external entity. Where external entities are used their declarations should take the form:

```
<!ENTITY % setname PUBLIC
        owner-identifier//ELEMENTS set-description//lc >
```

where:

- setname is the name of the parameter entity used to activate the set,

- owner-identifier is any valid form of owner identifier (see 'Formal public identifiers', in Section 4.3.2),

- set-description is a name describing the contents of the element set, and

- lc is a language code identifying the language in which the element set has been prepared.

The entity should be invoked within the same document type declaration subset by entry of a parameter entity reference of the form %setname;.

If a document type declaration subset contains element declarations, these will normally take precedence over any element declarations with the same name called from external entities. To illustrate this point, consider the following, slightly-improbable declaration:

```
<!DOCTYPE  general PUBLIC "ISO 8879-1986//DTD General Document//EN"  [
          <!ENTITY % AWbook PUBLIC
          "-//Addison-Wesley//DTD SGML: An Author's Guide to the Standard Generalized
          Markup Language//EN" >
    <!ELEMENT p    - O  (#PCDATA)                        >
    %AWbook; ]>
```

Here the initial document type declaration requested is the general set defined in Annex E of ISO 8879. This has been supplemented by the set of declarations defined in Appendix C of this book (called as the %AWbook; external entity) and by a specially entered element declaration for the paragraph element. Because both the externally stored entity sets are, in this case, recalled at the end of the document type declaration subset, the sequence in which these declarations are seen by the program is:

(1)   the individual element declaration,

(2)   the declarations called through the %AWbook; parameter entity reference, and

(3)   the declarations contained in the external set called by the 'optional-external-identifier' following the name given to the document type.

As the program only remembers the first definition it receives for each element, it will use the individual element declaration for the paragraph element (p). This declaration restricts the contents of the paragaph element to data characters, without any embedded elements.

If, however, the %AWbook; parameter entity reference had been placed in front of the element declaration, the definition used for the ‹p› tag would have been that declared in the 'SGML: An Author's Guide to the Standard Generalized Markup Language' document type definition. This is because this definition would have been inserted into the document type declaration subset in front of the element declaration. (The set associated with the DOCTYPE declaration itself is always added at the *end* of the subset, so its declarations never take precedence.)

It can be seen from the above example that the positioning of element declarations within the document type declaration subset is important. Provided that local element declarations precede any references to external entities, they will take precedence over other element declarations with the same name recalled from elsewhere. This makes updating existing element declarations a straightforward task and allows publicly declared element sets to be updated without direct modification of the stored declarations.

It should be noted that, when element sets are extended by the addition of other publicly declared or locally stored element declarations, not all of the elements mentioned in the model groups need to be formally declared within the DTD. In fact, provided the element is not a required subelement of the model, it only needs to be declared as part of the element set if the element is actually used in the context identified by a model group within the document.

5.5 Using elements

Within documents the contents of elements are specified by the use of **start-tags** and **end-tags**. A start-tag consists of the element's name between the currently declared **start-tag open** and **tag close** delimiters (‹ and › respectively in the reference concrete syntax – see Table 3.2). Optionally, the tag close code can be replaced by a **null end-tag** code (for example /) so that a matching null end-tag can be used in place of the normal end-tag (see Chapter 7). Where appropriate, the element name can be qualified by the entry of one or more of the attributes declared for the element (see Chapter 6) and by the name of an associated document type (see Chapter 9).

An end-tag consists of the element's name between the currently declared **end-tag open** and **tag close** delimiters (‹/ and › respectively in the reference concrete syntax). While document types can be associated with the element name in an end-tag (see Chapter 9), attributes can never be used in end-tags. Where a null end-tag has been used to close the element's start-tag, the whole of the end-tag *must* be replaced by a single null end-tag code.

Not all tags need to be present in a document. Provided that the OMITTAG feature has been allowed in the SGML declaration (see Chapter 10), tags can be omitted when their presence can be implied without ambiguity. Where the FEATURES clause of the SGML declaration also contains the statement SHORTTAG YES, tag names need not be entered within the delimiters where they can be implied unambiguously. (A full description of the minimization features available with the reference concrete syntax is given in Chapter 7.)

Unlike entity references, element names can normally be entered in any shift. (The NAMECASE section of the SGML declaration defaults to GENERAL YES. Where this entry is altered, document designers should take special care to warn users of the need to enter tags in the appropriate shift.)

The main problem that can occur when using elements is that their tags may be entered at a level for which they have not been declared. Where sophisticated SGML-based text entry terminals are being used to input text, the program will be able to tell users when an invalid element has been requested. For many users, however, such inconsistencies will not become apparent until the coded text is sent to a separate SGML parser for checking. As the parser checks the document's markup it will identify the error and output an appropriate message. The markup must then be checked and altered, as necessary, before the document is reprocessed.

In many cases, coded text will be easier to read if most of the markup tags are entered on separate lines. To facilitate this, SGML treats the record boundaries identified by the RS record start and RE record end characters in special ways.

5.5.1 The effect of record boundaries

A record is defined within SGML as any data between a record start code and a record end code. In the reference concrete syntax the record start code is the hexadecimal 0A (the ASCII line feed code) while the record end code is hexadecimal 0D (the ASCII carriage return code).

SGML does not restrict the length of a record and record boundaries do not *need* to be present. Where they are present within parsed text (as opposed to marked sections or markup declarations) their effect depends on their position.

When parsing data the SGML program ignores any record start codes (**RS**), using the record end code (**RE**) as the sole guide to record boundaries. Three rules control the effect of the record end code:

(1) The *first* RE in an element is ignored if it is not preceded by an RS code, some recognized data or a proper subelement (i.e. a subelement that

is specified in the model group for the element rather than in an inclusion clause associated with the element);

(2)   The *last* RE in an element is ignored if the record is not followed by data or a proper subelement; and

(3)   RE codes that do not immediately follow an RS code or another RE code are ignored unless the program identifies data or a proper subelement between the codes.

NOTE: When start-tag omission is in force (see Chapter 7) omitted markup recognition occurs before the above rules are applied.

The effect of these three rules can be seen in the following example:

Record	Contents
1	`<p>`
2	`Record end codes immediately after tags are ignored`
3	
4	`<hp1>`
5	`Highlighted phrases`
6	`</hp1> do not always start on a new line`
7	`</p>`

Each of the records shown above starts with a record start code and ends with a record end code (the record numbers are not part of the file – they are simply shown for reference).

The first element of the text is the paragraph element whose start-tag appears in line 1. As this start-tag is immediately followed by a record end code without any preceding text, rule (1) above will result in the record end code on line 1 being ignored. This means that the program will treat the first two lines of coding as if they had been entered in a single line reading:

`<p>Record end codes immediately after tags are ignored.`

The third record appears to consist simply of a record start code followed by a record end code, but it could also contain other hidden codes, such as Tab codes and Backspaces. If this was the case, rule (3) above may result in the record end code at the end of the line being ignored. If the line is a true blank line, consisting of a record start code followed immediately by a record end code, however, a single record end code will be retained when the document is parsed.

As with the first record, the record end code at the end of the fourth record will be ignored since no data for the embedded subelement precedes it. At the end of the fifth record, rule (2) will cause the last record end of the embedded subelement to be ignored since, in this case, it is followed by the end-tag of the subelement rather than data or another level of embedded subelement. The program will, therefore, treat records 4–6 as if a single record had been entered as:

```
<hp1>Highlighted phrases</hp1> do not always start on a new line.
```

As the record end code at the end of the sixth record is the last such code in the paragraph element, this will also be ignored (see rule (2)), so the whole example will be treated by the program as if it had been entered as:

```
<p>Record end codes immediately after tags are ignored.
```

```
<hp1>Highlighted phrases</hp1> do not always start on a new line.</p>
```

NOTE: The blank line will only be retained if the third record was actually blank.

By now you may be wondering what happened to the nice simple concept of elements introduced in Chapter 2. Don't worry! Behind all this complexity there is really a simple message – *the power of SGML makes it possible to handle both simple and complex situations by applying the same techniques.* Many of the features explained in this chapter will not be apparent to users – they are the province of the specialist document designer. If you have mastered this chapter you are well on the way to becoming a document designer. If you have not, there is no need to feel dismayed – the chances are that you will never need to make use of those features you did not fully understand.

Most of the declarations used in this chapter have been taken from the document type definition for this textbook, which is defined in Appendix C. As this textbook is a fairly complex type of document, study of this DTD, together with the accompanying brief description of the use of each element, will enable you to appreciate more fully the power of SGML elements.

6

Attributes

6.1   Overview

An attribute is a parameter (value) used to qualify an element's start-tag. Attributes are typically used to:

- identify the status of a document or element, for example `<memo status =draft>`;

- control how text is to be formatted, for example `<line type=centred>`;

- identify text to be generated by the system, for example `<li number=alpha>`;

- define the size or source of externally stored data to be added to the document, for example `<artwork sizex="120mm" sizey="90mm">`;

- uniquely identify a particular occurrence of an element, for example `<fig id="piechart1">`; and

- cross-refer to a previously identified element, for example `<figref refid ="piechart1", page=yes>`.

From the above examples it can be seen that there are two parts to an **attribute specification** – an **attribute name** and an **attribute value**. These two parts are joined by a **value indicator** (= in the reference concrete syntax) to give an attribute specification of the form:

```
<element-name attribute-name=attribute-value ... >
```

Attribute values are often entered as **attribute value literals**. A literal is a string of characters recognized as a single unit by the system because the characters have been entered between a matched pair of **literal delimiters**. The two alternative sets of literal delimiters provided in SGML are referred to within the standard as **lit** (literal) and **lita** (alternative form of literal). In the reference concrete syntax these are represented by the quotation mark (") and apostrophe ('), respectively.

The choice of which set of literal delimiters should be used is normally entirely a matter of user convenience. The only restriction is that the character chosen cannot appear in the entered attribute value. This means that attribute values such as Albert l'Ouvrier must be entered within quotation marks rather than apostrophes, as is shown in the following example:

```
<ix see="Albert l'Ouvrier">Albert-Alexandre Martin<ix>
```

Only one type of literal delimiter can be used to delimit a particular attribute value but the two types can be used interchangeably within the same tag, for example:

```
<fig id='pie127-87' frame="rule" align='centre' >
```

The basic format for the attribute specification can be modified in a number of ways. Where, as in the reference concrete syntax, the FEATURE section of the SGML declaration contains the statement SHORTTAG YES, the literal delimiters can be omitted if the only characters used in the value are those currently declared as **name characters** (for example alphanumeric characters in the reference concrete syntax), without any spaces. For example, the declaration shown above could also have been entered as:

```
<fig id=pie127-87 frame=rule align=centre>
```

as the values in it have all been defined using name characters.

NOTE: If SHORTTAG NO *has been specified in the* FEATURES *clause of the SGML declaration, the element's unique identifier will need to be entered within literal delimiters as it is not one of the declared values defined in the* <fig> *element's attribute definition list. The other two values will, however, never need literal delimiters as they have been defined as declared values for their attributes (see Section 6.2).*

When the entered attribute value has been declared as a member of a set of valid attribute values for the element, the attribute name with the associated value indicator can also be omitted when SHORTTAG YES has been specified in the FEATURES clause, giving an attribute specification of the form:

```
<li alpha>
```

In this case the attribute value must *not* be entered in delimiters because, if it is, the program will be unable to identify the attribute referred to.

Attribute values can also consist of *delimited* lists of values, each item of which is separated from the others by a space or another valid **separator character** (e.g. RE, RS or TAB). For example, the two size attributes shown above for the ‹artwork› element could be combined to give an attribute specification of the form:

```
<artwork size="120mm 90mm">
```

Each attribute can be given a default value when it is declared. If either OMITTAG YES or SHORTTAG YES has been specified in the FEATURES clause, this default value will be used whenever a specific attribute value is not entered as part of the start-tag. Where a general default value cannot be specified, a special keyword, such as #IMPLIED or #CURRENT, must be entered to tell the program what it should do when no value has been entered in the start-tag. Where an attribute value must be entered whenever the element is requested, the keyword #REQUIRED should be used as the default value.

A special type of attribute, called a **data attribute**, can be used to qualify notation declarations associated with non-SGML data entities. These attributes allow parameters to be passed to programs processing the externally stored data before it is added to the document.

6.2   Declaring attributes

Attributes are declared by adding **attribute definition list declarations** to the document type declaration subset. Normally, attributes will be declared with the associated elements, either immediately after the appropriate element declaration or as a separate set of attribute declarations at the end of the element set.

Each attribute definition list is declared as a separate markup declaration, delimited by the currently defined markup declaration delimiters (e.g. ‹! and › in the reference concrete syntax). The list starts with the reserved name ATTLIST or its previously declared replacement, followed immediately by details of the element(s) with which the list is to be associated. Once the **associated element type** has been declared, one or more **attribute definitions** can be entered before the closing delimiter to give the attribute definition list the general form:

```
<!ATTLIST elements attribute-definition-1
              ...
          attribute-definition-n >
```

Where more than one element is associated with a given list of attributes, the names of the associated element types can be entered as a bracketed name group, individual names being delimited by any valid connector to give an entry of the form:

```
<!ATTLIST (element1|...|elementn) attribute-definition-1
                              ...
                  attribute-definition-n >
```

Each attribute definition consists of an **attribute name**, a **declared value** and a **default value**. These elements are separated from each other by a **parameter separator** (**ps**) which, in the case of the reference concrete syntax, can be a space, a Record Start or Record End code, a Tab code, a special system-specific **entity end** (**Ee**) code, a comment delimited by pairs of hyphens or a valid parameter entity reference that starts with one of the other valid parameter separators.

Attribute names must start with a valid name start character and must contain only valid name characters in other positions. Their length must not exceed the current value of the NAMELEN quantity value (see Chapter 10). This means that in the reference concrete syntax, attribute names must consist of not more than eight alphanumeric characters, full stops or hyphens, starting with a letter. Attribute names do not need to be unique, though each name can only be used once in any attribute definition list declaration.

The declared value of an attribute is either a bracketed list of valid **attribute values** or a **keyword** identifying the types of entries that can be used as attribute values. Where specific attribute values are defined, each permitted attribute value must be unique to the attribute definition list, but where keywords are used, the same value can be used for a number of different attributes.

A list of valid keywords is given in Table 6.1. (Examples of the use of each of these keywords are given in Section 6.3.) As the token keywords (NMTOKEN, NMTOKENS, NUTOKEN and NUTOKENS in the reference concrete syntax) provide a slightly more flexible approach to attribute values they are often used in preference to their more specific equivalents (NAME, NAMES, NUMBER and NUMBERS), which restrict the entered values to a narrow set of characters.

The default value entry of the attribute definition consists of either a specific value or one of the keywords listed in Table 6.2. Note that for default values these keywords are preceded by the reserved name indicator (**rni** – # in the reference concrete syntax) to ensure that they are not mistaken for attribute values of the same name which have not been enclosed in literal delimiters.

Table 6.1 Keywords for attribute declared values.

Keyword	Purpose
CDATA	Attribute value consists of character data (valid SGML characters, including markup delimiters)
ENTITY	Attribute value can be any currently declared subdocument or data cntity name
ENTITIES	Attribute value is a list of subdocument or data entity names
ID	Attribute value is a unique identifier (ID) for the element
IDREF	Attribute value is an ID reference value (i.e. a name previously entered as the unique identifier of another element)
IDREFS	Attribute value is a list of ID reference values
NAME	Attribute value is a valid SGML name
NAMES	Attribute value is a list of valid SGML names
NMTOKEN	Attribute value is a name token (i.e. contains only name characters but, in this case, with digits and other valid name characters accepted as the first character)
NMTOKENS	Attribute value is a list of name tokens
NOTATION	Attribute value is a member of the bracketed list of notation names that qualifies this keyword (see 'Notation attributes' in Section 6.3.5)
NUMBER	Attribute value is a number
NUMBERS	Attribute value is a list of numbers
NUTOKEN	Attribute value is a number token (i.e. a name that starts with a number)
NUTOKENS	Attribute value is a list of number tokens

Table 6.2 Keywords for attribute default values.

Keyword†	Purpose
#FIXED	The following value is a fixed default value (i.e. cannot be changed by entry of another value in the start-tag)
#REQUIRED	The attribute value must be entered within the start-tag of the element
#CURRENT	If no attribute value is specified in the start-tag the current (last entered) value is to be used
#IMPLIED	If no attribute value is specified the program may imply a value
#CONREF	The element may contain either specific cross-reference text or an attribute whose value is a recognized ID reference value (i.e. a name that has previously been entered as the unique identifier to an element)

† The # preceding each keyword indicates the presence of the current reserved name indicator character.

The restrictions that apply to the use of the keywords listed in Tables 6.1 and 6.2 are:

- the ID and NOTATION keywords may be used only once in any attribute definition list;

- the NOTATION keyword cannot be used for attributes associated with an element whose contents have been declared as EMPTY;

- #CONREF cannot be used to specify the default value of attributes associated with EMPTY elements;

- the same token cannot appear in two lists of valid attribute values in the same declaration;

- the default value of an attribute declared using the ID declared value keyword must be either #REQUIRED or #IMPLIED; and

- an empty default value can only be specified for attributes whose declared value is CDATA.

Further restrictions also apply to names associated with attributes declared using the ID and NOTATION keywords. This will be explained below when examples of the use of these keywords are given.

6.3   Using attributes

6.3.1   Simple attributes

The simplest type of attribute is one with just two declared values, one of which is the default. For example, in the Addison-Wesley textbook document type definition in Appendix C, the ISBN element is specified as:

```
<!ELEMENT ISBN    - -  CDATA -- ISBN (or ISSN) number -- >
<!ATTLIST ISBN    type (book|serial)  book           >
```

This declaration shows that there are two valid entries (tokens) for the type attribute – book and serial. By default, type will use the value book to generate an International Standard Book Number (ISBN). Alternatively, this default value can be overridden by entry of a type=serial attribute within the <ISBN> start-tag if the document is one that has been assigned an International Standard Serial Number (ISSN). As both tokens only contain valid name characters, parameter literals do not need to be used to delimit the default value or an entered attribute value while the concrete syntax currently being used contains the SHORTTAG YES statement.

Two forms in which the required number can be entered are:

```
<ISBN>0 201 17535 5</ISBN>
<ISBN serial>0143-9472</ISBN>
```

In the first example no attribute value has been entered because the default value, book, is the one required and there is no point in entering an attribute when the value required is the one the program will default to in any case.

In the second example the attribute value, serial, has been added to the start-tag to generate the relevant ISSN. The attribute name and the associated value indicator have not been entered in this example because, when the short tags option has been switched on by use of SHORTTAG YES, they are not essential for entries selected from a list of valid attribute values. On the other hand, the </ISBN> end-tag (or a null end-tag replacement for it – see Chapter 7) is compulsory in both examples as elements declared using the CDATA option must have end-tags (see Chapter 5).

In a printed document the first of the above examples would generate an ISBN, the program automatically adding the letters ISBN to the entered number. For the second example the program would recognize the serial attribute as a request to modify its generated text to produce an ISSN number. Typically, the end results take the form:

```
ISBN 0 201 17535 5
ISSN 0143-9472
```

A list of declared values can contain as many names as required. For example, the list element defined in Appendix C is declared as:

```
<!ELEMENT li      - - (it+)  -- list of items -- >
<!ATTLIST li   number  (arabic|roman|alpha|default|none)  default
               form    (compact|spaced)                   spaced >
```

In this case the number attribute can have one of five values, the default option being the default value, while the form attribute can either be compact or the default value of spaced.

The number attribute of the list element controls the numbering of items in the list. The options available in this set are:

- arabic to number each item in the list with an arabic number (starting from 1);

- roman to number each item with a roman numeral (starting from i);

- alpha to use letters to number each item (starting with a);

- default to use the publisher's preferred method of marking list items (e.g. hyphens, bullets, numbers, etc.); and

- none   to specify that no printed character is to precede the text entered for each item (a space may still be left between entries).

Obviously, other options could be defined for a list, but these must depend on the particular house style.

The two options provided for the form attribute of the list element allow users to control whether or not lists can be compacted (e.g. printed without spaces between the entries in the list). By default each item will be preceded by a small separating space. If the compact attribute is specified, however, the formatting program will set the items with little or no intervening space to pack the entries closer together. The spaces above and below the list will, of course, still be retained.

In its simplest form a list could be entered as:

```
<li><it>item 1<it>item 2<it>item 3<it>item 4</li>
```

If the default house style called for bullets as the list item identifier, this list would be printed as:

- item 1
- item 2
- item 3
- item 4

If the start-tag was changed to `<li form="compact">` or just `<li compact>`, the list might appear as:

- item 1
- item 2
- item 3
- item 4

If the start-tag was `<li number='none' form="compact">` or simply `<li none compact>` the list might appear as:

    item 1
    item 2
    item 3
    item 4

If the start-tag was `<li alpha>`, the list would be numbered alphabetically as:

    a) item 1
    b) item 2
    c) item 3
    d) item 4

while an ‹li arabic› entry could result in a list of the form:

> 1 – item 1
> 2 – item 2
> 3 – item 3
> 4 – item 4

The ‹li roman› option might result in a list of the form:

> i. item 1
> ii. item 2
> iii. item 3
> iv. item 4

It should be noted that the format of the numbers generated in response to the number attribute is controlled by the text formatter. The decision to right align the item numbers in the last of the above lists is one that has been made by the text formatter – SGML does not control such features directly. For example, if a list's start-tag was entered as ‹li roman compact›, the formatter could quite legitimately decide to output the roman numerals as bracketed capital letters, rather than lower-case letters followed by full stops, for example:

> (I)   item 1
> (II) item 2
> (III) item 3
> (IV) item 4

Before using a particular text formatter you should, therefore, check how the program will handle such features as compacted lists, etc. (Unfortunately, there are at present no hard and fast guidelines about the best way to format lists, so each formatter has its own variations. Hopefully, in time, a consensus of opinion will emerge about the meaning of many commonly used attributes.)

6.3.2   Using tokens

In the above definitions it has been presumed that each list will start from the same initial number (1, i, a, etc.). If there is a likelihood that some lists may need to start from a different number (e.g. because they are part of larger set of numbered examples) it may be necessary to add another attribute to the attribute definition list for the ‹li› element to allow a start number to be defined for the list. Typically, this attribute will be declared by addition of an entry of the form:

```
start    NMTOKEN    1
```

The NMTOKEN keyword indicates that the attribute value for the start attribute must be a **name token**. A name token can be any character string consisting solely of name characters, e.g. alphanumeric characters and those characters defined in the UCNMCHAR and LCNMCHAR entries of the SGML declaration.

The start attribute has been defined as a name token rather than a number token so that both alphabetic and numeric entries can be used to define the starting point of the list. For example, if the list's start-tag was entered as ‹li alpha start="c"› our sample list might be output as:

(c) item 1
(d) item 2
(e) item 3
(f) item 4

Note that, because the start attribute has, in this case, been defined using the NMTOKEN keyword, its name and the associated value indicator are compulsory. (The facility to omit an attribute's name and the associated value indicator is restricted to attributes, such as the number attribute, for which a list of valid name tokens has been specified.)

If the NAMECASE GENERAL YES parameter of the SGML declaration is changed to NAMECASE GENERAL NO to prevent automatic substitution of capital letters for lower-case letters within tags, the attribute value entered for start could also be used to determine whether or not capitals are to be used to number lists. For example, the start-tag ‹li alpha start=A› could be used to produce a list of the form:

A. item 1
B. item 2
C. item 3
D. item 4

while ‹li alpha start=a› would produce:

a. item 1
b. item 2
c. item 3
d. item 4

The start attribute cannot, however, completely replace the number attribute because the program would be unable to distinguish between roman numerals and alphabetic entries entered as values for the start attribute. For instance, to generate a list of items numbered with roman numbers starting from v) requires a start-tag of the form ‹li roman start=v› to produce:

    v)   item 1
    vi)   item 2
    vii) item 3
    viii) item 4

If the default house style called for alphabetic numbering of items, however, entry of ‹li start=v› on its own would result in a list reading:

    v) item 1
    w) item 2
    x) item 3
    y) item 4

Except where the number attribute is alpha (or default if the default form of numbering is alphabetic) the start attribute can consist of any number of characters. For example, the start-tag ‹li arabic start=101› could be used to produce a list of the form:

    (101) item 1
    (102) item 2
    (103) item 3
    (104) item 4

NOTE: Multiple character alphabetic tags are ambiguous as the program would not know which character to increment. For example, if the entered value was word, should the following item begin wore or xord?

Another way of associating an initial value with the number attribute is to consider it as a second parameter in a **name token list**. For example, if the definition of the list element was amended to read:

```
<!ELEMENT li    - -  (it+)  -- list of items -- >
<!ATTLIST li    type NMTOKENS        "default 1"
                form (compactispaced) spaced     >
```

the start and number parameters could be entered as a single attribute, e.g.

‹li type="alpha m"›, to produce a list of the form:

    m) item 1
    n) item 2
    o) item 3
    p) item 4

As attribute names are compulsory when keywords have been used to indicate the types of attribute values that can be entered, type = must always precede the attribute value when the type attribute has been defined as shown above. Similarly, because the attribute value consists of more than one name in this case, the parameter literals surrounding the attribute value cannot be omitted, even though SHORTTAG YES has been specified in the SGML declaration. (A short form is still permitted for the form attribute.) For example, ‹li type='roman iii' compact› could be used to produce a list of the form:

    iii) item 1
    iv) item 2
    v) item 3
    vi) item 4

The order in which name tokens are entered in token lists may be important if the formatting program expects to receive parameters in a predefined sequence. Where attributes have been declared with specific names, the program can sort out the sequence in which the parameters should be passed to the text formatter. Lists of tokens, however, should be passed to the formatter in the order received because the program may not know which entry refers to which parameter. For example, the tag ‹li start=s compact alpha› would be valid if the first of the above attribute definition lists was used for the ‹li› element since each attribute value can be associated with a specific, if undeclared, attribute. The tag ‹li type="25 arabic" compact›, however, may not be valid if the second set of definitions applied because the text formatter may not be able to ascertain that the 25 was supposed to be the start number and arabic the type of number. The formatter would expect these two parameters to be presented to it in the correct order and may not be intelligent enough to try the parameters the other way round. Hence the need to check carefully the sequence in which such parameters are used.

NOTE: Before interpreting a list of attribute values, the program will replace any multiple spaces, record end codes or separator characters in the list with a single space. (Where the attribute has been declared to contain character data, however, all codes entered between the parameter literals will be retained.)

6.3.3   Numeric attributes

The only difference between the NUTOKEN and NUTOKENS **number token** declared value keywords and the name token keywords (NMTOKEN and NMTOKENS) used in the preceding examples is that the first character of any NUTOKEN must be numeric. In many cases the two sets of keywords are used together, as the following declaration for an ‹artwork› element shows:

```
<!ELEMENT artwork    - O EMPTY                                    >
<!ATTLIST artwork  sizex  NMTOKEN  textsize -- defaults to as text --
                   sizey  NUTOKEN  #REQUIRED                      >
```

In this case the horizontal width (sizex) of the artwork defaults to a special parameter value (textsize) known to the formatting program, unless a specific value is entered for the attribute. As this special name starts with a letter rather than a number, the NMTOKEN keyword has been used for the declared value. For the sizey attribute, however, the declared value is NUTOKEN to ensure that the first part of the compulsory vertical size parameter is always a number.

To see the differences between these two definitions compare these valid tags:

```
<artwork sizex=150mm sizey=100mm>
<artwork sizey = 8in>
<artwork sizex = "26-picas" sizey = '4-in'>
```

with these invalid ones:

```
<artwork>
<artwork sizex=mm150 sizey=mm100>
<artwork sizey = 8 in>
<artwork sizex = "26 picas" sizey = "4 in">
<artwork textsize sizey=24pi>
<artwork sizey = 6">
```

At first sight many of the entries in the invalid list may seem to be valid, so let's take a look at why they are actually invalid. In the first invalid example the problem is that the compulsory sizey attribute has not been entered. (Always remember that attributes whose declaration contains the keyword #REQUIRED rather than a specific default value must have their attribute values entered as part of the start-tag.)

The next example is invalid because the value entered for the sizey attribute does not start with a number. Because the NUTOKEN keyword has been used in the declaration, all values entered for the sizey attribute must start with at lcast one digit, rather than a letter. It should be noted, however, that the value for the sizex attribute, which has been entered in the same form, will be treated as valid by the SGML parser because this attribute has NMTOKEN for its declared value. (The text formatter may not be so happy about receiving values in this form though!)

The third and fourth invalid examples have a very subtle fault. Note that a space between the 8 and the in is the only difference between the third invalid example and the second of the valid examples. The difference between the third valid example and the fourth invalid one also concerns spaces, in this case in place of hyphens. Spaces are not – and never can be – valid entries in a name since they and other valid separator codes, including the Record Start and Record End codes, are specifically excluded from being added to the set of valid name characters defined in the SGML declaration (see Chapter 10). Because the third example has not been placed between literal delimiters, the program will not identify the in as part of the sizey attribute and, after treating the 8 as the illustration's depth expressed as a number of default units, it will try to use the in attribute as a sizex value. (At this point, it is not certain what the program's reaction will be. It may reject the value or presume a numeric value that is to be expressed in inches, or it may just ignore the entry altogether.) The fourth invalid entry will, however, always be treated as incorrect because the presence of a space identifies the entry within the literal as a list of tokens, which is invalid in this case because the attributes have been declared with NMTOKEN and NUTOKEN, not NMTOKENS and NUTOKENS.

For the fifth of the invalid entries, an attempt has been made to minimize the entry by omitting the sizex= attribute name and value indicator. This technique, however, is only allowed where a specific set of valid name tokens has been entered as the declared value, so the entered attribute value will not be recognized as valid for the ‹artwork› element.

The final example illustrates another subtle fault. Here an attempt has been made to use the quotation mark (") to represent inches. However, unless otherwise instructed by a change in the document's set of delimiter characters, the program will see the symbol as an unmatched literal delimiter and so flag the entry as invalid.

One way of simplifying the attribute definition list for the ‹artwork› element would be to treat both size values as part of a single number token list by using a declaration of the form:

```
<!ATTLIST artwork size NUTOKENS #REQUIRED >
```

In this case a valid start-tag for the artwork element might take the form:

```
<artwork size = "100mm 4.5inches">
```

Note that the two entries are separated by a space and that no other spaces occur in the list. As the full stop is part of the default set of name characters it can be used within the attribute value, but beware – it cannot be used at the start of a number token as the first character must be a number. If a fractional value is required it must be entered as:

```
<artwork size = "2cm 0.5inches">
```

rather than:

```
<artwork size = "2cm .5inches">
```

NOTE: Users of the European form of decimal point (the comma) should check that the comma has been added to the list of name characters (UCNMCHAR or LCNMCHAR) specified in the current SGML declaration.

In the above examples, we have freely mixed different measurement systems – a feature that is perfectly valid within SGML. One word of warning is necessary, however. Not all text formatters will allow you to enter mixed values and they may be fussy about the characters required to indicate the units of measurement. In particular, many typesetting systems will not accept values specified in inches or millimetres, requiring instead that all measurements be entered using the printer's traditional values of picas and points (see Chapter 1). If you are not given specific lists of the units that *can* be accepted, you should consult your publisher/typesetter before using size parameters.

Where only one unit of measurement is being used on the output system the NUTOKEN and NUTOKENS keywords can be replaced by NUMBER or NUMBERS to restrict attribute values to numeric values only. For example, if the attribute definition list for the <artwork> element was defined as:

```
<!ATTLIST artwork size NUMBERS #REQUIRED>
```

a valid entry might take the form:

```
<artwork size = "150 100">
```

There is, however, one danger with the NUMBER keyword. Since only digits can be entered for attributes declared in this way, decimal values cannot be defined. If decimal values are likely to be needed the NUTOKEN or NUTOKENS option should be specified so that full stops can be used as decimal points.

6.3.4   Alphabetic and other attribute values

Where numbers should never be entered as the first character in an attribute value, the NAME or NAMES keywords can be used as the declared value to restrict the range of valid entries. In this case, all entered attribute values will start with a letter, with following characters being restricted to the currently declared set of name characters (see Chapters 3 and 10).

Where attribute values need to contain characters not currently defined as name characters, the CDATA keyword should be used in the attribute definition. Whenever CDATA attribute values contain characters other than name characters, literal delimiters *must* be used to delimit the entered value. (This rule automatically applies to lists of tokens because spaces and separator characters cannot be declared as valid name characters.) For example, if the attribute definition list for the artwork element was defined as:

```
<!ATTLIST artwork size CDATA "150mm 100mm" >
```

the default size of 150 mm by 100 mm could be altered by entry of a start-tag of the form:

```
<artwork size = '8" 4"'>
```

If, however, the required size was specified as:

```
<artwork size = 100mm 200mm>
```

the start-tag would be treated as illegal because the attribute values are not enclosed by literal delimiters. Instead of leaving space for the artwork the program would probably, in this case, simply print the characters entered in the illegal tag.

When the CDATA keyword is used the default value can be an empty string, as the following declaration shows:

```
<!ELEMENT textbook   - 0    (front, body, back?) +(%floats;|ix) >
<!ATTLIST textbook version  CDATA    "1"
                   status   CDATA    ""
                   security CDATA    #IMPLIED                   >
```

If no specific attribute entries are made, the textbook will have a version number of 1, no status and an implied security value that will depend on how the system has been set up. Alternative values can be specified at the start of any book by entry of a start-tag, such as:

```
<textbook version="1987/2" status="draft" security="confidential">
```

The only restrictions on the contents of attributes declared using the CDATA keyword are that character strings declared to be short reference delimiters (see Chapters 3 and 10) will not be recognized as such within the literal delimiters, and codes defined as non-SGML characters may not be included in the attribute value.

6.3.5 Specialized attributes

Four special types of attribute values are catered for by SGML:

(1)   attributes referring to entities declared within the document,
(2)   attributes used as unique identifiers for start-tags,
(3)   attributes that cross-refer to entered unique identifiers, and
(4)   attributes that declare the notation used within an element or external entity.

Entity Attributes

In the declaration of the `artwork` element given above, it was presumed that supplied artwork would be pasted into a blank area whose size was defined as an attribute of the relevant start-tag. But what if the information required to generate the picture is already stored on the system? In this case, the file containing the coded picture could be declared as an external entity (see Chapter 4) by entry of a declaration of the form:

```
<!ENTITY pic12 SYSTEM "piechart" NDATA picture>
```

or

```
<!ENTITY pic13 SYSTEM NDATA picture>
```

within the base document type definition.

To recall these pictures at appropriate points in the text a general purpose `<artwork>` element could be declared as:

```
<!ELEMENT artwork - O    EMPTY        >
<!ATTLIST artwork sizex  NMTOKEN  textsize
                  sizey  NUTOKEN  #IMPLIED
                  file   ENTITY   #IMPLIED>
```

The attribute definition list shows that the `<artwork>` element can have its start-tag qualified by an attribute, called `file`, whose value is the name of an entity declared elsewhere in the document. By default the name of this entity can be implied by the system (typically to a value consisting of the letters `fig` followed by a number indicating the figure's relative position, e.g. `fig12`) and the default depth would, in such cases, be implied to be that of the generated artwork.

Once the `<artwork>` element has been declared in this way, illustrations can be called from any previously declared external file by entry of a start-tag, such as:

```
<artwork file="pic12">
```

Note, however, that as this start-tag has exactly the same effect as a straightforward entity reference to the external entity (e.g. &pic12;), its only advantage is that the purpose of the entity reference is slightly clearer when the entity name is used to qualify the element. But there are times when there are advantages in using attributes to recall external entities. For example, if the above attribute definition list was extended to read:

```
<!ELEMENT artwork - O   EMPTY                        >
<!ATTLIST artwork sizex NMTOKEN        textsize
                  sizey NUTOKEN        #IMPLIED
                  file  ENTITY         #IMPLIED
                  frame (box|rule|none) none        >
```

the additional parameter could, optionally, be used to place a frame around the recalled artwork, or to place a rule above and below the picture (an addition that could not easily be made using an entity reference). For example, the start-tag:

```
<artwork file="sleigh" hn>
```

could be used to call up the following illustration:

Note that, in this case, the size of the picture's frame has not been specified within the start-tag. The frame has been generated within the text formatter by application of one or more special procedures which automatically determine the size of the artwork and add an appropriate margin before placing the frame around it.

When using the ENTITY keyword to incorporate externally stored data into a document it is important to remember that the associated element must be declared as EMPTY and, therefore, requires no end-tag (see Chapter 5). It should also be noted that if the program encounters an ⟨artwork⟩ start-tag without a file name and then cannot find an external entity declaration whose name matches the value it implies for the attribute, the program will report an error.

Recalled entities do not have to contain non-SGML data. They could equally well contain an SGML subdocument (see Chapter 9) or text which does not contain SGML markup instructions (i.e. CDATA or SDATA entities – see Chapter 4). They may not, however, contain markup or other parsable text that requires parsing according to the document type definition currently in force.

Unique identifiers

The ID declared value keyword allows a unique identifier to be associated with specific start-tags. Once a particular start-tag has been given a unique identifier it can be cross-referred to by other attributes declared using the IDREF or IDREFS keywords (see the next section on 'Cross-references').

As mentioned in the list of restrictions on the use of keywords, the default value associated with an attribute that has the ID keyword as its declared value must either be #REQUIRED (to indicate that a unique identifier *must* be entered in all start-tags for the associated elements) or #IMPLIED (to indicate that the identifier can be implied by the system if not present).

NOTES:

(1)   While the #IMPLIED keyword does allow the use of an identifier attribute to be optional, cross-reference to elements with implied (unentered) identifiers will be difficult to control accurately.

(2)   Because each identifier must be unique to the document, the standard recommends that the same attribute name (e.g. id) be used for all identifiers. (This idea is not, however, compulsory.)

A typical use of the ID keyword would be to allow items in a list to be allocated unique identifiers. The item element (⟨it⟩) might be declared as:

```
<!ELEMENT it  0 0 (#PCDATA|%copy;|li|qi%phrases;)* -- items in list -- >
<!ATTLIST it  id  ID      #IMPLIED -- identifiers are optional -- >
```

Individual items within the list could then be identified by entry of a tag, such as:

```
<it id=item3>
```

Unique identifiers should be used wherever a reference may need to be made to the position at which an element occurred. Typically, they will be declared for elements, such as figures, footnotes, headings and tables, all of which can be referred to in the text by use of phrases, such as 'Figure 1.2, on page 88'.

Because each SGML identifier (known as an **id value**) must be a valid SGML name, each identifier must start with a letter. This means that entries such as:

```
<fig id=1.2>
```

are invalid. If you do want to use numbers as identifiers you must place at least one letter in front of the first digit, example:

```
<fig id=f1.2>
```

Unless the text-entry system checks each identifier as it is entered, it is the user's responsibility to ensure that the identifiers used in a document are unique. The identifier must not just be unique to the element concerned – it must be unique to the whole document. Though the identifier can be entered in either case any lower-case characters will be converted to upper-case before the uniqueness of the identifier is determined (unless the SGML declaration has been altered to contain the statement NAMECASE GENERAL NO). This means, for example, that the tag <fig id=F1.2> would be treated as identical to <fig id="f1.2"> and so would be rejected if already used (or implied by the program).

Cross-references

A unique identifier that has been entered as an attribute of a specific element can be referred to within the same document by use of an attribute with a declared value of IDREF or IDREFS. Normally, only one unique identifier will be involved, so the attribute can be declared using the singular IDREF keyword. Typically, the declaration will take the form:

```
<!ELEMENT fnref   - O  EMPTY              >
<!ATTLIST fnref refid  IDREF    #REQUIRED
                page  (yes|no) no         >
```

In this case the footnote reference element (fnref) has been declared as an empty element because its contents are automatically generated by the program. It has a compulsory attribute called refid (short for reference identifier) which must be a reference to a unique identifier used somewhere in the current document and an optional page attribute that defaults to no.

When a footnote is required within the text it will be entered at the point at which the footnote number is to appear in the form:

```
<p>This paragraph of text<fn id=note1>Copy for first
footnote</fn> contains two footnotes<fn>Copy for
footnote 2</fn>.</p>
```

If the identified footnote is to be referred to elsewhere in the text, a footnote reference should be entered in the form:

```
<p>As shown earlier<fnref refid=note1>, certain
footnotes may be referred to more than once. ...
```

The way in which footnotes are treated will depend on how the system being used has been set up (though, fortunately, this does not affect the way the ⟨fn⟩ and ⟨fnref⟩ elements are used). For instance, if footnotes are numbered consecutively throughout a book, the subsequent cross-reference will normally be simply a repeat of the (superior) number used to identify the footnote when it first occurred. If, however, the system has been set up so that symbols are used to identify the footnotes that occur on individual pages, the page attribute could be added to the footnote reference to give it the form:

```
<fnref refid=note1 page=yes>
```

This might generate a cross-reference of the form:

```
As shown earlier (see the first note on page 34),
certain footnotes may be referred to more than once. ...
```

Reference identifiers can also be associated with the items in a list. For example, cross-references for the item element's identifier have been defined in Appendix C as:

```
<!ELEMENT itref   - O EMPTY -- generated item reference -->
<!ATTLIST itref  refid  IDREF      #REQUIRED
                 page  (y|n)       y                      >
```

In this case the page attribute, which controls whether or not the page number is to be output as part of the reference, has been given a shortened form of y and n in its list of permitted values. The default value of y has been used to add the page number automatically to each reference. If the reference is made in the form:

```
<p>As shown in <itref refid=item3 page=y> ...
```

or, more simply:

```
<p>As shown in <itref refid=item3> ...
```

the output text might take the form:

```
As shown in entry c) on page 143 ...
```

Alternatively the reference could be entered in the form:

```
<p>As shown in <itref refid=item3 page=n> ...
```

or, more simply:

```
<p>As shown in <itref refid=item3 n> ...
```

to reduce the reference to the form:

```
As shown in c) ...
```

As well as being able to add the page numbers to cross-references, the program will also automatically update the format of the entry to reflect the format and position of the identified entry in the list. For example, alterations to the list could change the position of the entry originally called item3 so that it is now the fifth item in the list, and the number attribute could be set to arabic rather than alpha. Without the user making any change to the cross-reference entry, the program should automatically change the reference to read:

```
As shown in 5) on page 143
```

While attributes using the IDREF or IDREFS keywords will normally have a default value of #REQUIRED, there are circumstances in which entries of the form #CONREF and #CURRENT may apply. (For details of the use of the #CURRENT default value refer to Section 6.3.6.)

The #CONREF keyword is particularly useful where documents are being prepared as a number of individual files, which will be linked together as subdocuments to a master document prior to output. Because cross-references can only be made to identifiers entered in the same document, cross-references to identifiers used in subdocuments will need to be entered specifically by the author. To allow for this, the special #CONREF keyword permits references to be invoked in two forms:

(1)   by entering the wording required for the cross-reference as the contents of the element, and

(2)   by using a cross-reference attribute.

To see how this works, consider the following declaration for a figure reference:

```
<!ELEMENT figref - 0   (#PCDATA|%phrases;)* -- x-ref for fig -- >
<!ATTLIST figref refid IDREF        #CONREF
                 page  (yes|no)     no                          >
```

Because the refid has, in this case, been given a default value keyword of #CONREF rather than the #REQUIRED used for itref above, the contents of the associated element cannot be declared to be empty. Instead the element declaration has been given a content model that allows data to be entered, including embedded phrases if required.

When a cross-reference is required to an element in the current document the reference can be made in the form of a start-tag qualified by an attribute, for example:

```
(see <figref refid=pic87-12 page=yes>)
```

to generate a reference of the form:

```
(see Figure 3.12 on page 352)
```

When, however, the reference is to a figure in another subdocument the relevant entry should be entered as text within the start- and end-tags of the figure reference, for example:

```
<p>As shown in <figref>Figure A.1 in Appendix A</figref> ...
```

It can be seen from the above examples that when the attribute is present in the start-tag, the element is treated as an empty element (without content) and, therefore, no end-tag is present. When the attribute value is not specified, however, the element's end-tag must be entered to identify the end of the reference. Because the end-tag is present in some cases and not in others, the second of the tag omission indicators for any element associated with an attribute whose default value is #CONREF should be 0.

A word of caution is needed here, however. If the attribute list contains two #CONREF default value keywords, it is important that the text formatter is able to imply values for *both* attributes. This is because if either attribute is present the element will automatically become an empty one, any data within it being considered part of the next highest level in the document's structure. If either of the attributes is omitted the program will need to presume a value for it.

Notation attributes

The NOTATION declared value keyword can be used to identify elements whose content has been entered using a special coding notation. Attributes declared in this way are used to associate the element's contents with one of the notation declarations contained in the document type declaration subset. (The use of notation names to identify the notation used to code external entities was explained in Chapter 4.)

The format of the declared value statement changes slightly when the NOTATION keyword is used because the keyword needs to be qualified by a list of valid notation names. A typical entry might take the form:

```
<!ELEMENT eqn    - - RCDATA        -- equation -- >
<!ATTLIST eqn   type NOTATION (a-w|tex|setm) a-w >
```

The three types of notation that can be used in this example to qualify the eqn element could be defined as:

```
<!NOTATION a-w  PUBLIC "-//Addison-Wesley//NOTATION maths//EN">
<!NOTATION tex  PUBLIC "-//local//NOTATION TeX Formula//EN"   >
<!NOTATION setm PUBLIC "-//BSI//NOTATION SETM coding//EN"     >
```

If the equation was coded using the markup scheme described in Addison-Wesley's guide to preparing equations, the equation can simply be entered between <eqn> and </eqn> tags because the default notation is that identified by the name a-w. Alternatively, the equation could be coded using Donald Knuth's T$_E$X notation. In this case, the start-tag should be entered in the form <eqn type="tex"> or by using the minimized form of the attribute specification <eqn tex>. (Note that because a name group has been used to qualify the NOTATION keyword, the attribute value does not need to be preceded by the attribute name and value indicator.) If the equation is to be coded by reference to the typographic characteristics of each letter, the standard BSI method for specifying electronic typographic markup (SETM) can be used after a tag of the form <eqn setm>.

NOTE: Because elements with notation attributes should always contain some content coded in the relevant notation, the NOTATION *keyword cannot be used for attributes associated with elements whose contents have been declared by use of the* EMPTY *keyword. Similarly, if* #CONREF *has been used as the default value of another attribute in the same attribute list and a specific value is entered for that attribute, an attribute defined using the* NOTATION *keyword must not be present in the same start-tag since, in this instance, the element will be an empty element.*

Data attributes

When a notation declaration has been associated with a data entity by use of the CDATA, NDATA and SDATA entity type statement in the entity's external identifier (see Chapter 4) the notation name can, optionally, be qualified by the use of **data attributes**. These data attributes can either be passed to the system as parameters associated with the commands that activate the required notation interpreter or they can be used to determine which commands should be sent to the host system.

Data attributes are declared in the same way as other attributes but, in this case, the associated element type statement is replaced by the name(s) of the notation(s) with which the defined attributes are to be associated. To indicate the changed role of the attribute definition the reserved word #NOTATION must precede the notation name(s).

To see how data attributes can be used in practice, consider the following data attribute definition, which could be used to qualify the external entity declarations of entities containing equations coded using one of the notations defined above:

```
<!ATTLIST #NOTATION (a-w|tex|setm) align CDATA "" >
```

Here the data attribute called align has been associated, through the bracketed name group, with each of the three notation declarations defined above. The value entered for this attribute can consist of any sequence of data characters, no default value being specified. The purpose of this data attribute is to tell the program processing the external data entity, prior to its incorporation into the text, how the various parts of a formula defined using one of these notations should be aligned. It is presumed that, by default, the various parts of the formula will be run on one after another, for example:

$$a^x = (e^b)^x = e^{bx} = \exp(bx)$$

Alternatively, the program could be asked to use the equals signs to align the various parts of the formula to produce:

$$a^x = (e^b)^x$$
$$= e^{bx}$$
$$= \exp(bx)$$

In the latter case the original entity declaration of:

```
<!ENTITY eqn22 SYSTEM CDATA a-w >
```

would be extended to read:

```
<!ENTITY eqn22 SYSTEM CDATA a-w [align = "="] >
```

to produce the second format of the equation.

Note that, within the entity declaration, the **data attribute specification** uses the currently defined declaration subset open (**dso**) and declaration subset close (**dsc**) codes to delimit the entered list of attributes. In the reference concrete syntax these are the open and close square brackets, respectively.

If the program processing the external data entity was sophisticated enough, it might be possible to pass it a string of characters that could optionally be used as alignment points within the formula. For example, when using the above attribute declaration, an entity defined as:

```
<!ENTITY eqn57 SYSTEM CDATA a-w [align = "= + -;"]>
```

might be used to produce a formula of the format:

$$c(x) = b_0 + b_1(x - a)$$
$$+ b_2(x - a)^2$$
$$+ b_3(x - a)^3$$

Like normal attributes, data attributes can be minimized if the permitted values have been defined as a name token group. For example, if the attribute list had been defined as:

```
<!ATTLIST #NOTATION (a-w|tex|setm) align (left|right|centre) left >
```

an entity declaration could take the form:

```
<!ENTITY form3-4 SYSTEM "f34-eqn.txt" CDATA a-w [centre] >
```

Here the bracketed attribute list simply consists of an unqualified attribute value.

More than one data attribute can be associated with a particular notation, provided that all the attributes for a given notation are defined in the same attribute definition list declaration. (This is a general restriction on attributes – only one set of attributes can be associated with any element or notation.) The following data attributes could, for example, be associated with the piechart notation defined in Chapter 4:

```
<!ATTLIST #NOTATION piechart type   (colour|bw)      bw
                    detail (tone|stipple)   tone
                    rules  (outer|segments) outer >
```

An external entity containing a coloured pie chart whose segments were stippled and contained within rules could be then be declared as:

```
<!ENTITY pie34 SYSTEM NDATA piechart [colour stipple segments] >
```

When defining attributes for use with notations, however, the ENTITY, ENTITIES, ID, IDREF, IDREFS and NOTATION keywords must not be used since these keywords can only be used as declared values for attributes associated with elements. Similarly, the #CURRENT and #CONREF default value options cannot be used because data attributes are not optional.

6.3.6 *Controlling attribute values*

We have already seen how the default value entry of an attribute definition can be used to control the entry of attribute values by use of the #REQUIRED or #IMPLIED keywords, and how an entered default value can be used by the program when a specific value has not been entered. Two other keywords can also be used to control the entered values – #FIXED and #CURRENT.

If an entered default value is preceded by the keyword #FIXED its value can never be changed. For example, the textbook element could be defined as:

```
<!ELEMENT textbook    - 0  (front, body, back?) +(%floats;|ix) >
<!ATTLIST textbook version CDATA   "1"
                   status  CDATA   ""
```

```
security CDATA    #IMPLIED
textsize NUTOKENS #FIXED "27picas 45picas"    >
```

In this case the text area of the textbook has been declared to be a fixed attribute of 27 picas wide by 45 picas deep. By entering this fixed value as one of the attribute values declared in the document type definition, the relevant values can be passed to the text formatter with each document without the author having to enter a specific attribute value for every textbook in the series.

NOTE: #FIXED *attributes are normally associated with simple link declarations (see Chapter 9).*

When the SGML declaration contains both the SHORTTAG YES and OMITTAG YES statements, the #CURRENT keyword can also be used in place of a default value. This keyword tells users that, for the first occurrence of the associated element, a value must be entered (as if #REQUIRED had been used) but if no value is entered for subsequent occurrences of the element the last entered value will be used as the current default value.

Note, however, that only one current value is associated with each attribute. If an attribute is shared by a number of elements, the value used will be the last one entered for the specified attribute in any of the associated elements, not the last value used with the same element. For example, if the following attribute definition was added to the document type declaration subset:

```
<!ATTLIST (p|note) indent NUTOKEN #CURRENT>
```

and a section of text was coded as:

```
<p indent=0>This is an example of a normal, unindented
paragraph of text. Note that because the paragraph
tag was the first one that used the indent attribute a
value had to be entered, even though no indent was
required.
<note indent=3picas>This note has been set with a 3 pica
(&frac12;&inch;) indent.</note>
<p>Because no specific indent value has been stated this
paragraph has also been indented by 3 picas as this is
the value currently associated with the indent
attribute.
<p indent=0>To cancel the indent applied to the note it
is necessary to enter a new value for the indent
attribute as part of the paragraph's start-tag.
```

the set text should appear in the form:

> This is an example of a normal, unindented paragraph of text. Note that, because the paragraph tag was the first one that used the indent attribute, a value had to be entered even though no indent was required.
>
> *NOTE: This note has been set with a 3 pica (½″) indent.*
>
> Because no specific indent value has been stated this paragraph has also been indented by 3 picas as this is the value currently associated with the indent attribute.
>
> To cancel the indent applied to the note it is necessary enter a new value for the indent attribute as part of the paragraph's start-tag.

Note that, until the indent is specifically restated, the value entered at the start of the ‹note› element remains in force for the ‹p› element as well.

6.4   Attribute interpretation

While the applications of attributes are almost limitless, document designers should take care to ensure that attributes are easy to use. Wherever possible the most likely value of an attribute should either be its default value or a value that the program can imply from the current state of the document so that, on most occasions, the value does not need to be entered into the text.

Attribute names should be as self-explanatory as possible within the maximum name length permitted by the concrete syntax currently in force. It is unwise to use the same attribute name for attributes with different purposes as this can lead to users applying the wrong meaning to the attribute. While many attribute values may be shared with other attributes, it is advisable to allocate unique attribute values wherever possible. In particular, it must be remembered that the same attribute value cannot be associated with two attributes defined in the same attribute definition list declaration (a point I forgot, to my cost, when preparing the first version of the sample DTD shown in Appendix C!).

When changing document types it is important that you check the default values assigned to each of the attributes defined in the new document type declaration. In particular, look out for attributes flagged as being required. You must remember to enter values for such attributes every time you request the associated element (or notation). Special note should also be taken of other attributes where a keyword has been used for the default value since, in such cases, care must be taken to ensure that the right types of values are used within the start-tag.

As will be shown in Chapter 9, more than one set of attributes can be in force at the same time when concurrent document structures are being used. Using LINK statements, concurrent sets of attributes can be linked together to provide all the details needed to format the document prior to output. Alternatively, different sets of attributes may be provided for different purposes. For example, one set of attributes could provide the information required to add data to a database, while an alternative set could determine the route the document should take when it is transmitted to other users. Attributes can also describe the language in which the document has been written and define details, such as which characters are to be used around quoted text for each language. (An example of this type of use is given in Appendix A.) In fact, the uses of attributes are legion. By experimenting with this powerful facility you should be able to build up sets of parameters to cope with every situation you are likely to meet in producing a document.

7

Minimization

7.1 Types of minimization
7.2 Combining minimization techniques

SGML provides four main techniques for minimizing the number and length of a document's markup tags:

(1)   tag omission (OMITTAG),

(2)   tag shortening (SHORTTAG),

(3)   tag grouping (RANK), and

(4)   automatic tag recognition (DATATAG).

As minimization techniques are an optional feature of SGML, users must specifically declare their intention to use them by selecting the appropriate options from the FEATURES clause of the SGML declaration (see Chapter 3). In a basic SGML document only the OMITTAG and SHORTTAG options are available.

NOTE: While most SGML parsers will expand minimized tags before outputting a document, it should be noted that the ability to handle minimization is not a compulsory feature of an SGML parser. Because programs capable of handling element minimization must be able to track each element's position in the document structure, it is important to check that potential receivers of a minimized SGML document do have programs that can handle minimized tags properly before the techniques detailed in this Chapter are used. If you have any doubts on this score or are unable to check the capabilities of all the programs likely to handle your document, you would be well advised not to use minimization while preparing SGML-coded documents.

7.1   Types of minimization ─────────────────────────

7.1.1   Tag omission

The most commonly used form of minimization is **tag omission**. This optional SGML feature allows tags to be omitted when their presence can be implied by the program from the structure of the document declared in the document type definition.

Whenever the FEATURES clause of the SGML declaration contains the entry OMITTAG YES, as it does for the reference concrete syntax, all element declarations in the document type definition must contain two characters defining the type of **omitted tag minimization** permitted for the declared element(s). As explained in Chapter 5, the first of these two characters is set to O (the letter O rather than the number 0) if the element's start-tag can be omitted – otherwise a hyphen is entered. If the element's end-tag can be omitted the second character is set to O – otherwise a hyphen is entered. The two characters must be separated by a space (or any other valid separator character) and must be separated from the preceding element name, and following details of the element's contents, by further spaces or separator characters.

When tag omission has been permitted in the element declaration, users can opt to leave out any tag whose presence can be inferred *unambiguously* by the program. If, however, the program could infer the presence of more than one type of element at a particular point in the document, the relevant tag must be added to the document.

Start-tag omission

Start-tags can be omitted from a document when the element concerned is contextually required (i.e. must occur at that position) *and* any other element that could occur at the same point (such as an element specified in the inclusion clause of a higher level element) is contextually optional. Elements whose start-tags may be omitted should not be qualified by an occurrence indicator in the model group since such indicators normally make it impossible to identify which element should occur next.

Start-tags cannot be omitted when the element concerned has been declared with a content type of RCDATA, CDATA or EMPTY since problems could occur in such elements if the next character is a valid SGML delimiter. For similar reasons, start-tags should not be omitted where the first character in the element with the omitted short-tag is one of the short reference characters associated with the element in a short reference use (USEMAP) declaration, especially where the short reference would be associated with a different entity if the start-tag is not present.

When the presence of an omitted start-tag is implied by the parsing program, the currently defined default values will automatically be used for any attributes associated with the element. It is important, therefore, to ensure that the default values of any attributes associated with elements which may have their start-tags omitted are checked carefully before the OMITTAG option is used. If one or more of the applicable attributes is a required attribute, either because its default value has been declared using the #REQUIRED keyword or because the default value is #CURRENT and the element has not yet been used, the start-tag cannot be omitted. In such cases, the full tag – including all compulsory attributes – must be added to the text.

End-tag omission

The rules governing the use of end-tag omission are much less restrictive than those for start-tags. End-tags can be omitted wherever the tag is followed by the end-tag of another currently open element (i.e. one started at a higher level than the current element) *or* when the tag is followed by an element or data character that is not a permitted part of the element's content model. End-tags can also be omitted if their presence can be implied by the end of an SGML document or subdocument.

The only word of caution that needs to be given with respect to these straightforward rules is that users should remember that entry of a start-tag for an element defined as an exclusion in one of the currently open elements will cause the program to infer the presence of an end-tag for that element (and any nested subelements). Similarly, any text entered immediately after the start-tag of an element whose content model has been declared as EMPTY will be treated as a character that is not a permitted part of the element's content. In both cases, the parsing program will automatically assume that the following text belongs to the element at the next higher level in the document's structure.

Omitting tags

The elements defined in Appendix C for identifying sections within a Chapter illustrate how tag omission is used in practice. The main declarations involved are:

```
<!ELEMENT h2          - 0  (h2t, (%text;)*, h3*)     >
<!ELEMENT (%titles;)  0 0  (#PCDATA|%phrases;)*      >
<!ELEMENT p           - 0  (#PCDATA|%phrases;|q|
                           %element;|%lists;|%refs;)+>
```

where %titles; has been declared as:

```
<!ENTITY % titles  "h0t|h1t|h2t|h3t|h4t|h5t" >
```

If tag omission was not permitted by the current concrete syntax (i.e. OMITTAG NO had been specified in the SGML declaration), a section defined using the models detailed above would need to be coded as:

```
<h2><h2t>Section Headings</h2t>

<p>Section headings should indicate ...

... end of the paragraph.</p>
<p>An alternative use for section headings ...

... at the end of the section.</p></h2>
```

Here each start-tag is matched by an equivalent end-tag, the start of each compulsory element in the model group always being required.

When tag omission is allowed, however, the coding can be simplified to:

```
<h2>Section Headings
<p>Section headings should indicate ...

... end of the paragraph.
<p>An alternative use for section headings ...

... at the end of the section.</h2>
```

In this example, the tag minimization option has led to a halving of the number of tags that need to be added to the text. Let us look at how this was achieved.

The most important saving occurred in the section title, where both the start- and end-tags have been omitted. The start-tag can be omitted because the presence of this compulsory first embedded subelement could be inferred by the parsing program from the content model of the section element (<h2>). The parsing program knows from the content model that before it can accept any data for the section, it must receive a start-tag for the <h2t> element that contains the section's title. As soon as it sees a character other than a start-tag delimiter (<) it will automatically recognize that the character should be preceded by <h2t>. (It may or may not insert the required tag into the text string – it is up to the program to decide whether it needs to or not.)

The end-tag for the section title can be omitted because the <p> used to identify the start of the first paragraph in the section is not a valid part of the content model for the section title. As the section title can only consist of text or tags identifying the start or end of a highlighted phrase, the parsing program will automatically recognize that a </h2t> tag should precede the first of the <p> tags.

The two paragraph end-tags (</p>) have been omitted from the minimized version of the coded text for different reasons. At the end of the first paragraph the tag can be omitted because the content model for the paragraph element does not allow other paragraphs to be directly embedded within a paragraph. (Further paragraphs can be started within embedded elements, such as examples or items in a list, but only after entry of another tag.) As soon as the parsing program sees the second <p> it knows it can infer the presence of a paragraph end-tag for the preceding paragraph.

The second of the paragraph end-tags has been omitted because it is immediately followed by the end-tag of an element at a higher level in the document's structure. Providing the OMITTAG option has been activated, the parsing program will automatically close any currently open embedded element, which has been declared as having omissible end-tags, when it encounters an end-tag for a higher level element. (If an embedded element whose end-tag cannot be omitted is still open, however, the program will report an error in the coding.)

It should be noted that the presence of the </h2> tag is not compulsory. If the section shown in the above example was immediately followed by another section, its end-tag could be omitted to give an entry of the form:

```
<h2>Section Headings
<p>Section headings should indicate ...

... end of the paragraph.
<p>An alternative use for section headings ...

... at the end of the section.
<h2>Omitting Tags
<p>When specified in an element's declaration ...
```

When the parsing program analyses this part of the document the presence of the start-tag (<h2>) for the second section will cause it to infer the presence of an </h2> tag at the end of the first section. From the presence of this implied end-tag the program will also be able to identify the need for a </p> tag to close the last paragraph of the preceding section.

7.1.2 Short tags

Shortened versions of tags can be used whenever the FEATURES clause of the SGML declaration contains the statement SHORTTAG YES. There are three ways in which element tags can be shortened:

(1)   by omitting the generic identifier (name) of the element,

(2) by omitting the closing delimiter of the tag, and

(3) by using the **null end-tag** option.

NOTE: Start-tags can also be shortened by use of the attribute minimization techniques detailed in Chapter 6.

Empty tags

Empty tags are tags from which the element's name has been omitted. In its simplest form an **empty start-tag** consists of the currently defined start-tag open and tag close symbols (‹ and ›, respectively in the reference concrete syntax), without an intervening space. Similarly, an **empty end-tag** consists of the currently defined end-tag open and tag close symbols (e.g. ‹/›).

The way in which the program interprets an empty start-tag depends on whether or not tags can also be omitted from the document. If OMITTAG YES has been specified in the SGML declaration, the program will give the empty start-tag the generic identifier of the most recently started element in the base document type. Otherwise the generic identifier used will be that of the most recently ended element.

Where tag omission is permitted, the first of the above rules allows the program to infer which generic identifier it should use before determining whether or not a tag has been omitted from the markup. By presuming that the last opened element is to be repeated, the program has a value which it can use to check for the omission of end-tags. It can then determine whether the last element used should be closed by the addition of an implied end-tag or whether the new tag represents a further level of nesting within the document's structure.

When tags cannot be omitted, the last element to be closed is presumed to be the one to be repeated, even if the element is not a repeatable element. This can, unfortunately, lead to errors where the last element used is not repeatable (e.g. because it has not been given an occurrence indicator or the optional occurrence indicator, ?, has been used to restrict the number of times the element can occur) since the program will report the illegal empty start-tag as an error even when the content model unambiguously defines which element must occur next.

For empty end-tags the generic identifier added by the program is always that of the last element to be opened in the base document (i.e the document indicated by the document type name entered as the initial base document element).

Typically a piece of text coded using empty tags will take the form:

```
<p>This paragraph contains two lists. The first has four
entries:<li arabic>
<it>item 1
<>item 2
```

```
<>item 3
<>item 4</></>
while the second only has two:<li>
<it>first item
<>second item</>.</>
<>Multiple lists ...
```

In this example, the first three empty start-tags and the first empty end-tag will be given implied generic identifiers of it since this was the last element to be started. Once the last of the items in the first list has been formally closed by the first empty end-tag, the list item (<li>) becomes the currently active element. This list then has to be closed by the second empty end-tag before the second part of the paragraph element can be processed. The next empty start-tag and the first of the empty end-tags are linked to the <it> tag at the start of the second list, while the final empty end-tag closes the second list.

Provided OMITTAG YES has been specified in the SGML declaration and that the document type declaration shows that paragraph end-tags can be omitted, no empty end-tag is needed to close the paragraph. As soon as the program sees the next empty start-tag, it knows that the currently open element, the paragraph element, is to be repeated. The presence of the empty start-tag will cause the program to infer automatically the presence of </p> at the end of the preceding paragraph as well as the <p> required to start the new paragraph.

It should be noted that empty start-tags do not inherit any attributes entered for the last tag opened. Instead, the current default values for the element will be applied. This means that empty start-tags cannot be used to start any element whose attributes are required within the start-tag, e.g. because the #REQUIRED keyword was specified. The lists in the above examples illustrate the effect of this ruling. While the first list will be numbered using arabic numerals, the second list will use the document's default style for item identification to give a printed list of the form:

This paragraph contains two lists. The first has four entries:

    1) item 1
    2) item 2
    3) item 3
    4) item 4

while the second only has two:

    – first item
    – second item.

Multiple lists ...

Unclosed tags

Where two or more consecutive tags are required in a document, the end delimiters of all tags (except the last one in the sequence) can be omitted, if SHORTTAG YES has been specified. No restriction is placed on whether the next tag in the sequence is a start-tag or an end-tag. End-tags can be followed by start-tags, and vice versa. The four permissible combinations are illustrated by the following examples:

```
<p<hp1>
</q</p>
</q<p>
<artwork sizey = 120mm</p>
```

In the first case a new paragraph is to start with a highlighted phrase. The second example shows how the tags could be minimized if a paragraph ended with a quote. If another paragraph was to start immediately after, and tag omission was permitted, the third example would close down the quote at the end of the first paragraph and start a new paragraph (the omitted end-tag for the preceding paragraph element being implied by the program). The final example shows how the tags might be combined if the last tag in an element was an empty tag, such as the artwork tag. (If an embedded element is to be immediately followed by the end-tag for the element within which it is embedded, its content model must be EMPTY or optional if an error is not to be reported.)

Note that there is no restriction on the use of attributes in tags with omitted delimiters. Any number of valid attributes can be entered. As far as the program is concerned, the only action it is required to perform is to infer the presence of a tag close code in front of any start-tag open or end-tag open codes it encounters within a tag.

Null end-tags

Null end-tags provide a means of specifying the end of an element with a single character. In the reference concrete syntax the character defined as the **null end-tag** (**NET**) is the solidus (slash) but any code can be assigned to this role within the SGML declaration (see Chapter 10).

Two operations are involved in activating the null end-tag option. The first step involves creating a **net-enabling start-tag** by replacing the tag close code at the end of an element's start-tag with a NET code. The second step involves replacing the whole of the element's end-tag with a matching NET code. To see how this works in practice, look again at the <ISBN> element, which was defined in Chapter 6 as:

```
<!ELEMENT ISBN  - -  CDATA -- ISBN (or ISSN) number -- >
<!ATTLIST ISBN type (book|serial)  book            >
```

Instead of entering an ISBN number as:

```
<ISBN>0 201 14223 6</ISBN>
```

we can use the null end-tag option to enter the element in the form:

```
<ISBN/0 201 14223 6/
```

Note that by replacing the end delimiter of the start-tag with the special NET code, we have been able to reduce the end-tag to a single matching character. This feature is particularly useful when the content of the model has been declared, as in the above case, using the reserved name CDATA or the similar RCDATA keyword, since this makes the presence of some form of end-tag for the element compulsory.

Null end-tags can be used for any element declared in the base document that does not require the character assigned to the null end-tag role in its contents or those of any embedded elements. However, because care is needed to ensure that the relevant element is not prematurely ended by entry of the character assigned as the NET code, null end-tags are normally used only for elements that do not contain many embedded subelements. Typically, they are used around lower level elements, such as highlighted phrases, quoted text, etc., where the end-tag is always required.

Null end-tags can be nested to any level permitted for elements (typically, the default value of 24 levels). Each null end-tag identified by the program closes down the last element defined using a net-enabling start-tag (i.e. one whose tag ends with a NET code). The following example shows how null end-tags can, with care, be embedded within each other:

```
<p/This paragraph has been started with a
<hp1/net-enabling start-tag/, as has the <q/highlighted
phrase/ embedded within it./
```

The main point to note about this example is that the number of net-enabling start-tags exactly matches the number of individual null end-tags in the paragraph. The three slashes that are not part of a start-tag close the highlighted phrase, quoted text and paragraph elements, respectively.

The following is an example of an illegal use of a null end-tag:

```
<p/Paragraphs cannot contain either/or choices if
started with a net-enabling start-tag./
```

A program receiving this would automatically terminate the first paragraph after the word 'either'. It would then place the rest of the paragraph in the next higher open element, if permitted, treating the slash intended to end the paragraph as a normal text character.

One way of avoiding this problem is to use a character reference or an entity reference to generate the embedded slash. In this case, the paragraph could be amended to read:

```
<p/Paragraphs cannot contain either&#47;or choices if
started with a net-enabling start-tag./
```

or:

```
<p/Paragraphs cannot contain either&sol;or choices if
started with a net-enabling start-tag./
```

where / has been defined as:

```
<!ENTITY sol CDATA "/">
```

so that the expanded entity reference cannot be mistaken for a markup tag (see Chapter 4).

NOTE: When concurrent document structures are being used (see Chapter 9), null end-tags can only be used with elements defined in the document type definition of the base document type.

7.1.3   Tag grouping (rank)

When the current SGML declaration contains the statement RANK YES in the FEATURES clause, elements can be declared as ranked elements (see Chapter 5). When an element declaration contains a rank stem and a rank suffix, the element's start tag can be shortened by omission of the rank suffix, provided that the element concerned has been entered in full (i.e. with a numeric rank suffix) at some preceding point in the document.

Where a single element declaration has been used for a ranked group of elements, the rank suffix that is added to the end of a minimized ranked element is the last rank number entered for any member of that ranked group. (The effect of this rule was illustrated in Chapter 5.)

7.1.4   Automatic tag recognition (data tags)

Data tags are sequences of characters which, as well as forming part of the document, also mark the *end* of an element. Whenever the data tags option has been activated by entry of DATATAG YES in the FEATURES clause of the SGML declaration, the program will check the content of those elements whose declarations contain data tag definitions to see if it can automatically identify the end of the element from the presence of a specified string of characters.

Data tags are declared within the *content model* of an element in the base document's DTD by replacing the name of one or more of the embedded elements with a **data tag group**. (This technique allows more than one data tag to be associated with each element, as will be explained shortly.) Each data tag group is enclosed within a special pair of delimiters known as the **data tag group open** (dtgo) and **data tag group close** (dtgc) delimiters. In the reference concrete syntax these symbols are the left and right square brackets. The declaration within these delimiters has two main parts – the **generic identifier** of the element concerned and the **data tag pattern** to be checked for whenever the specified element has been opened. The data tag pattern can also consist of two parts. Each pattern must start with a **data tag template** or a **data tag template group** which defines the character sequences for which the program is looking. This can optionally be followed by a **data tag padding template** that identifies one or more characters which should be skipped if they occur immediately after a data tag. Each part of the data tag group is separated from the others by the currently defined sequence indicator (**seq** – , in the reference concrete syntax).

To see how data tags work consider the following set of declarations:

```
<!ELEMENT  members   - - (delegate+)                  >
<!ELEMENT  delegate  - 0 ([name, ", ", " "], body) >
<!ELEMENT  name      0 0 (#PCDATA)                    >
<!ELEMENT  body      0 0 (#PCDATA)                    >
<!SHORTREF map1      "&#RS;"   entry                  >
<!ENTITY   entry     STARTTAG delegate                >
<!USEMAP   map1      members                          >
```

Here a single data tag template, consisting of a comma followed by a space, has been associated with the element called ‹name› that forms the first embedded element of the ‹delegate› element. Optionally, this template can be followed by more spaces, which the program should treat as part of the data tag. To see how the addition of a data tag group in the above declaration affects the coding of a document consider the following list of members attending an SGML meeting:

```
<members>
James D. Mason,     ANSI
Charles F. Goldfarb, ANSI
Joan M. Smith,      BSI
Francis J. Cave,    BSI
Jacques Henry,      AFNOR
Craig Smith,        DIN
Anders Bergland,    ISO
</members>
```

As soon as the program encounters the ‹members› tag it will invoke the short reference map declared within the above set of definitions. This map will treat the record start code at the beginning of each line as a short reference to the start-tag of a ‹delegate› element.

Each ‹delegate› element starts with the name of a delegate, the end of the name being indicated by a comma and at least one space. When the program sees this data tag sequence it will automatically infer the presence of a ‹/name› end-tag. As the comma and any immediately following spaces are not part of the delegate's name, or part of the ‹body› element, the program automatically treats the data tag as an implied #PCDATA element; that is the ‹delegate› element is considered to be defined as:

```
<!ELEMENT delegate (name, #PCDATA, body) >
```

where #PCDATA can only consist of a comma followed by one or more spaces.

Because data tags act as real end-tags rather than omitted end-tags, once the program has identified the end-tag for the ‹name› element it will also be able to infer the presence of the next start-tag immediately after the data tag template because the declaration for the ‹delegates› element tells it that a ‹body› element must follow.

The combination of the data tag and the short reference for the ‹members› element means that the program would treat the uncoded text as if it had been coded:

```
<members>
<delegate><name>James D. Mason</name>,     <body>ANSI</body>
<delegate><name>Charles F. Goldfarb</name>, <body>ANSI</body>
<delegate><name>Joan M. Smith</name>,      <body>BSI</body>
<delegate><name>Francis J. Cave</name>,     <body>BSI</body>
<delegate><name>Jacques Henry</name>,       <body>AFNOR</body>
<delegate><name>Craig Smith</name>,         <body>DIN</body>
<delegate><name>Anders Bergland</name>,     <body>ISO</body>
</members>
```

It is important to realize the difference between the role of the data tag and the short reference in the above example. While the short reference *replaces* the record start character it is linked to, the characters defined in the data tag template are *retained as a special piece of (implied) parsed character data*. It should also be realized that the data tag is looked for only while the ‹name› element remains the currently open element, while the short reference applies to any embedded elements as well (unless they invoke their own short reference map).

When declaring data tag templates, it is important to ensure that the length of the data tag template or data tag padding template does not exceed that declared as the DTEMPLEN quantity in the SGML declaration (see

Chapter 10). Similarly, the data tags entered in the text, including any padding characters, must not exceed the DTAGLEN quantity. In the reference concrete syntax both of these quantities are set to 16 characters.

Data tag templates cannot include *numeric* character references to non-SGML characters or SGML function characters, though these are permitted in entity strings. This prohibits the use of the 	 sequence to identify a Tab code in a data tag, though it would be a valid part of the replacement text of an entity. If, for example, the Tab code had been used within the above example to position the second column, the declaration for the ‹delegate› element would need to be altered to:

```
<!ELEMENT delegate - O ([name, ",&#TAB;", " "], body) >
```

It should be noted, however, that if this declaration is to be used, all entries must be keyed without any spaces between the comma and the Tab code. If there is a likelihood that the typist may key one or two spaces after the comma, the range of permitted data tags should be extended by defining all the valid templates in a data tag template group. As with other groups within the content model, the data tag template group is enclosed by group open and group close symbols (left and right brackets in the reference concrete syntax). In the case of data tag template groups the entries within the group must be separated by **or** connectors. This gives the entry the form:

```
<!ELEMENT delegate - O ([name, (",&#TAB;"|", &#TAB;"|",  &#TAB;"), " "], body) >
```

Unfortunately, groups are not permitted for the data tag padding template, so if more than one Tab code is used to move to the start of the next column these and any following spaces will not be recognized as a part of the template, and so will not be removed from the data stream. If Tab codes are more likely to be used than spaces it would be possible to change the data tag padding template to a Tab code, but in this case you would not pick up those cases where the typist used spaces to move to the start of the column. To overcome this problem it may be necessary to extend the list of valid data tags even further to read:

```
<!ELEMENT delegate - O ([name,
                 (",&#TAB;"|",&#TAB;&#TAB;"|
                 ", &#TAB;"|", &#TAB;&#TAB;"|
                 ", &#TAB;"|",  &#TAB;&#TAB;"), " "], body) >
```

Because data tags are only associated with elements that are embedded within specific elements, it is possible to associate more than one data tag with a given element. For example, if the ‹name› element defined above is also used within a bibliographic reference, it may be followed by a colon rather than a comma. In this case, the data tag might be declared as:

```
<!ELEMENT bib-ref - 0 ([name, ": "], [date, ") "], title, details) >
```

Note that this time the optional data tag padding template has not been used. The end of the ‹name› element is identified within the ‹bib-ref› element by the first occurrence of a colon followed by a space. As the following ‹date› element is compulsory its start-tag can be omitted (provided start-tag omission has been permitted in the associated element declaration). On starting the new element, the program will automatically change its checks to look for the data tag template of the ‹date› element. This will cause the first right parenthesis and space combination in the ‹date› element to act as the end-tag for the element and, by implication, start the ‹title› element. Using such data tags allows bibliographic references to be entered as:

```
<bib-ref>Bryan, M: (1982) Photosetting Terminology</bib-ref>
```

rather than:

```
<bib-ref>Bryan, M: <date>(1982) <title>Photosetting Terminology</bib-ref>
```

Obviously, the shorter form involves much less keying and is also much more readable. It should be noted, however, that, when parsed by the program, the bibliographic reference would, for either of the examples given above, be expanded to the form:

```
<bib-ref><name>Bryan, M</name>: <(date>1982</date>) <title>Photosetting Terminology
</title></bib-ref>
```

because the data tag automatically forms an implied #PCDATA element within the model group. As can be seen, the use of the close parenthesis as the data tag for the ‹date› element leads to an illogical date entry containing an open, but no closing, parenthesis. There are two ways of overcoming this problem:

(1)   changing the data tag pattern associated with the ‹name› element to ": (" would generate an expanded sequence of the form:

```
<bib-ref><name>Bryan, M</name>: (<date>1982</date>) <title>Photosetting
Terminology</title></bib-ref>
```

(2)   changing the data tag associated with the ‹date› element to a single space (i.e. " ") would generate an expanded sequence of the form:

```
<bib-ref><name>Bryan, M</name>: <date>(1982)</date> <title>Photosetting
Terminology</title></bib-ref>
```

The preferred format will depend on the use to which the date field is to be put at a later stage.

More than one of the currently open elements may have the same sequence of characters in its data tag template. In such cases two rules apply:

(1)   the longest possible data tag template in the data tag pattern is matched; and

(2)   if more than one element could be satisfied by a data tag template the most recently opened element is satisfied first.

Only when the data tag's template has been recognized will the program look for one or more occurrences of the string entered as the data tag padding template.

NOTE: Data tags will only be recognized in contexts where end-tags are permitted. They will not, therefore, be recognized in a CDATA *element or marked section (see Chapters 5 and 8).*

7.2   *Combining minimization techniques* ⎯⎯⎯⎯⎯⎯

As has been shown in the preceding examples, it is possible to mix the minimization features allowed in the currently active SGML declaration. In doing so, users should be aware that SGML parsing programs are expected to resolve any data tags, shortened tags or entity references before looking for omitted tags. Only when all these features have been resolved can the program accurately determine the level to which a ranked element belongs.

NOTE: The standard does not allow the concept of an empty start-tag to be combined with that of unclosed start-tags or net-enabling start-tags, so you cannot have entries such as:

```
<<q/Roger and out/ and </Willco/.</>
```

To see how mixing the various forms of minimization (including short references and attribute minimization) can reduce the amount of coding required in a document, consider the effect of using the following set of declarations in a document where the FEATURES clause of the SGML declaration starts:

```
FEATURES MINIMIZE DATATAG YES OMITTAG YES RANK YES SHORTTAG YES


<!ELEMENT p        0 0 (#PCDATA|%phrases;|q|
                        %element;|%lists;|%refs;)+  >
<!ELEMENT li       0 0 ([it, (",&#RE;"|".&#RE;")]+) >
```

```
<!ATTLIST  li number
                  (arabiciromanialphaidefaultinone) default  >
<!ELEMENT  it          0 0  (#PCDATAiqi%phrases;)*    >
<!ELEMENT  hp 0        - 0  (#PCDATAiqi%phrases;)*    >
<!ELEMENT  hp 1        - 0  (#PCDATAiqi%phrases;)*    >
<!ELEMENT  hp 2        - 0  (#PCDATAiqi%phrases;)*    >
<!ELEMENT  hp 3        - 0  (#PCDATAiqi%phrases;)*    >
<!ELEMENT  q           - -  (#PCDATAiqi%phrases;)*    >
<!SHORTREF listmap     ":&RE;"  startli               >
<!ENTITY   startli     "<li roman>"                   >
<!USEMAP   listmap      p                              >
<!SHORTREF listmap2    ":&RE;"  startli2              >
<!ENTITY   startli2    "<li none>"                     >
<!USEMAP   listmap2     it                             >
```

The two short reference declarations, listmap and listmap2, are used to identify the start of lists and sublists from the presence of a colon at the end of a line of text. (This special sequence of codes will need to be declared as a valid short reference string in the DELIM clause of the SGML declaration associated with the document.) Within a list (li), a comma or full stop at the end of a line will be recognized as a data tag that identifies the end of a list item (it). Tag omission has been permitted on all elements except the quote and highlighted phrase definitions, where start-tags and, in the case of quoted text, end-tags (or null end-tags) are required.

The following would be a valid piece of minimized text for use with the above declarations:

```
<p>SGML markup is:
based on the <hp1/logical/ structure of the document
rather than its <hp/physical/ appearance,
capable of minimization by means of:
   <hp2/omitted tags/,
   <hp/short tags/,
   <hp/ranked elements/,
   <hp/data tags/.
<p>Each of these <q<hp3/SGML features/</> can be
combined as required.</p>
```

If none of the minimization techniques were available the same piece of text would need to be entered as:

```
<p>SGML markup is:
<li number="roman"><it>based on the <hp1>logical</hp1>
structure of the document rather than its
<hp1>physical</hp1> appearance,</it>
<it>capable of minimization by means of:<li number=none>
<it><hp2>omitted tags</hp2>,</it>
```

```
<it><hp2>short tags</hp2>,</it>
<it><hp2>ranked elements</hp2>,</it>
<it><hp2>data tags</hp2></it>.</li></li></p>
<p>Each of these <q><hp3>SGML features</hp3></q> can be
combined as required.</p>
```

In this very heavily coded section, the combination of minimization techniques and short references has reduced the amount of coding required to less than a third of that needed to code the text fully. While such figures are easily obtainable by thoughtful use of SGML's minimization features, it should be noted that keeping track of which elements are closed by which NET, short or implied tag is not always obvious, especially during text editing/updating performed some time after the text was originally coded. Therefore, careful thought needs to be given to likely future uses of the text before its markup is reduced in this manner.

In many cases, the techniques mentioned in this chapter will be combined with the short reference technique detailed in Chapter 4 to make markup transparent to the user. Typically, the start of a new paragraph can be identified by the entry of a single blank line in the text while the presence of a new list item will be linked to the fact that such lines start with the sequence space, hyphen, space, which is unlikely to occur immediately after a record start code in any other circumstance. By careful consideration of such factors, SGML document designers can reduce the amount of minimization required in the document *and* reduce the amount of coding needed to prepare a document to levels significantly below those required by most current word processors.

8

Other SGML Declarations

8.1 Marked sections
8.2 Processing instructions

This chapter covers two types of SGML declarations – **marked sections** and **processing instructions** – which differ from most of the declarations encountered so far in that they can occur within the text of the document.

Marked sections can be used to identify sections of text that need special handling. There are two principal reasons for marking sections of text:

(1)   because the text includes character sequences that could accidentally be interpreted as markup, and

(2)   because the text may not be needed in all versions of the document.

Where examples of SGML markup need to be included in a document they should be entered as part of a marked section to ensure that they are not misinterpreted as markup. (All the examples in this book were entered as marked sections.)

Where a single document contains more than one version of the text, either because the text has been updated or because alternative versions may be required, marked sections allow users to determine which sections should be printed. Notes which may or may not appear in the printed version can also be treated as marked sections so that they can, for example, be included in drafts or proofs of the text but be left out of printed versions of the text. '

Marked sections can also be used to identify text that has only been added on a temporary basis. By entering it as a temporary marked section, such text will be identified in a way that allows it to be deleted quickly when no longer required.

Processing instructions are instructions to the local system telling it, in its own language, how to process the document. Typically, processing instructions are used to define how the following text should be formatted. Because such instructions are system-specific, and also often application-dependent, they need to be specially identified so that, for example, when the document is sent to another system or its format is changed, any processing instructions incorporated in the document or its document type declaration can be changed accordingly.

8.1   Marked sections

Marked sections are sections of text that require special handling, either to determine whether or not they are to be output, or to identify certain codes in the section as text rather than markup delimiters. Such sections of text are enclosed between special **marked section start** and **marked section end** delimiter sequences. These delimiter sequences are both made up of a combination of two other delimiters. The marked section start delimiter sequence consists of the markup declaration open (**mdo**) delimiter immediately followed by a single declaration subset open (**dso**) delimiter. This initial **dso** is followed by a **status keyword specification** identifying the type of marked section required, which is followed by a second **dso** delimiter identifying the start of the marked section text.

The end of each marked section is indicated by a special **marked section close (msc)** delimiter sequence, which is immediately followed by a markup declaration close (**mdc**) delimiter. In most cases, the marked section close delimiter will consist of two matching characters which are obviously linked to the **dso** delimiters used in the marked section start sequence (e.g.]]).

When the standard delimiter set of the reference concrete syntax is being used, the overall form of a marked section is:

```
<![ status-keywords [ ... marked section ... ]]>
```

There are two special points to note about this declaration format:

(1)   status keywords *must* be preceded by (and can be followed by) a space or other valid parameter separator, such as a comment or parameter entity reference; and

(2)   no other spaces are allowed within the delimiter sequences used to identify the start and end of a marked section.

The five **status keywords** that can be used in the status keyword specification are:

(1)   CDATA, to indicate that the contents of the marked section are to be treated as **character data** which does not contain any resolvable SGML markup;

(2)   RCDATA, to indicate that the contents of the marked section are to be treated as **replaceable character data** in which any character references or embedded text, CDATA or SDATA entities are to be resolved before the marked section is output;

(3)   IGNORE, to indicate that the contents of the marked section are to be ignored during output;

(4)   INCLUDE, to indicate that the contents of the marked section are to be included during output; and

(5)   TEMP, to indicate that the section is a temporary part of the document that may be removed at a later date.

Where no keyword is specified the INCLUDE keyword is assumed.

Where marked sections are embedded within other marked sections the following order of precedence applies to the entered keywords (highest shown first)

IGNORE

CDATA

RCDATA

INCLUDE

Marked sections cannot, however, be embedded within sections defined using the CDATA or RCDATA keywords since within such sections the program looks only for the next marked section end delimiter sequence. As soon as it encounters this sequence, it will terminate the section that started with CDATA or RCDATA rather than any embedded marked section. This means that embedded marked sections are only recognized where INCLUDE, IGNORE and TEMP are the only keywords used in the status keyword specification.

It should also be noted that marked sections can only contain valid SGML characters since non-SGML data must always be called as part of an NDATA external entity (see Chapter 4). The fact that a marked section is flagged to be ignored does not mean that it may contain non-SGML (shunned) characters.

8.1.1   Using marked sections

The CDATA and RCDATA keywords are typically used in situations where the author wishes to output SGML tags as part of the text. For example, to include the sequence:

```
<hp1>highlighted phrase</hp1>
```

within a paragraph (without using an entity reference) you could enter it as:

```
<![ CDATA [
     <hp1>highlighted phrase</hp1>
]]>
```

It should be noted that the two record end codes within the marked section in the above example will be retained as character data. This ensures that the highlighted text will appear on its own line, indented by five spaces as shown above, even if the marked section is preceded or followed by other markup codes. (Compare this with 'The effect of record boundaries' in Section 5.5.1.)

If the section of text to be marked contains characters that cannot be entered directly (e.g. because they are not part of the document's character set and so have to be defined as character references) the RCDATA keyword can be used in place of CDATA to tell the program that it must resolve any general entity or character references within the marked section of text. For example, to generate the sequence:

```
<hp2>12µm</hp2>
```

you should enter it as:

```
<![ RCDATA [
     <hp2>12&#233;m</hp2>
]]>
```

to ensure that the chararacter reference will be correctly resolved to the µ character while the start- and end-tag of the highlighted phrase are retained as part of the text. If CDATA is used instead of RCDATA, the character reference will be printed in place of the character, for example:

```
<hp2>12&#233;m</hp2>
```

One small word of warning is necessary here – do not use the sequence]]> within a CDATA or RCDATA marked section, otherwise you will terminate it prematurely. (Guess how I came across this potential problem while preparing this chapter!) When entering the above examples I had to remember to change the last character of the marked section to >, and the first to <, to give an entry of the form:

```
<![ CDATA [
&lt;[[ RCDATA [
     <hp2>12&#233;m</hp2>
]]&gt;
]]>
```

to avoid the premature closure of the marked section.

NOTE: The less than sign was changed to avoid any possibility of a parser telling me that I could not nest a marked section within a CDATA marked section. Strictly speaking, this is not necessary but it is safer to make the change to avoid a possible problem later.

Ignored sections

The IGNORE and INCLUDE status keywords are normally used to identify which parts of a document are to be printed during a particular pass. To facilitate the output of multiple versions of a document the relevant status keywords are normally defined as parameter entities in the DTD at the start of the document so that they can be quickly redefined when the job is reprocessed. (This is the only circumstance in which a parameter entity references can be used within the text of a document.)

In a typical application the necessary parameter entities might be defined as:

```
<!ENTITY % mk1 "IGNORE"  -- Mark 1 version -- >
<!ENTITY % mk2 "INCLUDE" -- Mark 2 version -- >
```

The associated parameter entity references %mk1; and %mk2; can be used within a marked section declaration in the text to identify text that applies to a particular version of the product, as the following example illustrates:

```
<p>To connect the unit:
<![ %mk1; [- unscrew the retaining bolt holding the cover]]>
<![ %mk2; [- unclip the cover]]>
- undo the wing nut on Arm A ...
```

Normally, the first of the marked sections would be ignored so that the later Mark 2 version is printed. If, however, it became necessary to reprint the Mark 1 version of the instructions the only parts of the document that need to be changed are the two entity declarations in the DTD, which would be changed to read:

```
<!ENTITY % mk1 "INCLUDE" -- Mark 1 version -- >
<!ENTITY % mk2 "IGNORE"  -- Mark 2 version -- >
```

The above technique can be extended to any number of versions affecting many sections of text, as the following start to a newspaper article suggests:

```
<!ENTITY % con "IGNORE" -- Conservatives hold seat -- >
<!ENTITY % lab "IGNORE"                                 >
<!ENTITY % sdp "IGNORE"                                 >

<h1><![ %con; [Conservatives Retain]]><![ %sdp; [Watkinson
Regains]]><![ %lab; [Labour Steals]]> West Glos

<p><![ %con; [Paul Marland retained his]]><![ %sdp;
[John Watkinson regained the]]><![ %lab [In one of the
most surprising results so far announced, Peter Neilson
stole Paul Marland's]]> West Gloucestershire
parliamentary seat in yesterday's general election.
...
```

Here three options have been allowed for, the correct one being selected at the last minute by changing the entity declaration for the winning party to read INCLUDE rather than IGNORE.

The IGNORE keyword can also be used to prevent notes added to the text as reminders from being printed. While such notes can be flagged directly with the keyword so that they are never printed, it is better practice to use a parameter entity to determine whether or not they should be printed. For example, the parameter entity:

```
<!ENTITY % nb "IGNORE" >
```

could be used in conjunction with a declaration of the form:

```
<![ %nb; [Remember to say something about marked sections in Appendix A.]]>
```

If such notes are to appear in a draft all the author needs to do is change the entity declaration to read:

```
<!ENTITY % nb "INCLUDE" >
```

or even:

```
<!ENTITY % nb "" >
```

(Remember that when no keyword is specified the INCLUDE keyword is assumed.)

Temporary sections

There are occasions when part of a document may only be required temporarily. For example, you may need to add the phrase 'in preparation' to a citation until such time as the cited work is published. In this case, the TEMP keyword can be used to identify the marked section as one that will need to be removed later. Typically, the entry will take the form:

```
<cit>Bryan, M. T. (1988) <hp1>SGML: An Authors Guide to the Standard Generalized Markup
Language</hp1>, Wokingham: Addison-Wesley<![ TEMP [ (in preparation)]]></cit>
```

The TEMP keyword acts only as a flag – it does not affect the way in which the text is processed. In the above example the program treats the marked section in exactly the same way that it would treat a section for which no keyword has been entered – it acts as if INCLUDE had been specified. The only difference between the above declaration and a declaration of the form:

```
<cit>Bryan, M. T. (1988) <hp1> SGML: An Authors Guide to the Standard Generalized Markup
Language</hp1>, Wokingham: Addison-Wesley <![ [(in preparation)]]></cit>
```

is that requesting the removal of the section when it is no longer required will be easier when the TEMP keyword is present since the program can identify such marked sections as those that may need to be discarded.

Combining keywords

More than one keyword can appear at the start of a marked section declaration. For example, once the publication mentioned in the above citation has been published, the word IGNORE could be added to the marked section declaration to avoid having to delete the text. The stored citation could then have the form:

```
<cit>Bryan, M. T. (1988) <hp1> SGML: An Authors Guide to the Standard Generalized Markup
Language</hp1>, Wokingham: Addison-Wesley <![ IGNORE TEMP [ (in preparation)]]></cit>
```

By retaining the temporary section in this case, any future users of the citation will be able to see that it was prepared before the book was published, which should act as a warning that the citation may not be completely accurate.

The CDATA and RCDATA keywords, can also be combined with other keywords or entity references to keywords to give declarations such as:

```
<![ %mk1; CDATA [For model &#233 a 12mm ring spanner is
required.]]>
```

```
<![ %mk2; RCDATA TEMP [A 12&#233;m feeler gauge should
be placed at point <p> to check the clearance.]]>
```

Note how the potential problem of a model number with the same form as
a character reference has been overcome in the first of the above examples
using the CDATA keyword. In the second section, use of the same sequence of
characters as a character reference has been permitted by changing the
keyword to RCDATA in the section that is to be temporarily included, whenever
the %mk2; parameter entity is set to INCLUDE.

8.1.2 Storing marked sections as entities

Where a marked section is likely to be used more than once in a document
it can be stored as an entity. To speed up identification of the text as a
marked section the MS keyword should be used in the entity declaration.
The program will then automatically add the marked section open and
close delimiter sequences to the replacement text entered for the entity.
For example, if the temporary 'in preparation' marked section declaration
defined above was to be used in a number of citations it could be declared
as an entity by entering:

```
<!ENTITY inprep MS " TEMP [ (in preparation)" >
```

Once the entity has been defined in this way the citation can be
altered to read:

```
<cit>Bryan, M. T. (1988) <hp1> SGML: An Authors Guide to the Standard Generalized Markup
Language</hp1>, Wokingham: Addison-Wesley&inprep;</cit>
```

When storing marked sections as entities, however, it is important to
remember that all of the marked section must be defined in the same
entity. For example, the entity references:

```
<!ENTITY ignore  "<[ IGNORE ["                          >
<!ENTITY message "Remember to check this before publication" >
```

could not be used to create a marked section by entry of a definition such
as:

```
&ignore;&message;]]>
```

8.1.3 Nested marked sections

SGML allows marked sections to be nested up to the level defined by the currently active TAGLVL parameter (see Chapter 10). In the reference concrete syntax, up to 24 different levels of marked sections can be active at any point in the document. As was mentioned earlier, nesting is not allowed within CDATA or RCDATA marked sections, so only sections defined using the INCLUDE, IGNORE and TEMP keywords can contain nested marked sections. (Remember – if no keyword is present INCLUDE is assumed.)

To see how nesting might work, consider the following example:

```
<!ENTITY % bibliog "INCLUDE" >
<!ENTITY % nb "IGNORE" >
<!ENTITY inprep MS " TEMP [ (in preparation)" >
<![ %bibliog; [<h1>References</h1t>
<cit>Bryan, M. T. (1988) <hp1>SGML: An Authors Guide to the Standard Generalized Markup
Language</hp1>, Wokingham: Addison-Wesley&inprep;</cit>
.
.
<![ %nb; [Need to cite Robinson's paper here&inprep;]]>
.
.
]]>
```

Here the bibliography is to be included in the document but, because in some cases it will not be required, it has been treated as a marked section whose presence can be controlled by use of the %bibliog; parameter entity. Within the bibliography further marked sections have been used to define temporary additions to the citation (via the &inprep; entity declaration) and to add a note for the author. Note that, within the note the &inprep; entity reference has been used as a reminder of why the details still need to be added. This reference to an embedded marked section will, however, only be expanded if the keyword stored in the %nb; parameter entity reference is changed to INCLUDE.

If the entity declaration for the %bibliog; entity reference is changed to:

```
<!ENTITY % bibliog "IGNORE" >
```

all the marked sections embedded within the bibliography will be ignored because the IGNORE keyword in the outermost marked section has precedence over all other embedded keywords.

8.2   *Processing instructions*

Processing instructions can be used to tell the local system how it should process the data contained within a document. Because processing instructions are normally written in a language that is known only to the current system or to those using a similar set of instructions, they cannot be entered as part of the generalized coding used for SGML. To distinguish the processing instructions from other markup, therefore, they are enclosed in a special set of delimiters known as the **processing instruction open (pio)** and **processing instruction close (pic)** delimiters. In the reference concrete syntax **pio** is ‹? and **pic** is ›.

The format of the data within the processing instruction is determined by the processing system. The only restrictions placed on the format of processing instructions by SGML are that:

- they may only contain characters recognized as SGML characters in the currently defined concrete syntax, and

- they may not contain the character used as the processing instruction close delimiter in the current concrete syntax.

It should be noted that, once a processing instruction has been started, the SGML parser will ignore all characters up to and including the currently defined processing instruction close sequence.

The maximum length of individual processing instructions is controlled by the PILEN quantity in the SGML declaration (see Chapter 10). In the reference concrete syntax PILEN is set to 240.

To illustrate how processing instructions can be used to control the format of data stored in a document, consider the following example:

```
<p><?[s24][sec][rm]>T<?[pri][rm]>his paragraph requires
a special character (<?[f318][gB][rm]>) which has not
been defined in any of the entity sets currently in
force.</p>
```

Here the required processing instructions have been specified using the British Standard Method for Specifying Electronic Typographic Markup (SETM) which is due to be published in 1988. As this standard defines a 'starter set' of instructions common to most typesetters, together with a method of extending this set as required, it provides a useful way of standardizing formatting instructions in the absence of an internationally agreed way of specifying such details.

NOTE: The starter set of instructions defined in SETM is:

[Sn]	*Type size†*
[ONn]	*Leading (interlinear space)†*
[Wn]	*Type width*

[Mn]	*Measure*
[PTFname]	*Primary type family*
[STFname]	*Secondary type family*
[Fname]	*Alternative type face*
[PRI]	*Select primary type family*
[SEC]	*Select secondary type family*
[RO]	*Select roman font of current family*
[I]	*Select italic font of current family*
[B]	*Select bold font of current family*
[BI]	*Select bold italic font of current family*
[SC]	*Select small capitals font of current family*
[RTY]	*Create reversed-out type*
[/RTY]	*Terminate reversed-out type*
[CLRn]	*Print text in colour n*
[HDdn]	*Move horizontally in direction d (d = + or −)*
[VDdn]	*Move vertically in direction d (d = + or −)*
[HP]	*Memorize current horizontal position*
[RHP]	*Return to memorized horizontal position*
[LSdn]	*Add or subtract inter-character space (d = + or −)*
[/LS]	*Cancel letter-spacing*
[KERN]	*Kern subsequent text*
[/KERN]	*Cancel kerning*
['x]	*Set x as first order superior*
[,x]	*Set x as first order inferior*
[''x]	*Set x as second order superior*
[',x]	*Set x as second order inferior to superior*
[,'x]	*Set x as second order superior to inferior*
[,,x]	*Set x as second order inferior*
[SU]	*Set subsequent text using first order superiors*
[IN]	*Set subsequent text using first order inferiors*
[/SI]	*Cancel superiors/inferiors*
[L]	*Terminate line here and align left*
[R]	*Terminate line here and align right*
[C]	*Terminate line here and centre*
[E]	*Terminate line here and align as per set alignment tag*
[ZAj]	*Set alignment of following text*
[]	*Terminate line here, align as per set alignment tag and indent as per indent first line tag*
[IPn]	*Indent first line on left*
[/IP]	*Cancel indent of first line*
[IHn]	*Indent all but first line on left*
[ILnLo]	*Indent left (optionally) for o lines*
[/IL]	*Cancel indent left*
[IRnLo]	*Indent right (optionally) for o lines*
[/IR]	*Cancel indent right*

`[/II]`	*Cancel all indents*
`[Adn]`	*Additional interlinear space (d = + or −)*
`[PJ]`	*Vertical expansion point for current page*
`[RHnw]`	*Horizontal rule, length n, width w*
`[BOX WEIGHT=n, WIDTH=n, HEIGHT=n]`	
`[LSQ]`	*Start of leader sequence*
`[/LSQ]`	*End of leader sequence*
`[LDR]`	*Set leader sequence*

† May be concatenated to give an instruction of the form [s10on12pt]

The units of measurement for the numeric (n) parameters of the SETM instructions can be expressed in picas (pi) and points (pt), ciceros (ci) and didot points (di), centimeters (cm), millimetres (mm) or inches (in). Where subunits are permitted, matched pairs of unit identifiers must be used, for example [m12pi6pt].

An SGML parser will ignore the processing instructions in the above example, simply passing the entered data on as part of the text string. When the document is formatted by the system, however, the entered instructions will be recognized by the formatting program as instructions that it needs to format the document. In the case illustrated above the program will recognize that the first character of the entered paragraph is to be treated as a 24pt initial letter to be set using the roman version of the face currently defined as the secondary type family. The rest of the paragraph is to be set in the roman face of the primary type family. Within the brackets in the middle of the paragraph a special typeface is requested before a character which is not available in the SGML character set is requested as part of the processing instruction. Figure 8.1 shows how this paragaph might appear after processing.

𝕿his paragraph requires a special character (ß) which has not been defined in any of the entity sets currently in force.

Figure 8.1 Paragraph set using processing instructions.

Processing instructions can always be entered on a line of their own if preferred. In this case, the rules for record boundary recognition detailed in Chapter 5 will automatically suppress the record end code following the processing instruction. For example, the entry:

```
<p>
<?[s11on13][pr][i]>
The first paragraph of a section ...
```

is equivalent to:

```
<p><?[s11on13][pr][i]>The first paragraph of a section ...
```

because the first record end of the paragraph element will be ignored since it has not been preceded by data or a proper subelement, and the record end following the processing instruction will be ignored because it represents a record end that does not immediately follow an record start or another record end and there is no intervening data or subelement.

8.2.1 *Storing processing instructions as entities*

Because processing instructions reduce the portability of SGML documents, their use outside the document prolog is deprecated within ISO 8879. For this reason it is recommended that, wherever possible, processing instructions should be declared as entities, within the document type declaration.

The PI keyword can be used to identify the replacement text of an entity as a processing instruction that should be passed directly to the host system. (The processing instruction opening and closing delimiters are, as usual, omitted from the replacement text.) For example, the processing instructions used to create the large initial letter in Figure 8.1 could be declared in the document prolog by entry of the following entity declarations:

```
<!ENTITY initial PI "[s24][sec][rm]" >
<!ENTITY main    PI "[pri][rm]" >
```

These entities can either be used directly within the relevant paragraphs, for example:

```
<p>&initial;T&main;his paragraph requires a special
character (<?[f318][gB][rm]>) which has not been defined
in any of the entity sets currently in force.</p>
```

or can be linked with short references such as:

```
<!SHORTREF paramap "@" initial "#" main >
<!USEMAP   paramap p>
```

to allow the paragraph definition to be further shortened to:

```
<p>@T#his paragraph requires a special character
(<?[f318][gB][rm]>) which has not been defined in any of
the entity sets currently in force.</p>
```

Note that the one-off processing instruction used to generate the special character in the above examples has not been defined as an entity. Whilst this reduces the need to declare entities for a special case such as this, it does mean that if the document is transmitted to another system there is a chance that the embedded processing instruction could be missed when the definitions are being changed to suit the new system.

NOTE: If one or more of the entered processing instructions is to return data to the system the SDATA *keyword must be used in preference to* PI *in the entity declaration since only* SDATA *entities can accept returned data. In such a case, the returned data will become the replacement text for the entity in place of the entered processing instruction.*

8.2.2   Using processing instructions in marked sections

Where two different systems may to be used to format a document, the marked section facility can be used to control the processing instructions used on each system. For example, two sets of processing instructions could be entered in the text as:

```
<![ %systema; [<?processing instructions for system A>]]>
<![ %systemb; [<?processing instructions for system B>]]>
```

While the document is being processed on system A the associated parameter entities would be defined as:

```
<!ENTITY % systema "INCLUDE" >
<!ENTITY % systemb "IGNORE"  >
```

When the document is transferred to system B the processing instructions used can be quickly changed by altering the entity declarations to read:

```
<!ENTITY % systema "IGNORE"  >
<!ENTITY % systemb "INCLUDE" >
```

As with most of the advanced SGML features, the uses to which marked sections and processing instructions can be put are legion, but their use is entirely optional. If, however, the author feels that they would be useful for marking up a particular piece of text a check should be made to ensure that the programs processing the document are able to handle them. (SGML programs will always be able to recognize marked sections and processing instructions as such, but you must check that the text formatter is able to process the embedded coding correctly.) Before making extensive use of these facilities it is advisable to prepare a small test document to ensure that any processor-specific instructions are correctly interpreted by receiving systems.

CHAPTER 9

Multiple Document Structures

9.1 SGML subdocuments
9.2 Concurrent document structures

More than one document structure may be required to cope with the varying roles of the elements making up an SGML document. Sometimes the different document structures are used individually; at other times concurrent multiple roles can be allocated to a single piece of text.

Where a document is made up from a number of previously prepared subsections, each of which has its own document structure, the individual subsections can be treated as externally stored **subdocuments** of the main document. Such subdocuments must be declared as external entities in the document type declaration at the start of the main document. At the appropriate point in the text, an entity reference (or attribute) is used to call the previously declared subdocument into the main document.

Concurrent document structures can be used, for example, to distinguish between the different purposes to which data may be put (e.g. for database retrieval or book production) or to identify structures generated during the processing of a document (e.g. the layout structure of a formatted book). Each concurrent structure used within the document must be declared in a document type declaration entered immediately after the SGML declaration at start of the document.

The use of SGML subdocuments and concurrent document structures is controlled by the FEATURES clause of the document's SGML declaration (see Chapter 3). If subdocuments are to be used the SUBDOC NO entry in the last line of the FEATURES clause must be changed to SUBDOC YES n, where n indicates the maximum number of subdocuments that will be open at any point in the document. If concurrent document structures are required the CONCUR NO entry must be changed to CONCUR YES n, where n indicates the number of document structures that are to be associated with the base document type.

9.1 SGML subdocuments

SGML subdocuments are self-contained, externally stored entities which consist of a document type declaration followed by text marked up using the entities, elements and attributes defined in the local declaration.

SGML subdocuments are particularly useful where a document is to consist of contributions from a number of sources. Each contributor can prepare their section of the overall document using tags and entities that suit the particular contribution. The files containing each contribution can then be declared as subdocument entities within the overall document.

Before preparing text for use as a subdocument of another document it is important to ensure that the same SGML declaration will be used for each subdocument in the overall document. *It is the SGML declaration of the main document that applies to an SGML subdocument since the subdocument may not contain its own SGML declaration.* Although a local SGML declaration may be added to the subdocument while it is being prepared, this will need to be removed before the file can be used as a subdocument within another document.

Once a subdocument file has been prepared it must be declared as an external entity before it can be called within the main document. As explained in Chapter 4, there are two main types of external entities – system-specific and publicly declared. If the subdocument is stored locally it can be declared as a system-specific entity by entry of an entity declaration such as:

```
<!ENTITY paper1 SYSTEM "c:\book10\freedom.txt" SUBDOC>
```

If the system can automatically recognize the name of the file from the entity's name, the optional **system identifier** (e.g. `"c:\book10\freedom.txt"`) can be omitted to give an entity declaration such as:

```
<!ENTITY freedom SYSTEM SUBDOC>
```

Where the subdocument's contents are already known to all systems likely to receive the document, the entity can be publicly declared by entry of a declaration, such as:

```
<!ENTITY waiver PUBLIC "waiver.doc" SUBDOC >
```

If the FEATURES clause of the SGML declaration for the main document contains the statement FORMAL YES, however, it will be necessary to use formal names for any publicly declared subdocuments (see 'Formal public

identifiers' in Section 4.3.2). A typical formally declared public subdocument entity might be defined as:

```
<!ENTITY warranty PUBLIC
    "-//ABC Inc//SUBDOCUMENT General Warranty//EN" >
```

It should be noted that, even though they contain markup declarations, SGML subdocuments are defined as general entities rather than
parameter entities. This is because the entity reference for the subdocument must occur at the appropriate point within the text of the
document, rather than within the document type definition.

The name of the external entity containing the subdocument need
not reflect the name of the document type used within the subdocument.
Within the subdocument, however, the first start-tag entered must have the
same name as the subdocument's document type declaration, since this
defines the base document element for the subdocument.

A previously defined subdocument can be recalled by entering an
entity reference, such as &warranty;, at the appropriate point in the text.
Alternatively, the external entity can be requested by associating an
appropriate entity attribute with an empty element, as the following
example shows:

```
<!ENTITY  paper1  SYSTEM "c:\book10\freedom.txt" SUBDOC>
<!ELEMENT article - 0     EMPTY>
<!ATTLIST article file   ENTITY #REQUIRED>
<textbook><titlep><title>It's A Free World</title>
.
.
.

<body>
<h0>Personal Freedom
<article file=paper1>
```

In this example, the external entity referred to as paper1 has been
stored on the local system in a file called freedom.txt in directory book10 on disk
drive C. This file is to be output as the first file in the 'Personal Freedom'
part of a textbook called 'It's A Free World'. To achieve this, the declared
name of the external entity has been entered as the compulsory value of
the file attribute for the <article> element. The <article> element has been
declared to be an empty element because it contains no text, since it is only
used to call external entities into the main document. And, because it is an
empty element, it needs no end-tag to identify the end of its contents, so
the end-tag has been declared as omissible (see Chapter 5).

Before requesting a subdocument from the system, an SGML parser
will record the current state of all its parameters and declarations for recall
after the subdocument has been processed. Within the subdocument only
the locally defined markup declarations will apply. This means that

features such as current rank will start from the base level within the subdocument rather than at any existing rank level and that entities declared in the main document cannot be referred to in the subdocument. It also means that you cannot use an identifier declared in the main document to create a cross-reference in the subdocument or vice versa.

9.2   *Concurrent document structures*

Where two or more 'views' of a document's contents can exist, more than one document type declaration can be specified at the start of a document. For example, if the text for a catalogue was also to be used in an on-line database, it may be necessary to indicate two different roles for a piece of text in its markup, as the following example shows:

```
<product>
<(dbs)item no=12963>
<hp2>250 Fibre Washers (large mixed pack)</hp2>
</(dbs)item>
A wide range of metric and imperial sizes suitable
for most applications
<price><(dbs)gross>1.90</(dbs)gross></price>
</product>
```

In this case, the first highlighted line of the printed product description is to form the item name in the database system (dbs), where it will be referred to as item number 12963. Similarly, the printed price will become the gross value in the database system. Notice how the name of the elements associated with the database system have been preceded by a bracketed **document type specification** to indicate that they are associated with a document type declaration other than that specifed as the base document type declaration.

Normally, however, concurrent document structures will not be used directly by authors or other end-users but will be used by the document designer to tell the system how it should store details of the way in which text has been processed. For example, in a typical publishing application, a document will pass through a number of production stages to produce galley proofs, paginated text, imposed sheets, etc. Traditionally, each of these stages has resulted in an output file which is coded to suit the use to which it will be put. The problem with this is if changes are required to the text, more than one version of the file may need to be updated. To avoid having to create different files at each stage in the production process SGML allows the details required for each structure to be stored in the same file.

Before SGML's concurrent document structure can be used, however, the document designer must decide the maximum number of concurrent structures that will be allowed in the document. The FEATURES clause of the SGML declaration must then be altered so that it contains the entry CONCUR YES n, where n is the number of document structures to be declared in the document's **prolog** *in addition to* that of the base document type.

Each of the allowed document structures is declared at the start of the document by entry of a document type declaration immediately after the document's SGML declaration. The first document type declaration entered must be that for the base document. This initial DTD is referred to as the **base document type declaration**. (Its name is used as the document's initial **base document element** start-tag – see Chapter 5). The document type declarations for the other concurrent document structures can be defined in any order but they must be entered before any text or document markup.

Each document type declaration starts with the current markup declaration open (**mdo**) delimiter followed by the reserved word DOCTYPE (or its nominated replacement in the current concrete syntax) and the name of the document type. This **document type name** must not match that used for any other document structure or **link type name** (see 'Explicit links' in Section 9.2.1), in the same prolog. Where necessary, the document type name can be followed by an optional-external-identifier that identifies an external file containing some or all of the DTD's markup declarations. Locally defined declarations for the required document structure are entered as a **document type declaration subset** between declaration subset open (**dso**) and declaration subset close (**dsc**) delimiters. The declaration is completed by entry of a markup declaration close (**mdc**) delimiter to give the declaration the overall form:

```
<!DOCTYPE docname optional-external-identifier
        [ ... local declarations ... ] >
```

Typically, a document with three concurrent document structures might start:

```
<!SGML    "ISO 8879-1986"
 BASESET "ISO 646-1983//CHARSET
          International Reference Version (IRV)//ESC 2/5 4/0"
    .

    .

    .
 FEATURES MINIMIZE DATATAG NO   OMITTAG  YES   RANK    NO SHORTTAG YES
          LINK     SIMPLE  NO   IMPLICIT NO    EXPLICIT NO
          OTHER    CONCUR YES 2 SUBDOC   YES 1 FORMAL   NO
 APPINFO NONE
  >
```

```
<!DOCTYPE textbook PUBLIC "-//Addison-Wesley//DTD SGML:
               An Author's Guide to the Standard Generalized Markup Language//EN"
[<!ENTITY % AWacc PUBLIC "-//Addison-Wesley//ENTITIES Accented Characters//EN">
   %AWacc;]>
<!DOCTYPE galley [
<!ELEMENT galley - O     (block)+                    >
<!ELEMENT block  - -     (#PCDATA|phrase|quote)* >
<!ATTLIST block  family  NUTOKEN   "Times"
                 face    NAME      "roman"
                 measure NUTOKEN   "27pi"
                 ptsize  NUTOKEN   "10on12pt"
                 lead-out NUTOKENS #IMPLIED
                 flind   NMTOKEN   "0" --first line indent--
                 l-indent NUTOKEN  "0"
                 r-indent NUTOKEN  "0"
                 relateto (last|next|current)  "last"
                 atpoint  (left|right|bottom)  "bottom"
                 pref-sep NUTOKENS         #IMPLIED
                 min-sep  NUTOKENS         #IMPLIED
                 max-sep  NUTOKENS         #IMPLIED
                 number   NUTOKEN          #IMPLIED
                    .
                    .
                    .                                          >
     .
     .
     .
]>
<!DOCTYPE pages [
<!ELEMENT pages - O     (page)+                              >
<!ELEMENT page  - -     (header?, textarea, notes*, footer?, trimmark*)>
<!ATTLIST page  id      ID              #IMPLIED
                page-no NMTOKEN         #IMPLIED
                way-up  (0|90|180|270)  "0"                   >
     .
     .
     .
]>
```

The first element entered after the above declarations must be that for the ‹textbook› element since this is the base document element for the first of the entered document type declarations, which is automatically taken by the SGML parser as the base document type declaration for the document. Until the textbook is processed to produce galley proofs, the only tags in the document will be those declared in the base document type declaration. (Elements in this set do not need to be preceded by a bracketed document type specification.)

When the document is formatted to produce galley proofs a second, physical, structure can be *added* to the logical structure used by the author to code the document. For a typical paragraph the resultant markup might take the form:

```
<p><(galley)block flind="18pt">Many paragraphs of
text have their first line indented by one or two ems.
This technique allows paragraphs to be set without
intervening space, so increasing the density of the
page.</(galley)block>
```

When the document is paginated the one-to-one relationship between the logical structure and the physical structure will begin to break down at all but the highest level. (Chapters will normally equate to page sets but most pages will start and stop in the middle of an element.) The start of a typical page might take the form:

```
<(pages)page id="p144">
<(pages)folio size="9pt" face="bold">144
<(pages)header size="9pt" face="small-caps">
introduction to expert systems
<(pages)textarea>
differentiate between the different kinds of knowledge,
which may need to be represented and applied in
different ways.</(galley)block>
<h2><(galley)block family="Helvetica" face="bold"
pref-sep="18 6" max-sep= "24 6" number="10.1.1">
The structure of prototypes</(galley)block>
<p><(galley)block>In order ...
```

Note how, in this example, the text at the start of the ⟨textarea⟩ element on the page is not preceded by tags from the base (textbook) document set or from the galley document type declaration. Because the paragraph that ends on page 144 of this book starts on page 143, the ⟨p⟩ and ⟨(galley)block⟩ elements for the paragraph appear on that page rather than this one. This fact is only registered by inclusion of the compulsory end-tag for the ⟨(galley)block⟩ element, which has been placed at the end of the paragraph. (As the end-tag for the ⟨p⟩ element is optional in the base document type declaration it has been omitted here.)

The above example also illustrates how the default entries for the attributes associated with the ⟨block⟩ element in the galley document type declaration control the default format of the text. The default attributes apply whenever no other values are entered. By setting the default values to those used for the most common version of a block (in this case that used for text paragraphs) only elements which require other setting parameters need to have specific values defined within the automatically generated start-tags. For example, the start-tag for the subheading following the first paragraph on page 144:

```
<(galley)block family="Helvetica" face="bold"
pref-sep="18 6" max-sep="24 6" number="10.1.1">
```

shows that this heading is to be set in the default size (10 on 12pt) using Helvetica bold, with preferably 18pt space above the heading and 6pt space below the heading. (The space above the heading can be expanded to 24pt during pagination.) The number attribute shows the form of the number that the system has generated for this heading.

Just as the start of a page can occur in the middle of a paragraph, so the end of a page can occur within a logical element/physical block, as the following example shows:

```
...
<p><(galley)block flind="18pt">As it happens, conflict
resolution will do the right thing. Because the
<hp2><(galley)phrase family="OCR" setwidth="8pt">
modify</(galley)phrase></hp2> action has made
<hp2><(galley)phrase family="OCR" setwidth="8pt">
(brick^name C^size 30^place hand)</(galley)phrase></hp2>
the most recent</(pages)page><(pages)page id="p49">
...
```

In this example the paragraph's formatted block has two OCR programming phrases embedded within it. Note, however, that neither of the elements defined at the start of the paragraph have been closed before the end of the page. Both the paragraph element (<p>) and its associated galley element (<(galley)block flind="18pt">) will, in this case, still be in force when the <(pages)textarea> element starts after the running head for the new page.

By now you are probably wondering how the program knows which attributes of the <(galley)block> element to associate with each of the elements in the logical structure. On some systems, providing this information will be an integral part of the role of the text formatter but SGML also allows this information to be defined by the document designer via the addition of **link declarations** to the document type declaration.

9.2.1 Linking document structures

SGML uses three types of declarations to link concurrent document structures:

(1)   **link type declarations** to set up links between different document types,

(2)   **link set declarations** to control how individual elements are to be linked, and

(3)   **link set use declarations** to switch from one set of links to another.

While link set use declarations can, like short reference use (USEMAP) declarations, be entered directly within the text to override the currently active link (see later sections), link declarations are normally only found in the prolog, after the associated document type declarations. (In this context it is important to remember that the link declarations must be entered after all the document type declarations required for the document have been declared. The link declarations may be separated from the DTDs by comment declarations, spaces, record start and end codes, valid separator characters or processing instructions, which are collectively referred to within ISO 8879 as **other prolog**.)

Three types of link are recognized by SGML·

(1)   **simple links** controlled by attributes associated with the base document element,

(2)   **implicit links** whose resultant elements are implied by the formatting program, and

(3)   **explicit links** where each link is explicitly controlled by the document designer.

Only one type of link is used to link any pair of document structures defined in the document prolog.

The types of links that can be used within a document are controlled by the LINK entries in the FEATURES clause of the SGML declaration (see Chapter 3). In the reference concrete syntax the LINK features are disabled by entry of the following line:

```
LINK    SIMPLE NO    IMPLICIT NO    EXPLICIT NO
```

If simple links are required in a document, the first entry in this line must be changed to SIMPLE YES followed by a number indicating the maximum number of simple links to be used in the document. If implicit links are to be used, the second entry changes to IMPLICIT YES (without a qualifying number). Where explicit links are required, the maximum number of links to be used within a single chain in the document must be stated after the entry EXPLICIT YES, giving a composite entry of the form:

```
LINK    SIMPLE YES 4  IMPLICIT NO    EXPLICIT YES 2
```

If EXPLICIT YES is specified, multiple DTDs can be declared in the prolog (even if concurrent document types are not permitted by the SGML declaration). The number of explicit links allowed in the FEATURES clause must be, at least, one less than the number of document type declarations in the longest chain of linked documents declared in the prolog.

Explicit links

To see how link declarations can be used, consider the following (very much simplified) link type declaration, which shows how **explicit links** could be used to produce justified galleys of text from an SGML-coded source document that only contains text in elements tagged as paragraphs, notes and list items:

```
<!LINKTYPE justify textbook galley
[<!ATTLIST p       align    (sielcij)  j
                   hyphens  NAME       English
                   consechy NUMBER     3
                   wordlims NUMBERS    "7 3 3"   >
  <!ATTLIST note   align    (sielcij)  j
                   hyphens  NAME       English
                   consechy NUMBER     3
                   wordlims NUMBERS    "7 3 3"
                   keep     NUMBER     3         >
  <!ATTLIST it     default  RCDATA     "&bull;"
                   align    (sielcij)  s
                   hyphens  NAME       English
                   consechy NUMBER     2
                   wordlims NUMBERS    "9 3 5"   >
  <!LINK #INITIAL p block [family="Times"       face="roman"
                   ptsize="10on12pt"   measure="27pi"
                   lead-out="11pt 13pt" flindent="18pt"
                   l-indent="0"        r-indent="0"
                   relateto=last       atpoint=bottom
                   pref-sep="0 0"      max-sep="2pt 2pt" ]
              note block [family="Times"        face="italic"
                   ptsize="9on11pt"    measure="27pi"
                   flindent="0"
                   l-indent="0"        r-indent="0"
                   relateto=last       atpoint=bottom
                   pref-sep="3pt 3pt"  max-sep="6pt 6pt"
                   min-sep="2pt 2pt"   precede="NOTE: " ]
  it #USELINK link2 block [family="Times"       face="roman"
                   ptsize= "10on12pt"  measure="27pi"
                   flindent="-13pt"
                   l-indent="18pt"     r-indent="0"
                   relateto=last       atpoint=bottom
                   pref-sep="2pt 2pt"  max-sep="3pt 3pt"
                   min-sep="1pt 1pt"                   ]>
```

```
<!LINK link2  p   block [family="Times"       face="roman"
                        ptsize ="10on12pt" measure="27pi"
                        flindent="0"
                        l-indent="18pt"    r-indent="0"
                        relateto=last      atpoint=bottom
                        pref-sep="2pt 2pt" max-sep="3pt 3pt"
                        min-sep="1pt 1pt"                    ]
          note [keep=1] block [family="Times"    face="italic"
                        ptsize="9on11pt"   measure="27pi"
                        flindent="0"
                        l-indent="18pt"    r-indent= "0"
                        relateto=last      atpoint= bottom
                        pref-sep="2pt 2pt" max-sep="3pt 3pt"
                        min-sep="1pt 1pt"  precede="NB: "   ]>] >
```

The first line of the declaration starts with a markup declaration open delimiter followed by the keyword used to identify link type declarations (<! and LINKTYPE in the reference concrete syntax). This is followed by a **link type name** that should uniquely identify the role of the link. (Link type names must not be duplicated or match any of the names allocated to document types declared within the document.) In this example, the link type name is justify. When explicit links are being used, the link type name is followed by the names of the two document type declarations to be linked by the declaration, the **source document type name** (e.g. textbook) preceding the **result document type name** (e.g. galley).

The rest of the link type declaration forms a **link type declaration subset**. As with other subsets within SGML, the set is delimited by declaration subset open and close delimiters (square brackets in the reference concrete syntax).

Four types of declarations are permitted within a link type declaration subset:

- **link attribute set** declarations defining the sets of attributes that can be used to control the link process;
- **link set declarations** and **ID link set declarations** defining the links between elements; and
- **entity set** declarations defining parameter entities that are used within the link type declaration subset.

The link attribute set consists of an optional set of **attribute definition list declarations**. The attributes declared in these definitions can be used to pass parameters to routines that link the two document type definitions. You will remember from Chapter 6 that, when the reference concrete syntax is in force, each attribute definition list declaration starts with <!ATTLIST, followed by the name of the source document element(s) to which the following list of attributes applies, and ends with a markup declaration close delimiter (>). When used in link type declaration subsets, the attribute's declared value cannot be defined by use of the ID, IDREF, IDREFS or NOTATION keywords, and the #CURRENT and #CONREF options cannot be used for the default value. (These restrictions apply because link attributes cannot be used within an element's start-tag. In each of the above cases, users would need to specify the applicable attribute values or supply the contents to which the attributes are to apply.)

Only three sets of attribute definitions have been specified in the simplified example above. For a paragraph of text the attributes declared are:

```
<!ATTLIST p align    (s|e|c|j) j
            hyphens  NAME     English
            consechy NUMBER   3
            wordlims NUMBERS  "7 3 3"  >
```

The four attributes declared here allow the document designer to control:

(1)   the form of alignment (justification) to be applied to the element (start-of-line, end-of-line, centred or justified);

(2)   the hyphenation algorithm to be used during justification;

(3)   the maximum number of consecutive hyphenated lines; and

(4)   the minimum size of a hyphenatable word, and the minimum number of characters that can be left on the first line and carried to the next line.

The same four attributes have been used for notes, but this time an extra attribute has been declared to allow the document designer to control the number of lines to be retained on the page before a note is split. The default entry used here is three lines. (Shortly, we will show how this default value can be overridden.) The final form of the attribute definition list declaration associated with the <note> element is:

```
<!ATTLIST note align    (s|e|c|j) j
              hyphens  NAME     English
              consechy NUMBER   3
              wordlims NUMBERS  "7 3 3"
              keep     NUMBER   3       >
```

This entry, and the one for the paragraph element, can be shortened by use of parameter entity declarations within the link type declaration subset, as the following example shows:

```
<!ENTITY % group1 'align    (s|e|c|j) j
                   hyphens  NAME      English
                   consechy NUMBER    3
                   wordlims NUMBERS   "7 3 3"'>
<!ATTLIST p        %group1;                 >
<!ATTLIST note     %group1;
                   keep     NUMBER    3     >
```

For the list item (`<it>`) element, however, the above parameter entity declaration cannot be used because the default values are different for this element. In this case, the declaration reads:

```
<!ATTLIST it default RCDATA    "&bull;"
             align   (s|e|c|j) s
             hyphens NAME      English
             consechy NUMBER   2
             wordlims NUMBERS  "9 3 5" >
```

Here, the default version of the symbol to precede each list item is to be a bullet (solid circle), each entry being aligned at the start of the line only (ragged right). The maximum number of consecutive hyphenated line endings has been reduced to two, while the smallest size word that can be hyphenated has been increased to nine characters, three of which must remain on the first line and at least five of which must be placed on the second line.

It should be noted that, in most practical situations, more than four attributes will be needed to control the requested process. The number of attributes used in a particular application of SGML will depend on the degree of control that the document designer can exert over the process. Processes such as justification and pagination typically require a wide range of parameters, but for the sake of clarity these have been left out of this simplified example.

Two link set declarations have been specified in the example link shown on p.208. The first is the *compulsory* initial link set declaration. The use of the #INITIAL keyword as the **link set name** tells the program that this link set declaration is to be treated as the current link set when the document instance begins (i.e. when the start-tag for the element whose name matches that specified as the source document type name in the link type declaration is encountered).

The link set name is followed by the first **source element speci-fication** in the link set, which starts with the name(s) of the elements that are to use the link. This name can be qualified by one or more attributes forming a **link attribute specification**, which may be preceded by a link usage qualifier (#USELINK or #POSTLINK). The source element specification is followed by a **result element specification**, which also starts with an element name – this time taken from the list of generic identifiers defined in the DTD for the result document. This element name will normally be followed by a **result attribute specification** showing the attributes to be associated with the selected element in the result document. Each link set in an explicit link consists of repeated pairs of source element specifications and result element specifications (a pair forming an **explicit link rule**).

Three explicit link rules have been declared in the initial link set declaration shown above. The first two link the paragraph and note elements to the block element defined in the document type declaration identified by the result document type name entered at the start of the link type declaration (i.e. ⟨(galley)block⟩). These links also define specific values for some of the attributes associated with the ⟨(galley)block⟩ element in its declaration. (In practice, the range of attributes for a block is likely to be much greater than that shown in this example.)

For the justify link, a paragraph of text is to be set in 10/12pt Times roman, on a measure of 27 picas, with an 18 point (18pt) indent for the first line of the paragraph. The block is to be positioned relative to a point defined by the bottom of the last element set, from which it will normally not need to be separated (pref-sep = preferred separation) but, in certain circumstances known to the pagination program, it can be separated from adjacent paragraphs by as much as 2pt. (Its default 12pt leading value can also, if required, be adjusted in the range between 11pt and 13pt to avoid a bad page break.)

By contrast, a note is to be set in 9/11pt Times italic without an initial indent, and with a preferred separation of 3pt from adjacent blocks. (The pagination program may reduce this to 2pt, or enlarge it to 6pt, to avoid bad page breaks.) The entered text is to be preceded by the word NOTE:, followed by a space.

For list items the initial link set declaration entry reads:

```
it #USELINK link2 block [family="Times"    face="roman"
                         ptsize= "10on12pt" measure="27pi"
                         flindent="-13pt"
                         l-indent="18pt"   r-indent="0"
                         relateto=last     atpoint=bottom
                         pref-sep="2pt 2pt" max-sep="3pt 3pt"
                         min-sep="1pt 1pt"                  ]
```

Here the text face of 10/12pt Times roman is to be set across a measure of 27 picas reduced by a left indent of 18pts, except on the first line of each item, which is only to be indented by 5pts (18pt−13pt) before the bullet specified by the default attribute (in the link attribute set) is printed. By preference, there should be a 2pt gap between items in a list, but this can be varied during pagination between 1pt and 3pt if necessary.

The #USELINK link2 statement that, in this case, follows the name of the element being linked, tells the program to switch over to using the link set declaration identified by the link set name link2 when looking at elements that are embedded within list items. This declaration will remain current until the end of the list item is recognized by the program (either from the presence of an explicit end-tag or implicitly when a tag of a higher or equal level is encountered). At this point, the link in force when the list item was encountered will be restored.

Within the link2 link set declaration, paragraphs and notes have again been linked to the <(galley)block> element, but this time a different set of attribute values have been specified. When embedded within a list item, paragraphs are to be set with an 18pt left indent but without a first line indent. Instead, each paragraph is to be separated from its neighbours by a 2pt space, which can be reduced to 1pt or increased to 3pt during pagination. Within a list, the paragraph's leading may not be varied (unless the default value for the lead-out attribute in the galley document type declaration contains a variation range).

In link2 the link specified for notes is:

```
note [keep=1] block [family="Times"    face="italic"
                     ptsize="9on11pt"   measure="27pi"
                     flindent="0"
                     l-indent="18pt"    r-indent="0"
                     relateto=last      atpoint=bottom
                     pref-sep="2pt 2pt" max-sep="3pt 3pt"
                     min-sep="1pt 1pt"  precede="NB: " ]
```

The main thing to note about this declaration is the addition of a **link attribute specification** to the source element specification identifying the element in the source document to which the link is to apply. The attribute used here must be one of the control parameters specified in the link attribute set at the start of the link type declaration subset. (It is important to remember that *the attribute cannot be one of those associated with the source element when it was declared in the document type declaration*.) In this case, the entered attribute tells the program that it only needs to keep one line on the page when it splits a note embedded within a list item.

Within a list item, notes are to be identified by the letters NB: followed by a space, rather than by NOTE:, and are to be indented by 18pt to align with the text of the item entry. Notes will preferably be separated from the preceding text by a 2pt space, which can be reduced to 1pt or increased to 3pt during pagination. Otherwise the typographic parameters of the embedded notes are the same as those of ordinary notes.

Alternative link points

The link set change shown in the above example will be activated by the parser immediately after the start-tag of the identified element, before any of the characters within the element are processed. There are, however, times when it is necessary to change the rules that apply to a link at the point immediately after an element has been processed, or when a specific instance of an element is encountered. During 1988 the SGML standard (ISO 8879) was extended to provide these facilities.

The new #POSTLINK option can be used in place of #USELINK to specify that a new link set is to be activated when the end-tag for the specified element is encountered or implied by the program. Where specific instances of an element require special link sets, an ID link set declaration can be used to specify the rules to be applied for each instance.

A classic example of the need to change the link rules immediately after a specific element is provided by books in which the first paragraph of text after a chapter heading starts with a larger letter than is used for other paragraphs. This could be handled using a link set of the following type:

```
<!LINKTYPE justify textbook galley
[<!ATTLIST h1     align    (s|e|c|j)  c
                  consechy NUMBER     0          >
<!ATTLIST p       align    (s|e|c|j)  j
                  hyphens  NAME       English
                  consechy NUMBER     3
                  wordlims NUMBERS    "7 3 3"
                  keep     NUMBER     3          >
<!LINK #INITIAL
   h1 #POSTLINK firstpar block [family="Helvetica"   face="bold"
                               ptsize="18on24pt"     measure="27pi"
                               l-indent="0"          r-indent="0"
                               pref-sep="0 48pt"     max-sep="0 72pt" ]
                     p block [family="Times"         face="roman"
                              ptsize="10on12pt"      measure="27pi"
                              lead-out="11pt 13pt"   flindent="18pt"
                              l-indent="0"           r-indent="0"
                              relateto=last          atpoint=bottom
                              pref-sep="0 0"         max-sep="2pt 2pt" ]
    ...
                                                     >
<!LINK firstpar
    p #POSTLINK #INITIAL block [family="Times"       face="roman"
                               ptsize ="10on12pt" measure="27pi"
                               initcap="22pt"        flindent="0"
                               l-indent="0"          r-indent="0"
                               relateto=last         atpoint=bottom
                               pref-sep="0 0"        max-sep="2pt 2pt" ]
    ...
                                                     >
    ] >
```

In the initial link set the first level of heading, for example the chapter heading, has been declared in such a way that, when the end-tag for the heading (</h1>) is encountered, the parser will switch to a special link set (firstpar) before processing the following text. The first paragraph differs from other paragraphs in that it has no first line indent but, instead, has a 22pt initial capital letter (which may or may not be a dropped capital, depending on the way the formatter interprets the initcap instruction), and its leading cannot be adjusted during pagination (to ensure that dropped caps will be positioned correctly).

When the end-tag for the first paragraph (</p>) is detected by the parser, the #POSTLINK #INITIAL entry associated with the paragraph element name (p) in the firstpar link set will cause the parser to revert to using the link definition for paragraphs given in the initial link. This will ensure that subsequent paragraphs have a first line indent of 18pt and no initial capital letter.

Where special instructions are to be associated with specific instances of an element, the source document type definition must include an attribute definition list declaration for that element which contains an attribute declared using the ID keyword as its declared value. In the source document instance each element that is to be treated differently must be given a unique identifier that the system can use to determine where the associated rule is to apply.

Special **ID link set declarations** are used to set up links for specific instances of an element. When the reference concrete syntax is being used, these links are defined within the link type declaration in a declaration that begins <!IDLINK and ends >. The unique identifier used to distinguish the first of the element instances to be specially treated is placed immediately after the IDLINK keyword, and this is followed by the name of the associated element type. (A space or comment should be used as a separator between the two names.) As with other link set declarations, the element name can be followed by a link attribute specification before details of the result element specification are entered. This sequence of unique identifier followed by link rule can be repeated as many times as is required for the document being processed.

The following example shows how a ID link set declaration might be used to set a specially identified paragraph in a different typeface (Bembo), without otherwise altering the format of the paragraph:

```
<!IDLINK bembopar p block [family="Bembo"      face="roman"
                           ptsize="11on12pt"   measure="27pi"
                           lead-out="11pt 13pt" flindent="18pt"
                           l-indent="0"        r-indent="0"
                           relateto=last       atpoint=bottom
                           pref-sep="0 0"      max-sep="6pt 6pt"
                           min-sep="2pt 2pt"                ] >
```

When preparing special links it is important to remember that each link set must cater for any subelements that the model allows to be embedded within the element being linked to the result document (hence the ellipses in the previous examples). Failure to do so may result in embedded elements not being formatted properly and, at best, will result in their being given default formatting parameters. This problem can be particularly important when ID link set declarations are being used, as these only affect one instance of the element. To overcome this problem, the #USELINK option can be combined with the IDLINK option to give a declaration of the form:

```
<!IDLINK bembopar p
   #USELINK bem-link block [family="Bembo"       face="roman"
                           ptsize="11on12pt"     measure="27pi"
                           lead-out="11pt 13pt" flindent="18pt"
                           l-indent="0"          r-indent="0"
                           relateto=last         atpoint=bottom
                           pref-sep="0 0"        max-sep="6pt 6pt"
                           min-sep="2pt 2pt"                 ] >
<!LINK bem-link hp1 block [family="Bembo"        face="italic"
                          ptsize="11on12pt"                  ]
                hp2 block [family="Bembo"        face="bold"
                          ptsize="11on12pt"                  ]
                hp3 block [family="Bembo"        face="bold-it"
                          ptsize="11on12pt"                  ]
                hp0 block [family="Bembo"        face="roman"
                          ptsize="11on12pt"                  ]
   ...                                                       >
```

In this example, the four types of highlighted phrase that might be encountered within the specially identified block have been defined in a separate link set declaration to ensure that they will be set in a matching type style.

Short cuts

As will be obvious from the complexity of the above simplified examples, preparing link type declarations for a document structure of the complexity of that defined for a textbook in Appendix C is going to be a time-consuming task. Fortunately, a number of short cuts are available.

As with the attribute declarations for the link attribute set shown above, parameter entities can be used to reduce the amount of keying required. As the following example shows, this can greatly reduce the length of link declarations:

```
...
<!ENTITY % times 'family="Times" face="' >
```

```
<!ENTITY % point 'relateto=last atpoint=bottom
                  pref-sep = ' >
<!ENTITY % noindnt 'flindent="0"
                    l-indent="0" r-indent="0"
                    %point;' >
...
<!LINK link3  h3    block [%times;bold"
                          %noindnt;"9pt 3pt"]
       ...                               >
```

Here, the link to be used for third-level headings uses three parameter entities and the default values of many of the attributes of the <(galley)block> element. Note, however, that only two of the parameter entities have been included in the link set declaration since the third one is automatically called within the %noindnt; parameter entity declaration. Also note that the quotation mark for the start of the bold attribute value must not be entered within the link set declaration since, in this case, it has been included in the declaration for the %times; parameter entity. On the other hand, the quote has not been included at the end of the declaration for %point;, so must be entered in the link set declaration. A further point to notice is how the alternative literal delimiters (**lita**) have been used to delimit the entity text where this contains embedded quotation marks.

NOTE: The above example is designed to show the maximum extent to which parameter entities might be used. It would be better practice to leave the quote preceding the face attribute (and the name of the preferred separation attribute) out of the entity declarations so that they must be entered in the link set declaration as this would make the link set declaration easier to interpret.

Entity declarations defined within the document type declaration subset of the document identified in the link type declaration as the source document type for the current link type declaration, can also be used within the link type declaration subset if they are appropriate, as can those defined in the base document type. If entity declarations of the same name occur in both the link type declaration and the document type declaration, however, the one in the link type declaration will have priority while the link is active.

Another short cut is to use a **name group** for the **associated element type** part of a source element specification in the link set declaration (or in the link attribute set declarations). For example, if text for glossary and term definitions is to have the same format, they could be declared as:

```
...
<!ATTLIST (gd|dd) align    (s|e|c|j)  j
                  consechy NUMBER    3          >
<!LINK  def-link  (gd|dd)  block [%times;roman"
                                 %noindnt;"3pt 3pt"]
        ...                                   >
```

Care must be taken, however, in using this technique. In particular, it is important to check that both the linked elements do actually use identical attributes for both the source and result elements. If different sets of attributes apply on either side of the link, this technique cannot be used.

Where a number of elements share the same output features these should be declared as the default values for relevant result element attributes. This will allow the attribute specification list to be omitted where the result element only requires these default values, giving a link set declaration of the form:

```
<!LINK linkname source-elements result-elements>
```

for example:

```
<!LINK link1   p     block >
```

Another useful short cut is to let the program imply the elements to which a link applies, and the relevant attribute values. The simplest way of doing this is to replace the details of the result element specification with the keyword #IMPLIED to give a link set declaration of the form:

```
<!LINK linkname element [attributes] #IMPLIED>
```

Here, the result of the link process will automatically be implied by the formatting program whenever the specified element is encountered, the optional link attribute specification associated with the source element specification defining the parameters to be passed to the program.

Alternatively, the program may be able to link all source elements to a specified result element using a set of attributes relevant to the link process, for example:

```
<!LINK linkset1 #IMPLIED block [textface= "Times roman"
                          display = "Swiss bold"
                          ptsize  = "9on10pt"
                          measure = "6inches"
                          lev1ind = "9pt"
                          lev3ind = "18pt"
                          lev3ind = "27pt"]>
```

It should be noted, however, that when used as a replacement for the source element name, the #IMPLIED keyword can be linked to only one result element.

Implicit links

The concept of implying links can be taken a stage further by the use of **implicit links**. When the LINK entries in the FEATURES clause of the SGML declaration contain the entry IMPLICIT YES, the result document type name at the start of the link type declaration can be replaced by the word #IMPLIED, no result element specifications being entered in the associated link set declarations. To see the implications of this, consider the following example:

```
<!LINKTYPE format textbook #IMPLIED
[<!ENTITY % list  "(p|note|li|it|h0|h1|h2|h3|q|lq|xmp|etc...)">
 <!ATTLIST %list; align    (s|e|c|j)  j
                  hyphens  NAME      English
                  consechy NUMBER    3
                  wordlims NUMBERS   "7 3 3"
                  family   NMTOKEN   "Times"
                  face     NAME      "roman"
                  ptsize   NUTOKEN   "10on12pt"
                  measure  NMTOKEN   "27pi"
                  flindent NMTOKEN   "0"
                  l-indent NUTOKEN   "0"
                  r-indent NUTOKEN   "0"
                  ...
                                                            >
        <!LINK #INITIAL  p    [flindent="18pt"]
                         note [l-indent="1pi" r-indent="1pi" face="italic"]
                         it   #USELINK link2 [l-indent="18pt" flindent="-13pt"]
                         h0   [ptsize="18on22pt" family="Univers"]
                         h1   [ptsize="14pt" family="Univers" face="bold"]
                         ...                                 >
        <!LINK link2     p    [l-indent="18pt"]
                         note [l-indent="18pt" r-indent="1pi" face="italic"]
                         xmp  [l-indent="2pi" justify="left"]
                         lq   [l-indent="2pi" r-indent="6pt" ptsize="9on10pt"]
                         ...                                 >
        ...                                                 ]>
```

Here, all that the document designer states is the names of the elements that are to be linked to a standard result element when the link is invoked and the parameters that are to be applied when the link is made.

One thing that should be noted here is that, when links are being set up for text formatting, only elements that can contain parsable data (indicated by #PCDATA in the associated model group or EMPTY where the text is generated by the program) need to be included in the list of source elements since only these elements contain text that can be processed. For implicit links, these source elements must all come from the document type identified by the **source document type name** entered immediately after the link type name.

Where style sheets are used to record the details of the parameters to be associated with each element, implicit links provide a natural route for linking elements to style sheets. As the following example shows, the name of the style sheet (e.g. chapter head) is the only attribute needed to control the link process:

```
<!LINKTYPE format textbook #IMPLIED
[<!ENTITY % list (p|note|li|it|h0|h1|h2|h3|q|lq|xmp|etc...) >
  <!ATTLIST %list; style    CDATA    "para"              >
  <!LINK #INITIAL  p
                   note [style="n"]
                   it   #USELINK link2 [style="list item"]
                   h0   [style="chapter head"]
                   h1   [style="main heading"]
                   ...                                    >
  <!LINK link2     p    [style="embedded para"]
                   note [style="embedded note"]
                   xmp  [style="embedded example"]
                   lq   [style="embedded quotation"]
                   ...                           >
  ...                                            ]>
```

In this case, the style sheet name, which is passed through to the text formatting routines, activates a predefined set of formatting instructions (the style sheet) which controls the appearance of the element's text. The formatter will automatically add any structure or coding required by the output device.

It should be noted, however, that implied links must always form the last link in a chain since you cannot use an implied structure as the source document for later explicit links that might, for example, paginate or impose the text.

Simple links

The final reduction in the process of implying links between document types involves the use of a **simple link**. When the LINK entries in the FEATURES clause of the SGML declaration contain the entry SIMPLE YES (followed by a number indicating the maximum number of such links permitted) the link type declaration can take the form:

```
<!LINKTYPE proof #SIMPLE #IMPLIED
[<!ATTLIST textbook status CDATA #FIXED "draft">]>
```

Here, the link type name is followed by two compulsory keywords and the link type declaration subset contains a single attribute definition list declaration, which defines certain *fixed* attributes associated with the base document type element.

Basically what the above declaration says is 'use the pre-defined set of links known as proof whenever the status attribute of the textbook element is set to draft'.

More than one simple link can be specified in a prolog. For example, the following additional link types could be declared for a textbook:

```
<!LINKTYPE review #SIMPLE #IMPLIED
[<!ATTLIST textbook status CDATA #FIXED "review">]>
<!LINKTYPE paginate #SIMPLE #IMPLIED
[<!ATTLIST textbook status CDATA #FIXED "final">]>
```

to specify the way the document should be processed before being sent for review or printing. With simple links, however, only the base document type can be linked to the implied structure and no further links in the chain are permitted.

Overriding link declarations

Link type declarations can be controlled from within the text by use of **link set use declarations**. (These have a very similar form to the short reference map use declarations explained in Chapter 4.) The general form of such declarations is:

```
<!USELINK setname linkname>
```

where USELINK is the default version of the keyword defined in the reference concrete syntax, setname is the name given to one of the link set declarations (<!LINK ...>) in the document's prolog and linkname is the link type name used to identify the link type declaration (<!LINKTYPE ...>) that contains the relevant link set declarations. A typical entry would be:

```
<!USELINK #INITIAL justify>
```

As with the USEMAP declaration, the special #EMPTY keyword can be used to switch off a link. To disable the justify link once it has been enabled, for example, you could enter the following declaration at any point in the text:

```
<!USELINK #EMPTY justify>
```

If the link set map is changed within an element by entry of a link set use declaration, the original link set can be restored by entering a declaration of the form:

```
<!USELINK #RESTORE linktype>
```

On seeing this markup declaration, the program will restore the link set that was associated with the current element prior to the preceding link set use declaration (e.g. the one that was current when the element began).

Using publicly declared link type declaration subsets

Where a publicly declared link type declaration subset is already known to the receiving system it can be invoked, like other publicly declared declaration sets, by use of a formal public identifier. In this case, the public identifier qualifies a link type declaration and so the public text class keyword used in the formal public identifier is LPD. A typical declaration might be:

```
<!LINKTYPE justify textbook galley
    "-//Addison-Wesley//LPD Justification links//EN">
```

If the publicly declared link set is to be extended by local definitions, which may override some of the definitions in the publicly declared set, the formal public identifier can be followed by a link type declaration subset. Typically, the prolog of a document using the example DTD shown in Appendix C and a modified version of the style sheet link type declaration shown above, will start:

```
<!DOCTYPE textbook PUBLIC "-//Addison-Wesley//DTD SGML:
An Author's Guide to the Standard Generalized Markup Language//EN"
    [<!ENTITY % AWacc PUBLIC
            "-//Addison-Wesley//ENTITIES Accented characters//EN">
    %AWacc; ]>
<!LINKTYPE format textbook #IMPLIED PUBLIC
            "-//Addison-Wesley//LPD Style sheet formatting//EN"
            [<!ATTLIST p style CDATA "indented para" ]          >
```

In this example, the default style for paragraphs has been specifically declared as indented para to override the value normally implied for this attribute in the public declaration. This locally defined default value will become the standard way of formatting paragraphs as no style attribute has been specified for paragraphs in the #INITIAL link of this set.

It should be noted that, as with DTDs, externally stored link declarations are added to the end of the local definitions, the first definition always taking precedence. To ensure the proper handling of entity references, all entities declared within the link are treated as preceding entities declared in the source DTD. This means that any entity declarations within the link with the same name as entities declared in the DTD will take precedence. Similarly, if the link declarations contain attributes which reference general entities not declared in the link type declaration or the link's source DTD, they will, if no default entity has been defined in the link's source DTD, be taken from the declarations within the base document set.

9.2.2 Associating entities and marked sections with concurrent document structures

Before we leave the subject of concurrent documents we need to consider briefly the relationships of entity references and marked sections to concurrent document structures.

Where the declaration associated with a general entity reference occurs in a document type definition other than the one used as the base document type declaration, the entity name must be qualified by a bracketed name group containing the name of the document type declaration in which the entity has been declared. For example, if the following entity occurred in the database (dbs) document type declaration:

```
<!ENTITY pno CDATA "Part No: AC 0-15-">
```

the relevant entity reference should be entered as &(dbs)pno; so that the program knows that the declaration it requires is part of the dbs document type declaration.

When marked sections (see Chapter 8) are being used within a document with more than one concurrent document structure, parameter entities used to store status keywords can be similarly qualified. This facility is useful when you need to restrict the application of a marked section. For example, when the following entity declaration has been entered in the appropriate concurrent document type definitions:

```
<!ENTITY % not "IGNORE" >
```

marked sections can be flagged to be ignored within certain document types by entry of a suitably qualified parameter entity, for example:

```
<![%(galley|pages)not; CDATA [
   Remember to add details about the winner here
]>
```

In this example, the marked section (which in this case contains an editorial note that appears on a separate line) will not be output when galley or page proofs are requested but will be included in all other versions of the document.

Where appropriate, link type names can also be used to qualify entity references. For example, if a processing instruction had been declared, as suggested in Chapter 8, as an entity of the form:

```
<!ENTITY italtext PI "[s10on12pt][m24pi][pri][i]">
```

in, say, the justify link type declaration, it can be activated by entry of an entity reference of the form &(justify)italtext; in the text. This tells the program that the parameters needed to process the text during justification should only be included within the document when the justify link is active. The typesetting parameters specified as part of the link process will then be (partly) overridden by the typesetting instructions entered within the processing instruction.

From the above examples it can be seen that SGML provides both document creators and document designers with a number of techniques for controlling how entered text is to be formatted. It should not, however, be thought that link statements and concurrent document types provide all the tools needed to produce paginated text. Fully paginated text requires a powerful text formatter, which will normally need to be set up for specific applications. The degree of interaction possible between the SGML document designer and the text formatter will depend on the skill of the system's designers in linking the formatter to the information stored as an integral part of the SGML document. As not all systems will be able to process links, users of SGML systems should ensure that they know the capabilities of the systems on which their documents will be processed before making use of these powerful facilities.

One final word of warning. Not all SGML features can be used within concurrent document structures. In particular, those SGML features that may only be used within the base document type, such as empty start-tags and net-enabling start-tags, cannot be used within concurrent document types. Similarly, care must be taken to ensure that notation names associated with entities or attribute lists are declared in each of the DTDs with which the entities are associated. Since such techniques are principally associated with text entry rather than text processing, however, they should not limit the use of concurrent document structures. Provided you restrict their use to text entry within the base document type you will not run into any problems.

10

Altering the Concrete Syntax

Where text entry or document processing is being performed on systems that are not based on the International Reference Version (IRV) character set defined in ISO 646, some alteration to the SYNTAX clause of the SGML declaration will be required. Where such changes have taken place, the concrete syntax is said to be a **variant concrete syntax**. All documents produced using a variant concrete syntax will require a certain degree of interpretation before they can be processed by an SGML parser that conforms to the reference concrete syntax defined in ISO 8879.

There are three basic ways of specifying a variant concrete syntax within a document:

(1) by requesting, in the SYNTAX clause of the SGML declaration, a **public concrete syntax** that is itself a variant concrete syntax;

(2) by using the SWITCHES option to modify the reference concrete syntax (or another publicly declared syntax); and

(3) by completely redefining the SYNTAX clause in the SGML declaration.

10.1 Using publicly declared variant concrete syntaxes

If the variant syntax required is known to all systems that will be used to process a document, it can be specified in the SGML declaration by entry of a public concrete syntax declaration of the form:

```
SYNTAX PUBLIC "public identifier"
```

225

Where FORMAL YES has been specified in the FEATURES clause of the SGML declaration the public identifier must be a formal public identifier (see Chapter 4). Typically, this will result in the SYNTAX clause having the form:

```
SYNTAX PUBLIC "ISO 8879-1986//SYNTAX Multicode Basic//EN"
```

10.1.1   The SWITCHES option

Where the variant concrete syntax required varies only slightly from that of the reference concrete syntax or another publicly declared concrete syntax, it may be possible to use the SWITCHES option associated with the public concrete syntax production in ISO 8879 to avoid having to define a complete SYNTAX clause.

The SWITCHES option allows specific pairs of characters within the declared syntax to be switched. For example, if the only difference between the reference concrete syntax and the required variant concrete syntax was the fact that the position of the square brackets and the curly brackets had been switched, the SYNTAX clause could be defined as:

```
SYNTAX PUBLIC    "ISO 8879-1986//SYNTAX Reference//EN"
         SWITCHES 91 123
                  93 125
```

Here, the codes defined in positions 91 and 93 (the square brackets) in the reference concrete syntax have been switched with those in positions 123 and 125 (the curly brackets).

The one restriction placed on the use of the SWITCHES option is that the standard alphanumeric characters (codes 48-57, 65-90 and 97-122) cannot be switched (otherwise names may not be detected).

It should be noted that not all parsers support the SWITCHES option. The system declaration (see Chapter 11) should be checked to ensure that the option is supported on both local and receiving systems before it is used.

10.2   Declaring a new variant concrete syntax ─────────

As was explained briefly in Chapter 3, the SYNTAX clause of the SGML declaration consists of eight main sections, which define:

● the numbers of any codes that are to be ignored because they are control or other non-SGML characters rather than data characters (**shunned character number identification**);

- the **character set description** for the **syntax-reference character set**, consisting of a **base character set** (BASESET) declaration and a **described character set portion** (DESCSET);

- codes that represent functions recognized by the parser (**function character identification**);

- the **naming rules** to be applied when defining tag and entity names;

- the markup delimiters required by the syntax (**delimiter set**);

- naming conventions to be used within markup declarations (**reserved name use**); and

- the **quantity set** required for the document.

The start of each section of the SYNTAX clause is identified by entry of one of SGML's **reserved names**. Within the SGML declaration these names, and all other declarations, must be entered using the IRV code set defined in ISO 646 (see Table 3.1) since any changes to this default character set that are declared within the SYNTAX clause will not take effect until the end of the SGML declaration has been detected (see Chapter 11).

Each part of the syntax declaration must be separated from its neighbours by at least one valid SGML **parameter separator** (see Chapter 6). Within the SGML declaration parameter separators can be:

- a separator character, such as a space, record start or record end code, or the Tab code defined for the reference concrete syntax; or

- an SGML comment, bracketed by pairs of hyphens.

10.2.1 Shunned characters

Shunned characters are characters that do not form part of the data entered within the document. There are two types of character that may need to be 'shunned' in an SGML document:

(1) **control characters** that tell the program how to format, transmit or interpret data, and

(2) **non-SGML characters** that never occur in text (but which can occur in non-SGML entities – see Chapter 4).

Not all codes defined as shunned characters are, however, ignored during processing. Codes which have been identified as representing SGML functions will retain the purpose declared in the FUNCTION section of the SYNTAX clause (see Section 10.2.3), irrespective of the fact they have been declared as shunned characters. Other, unassigned, shunned characters will be ignored by an SGML parser though.

The SHUNCHAR section of the SYNTAX clause can take one of three forms:

SHUNCHAR NONE *or*

SHUNCHAR n1 n2 ... *or*

SHUNCHAR CONTROLS n1 n2 ...

The first of these forms shows that the document contains no characters that need to be shunned by the parser. For the second form, the decimal value of each code to be shunned is entered after the reserved name SHUNCHAR, with at least one space or alternative parameter separator code preceding each number.

The most common form of shunned character number identification, however, is the third form, where the reserved name CONTROLS precedes the list of shunned characters. The inclusion of this reserved name tells the SGML parser that any code defined by the system as a control character should be added to the following list of shunned characters (which may be blank). This means that the system can be sure that any code it needs to control the processing of data will be passed through the SGML parser without alteration.

10.2.2   The syntax-reference character set

The **syntax-reference character set** defined in the SYNTAX clause of the SGML declaration must contain a coded representation of each significant SGML character. A character is considered to be a significant SGML character if it is (or could be) used in a markup declaration within the document. This includes all valid name characters, markup delimiters (including short reference delimiters), codes declared to be function characters (including record start and end codes and the space code) and those special characters allowed in minimum data literals within declarations (e.g. '()+-,./:= and ?).

The syntax-reference character set contains one or more two-part **character set descriptions**. The first part of each character set desciption defines, in human readable form, the **base character set** used as a reference source for part or all of the character set. The second part of the character set description consists of a formal description of the role allocated to each code used within the syntax in the form of a **described character set portion** statement.

The base character set description consists of the reserved name BASESET followed by a **public identifier** indicating the name of a reference character set. As explained in Chapter 4, public identifiers are names agreed between users as sufficient to identify data known to both the receiving and transmitting systems. Public identifiers must be entered within literal delimiters and, within the SGML declaration, can only consist of upper- and lower-case characters, numbers, spaces (or record start and end codes) and the special characters listed above (e.g. decimal values 10, 13, 32, 39–41, 43–58, 61, 63, 65–90 and 97–122). A typical privately-agreed entry might be:

```
BASESET "Linotron Code Set"
```

Where the FEATURES clause at the end of the SGML declaration contains the statement FORMAL YES, the public identifier must be a formal public identifier (see 'Formal public identifiers' in Section 4.3.2). In this case, the public text class keyword must be CHARSET. Where the character set has been defined by ISO a typical entry will have the form:

```
BASESET "ISO 646-1983//CHARSET International Reference Version (IRV)//ESC 2/5 4/0"
```

Formal declarations can also be used to request agreed code sets identified by registered or unregistered public identifiers such as:

```
BASESET "+//IBM//CHARSET EBCDIC//ESC 2/5 4/0"
```

and:

```
BASESET "-//Quorum//CHARSET CORA//ESC 2/5 4/0"
```

It should be remembered that, for all non-ISO coding schemes, the public text designating sequence entry at the end of the formal declaration should read ESC 2/5 4/0 since this special sequence will allow the SGML parser to return to its standard coding scheme at the end of the document.

The base character set declaration must be followed, after a valid parameter separator, by the described character set portion of the character set description. It is this part of the SYNTAX clause that defines the role of the characters used to markup the document. The start of the described character set portion is identified by the reserved name DESCSET.

The described character set portion of the character set description consists of a set of **character descriptions**, each of which is preceded by at least one parameter separator (e.g. a space or Tab code). These character descriptions describe the purpose of specific codes within the document or identify groups of codes that can be mapped to a sequence of characters defined within the previously specified base character set. Each character description consists of:

- a **described set character number** indicating the initial decimal value of the code sequence being described;

- a figure indicating the **number of characters** the description applies to; and

- either a **base set character number** indicating the equivalent character number(s) in the base character set *or* a **minimum literal** describing the role of the character *or* the reserved name UNUSED to indicate that the character is a non-SGML character that does not occur within the document or its markup.

In the reference concrete syntax, the described character set portion of the document character set consists of the single entry:

```
DESCSET 0 128 0
```

This description tells potential users that, in the reference concrete syntax, the 128 characters starting from decimal value 0 in the described character set are to have the same role as the 128 characters starting from position 0 in the character set identified as the base character set (i.e. in the International Reference Version code set described in the 1983 version of ISO 646).

NOTE: I have seen DTDs where the 128-character base character set described in ISO 646 has been associated with the entry DESCSET 0 256 0. *While this is not, strictly speaking, illegal it is, to say the least, ambiguous as it does not assign specific characters to codes in the range 128–255. It would be better if these codes were explicitly excluded by use of an entry of the form:*

```
DESCSET   0   128   0
         128  128  UNUSED
```

Defining an alternative character set (EBCDIC)

To change the reference concrete syntax to the International version of IBM's EBCDIC coding scheme, without changing the base character set, the following syntax-reference character set description could be used:

```
BASESET "ISO 646-1983//CHARSET International Reference
         Version (IRV)//ESC 2/5 4/0"
   DESCSET 0 1    0
          1  4    UNUSED
          5  1    "PT"
          6  2    UNUSED
          8  1    "GE"    -- Certain countries only --
          9  3    UNUSED
         12  2    12      -- CR in certain countries only--
         14  3    UNUSED
         17  1    "SBA"
```

```
18  1   "EUA"
19  1   "IC"
20  1   UNUSED
21  1   "NL"    -- New Line --
22  3   UNUSED
25  1   "EM"
26  2   UNUSED
28  1   "DUP"
29  1   "SF"
30  1   "FM"
31  9   UNUSED
40  1   "SA"
41  1   "SFE"
42  2   UNUSED
44  1   "MF"    -- Certain countries only --
45  15  UNUSED
60  1   "RA"    -- Certain countries only --
62  1   UNUSED
63  1   "SUB"
64  1   32
65  9   UNUSED
74  1   91      --[, country specific --
75  1   46
76  1   60
77  1   40
78  1   43
79  1   33      -- !, country specific --
80  1   38
81  9   UNUSED
90  1   93      -- ], country specific --
91  1   36      -- $, country specific --
92  1   42
93  1   41
94  1   59
95  1   94      -- ^, country specific --
96  1   96      -- ', country specific --
97  1   47
98  8   UNUSED
106 1   124     -- |, country specific --
107 1   44
108 1   37
109 1   95      -- _, country specific --
110 2   62
112 10  UNUSED
122 1   58
123 1   35      -- #, country specific --
124 1   64      -- @, country specific --
125 1   39
126 1   61
```

```
127  1    34      -- ", country specific --
128  1    UNUSED
129  9    97
138  7    UNUSED
145  9    106
154  7    UNUSED
161  1    45      -- -, country specific --
162  8    115
170 22    UNUSED
192  1    123     -- {, country specific --
193  9    65
202  6    UNUSED
208  1    125     -- }, country specific --
209  9    74
218  6    UNUSED
224  1    92      -- \, country specific --
225  1    UNUSED
226  8    83
234  6    UNUSED
240 10    48
250  5    UNUSED
255  1    "EO"    -- Certain countries only --
```

As can be seen from the above description, EBCDIC uses a wider range of values than ISO 646 or ASCII, being based on an 8-bit code rather than a 7-bit code. Though EBCDIC has 256 code positions available to it, only 94 are actually used for characters, a further 19 being defined as EBCDIC control codes, leaving a total of 143 codes being declared as UNUSED within the described character set portion of the character set description.

Because, within EBCDIC, most of the control codes differ from the control codes used by ISO 646, many of the initial entries in the above description only deal with a single character. Where the control code exists in both ISO 646 and EBCDIC, the third column contains the decimal value of the code within the base character set (ISO 646 in this case). Where the code is one of the control codes available only within EBCDIC, the entry in the third column consists of a delimited literal that contains the name assigned by IBM to the control code being described.

The printable characters used in the International version of EBCDIC are the same as those used in ISO 646, though the positions in which they occur are different. In many cases, though, similar sequences of characters can be identified in both sets, thus reducing the number of entries required in the described character set portion of the character set description.

Where required, comments have been added to the declaration to describe the role of the EBCDIC characters further, or to identify positions where characters may differ from those shown on some national layouts.

Multiple code sets

Where multiple code sets are required within a document, one or more codes will be allocated a role that controls which code set is being used at a particular point in the document. For example, if the conventions defined in ISO 2022 are being used to increase the available character set, the character set description could be extended to the form used for the **multicode basic concrete syntax** in Annex D of ISO 8879:

```
BASESET   "ISO 646-1983//CHARSET International Reference
          Version (IRV)//ESC 2/5 4/0"
DESCSET    0  14  0
          14   1  "LS1 in ISO 2022"
          15   1  "LS0 in ISO 2022"
          16 112  16
         128  14  UNUSED
         142   1  "SS2 in ISO 2022"
         143   1  "SS3 in ISO 2022"
         144 112  UNUSED
```

In this case, codes 14 and 15 are codes which lock the shift state to state 1 or 0 (the default state), respectively, while codes 142 and 143 are used to access single characters in shift states 2 and 3. (These roles are assigned in the FUNCTION section of the SYNTAX clause, as described in the next section.) The 112 codes starting at position 16 in ISO 646 are retained as valid character codes within the document, other codes in the range 0 to 255 being treated as non-SGML codes.

NOTE: An example of the use of multiple character set descriptions is given in Chapter 11.

Before leaving the subject of concrete syntax character set definition, one word of warning needs to be given. Because of the way character sets and code sets are defined in Section 4 of ISO 8879, no gaps are allowed *within* the syntax-reference character set. This means that the number in the first column of each entry must always match the sum of the entries in the first two entries in the preceding column.

10.2.3   Function characters

The **function character identification** section of the SYNTAX clause of the SGML declaration defines the codes allocated to three compulsory function characters (those for the record start, record end and space characters) and any number of other additional function characters required by the SGML parser.

The start of the section is indicated by entry of the reserved name FUNCTION. This must be followed, after one or more valid SGML parameter separators, by the letters RE, a second parameter separator and the (decimal) **character number** of the code used as the record end code, for example:

```
FUNCTION RE 10
```

The next two entries similarly define the codes used to represent the record start and space codes, for example:

```
FUNCTION RE 10 RS 13 SPACE 32
```

Once these three compulsory function codes have been defined any additional function characters used within the document can be declared. For each such character you must specify:

- the name to be used to identify the **added function**,
- the **function class** to which the function belongs, and
- the **character number** of the code to be used to request the function.

The function classes recognized by SGML are:

- SEPCHAR for codes to be recognized as valid SGML **separator characters**;
- MSOCHAR for **markup-scan-out characters** that suppress the recognition of SGML markup until a valid markup-scan-in character or an entity end code (see Chapter 6) is received;
- MSICHAR for **markup-scan-in characters** that re-enable recognition of SGML markup after receipt of a markup-scan-out character;
- MSSCHAR for **markup-scan-suppress characters** that suppress the recognition of markup for the immediately following character; and
- FUNCHAR for otherwise inert **function characters** (i.e. one that does not affect the parsing of an SGML document).

Within the reference concrete syntax only one added function is defined, that for the Tab code (decimal value 9 in ISO 646). This is defined as a valid SGML separator by thc following addition to the FUNCTION section of the SYNTAX clause:

```
TAB SEPCHAR 9
```

The three markup suppression function classes are often used where multiple code sets are required within a document. For example, if the shift codes defined in ISO 2022 are to be used to call the G1, G2 and G3 character sets associated with the multicode basic concrete syntax, the following additional function codes could be defined:

```
LS1  MSOCHAR   14 --Locking shift 1 (G1 set)--
LS0  MSICHAR   15 --Locking shift 0 (return to G0 set)--
ESC  MSOCHAR   27 --Escape (used to call other code sets)--
SS2  MSSCHAR  142 --Single shift two (G2 set)--
SS3  MSSCHAR  143 --Single shift three (G3 set)--
```

These definitions indicate that:

- code 14 will lock in code set G1, suppressing markup until such time as a markup-scan-in character is received;
- code 15 restores the basic G0 code set, allowing markup scanning to begin again;
- code 27 is the Escape code, which may mark the start of a sequence of codes calling an alternative code set (this code also suppresses markup recognition until an MSICHAR function code is encountered);
- code 142 causes the program to take the next character (only) from the alternative G2 character set (markup recognition needs to suppressed to prevent the second part of the two code sequence from being treated as a markup character); and
- code 143 similarly calls characters from the alternative G3 character set (again markup recognition needs to be suppressed for the second part of the code sequence).

It should be noted that, if the MSOCHAR option is used for any added function, at least one MSICHAR definition *must* be present in the same set to ensure that users can return to the original character set so that markup can be entered.

The MSSCHAR option can be very useful for suppressing markup recognition where the text contains strings of characters which are also used as markup tags. For example, if the following entry was added to the function character identification section of the SYNTAX clause:

```
SUP MSSCHAR 48 -- a sign suppresses markup --
```

a markup tag, such as ‹p›, can be entered in the text as a‹p› rather than as a CDATA marked section. Because the a sign (decimal 48) has been reassigned as a markup suppression code, the following less than sign will not be recognized as an SGML delimiter and will be passed, with the rest of the tag's characters, through the system as normal character data.

NOTE: The FUNCHAR option only needs to be used in the SYNTAX clause of the SGML declaration when the system requires special function characters to be included in the document at points at which they have particular significance to the SGML parser. Annex E of ISO 8879 illustrates how this technique can be used to produce a device-independent multicode concrete syntax.

Provided that the SCOPE clause of the SGML declaration reads SCOPE DOCUMENT (see Chapter 11), the names of added functions can be used as a qualifier for character references within document type declarations, as well as being used within the text. In both cases, the character references have the form &#abc;, where abc is the name allocated to the added function.

10.2.4   Naming rules

The **naming rules** defined within the SYNTAX clause of the SGML declaration allow users to extend the range of characters that can be used to create SGML names. This section of the declaration also controls whether entity and element names will or will not be case-specific.

Two sets of naming characters are recognized by SGML:

(1)   **name start characters** that can be used as the first character of a name, and

(2)   **name characters** that can be used at any position other than the first character of a name.

In both cases these sets are divided into two groups defining:

(1)   the lower-case form of the character, and

(2)   the associated upper-case form.

As will be shown later, it is very important that these two groupings be kept constantly in mind as they affect the way in which naming characters can be used.

Certain characters are automatically defined as naming characters by SGML. These are shown in Table 10.1. Of these characters, only the upper-case and lower-case letters are permitted as name start characters. One unfortunate consequence of this preassignment of roles is that, because SGML forbids preassigned characters being allocated to other roles, digits cannot be defined as valid name start characters. Consequently, all attribute values defined by use of the keywords NAME, NAMES, ID, IDREF or IDREFS must start with a letter or one of the alternative name start characters defined in the SYNTAX clause. (Because name tokens can start with any name character this rule does not apply to attributes defined using the NMTOKEN or NMTOKENS keywords.)

Table 10.1   Default naming characters.

Role	Characters	ISO 646 values
Lower-case letters	a–z	97–122
Upper-case letters	A–Z	65–90
Digits	0–9	48–57

      The start of the naming rules of the SYNTAX clause is identified by entry of the reserved name NAMING. This is followed by six compulsory entries defining:

(1)   additional lower-case name start characters (LCNMSTRT),

(2)   additional upper-case name start characters (UCNMSTRT),

(3)   additional lower-case name characters (LCNMCHAR),

(4)   additional upper-case name characters (UCNMCHAR),

(5)   whether reserved, element and attribute names can be entered in either case (NAMECASE GENERAL), and

(6)   whether entity names can be entered in either case (ENTITY).

Each of these clauses must be present even if no extra characters are to be added to the document (i.e. an empty list must be specified if the default characters are the only ones to be used.)

      Within each of the four lists of additional naming characters the following codes must not appear:

- upper-case or lower-case letters (codes 65–90 and 97–122),
- digits (codes 48–57), and
- function codes defined in the reference concrete syntax (codes 9, 10, 13 and 32).

Care should also be taken to ensure that none of the codes declared as valid SGML delimiters in the delimiter set specification that follows this naming specification is included in the set of valid name characters.

      The list of lower-case name start characters can be extended by entering the required codes as a delimited **parameter literal** after the reserved word LCNMSTART. The required characters can be entered as:

- the equivalent ISO 646 code (not that defined in the syntax-reference character set as this does not come into force until the end of the SGML declaration), and
- as character references (numbers entered using codes 48 to 57 for 0 to 9, preceded by codes 38 and 35 for & and #, and followed by code 59 for ;).

A consequence of this is that, if the code set has been extended beyond the 128 character set defined in ISO 646, codes with values above 128 can only be defined by entry of character references such as .

In the reference concrete syntax no additional name start characters have been defined, so the first entry reads:

```
NAMING LCNMSTRT ""
```

The default list of valid name start characters can be extended by entry of a string such as:

```
NAMING LCNMSTRT "a$&#129;"
```

The list of additional lower-case name start characters must be matched by a list of valid upper-case name start characters. For each character listed in the lower-case set, a matching upper-case entry must be stated or the lower-case entry must be repeated. This means that the list for the reference concrete syntax must be empty, to match that of the lower-case set, giving it the form:

```
UCNMSTRT ""
```

while three characters must be entered in the upper-case name start character set matching the extended set of lower-case characters defined above, for example:

```
UCNMSTRT "a$&#193;"
```

The list of name characters that can occur at positions other than the first position in a name can be extended to include any non-alphanumeric character not defined as a name start character. In the reference concrete syntax two additional characters have been defined (for both the upper-case and lower-case sets) by entry of the statements:

```
LCNMCHAR "-."
UCNMCHAR "-."
```

If this set is to be extended, rather than altered, it is important to remember that the hyphen and full stop must be included in the revised list, for example:

```
LCNMCHAR "-.,/&#163;"
UCNMCHAR "-.,/&#163;"
```

As with the list of additional name start characters, the number and sequence of additional upper-case name characters must exactly match those of the associated lower-case entries.

It is the last two naming rule entries that control how SGML parsers use the upper- and lower-case name character lists. In the reference concrete syntax these entries read:

NAMECASE GENERAL YES ENTITY NO

This tells you that, for general names (such as those used for reserved names, keywords, declaration names, element names, attribute names and any attribute values defined to be name tokens, number tokens or id references), any letter listed as a lower-case character is to be replaced by the equivalent character in the matching upper-case string before its validity is checked. By contrast, substitution is not permitted for names used in entity declarations or references, which means that variations such as &ISO; and &iso; can be occur in the same document.

In most cases, the default settings for the NAMECASE part of the naming rules will be the one required. Document designers are recommended not to change these settings without careful thought to the consequences. In particular, it should be noted that switching off GENERAL case sensitivity may make it difficult to deal with mixed shift tags that would otherwise be valid. (It should always be remembered that users may forget to enter the correct shift state before keying tags.)

10.2.5   *Alternative delimiters*

The **delimiter set** specification in the SYNTAX clause of the SGML declaration allows users to:

- redefine the codes used as markup delimiters, and
- extend or completely redefine the short reference sequences recognized by the parser.

While any sequence of codes *can* be defined as a delimiter, the use of alphabetic name start characters and digits is deprecated. In particular, the use of the character B within short references is restricted to that of a blank sequence identifier (as will be shown in the next section).

The recognition of SGML delimiters is formally restricted within the standard to those modes in which the delimiter is valid. In particular, each delimiter string must be part of the same entity if it is to be recognized by the parser (though the first character of the string can be entered as a named character reference if the character is one of the function characters declared in the SYNTAX clause of the SGML declaration).

NOTE: Details of delimiter recognition modes are given in Chapter 12.

Each delimiter defined in the SGML declaration must differ from every other delimiter that can be recognized in the same mode. The safest way to ensure that this is so is to make each delimiter different, but in practice only those delimiters that identify the start of a declaration, element or entity need to differ since, once the program has recognized the start of the delimited sequence, it will always look for the correct end delimiter.

The default form of the delimiter set specification, as used in the reference concrete syntax, is:

```
DELIM GENERAL SGMLREF SHORTREF SGMLREF
```

This defines the required **general delimiters** set as the SGML reference set shown in Table 3.2, and the set of **short reference delimiters** as the SGML reference set shown in Table 3.3.

General delimiters

To change the default set of general delimiters, the name of the delimiters to be amended (as shown in the second column of Table 3.2) and a parameter literal defining the character(s) to replace it should be entered after the GENERAL SGMLREF entry, for example:

```
DELIM GENERAL SGMLREF STAGO "["
                       ETAGO "[/"
                       TAGC  "]"
                       LIT   "''"
```

The last of the above entries illustrates one area of potential confusion in the definition of delimiter tags. Because the SYNTAX clause does not take effect until after the SGML declaration has been completely read and interpreted by the SGML parser, the quotation mark (decimal value 34) remains the LIT delimiter within the SGML declaration. Within that part of the document identified by the SCOPE clause of the SGML declaration, however, literal delimiters must be entered as pairs of apostrophes to conform with the revised delimiter definition given above.

When defining new delimiters it is important to remember that:

- character references can be used to define codes with values greater than 127,
- delimiter roles that are not redefined in this section take the values assigned in the reference concrete syntax, and
- only the first character of a delimiter can be entered as a named character reference (any other function codes in the sequence must be generated by the keyboard or entered as numbered character references).

Short reference delimiters

When altering the list of valid short reference delimiters two options are available for the reserved name following the initial SHORTREF section identifier:

- SGMLREF where the delimiter sequences that follow the reserved name are to be added to the default set defined for the reference concrete syntax (as shown in Table 3.3), and

- NONE where the entered delimiters are to replace the default set completely.

Each short reference delimiter added to the selected default set is defined in the form of a parameter literal, that is as a string of codes or character references between matched pairs of literal delimiters, which must be the apostrophe or quotation mark codes defined in ISO 646. Each parameter literal entered must be preceded by one or more spaces, or another valid parameter separator.

As with the parameter literals used to declare general delimiters, the codes entered must be the reference concrete syntax representation of the codes required, not the revised allocation declared in the described character set portion of the syntax-reference character set description. Character references can be used where necessary.

While short reference delimiters consisting of more than one code are deprecated by the standard, unless the string used represents a common keyboarding convention or coding sequence, the use of multiple character short references based on function codes can be very useful. A typical sequence might consist of two consecutive sets of record start and record end codes, for example:

```
SHORTREF SGMLREF "&#RE;&#RS;&#RE;&#RS;"
```

If multiple code short reference delimiters are to be defined, it should be remembered that only the longest delimiter string starting with a particular character sequence will be recognized at any point, even when the longer delimiter is not currently mapped to an entity. For example, if ## and # have both been defined as short reference delimiter strings, but the current map only contains a mapping for #, this mapping would not be used for the sequence ##, which would be treated as an unmapped short reference rather than as two occurrences of a mapped short reference.

The use of strings of characters that have previously been defined as general delimiters within a short reference delimiter is also deprecated within the standard because, once recognized as part of a valid – if unmapped – short reference, the same characters cannot then be recognized as part of a general markup delimiter. In particular, care should be taken to ensure that:

- none of the strings defined as the opening sequences for general delimiters in the reference concrete syntax are used as short reference delimiters unless they have been redefined in the preceding list of general delimiter changes, and
- that none of the strings defined as opening sequences for general delimiters match the default short reference strings when SGMLREF has been entered immediately after SHORTREF.

One special SGML feature that only applies to short reference delimiters is the concept of **blank sequences**. A blank sequence is an uninterrupted sequence of space or separator characters. The character B is used to indicate a blank sequence in a short reference delimiter. If only one B is entered the blank sequence can be of any length. If more than one B is entered the *minimum* number of space and/or separator characters that can occur in the string is defined by the number of Bs entered (with no upper limit). For example, the short reference delimiter defined in the reference concrete syntax set shown in Table 3.3 as B&#RE; can be used to identify any sequence of space, Tab or other specified separator characters that occurs at the end of a record, while the sequence BB&#RE; would only be recognized as a short reference if two or more spaces or Tab codes preceded the record end code.

When looking for short reference sequences, however, the program will recognize any direct references to a space or separator character before looking for blank sequences. The effect of this is that, although a sequence such as BBB will take precedence over the shorter BB sequence, a single Tab code will take precedence over both if &#TAB; has been defined as a short reference in the same document.

Only one blank sequence can occur in any short reference string. This blank sequence cannot be immediately preceded or followed by a reference to a character that could form part of a blank sequence (e.g. &#SPACE; or &#TAB;) as the program would be unable to distinguish between such a string and one containing one more B.

10.2.6 Reserved names

The **reserved name use** section of the SYNTAX clause can be used to change many of the reserved names used by SGML. The start of this part of the SGML declaration is indicated by entry of the reserved words NAMES SGMLREF. This indicates that, initially, the reference set of SGML reserved names, as defined in ISO 8879, applies. If no other entries occur in this clause all markup declarations must use these default names.

To alter one or more of the standard reserved names shown in Table 10.2 (i.e. those without a dagger) simply enter the name to be changed followed, after a space or other valid parameter separator, by the name you wish to use within the following document. There is no limit to the number of changes you can make, but each alteration must be separated from its predecessor or from the NAMES SGMLREF sequence by one or more spaces, or another valid parameter separator.

As usual within the SGML declaration, each existing and revised name must be entered using the ISO 646 character set defined in the reference concrete syntax. Where the new name requires a character outside the normal (ASCII) character set range the relevant code should be entered as a character reference.

Because the changes detailed in this clause only take effect when the end of the SGML declaration is recognized, reserved names that only occur within the SGML declaration or the system declaration (see Chapter 11) cannot be changed within the NAMES section of the SYNTAX declaration. However, care must be taken to ensure that any replacement names do not match existing reference reserved names, including those that cannot be changed, and that no other entry in the list of altered names is allocated the same replacement name. One effect of this limitation is that the default names of delimiters roles, and quantity set and capacity set names, cannot be used as replacement reserved names. (Such 'unalterable' names are indicated by a dagger in Table 10.2.)

Where a reserved name is used for more than one role it will be listed more than once in Table 10.2. It should be noted that any changes made to a name with multiple entries will apply to all situations where the reserved name might apply (except those flagged by a dagger, which can only be defined using the reference concrete syntax).

SGML reserved names will normally only need to be changed when documents are being prepared in a language other than English. In such circumstances commonly used reserved names, such as ENTITY, ELEMENT and ATTLIST may be redefined. A typical entry might be:

```
NAMES SGMLREF   ELEMENT   ELEMENTO
          ·     ENTITY    ENTIDAD
                ATTLIST   ATRLISTA
```

Before redefining reserved names, however, it is advisable to check if the standards authority for the country concerned has already defined a set of names suitable for use within that country since, wherever possible, these names should be adopted for the sake of uniformity. It should be noted, with respect to this, that little time will be saved by redefining the less commonly used reserved names (unless the codes required are not available on local keyboards) so many countries will retain the standard reserved words for many names.

Table 10.2 Reserved names used in SGML.

Reserved name	Role
AND	And connector†
ANY	Any content model
APPINFO	Application-specific information identifier†
ATTCAP	Attribute capacity indicator†
ATTCHCAP	Attribute character capacity indicator†
ATTCNT	Attribute count limit†
ATTLIST	Attribute definition list identifier
ATTSPLEN	Attribute specification length limit†
AVGRPCAP	Attribute value capacity indicator†
BASESET	Base character set identifier†
BSEQLEN	Blank sequence length limit†
CAPACITY	Public text class identifier
CAPACITY	Capacity set identifier†
CAPACITY	Capacity error report indicator†
CDATA	Status keyword (for marked section)
CDATA	Character data (for entity)
CDATA	Character data (in declared content)
CDATA	Character data (for attribute value)
CHANGES	Concrete syntax changes identifier†
CHARSET	Public text class identifier
CHARSET	Document character set identifier†
COM	Comment start or end sequence†
CONCUR	Concurrent document feature use indicator†
CONREF	Content reference attribute value
CONTROLS	Shun system control characters†
CRO	Character reference open sequence†
CURRENT	Current value (for attribute value)
DATATAG	Data tag feature use indicator†
DEFAULT	Default entity name
DELIM	Delimiter set identifier†
DELIMLEN	Delimiter length indicator†
DESCSET	Described character set portion identifier†
DOCTYPE	Document type declaration identifier
DOCUMENT	Public text class identifier
DOCUMENT	Syntax scope indicator†

† Must be entered using reference concrete syntax – cannot be redefined.

Table 10.2 (cont.)

Reserved name	Role
DSC	Declaration subset close sequence†
DSO	Declaration subset open sequence†
DTAGLEN	Data tag length limit†
DTD	Public text class identifier
DTEMPLEN	Data template length limit†
DTGC	Data tag group close sequence†
DTGO	Data tag group open sequence†
ELEMCAP	Element capacity indicator†
ELEMENT	Element declaration identifier
ELEMENTS	Public text class identifier
EMPTY	Empty content model indicator
EMPTY	Empty short reference map indicator
EMPTY	Empty link set indicator
ENDTAG	Bracketed end-tag entity
ENTCAP	Entity capacity indicator†
ENTCHCAP	Entity characters capacity indicator†
ENTITIES	Public text class identifier
ENTITIES	General entity name list (for attribute values)
ENTITY	Entity declaration identifier
ENTITY	General entity name (for attribute value)
ENTITY	Entity name case rules†
ENTLVL	Entity nesting level limit†
ERO	Entity reference open sequence†
ETAGO	End-tag open sequence†
EXCLUDE	Exclusion error report indicator†
EXGRPCAP	Exclusion/inclusion group capacity indicator†
EXNMCAP	Exclusion/inclusion name capacity indicator†
EXPLICIT	Explicit link feature use indicator†
FEATURES	Feature use identifier†
FIXED	Fixed entry (for attribute value)
FORMAL	Formal public identifiers indicator†
FORMAL	Formal public identifier error report indicator†
FUNCHAR	Inert function character†
FUNCTION	Function character set identifier†
GENERAL	General naming case rules†
GENERAL	General delimiters identifier†

† Must be entered using reference concrete syntax – cannot be redefined.

Table 10.2 (cont.)

Reserved name	Role
GENERAL	General validation feature indicator†
GRPC	Group close sequence†
GRPCAP	Group capacity indicator†
GRPCNT	Group token count limit†
GRPGTCNT	Grand total of group tokens limit†
GRPLVL	Group nesting level limit†
GRPO	Group open sequence†
ID	Unique identifier (for attribute value)
IDCAP	ID capacity indicator†
IDLINK	ID link set identifier
IDREF	Identifier reference (for attribute value)
IDREFCAP	ID reference capacity indicator†
IDREFS	Identifier reference list (for attribute values)
IGNORE	Status keyword (for marked section)
IMPLICIT	Implicit link feature use indicator†
IMPLIED	Implied attribute value
IMPLIED	Implied link type indicator
INCLUDE	Status keyword (for marked section)
INITIAL	Initial link identifier
INSTANCE	Syntax scope indicator†
LCNMCHAR	Lower-case name character†
LCNMSTRT	Lower-case name start character†
LINK	Link set declaration identifier
LINK	Link feature use indicator†
LINKTYPE	Link type declaration identifier
LIT	Literal start or end sequence†
LITA	Alternative literal start or end sequence†
LITLEN	Literal length limit†
LKNMCAP	Link/document type name capacity indicator†
LKSETCAP	Link set capacity indicator†
LPD	Public text class identifier
MAPCAP	Short reference map capacity indicator†
MD	Bracketed markup declaration entity
MDC	Markup declaration close sequence†
MDO	Markup declaration open sequence†
MINIMIZE	Markup minimization feature identifier†
MINUS	Exclusion indicator sequence†

† Must be entered using reference concrete syntax – cannot be redefined.

Table 10.2   (cont.)

Reserved name	Role
MODEL	Ambiguous model error report indicator†
MS	Bracketed marked section entity
MSC	Marked section close sequence†
MSICHAR	Markup-scan-in character†
MSOCHAR	Markup-scan-out character†
MSSCHAR	Markup-scan-suppress character†
NAME	Name (for attribute value)
NAMECASE	Naming rules case indicators†
NAMELEN	Name length limit†
NAMES	Name list (for attribute values)
NAMES	Reserved name use list identifier†
NAMING	Naming rules identifier†
NDATA	Non-SGML data entity
NET	Null end-tag sequence†
NMTOKEN	Name token (for attribute value)
NMTOKENS	Name token list (for attribute values)
NO	Negative feature use indicator†
NONE	No shunned characters†
NONE	No short references†
NONSGML	Public text class identifier
NONSGML	Non-SGML character report indicator†
NORMSEP	Normalized separator length†
NOTATION	Public text class identifier
NOTATION	Notation name (for attribute value)
NOTATION	Notation declaration identifier
NOTATION	Associated notation name (for data attribute)
NOTCAP	Notation capacity indicator†
NOTCHCAP	Notation character capacity indicator†
NUMBER	Number (for attribute value)
NUMBERS	Number list (for attribute values)
NUTOKEN	Number token (for attribute value)
NUTOKENS	Number token list (for attribute values)
0	Omittable tag identifier
OMITTAG	Omit tag feature use indicator†
OPT	Optional occurrence indicator sequence†

† Must be entered using reference concrete syntax – cannot be redefined.

Table 10.2 (cont.)

Reserved name	Role
OR	Or connector†
OTHER	Other features list identifier†
PCDATA	Parsed character data (in content model)
PERO	Parameter entity reference open sequence†
PI	Processing instruction (in entity)
PIC	Processing instruction close sequence†
PILEN	Processing instruction length limit†
PIO	Processing instruction open sequence†
PLUS	Inclusion indicator sequence†
PLUS	Required and repeatable occurrence indicator†
POSTLINK	Post-element link set use declaration identifier
PUBLIC	Publicly declared external identifier
PUBLIC	Public capacity set indicator†
PUBLIC	Public concrete syntax indicator†
QUANTITY	Quantity set identifier†
RANK	Rank feature use indicator†
RCDATA	Replaceable character data (in declared content)
RCDATA	Status keyword (for marked section)
RE	Record end function name
RE	Record end function character†
REFC	Reference close sequence†
REP	Optional and repeatable occurrence indicator†
REQUIRED	Required attribute value
RESTORE	Restore previous link set use declaration
RNI	Reserved name indicator†
RS	Record start function name
RS	Record start function character†
SCOPE	Syntax scope identifier†
SDATA	Specific character data (for entity)
SEPCHAR	Markup separator character†
SEQ	Sequence connector†
SEQUENCE	Blank sequence use indicator†
SGML	SGML declaration identifier†
SGML	SGML declaration error report indicator†
SGMLREF	SGML reference values†
SHORTREF	Public text class identifier
SHORTREF	Short reference mapping declaration identifier

† Must be entered using reference concrete syntax – cannot be redefined.

Table 10.2 (cont.)

Reserved name	Role
SHORTREF	Short reference delimiters identifier†
SHORTTAG	Short tag feature use indicator†
SHUNCHAR	Shunned character number identifier†
SIMPLE	Simple link type indicator
SIMPLE	Simple link feature use indicator†
SPACE	Space function name
SPACE	Space function character†
SRCNT	Short reference count†
SRLEN	Short reference maximum length†
STAGO	Start-tag open sequence†
STARTTAG	Bracketed start-tag entity
SUBDOC	Public text class identifier
SUBDOC	Subdocument entity
SUBDOC	Subdocument feature use indicator†
SWITCHES	Public concrete syntax indicator†
SWITCHES	Public concrete syntax use indicator†
SYNTAX	Public text class identifier
SYNTAX	Concrete syntax identifier†
SYSTEM	System related external identifer
SYSTEM	System declaration identifier†
TAGC	Tag close sequence†
TAGLEN	Undelimited tag length limit†
TAGLVL	Tag nesting level limit†
TEMP	Status keyword (for marked section)
TEXT	Public text class identifier
TOTALCAP	Total capacity indicator†
UCNMCHAR	Upper-case name character†
UCNMSTRT	Upper-case name start character†
UNUSED	Unused character indicator†
USELINK	Link set use declaration identifier
USEMAP	Short reference use declaration identifier
VALIDATE	Validation services identifier†
VI	Value indicator sequence†
YES	Positive feature use indicator†

† Must be entered using reference concrete syntax – cannot be redefined.

10.2.7 Quantity sets

The last part of the SYNTAX clause of an SGML declaration defines the limits to which elements, entities and model groups can be nested, together with the maximum length of such things as attribute definitions, entities, tag names, short reference delimiters, data tags, blank sequences, processing instructions, etc. These details are entered in the form of a **quantity set** declaration.

The start of the quantity set declaration is indicated by the presence of the reserved words QUANTITY SGMLREF. As elsewhere, the presence of SGMLREF indicates that, in the absence of further declarations, the values used will be the values laid down for the reference concrete syntax as shown in Table 10.3.

To alter one of the default values, the name of the parameter to be altered (as shown in the first column) should be entered followed by the revised value. As usual, a space or other valid parameter separator should be used to separate the entered values from the preceding reserved name or entry, and from each other.

Table 10.3 Quantity set of reference concrete syntax.

Reserved name	Value	Purpose
ATTCNT	40	Maximum number of attribute names and name tokens in an attribute definition list
ATTSPLEN	960	Maximum length of start-tag's attribute specifications
BSEQLEN	960	Maximum length of blank sequence mappable to a short reference string
DTAGLEN	16	Maximum length of data tag string
DTEMPLEN	16	Maximum length of data tag template or pattern template
ENTLVL	16	Maximum number of nesting levels for entities
GRPCNT	32	Maximum number of tokens in group (one level)
GRPGTCNT	96	Maximum number of tokens at all levels in a model group (data tag groups count as 3 tokens)
GRPLVL	16	Maximum number of nesting levels in a model group
LITLEN	240	Maximum length of a delimited literal (within delimiters)
NAMELEN	8	Maximum length of names, numbers, tokens, etc.
NORMSEP	2	Default separator length when calculating the normalized length of names, tokens, etc.
PILEN	240	Maximum length of processing instructions
TAGLEN	960	Maximum length of start-tags
TAGLVL	24	Maximum number of open elements

The values that are most likely to need to be altered are those for the maximum length of a name, number or token, and the count defining the maximum number of attribute names and name tokens that can be associated with a particular element. To alter these values the standard entry of QUANTITY SGMLREF can be amended to read, for example:

QUANTITY SGMLREF NAMELEN 12 ATTCNT 60

where the number 60 indicates the maximum number of attributes and/or attribute value names of up to 12 characters that may be entered in any attribute definition list declared within the document.

It should be noted that any value that is not specifically redefined within the syntax clause will be allocated the default value shown in Table 10.3. If you want to make it clear which values will be applied to the document, all values can be redefined by entry of a description of the form:

```
QUANTITY SGMLREF ATTCNT   60        ATTSPLEN  960
                 BSEQLEN  960        DTAGLEN   16
                 DTEMPLEN 16         ENTLVL    16
                 GRPCNT   32         GRPGTCNT  96
                 GRPLVL   16         LITLEN    240
                 NAMELEN  12         NORMSEP   1
                 PILEN    240        TAGLEN    480
                 TAGLVL   24
```

The quantity set declaration ends the SYNTAX clause of the SGML declaration. The role of the other clauses in the SGML delaration is explained in Chapter 11, which also shows how the redefined concrete syntax affects the following document. When changing the default values of the reference concrete syntax it is important that the other values in the SGML declaration are also checked carefully for applicability. In particular, it is important to make sure that the document character set description at the start of the SGML declaration does not conflict with the redefined syntax-reference character set.

The SGML Declaration

Each transmitted SGML document should be accompanied by an **SGML declaration** that defines:

- the document's character set,
- the storage capacity needed to process the document,
- the scope of the concrete syntax,
- the concrete syntax used within the document,
- which SGML features are used within the document, and
- any application-specific information needed to process the document.

This SGML declaration enables the recipient of an SGML document to determine whether their system can process the document 'as received' or whether character translation or other algorithmic conversion will be required before the document can be processed locally. It may also indicate the need for manual editing of the markup before the document can be processed.

Because the SGML declaration is intended for human consumption in printed form, as well as for machine processing, the reference concrete syntax must be used to prepare it, regardless of the concrete syntax used in the remainder of the document. Where the SGML declaration is not

Table 11.1   Characters permitted in SGML declarations.

Code(s)	Characters	Code(s)	Characters
32	Space	47	/
33	!	48-57	0 - 9
34	"	58	:
35	#	59	;
37	%	60	<
38	&	61	=
39	'	62	>
40	(	63	?
41	)	65-90	A - Z
42	*	91	[
43	+	93	]
44	,	97-122	a - z
45	-	124		
46	.		

provided in printed form, the receiving program must be able to convert the SGML declaration from its reference concrete syntax format to a form that can be read by the operator and/or to a form that can be used to call or generate the necessary translation tables automatically.

Only those characters declared as markup characters or minumum data characters in the reference concrete syntax (as shown in Table 11.1) can be used within the SGML declaration. Any other characters that need to be referred to within the SGML declaration must be specified in the form of numeric character references (e.g. ).

Because entity declarations cannot be entered within the SGML declaration, parameter entities cannot be used within the declaration. However, formal public identifiers can be used to add prestored sets of character, capacity, syntax and short reference details to an SGML declaration.

The start of each SGML declaration consists of the standard markup delimiter open sequence (<!) followed by the letters SGML, a space (or other valid parameter separator) and the delimited minimum literal "ISO 8879-1986", the final date indicating the version of the standard referred to when preparing the SGML declaration.

The rest of the SGML declaration is split into six main clauses, identified by the reserved names:

(1)   CHARSET, for the **document character set** details;

(2)   CAPACITY, for the **capacity set** statement;

(3)   SCOPE, for the **concrete syntax scope** statement;

(4)   SYNTAX, for the **concrete syntax** details;

(5)   FEATURES, for **feature use** details; and

(6)   APPINFO, for **application-specific information**.

NOTE: For details of the SYNTAX clause refer to Chapter 10.

The end of the SGML declaration is marked by a single markup delaration close character ($>$, decimal 62).

11.1   The document character set

The **document character set** clause of the SGML declaration defines all of the characters used within the following document. Because the document might contain characters that are not used for document markup, the document character set description can include characters that are not defined in the document's concrete syntax. (The clause can also be used to restrict the use of characters that are otherwise permitted according to the rules laid down in the concrete syntax.)

The document character set clause consists of the reserved name CHARSET followed, after a space (or alternative parameter separator), by one or more **character set descriptions**. Each character set description consists of a **base character set** statement followed by a **described character set portion** identifying the roles of individual characters. The format of the character set description is identical to that used in the SYNTAX clause of the SGML declaration (see Chapter 10), though the two character set descriptions need not be exactly the same.

NOTE: The rule about character set entries being consecutive (see Chapter 10) also applies to the document character set.

As the following example shows, more than one reference (base) character set can be used to build up a character set description:

```
<!SGML "ISO 8879-1986"
   CHARSET BASESET "ISO 646-1983//CHARSET International
                    Reference Version (IRV)//ESC 2/5 4/0"
            DESCSET 0    9  UNUSED
                    9    2  9
                    11   2  UNUSED
                    13   1  13
                    14  18  UNUSED
                    32  95  32
                    127  1  UNUSED
            BASESET "ISO Registration Number 109//CHARSET
                     ECMA-94 Right Part of Latin Alphabet
```

```
                    Nr. 3//ESC 2/9 4/3"
          DESCSET 128 32 UNUSED
                  160 5  32
                  165 1  "SGML Users' Group Logo"
                  166 88 38
                  254 1  127    --Moved from normal position--
                  255 1  UNUSED --as code 255 is shunned   --
     ...
```

In this example, the first part of the character set has been based on the code set defined in the 1983 version of ISO 646. Only codes 9, 10, 13 and 32 of ISO 646's control codes have been retained as SGML function codes recognized within the document. The 94 character codes starting at position 33 in ISO 646 have been mapped to the same positions in the document's character set.

The ISO 646 character set has, in this case, been extended by use of a formally registered set of characters that have been allocated registration number 109 by ISO. (This form of **ISO owner identifier** is only used for publicly registered character sets. It requires the use of a formal public identifier whose public text class entry is CHARSET.) The ECMA (European Computer Manufacturers' Association) 94 character G1 Latin alphabet extension character set has, as part of its ISO registration procedure, been allocated a formal public text designating sequence of ESC 2/9 4/3. This sequence, which shows how you should return from the ECMA code set to the ISO 646 code set if both are used as G0 character sets, forms the last part of the registered name used as the formal public identifier for the extension set. The character set descriptions following this change of base character set show that:

- the 32 codes starting at position 128 are not used within the following document,

- the five codes starting at position 32 in the ECMA code set are to be used in positions 160 to 164 of the document's character set,

- code 165 is to be used within the document to request a special symbol, the SGML Users' Group logo,

- codes 166 to 253 are to be matched to codes 38 to 125 in the ECMA-defined character set, and

- code 254 is to be matched to code 127 in the ECMA set since code 255 cannot be used because it has been defined as a shunned character within the SYNTAX clause, and has not been declared as a valid function character.

Note how comments can be embedded within the SGML declaration to explain the relevance of one or more of its entries. As a general rule, comments can be used anywhere a space, Tab code, record end or record start code could otherwise occur as a parameter separator within the SGML declaration.

Characters defined as UNUSED in the document character set will be treated as non-SGML characters. Such characters can only be incorporated into an SGML document as part of a non-SGML data (NDATA) external entity (see Chapter 4). Care should be taken to ensure that any characters declared as UNUSED in the document's concrete syntax are also declared as UNUSED in the document character set. By the same token, characters declared as shunned characters in the SYNTAX clause, which have not subsequently been assigned as function characters, cannot be used as the described set character number in the first column of a character description.

When using the document character set clause to create a translation table for an incoming document it is important to remember that character references to reassigned codes will also need to be changed during translation. For example, if a document prepared using the SGML declaration shown above is to be transferred to an EBCDIC-based system, an ISO 646 character reference such as " in an entity declaration will need to be changed to }, the EBCDIC code for a quotation mark.

When using more than one base character set in a document character set, it is important to ensure that each code in the set is referred to only once in the described character set portion of the declaration. For example, the following declaration would be illegal because code 126 has, accidentally, been defined as the last character to be used from ISO 646 before being re-assigned to hold the last character from the ECMA code set, and because there is a gap in the code set between 253 and 255:

```
<!SGML "ISO 8879-1986"
 CHARSET BASESET "ISO 646-1983//CHARSET International
                 Reference Version (IRV)//ESC 2/5 4/0"
         DESCSET 0   9  UNUSED
                 9   2  9
                 11  2  UNUSED
                 13  1  13
                 14  18 UNUSED
                 32  95 32
                 127 1  UNUSED
         BASESET "ISO Registration Number 109//CHARSET
                 ECMA-94 Right Part of Latin Alphabet
                 Nr. 3//ESC 2/9 4/3"
         DESCSET 128 32 UNUSED
                 160 5  32
                 165 1  "SGML Users' Group Logo"
                 166 88 38
                 126 1  127 --moved because 255 is--
                 255 1  UNUSED -- a shunned position --
 ...
```

11.2   Capacity sets ⎯⎯⎯⎯⎯⎯⎯⎯⎯⎯⎯⎯⎯⎯⎯⎯

The **capacity set** clause of the SGML declaration can be used to control the amount of space reserved by the SGML parser for the storage of document structure models, entities, short references, and so on. By default, the compulsory SGMLREF keyword at the start of the capacity clause will reserve 35 000 characters (bytes) of space. If the capacity set clause of the SGML declaration is left at this default setting of SGMLREF, each of the capacity sets listed in Table 11.2 will be able to take up as much of this room as is required.

In calculating the amount of storage required for most of the forms of SGML markup listed in Table 11.2, the current maximum length of an SGML name, as defined by NAMELEN in the QUANTITY section of the SYNTAX clause, is

Table 11.2   Reference capacity set.

Name	Default value	Points counted†	Purpose
TOTALCAP	35000	All	Grand total of capacity points
ENTCAP	35000	NAMELEN	Entity name capacity
ENTCHCAP	35000	††	Number of entity replacement characters
ELEMCAP	35000	NAMELEN	Element name capacity
GRPCAP	35000	NAMELEN	Tokens within model groups (data tag groups count as 3 tokens)
EXGRPCAP	35000	NAMELEN	Number of exception groups
EXNMCAP	35000	NAMELEN	Tokens within exception groups
ATTCAP	35000	NAMELEN	Attribute name capacity
ATTCHCAP	35000	††	Attribute default values capacity
AVGRPCAP	35000	NAMELEN	Attribute value token capacity
NOTCAP	35000	NAMELEN	Data content notation name capacity
NOTCHCAP	35000	††	Number of characters in notation identifiers
IDCAP	35000	NAMELEN	Explicit or default ID value capacity
IDREFCAP	35000	NAMELEN	Explicit or default IDREF value capacity
MAPCAP	35000	NAMELEN	Short reference map declaration capacity
LKSETCAP	35000	NAMELEN	Link set/type declaration capacity
LKNMCAP	35000	NAMELEN	Link/document type name storage capacity

† Per unit used
†† Per character declared

multiplied by the number of names, tokens, values, etc., declared within the document's prolog. If no specific value is declared in the SYNTAX clause the default NAMELEN value of eight characters, as used in the reference concrete syntax, must be used.

When calculating the length of attribute default values, however, the *actual* length of the entry must be increased by the current NORMSEP normal separator length (two in the reference concrete syntax). Where the attribute value is defined as a general entity name list, an id reference list, a name list, a name token list, a number list or a number token list, the NORMSEP length is added to the length of each default value in the list and is also counted a further time at the start of the list (even if the default value only contains one entry in the list). For entities declared using the CDATA or SDATA keywords the current NORMSEP value must also be allowed for at both the start and end of the entered parameter literal†. The maximum length of a normalized string (i.e. the string with its added normal separators) must not exceed the value specified for LITLEN in the quantity set part of the SYNTAX clause (240 characters in the reference concrete syntax – see Figure 10.3). When the default value of an attribute is #CONREF, #REQUIRED or #IMPLIED, however, the normalized length of the attribute value is 0. Where #CURRENT is used, the value required will be the normalized length of the largest value specified for the attribute in the document, that is the largest value that will need to be stored. (In case of doubt, allow the current maximum LITLEN value, for example 240+2).

When calculating ENTCHCAP, the length of an external entity is simply the sum of the undelimited public and system identifiers entered in the entity declaration. For embedded entities all replacement characters, including those defined in the default entity and the literal delimiters of the entry, count towards ENTCHCAP.

When calculating GRPCAP, each level of bracketed model group within all concurrent document types must be counted as a token, and each data tag group must be counted as three tokens. The simplest way to ensure that this value is calculated correctly is to treat each opening bracket in a model group (including the first one but excluding any entered as part of data tag definitions) as one token, any square bracket at the start of a data tag group as two tokens, and then add to this the total number of element names (generic identifiers) defined in the relevant document type definitions (ignoring any strings entered in data tag groups).

When calculating the value of MAPCAP, the number of short reference delimiters declared in the currently applicable concrete syntax must be taken into account. For this purpose, each declared short reference delimiter string is considered to have a maximum length defined by NAMELEN.

---

† It is important that these rules are also applied for those attributes where a null value has been specified as the default value by entering two adjacent string literal delimiters.

The MAPCAP value required for *each* declared short reference map is calculated by multiplying the number of delimiter strings by NAMELEN, and then adding a further NAMELEN value to allow for the name of the map. As the reference concrete syntax contains 32 delimiter strings, the default length of each short reference map used when the reference concrete syntax is in force is $(32 \times 8) + 8 = 264$ characters.

When calculating the required storage capacity it is important to take into account all document type declarations declared in the prolog, together with any associated link type definitions. The total of all capacity values likely to occur in the longest imaginable chain of linked concurrent documents must not exceed the TOTALCAP entry (or 35 000 if no specific entry occurs).

To see how the capacity requirements of a typical document would be calculated, consider the values required for the document type declaration detailed in Appendix C. This document type declaration contains 10 parameter entities and three general entities, each of which may have the default maximum name length of eight characters. The ENTCAP value for this declaration is, therefore, $8 \times 13 = 104$. The number of characters used in the entity strings is, in this case, 222. The total storage capacity required for the ENTCAP and ENTCHCAP values is, therefore, 326 characters.

Appendix C defines a total of 99 elements, which contain a total of 733 nested elements in 93 groups. Eight exception groups have been used, containing a total of 14 elements. The values required for ELEMCAP, GRPCAP, EXGRPCAP and EXNMCAP are, therefore, $99 \times 8 = 792$, $(93 + 733) \times 8 = 6608$, $8 \times 8 = 64$ and $14 \times 8 = 112$ respectively.

The document declaration defines a total of 56 attributes, which use 48 tokens. The values required for ATTCAP and AVGRPCAP are, therefore, $56 \times 8 = 448$ and $48 \times 8 = 384$ respectively. For ATTCHAP the values required, when NORMSEP has been added to both the start and end of lists and CDATA attributes, is 212.

Three notation declarations have been included in the DTD, so the required NOTCAP value is 24. The total number of characters in the notation identifiers (NOTCHCAP) is only 104.

While the declaration contains only nine ID attributes and six IDREF attributes, the total number of unique ID and IDREF entries in a document could well reach 1000. A total of 8000 characters of IDCAP storage space would be needed to store these unique references, with perhaps a further 8000 characters being needed to store cross-references (IDREFCAP).

As the reference concrete syntax contains 32 different short reference delimiter strings, the three non-empty maps declared in Appendix C require a total of $3 \times 264 = 792$ characters of storage space. The empty map simply requires space for the map name (eight characters).

As no links have been declared in Appendix C, LKSETCAP is 0 but LKNMCAP must be set to at least eight since this value must also allow for the length of all document type names declared in the prolog.

The total storage capacity required by our example DTD is, therefore,

104 + 222 + 792 + 6608 + 64 + 112 + 448 + 384 + 212 + 24
+ 104 + 8000 + 8000 + 792 + 8 + 8 = 25 882.

As this represents only 74% of the default capacity of 35 000 characters allowed for TOTALCAP when the standard capacity set entry of:

```
CAPACITY PUBLIC "ISO8879-1986//CAPACITY Reference//EN"
```

is used in the SGML declaration, it can be seen that textbooks that do not require a large number of cross-references should fall within the limits set by the default capacity set.

When an SGML declaration containing a redefined capacity set is received, the entries in it should be checked against the capacity set details in the system declaration of the system on which it is to be processed (see Section 11.6) to ensure that the requested storage capacity can be allocated on the receiving system.

Alternative capacity sets declarations can be publicly declared. To recall a previously defined alternative capacity set in an SGML declaration you must use the keyword CAPACITY as the public text class keyword, giving the statement the form:

```
CAPACITY PUBLIC "-//Western Electrics//CAPACITY System 9//EN"
```

11.3 Concrete syntax scope

The SCOPE clause of the SGML declaration defines the part of the document in which the following concrete syntax is to apply. If SCOPE is followed by the reserved name DOCUMENT the declared syntax applies to all parts of the document (except, of course, the SGML declaration itself). If the alternative INSTANCE keyword is used, the declared concrete syntax only applies within the text of the document itself, any declarations in the prolog being defined using the reference concrete syntax.

If the INSTANCE option is selected, three rules must be applied to the following SYNTAX clause:

(1)   the syntax-reference character set must define all the characters defined in the reference concrete syntax (in the same positions);

(2)   the significant SGML characters (as used in markup and minimum data strings) must be such that the start of the document instance is always distinguishable from the end of the prolog; and

(3)   any quantity values declared in the SYNTAX clause must equal or exceed those of the quantity set defined for the reference concrete syntax (see Table 10.3).

11.4   *The* FEATURES *clause*

The FEATURES clause of the SGML declaration is used to define which of SGML's optional features can be used within a document. The clause starts with the reserved word FEATURES. This is followed by details of the three main groups of features:

(1)   markup minimization features,

(2)   link type features, and

(3)   other features.

The markup minimization section of the FEATURES clause starts with the reserved word MINIMIZE. This part of the FEATURES clause allows users to declare whether or not the document's markup uses any of the minimization techniques detailed in Chapter 7. The optional techniques that can be declared in this clause are:

- data tag minimization (DATATAG),
- tag omission (OMITTAG),
- element ranking (RANK), and
- short tags (SHORTTAG).

If the feature has been used (or could be used) in the document, the relevant keyword must be followed by the word YES. If the feature has not been used in the DTD the keyword should be followed by NO.

If link type declarations are included in the document's prolog or in any declaration associated with the prolog, one or more of the options in the link type features list that follows the reserved word LINK must be followed by the word YES rather than the default NO value. As explained in Chapter 9, there are three basic types of links

(1)   simple links (SIMPLE),

(2)   implicit links (IMPLICIT), and

(3)   explicit links (EXPLICIT).

In the case of the SIMPLE and EXPLICIT options, the maximum number of permitted links must be specified immediately after a YES response.

The final section of the FEATURES clause starts with the reserved word OTHER. This section is used to declare any other SGML features used in the document. The section contains three entries:

(1)   CONCUR to declare whether or not concurrent document structures can be set up within the document,

(2)   SUBDOC to define whether or not SGML subdocuments can be called from within the document, and

(3)   FORMAL to define whether or not formal public identifiers are being used within the document's prolog.

If the CONCUR or SUBDOC options are set to YES (rather than the default entry of NO) they must be followed by a number indicating the maximum number of subdocuments or concurrent document types to be catered for.

By default, the FEATURES clause will take the form:

```
              FEATURES
MINIMIZE DATATAG NO  OMITTAG  YES  RANK     NO   SHORTTAG YES
LINK     SIMPLE  NO  IMPLICIT NO   EXPLICIT NO
OTHER    CONCUR  NO  SUBDOC   NO   FORMAL   NO
```

to indicate that, in the reference concrete syntax, only the omit tag and short tag features may be used.

11.5   Application-specific information ⎯⎯⎯⎯⎯⎯⎯⎯

The APPINFO clause of the SGML declaration can be used to add application-specific information to the SGML declaration. The only restriction placed on this information by SGML is that it must be entered as a delimited minimum literal, using the minimum data characters and codes shown in Table 11.1. Where no application-specific information is required, the APPINFO reserved word identifying the start of this clause must be followed by the reserved word NONE.

A typical use of this clause is illustrated in the following example:

```
APPINFO "To be processed on the Mark II in Washington"
```

11.6   System declarations ⎯⎯⎯⎯⎯⎯⎯⎯⎯⎯

A **system declaration** containing details of the system's capacity for processing SGML documents should be prepared for each system that conforms to ISO 8879. Like the SGML declaration, this must be created using the character set defined in the reference concrete syntax to ensure that it can be correctly interpreted by any user or system to which it is passed.

A system declaration contains five subsections:

(1)   a **capacity set** clause,

(2) a **feature use** clause,

(3) a **concrete syntax scope** clause,

(4) a list of **concrete syntaxes supported**, and

(5) a list of available **validation services**.

The capacity set clause has the same form as that used in the SGML declaration but, in this case, the numbers entered define the maximum values that can be accepted in an incoming SGML declaration.

The feature use clause also has the same format as that used in the SGML declaration but, in this case, the reserved word NO indicates that the system does not support the feature, while the reserved word YES indicates that the feature can be requested in documents to be processed by the system (qualifying numbers indicating the maximum number of links, subdocuments or concurrent documents that can be handled by the system).

As with the SGML declaration, the concrete syntax scope clause in the system declaration can be qualified by the word DOCUMENT or the word INSTANCE but in this case INSTANCE indicates that the system can handle more than one syntax at a time, while DOCUMENT indicates that only one concrete syntax can occur in any document sent to the system.

The list of **concrete syntaxes supported** in the system declaration contains details of each concrete syntax known to the system, in the form of a formal syntax clause for each syntax supported; the list also contains details of the type of **concrete syntax changes** that can be associated with each syntax. Where the system uses publicly declared concrete syntaxes, the relevant public concrete syntax declaration can be followed by CHANGES SWITCHES if the system supports the SWITCH option (see Chapter 10). Alternatively, the CHANGES option can be used to define:

- the maximum permitted delimiter length (DELIMLEN),
- whether or not blank sequences are supported (SEQUENCE),
- the maximum number of short reference strings that can be recognized (SRCNT), and
- the maximum length allowed for short references on the system (SRLEN).

The list of concrete syntaxes supported must include either the reference concrete syntax or, if the system does not support short references, the core concrete syntax. These may, optionally, be qualified by the CHANGES SWITCHES statement, if switches are permitted on the system, to give entries of the form:

```
SYNTAX PUBLIC "ISO 8879-1986//SYNTAX Reference//EN"
CHANGES SWITCHES
```

and:

```
SYNTAX PUBLIC "ISO 8879-1986//SYNTAX Core//EN"
```

The last part of the system declaration, identified by the reserved name VALIDATE, identifies the validation services provided by the system. Seven types of SGML validation may be specified as available:

(1)   general validation of markup errors within the document (GENERAL),

(2)   validation of content models (MODEL),

(3)   validation of models containing exclusions (EXCLUDE),

(4)   validation to ensure that capacity limits are not exceeded (CAPACITY),

(5)   validation to ensure that the document does not contain non-SGML characters (NONSGML),

(6)   validation of SGML declarations (SGML), and

(7)   validation of public identifiers to ensure they are formal public identifiers (FORMAL).

If an option is declared as being validatable by entry of the keyword YES after the approriate reserved name, the program will check the relevant part of the document for validity and report any errors in the normal way (which will depend on the system). If the relevant keyword is followed by NO, the system will not attempt to check the validity of the relevant productions.

A typical system declaration might take the form:

```
<!SYSTEM CAPACITY SGMLREF TOTALCAP 40000
                          ENTCAP    8000
                          ENTCHCAP 10000
                          ELEMCAP   4000
                          GRPCAP   10000
                          EXGRPCAP  1000
                          EXNMCAP   2000
                          ATTCAP    5000
                          ATTCHCAP  5000
                          AVGRPCAP  3000
                          NOTCAP    1000
                          NOTCHCAP  1000
                          IDCAP     8000
                          IDREFCAP  5000
                          MAPCAP    4000
                          LKSETCAP     0
                          LKNMCAP      0
```

```
                        FEATURES
MINIMIZE DATATAG  YES  OMITTAG  YES  RANK    YES  SHORTTAG YES
    LINK SIMPLE    NO  IMPLICIT NO  EXPLICIT NO
   OTHER CONCUR    NO  SUBDOC YES 4 FORMAL   YES
SCOPE    INSTANCE
SYNTAX   PUBLIC "ISO 8879-1986//SYNTAX Reference//EN"
         CHANGES SWITCHES
SYNTAX   PUBLIC "ISO 8879-1986//SYNTAX Multicode Basic//EN"
SYNTAX   PUBLIC "+//IBM//SYNTAX EBCDIC//EN"
         CHANGES DELIMLEN 3
                 SEQUENCE YES
                 SRCNT    100
                 SRLEN    10
VALIDATE GENERAL  YES
         MODEL    YES
         EXCLUDE  NO
         CAPACITY NO
         NONSGML  YES
         SGML     NO
         FORMAL   YES                       >
```

As the format of a system declaration closely matches that of a document's SGML declaration, it is a simple matter to check whether or not the document can be processed by the receiving system. Where a mismatch is identified, the transmitter can normally be informed before the text of the document is transmitted, so preventing unnecessary expense being incurred.

12 *Document Parsing*

In the preceding chapters we have seen how SGML tags and their associated declarations can be used to mark up electronically-coded text in an unambiguous way. This final chapter gives a brief overview of what happens when an SGML-coded document is *parsed* by an SGML parser.

An **SGML parser** is a program or a suite of programs that breaks down an SGML-coded document into a series of logical elements and checks that these elements conform to the model defined in the associated document type declaration.

When parsing a document, the SGML parser:

- checks each new character to see if it is part of a general delimiter string that identifies the start or end of a piece of markup,

- checks whether or not the character is a short reference delimiter that needs to be expanded,

- checks if the character is a separator character that should be ignored,

- checks if the character is a valid part of a markup tag,

- identifies the various markup tags, identifying any entities that need to be expanded or recalled from external sources, and

- checks if identified markup tags are valid according to the declared model.

12.1   Delimiter recognition

When looking for general delimiters the SGML parser will recognize the delimiter only in an appropriate context. For example, it will not recognize [as a markup delimiter until a markup declaration that could contain a subset has been started. The ten delimiter recognition modes defined in the standard are:

(1)   CON for delimiters recognized within the content of a document or a marked section,

(2)   CXT for delimiters that are only recognized in specific contexts,

(3)   DS for delimiters that are only recognized within a markup declaration subset,

(4)   DSM for delimiters that are recognized in markup declaration subsets and within the marked section of a marked section declaration within the document,

(5)   GRP for delimiters that are only recognized within model groups,

(6)   LIT for delimiters recognized within literal strings,

(7)   MD for delimiters recognized within a markup declaration,

(8)   PI for delimiters recognized within a processing instruction,

(9)   REF for delimiters recognized within an entity or character reference, and

(10)   TAG for delimiters recognized as a valid part of a start-tag or end-tag.

Table 12.1 shows the delimiters recognized in each of these modes when the reference concrete syntax is being used.

Table 12.1   Delimiter recognition modes.

Mode	Recognized delimiters
CON	&# & < </ > <! <?]] / (and short references)
CXT	-- [(> (as markup declaration or tag close)
DS	]
DSM	<!]] % <?
GRP		, & (as connector) [ ] ( ) ? + * " ' % #
LIT	&# & " ' %
MD	-- [ ] (" ' - + # % >
PI	>
REF	; (and any separator characters)
TAG	= " ' / </ < >

In content (CON) mode the following contextual constraints apply:

- character references are only valid if the &# sequence is followed by a name start character or a digit;

- markup declaration open sequences (<!) are only valid when followed by a name start character, a comment delimiter (--), a declaration subset open delimiter ([) identifying the start of a marked section or a markup declaration close delimiter (>) indicating an empty comment;

- start-tag open (<) and end-tag open (</) delimiters are only valid if followed by a name start character or, for SHORTTAG YES, by a tag close delimiter (>) identifying the presence of an empty tag or, for CONCUR YES, by a group open delimiter (() indicating the start of a document type specification;

- marked section close delimiters (]]) are only recognized if immediately followed by a markup declaration close delimiter (>);

- entity reference open delimiters (&) are only valid if followed by a name start character or, if CONCUR, SIMPLE, IMPLICIT or EXPLICIT are followed by YES in the FEATURES clause of the SGML declaration, by a group open delimiter (() indicating the start of a document type specification name group; and

- a null end-tag is only recognized within an element whose start-tag was a net-enabling start-tag.

Within a markup declaration the following contextual constraints apply:

- declaration subset close delimiters (]) are only recognized if a subset has been opened in the same entity;

- plus and minus signs are only recognized as exclusion delimiters if immediately followed by a group open delimiter ((); and

- parameter entity reference open delimiters (%) are only valid if followed by a name start character or, if CONCUR, SIMPLE, IMPLICIT or EXPLICIT are followed by YES in the FEATURES clause of the SGML declaration, by a group open delimiter (() indicating the start of a name group qualifying the use of a marked section.

Where two or more delimiters start with the same sequence of characters the parser should always identify the longest possible match first, even if the longer string is semantically incorrect, or a short reference string that has no mapping and is thus treated as data. Similarly, short reference strings and general delimiters are recognized in the order in which they occur, with no overlap. To see the effect of these rules, consider

what would happen if the following addition was made to the short
reference section of the SGML declaration:

```
SHORTREF SGMLREF "]]>"
```

As this short reference delimiter is the same as the sequence used to
close a marked section, its addition to the SGML declaration would
preclude the use of normal marked sections within the document. This is
because, being longer than the two markup delimiters, the string's role as a
short reference will be recognized before either of the smaller general
delimiters can be recognized, and so the sequence will always either be
mapped to an entity or treated as data. (If, however, the marked section
contained the CDATA or RCDATA keywords, the string would be treated as a
marked section close because short references are not recognized within
such marked sections.)

When a short reference delimiter is encountered in the document,
the parser will replace it by an entity reference if one has been declared in
the current short reference map. Otherwise, it will pass the string on as
data, performing no other parsing on the string once it has been recognized
as a short reference delimiter. If the short reference delimiter string
contained one or more record start or record end codes, the following rules
will apply to the form of the added entity reference:

- if the string contained one or more record start codes but no record
  end codes, a single RS code will be output in front of the entity
  reference;

- if the string contained one or more record end codes but no record
  start code, a record end code will replace the reference close
  delimiter (;) normally placed at the end of the added entity
  reference; and

- if the string contains both record start and record end codes, the
  entity reference will be preceded by a record start code and ended
  by a record end code (in place of the normal reference close
  delimiter).

12.2   Tag recognition ─────────────────────────────────

Before checking the validity of markup tags the parser must identify any
markup minimization used within the document, after expanding any
entity references to ensure that they do not contain markup declarations.
Only when any hidden tags, including data tags, have been identified can
the parser begin to check that the document conforms to the declared
model.

When checking the validity of a markup tag the parser will first check that it is allowed at the current point in the document model. Provided that the element is not one of those specifically excluded at the current point in the model, the parser will first try to treat the tag as one identifying a subelement within the currently open element. If the current model contains sequence connectors (,) the tag should represent the next tag in the listed sequence. Otherwise, the parser will check if the element's generic identifier matches one of the elements listed at the current nesting level within the model. If it is, and the element is not one that has previously been used but which can only appear once in the group, the parser will accept it.

If the new element is not one of those declared as part of the current nesting level of the model, the parser will check to see if it is a valid inclusion in the current model. If it is not a valid inclusion, the parser will then check to see if all compulsory elements at the current nesting level have been satisfied. If they have, the parser can return to the next highest level in the model to see if the new tag matches one of those at that level. (This process of moving back to the preceding level can continue as long as any model constraints are observed.)

Once the element has been identified as one that is appropriate for the current point in the model, its attribute values can be checked and default attributes added to the attribute list for any attributes whose entries have been minimized. If any of the entered attribute values are invalid, or if the element is not permitted at the current point in the model, the parser should issue an appropriate message indicating the point in the document at which the error was identified.

When checking attributes, the parser should check the uniqueness of each identifier and the validity of each cross-reference to a unique identifier. It will also resolve any attribute lists into identifiable components, separated by a single space, so that they can be passed on to a text formatter. (The parser will not resolve cross-references, however, as these may require a knowledge of the way the text is to be formatted.)

One consequence of the above parsing sequence of which authors need to be aware is that an element will always be treated as part of the current model group if it can be. If the same element is declared to be part of the model group and an allowable inclusion within the model, it will always be treated as part of the model group rather than part of the inclusion.

When analysing a model group, an SGML parser distinguishes between those model groups containing the #PCDATA keyword or data tags and those which do not. Where data is not permitted within the model, the group is said to contain only **element content**. If data can be entered within the element, the model is said to contain **mixed content**. The significance of this distinction is that, within element content, separator characters such as spaces, record starts, record ends and Tabs are ignored. Within sequences connected by **or** connectors and model groups linked by **and** connectors the difference between the two types of model is unlikely to cause any significant problems, but if the **seq** sequence connector (,) has been used problems can occur. For example, an element whose model has been defined as:

```
<!ELEMENT x    - 0   (y, #PCDATA) >
<!ELEMENT y    0 0   (#PCDATA)    >
```

might have its text entered in the form:

```
<x>   <y>Title</y>
Text .....
</x>
```

If a separator character, in this case a Tab code, has been entered before the start-tag for the first embedded element (<y>), the parser will treat it as a data character and use its presence to imply an omitted start-tag for the embedded element. On encountering the following start-tag for the embedded element immediately after the separator character, however, it would indicate an error in the document's markup because, according to the model, the embedded element is permitted to occur only once.

If, however, the model group definition was changed to:

```
<!ELEMENT x     - 0  (y, z)   >
<!ELEMENT (y,z) 0 0  (#PCDATA) >
```

the same sequence could not be misconstrued by the program since the fact that the element's model is purely element content will cause the initial Tab code to be treated as a separator character (and therefore be ignored). Where sequence connectors (,) or and connectors (&) are being used, the updated standard recommends the use of a separate, omissible, sub-element to contain the parsed character data.

12.3   *The parsed document*

An SGML parser only checks the logical structure of the document's markup and reports any errors it finds. It does not correct errors, format the text or resolve the cross-references, though these functions may be carried out by programs linked directly to the parser. The parser will, however, expand the entity references within the document and, in many cases, remove any minimization by adding any omitted tags or replacing short tags by the full version, before passing the expanded version of the tagged text to the text formatter.

It is the text formatter that determines how the contents of each element are to be laid out on the page and what form any cross-references should take. Where automatic generation of index entries, table of contents, etc., has been requested, this must also take place in the text formatter. Control of simple text formatters could be through the use of link type declarations, but, for many applications, control of the text formatter will be a manual or, at best, semi-automatic operation.

It should always be remembered, however, that SGML documents can be prepared without the aid of an SGML parser, or an SGML-sensitive text formatter. In many applications, provided that the text formatter can handle cross-references and generate indexes, and so on, a simple code conversion procedure will be all that is required to turn an SGML-coded document into a printed book.

By now you should have a good idea of how the powerful techniques provided by SGML can be used to simplify and speed up the production of textbooks and other types of multimedia publications. The application of logical coding techniques during text capture can greatly simplify the amount of coding needed to achieve a specific effect, and will allow the production of printed text to be divorced from the equipment used to key the text. By adopting these techniques during text preparation you will be equipping yourself for the future and ensuring that text keyed today will be useful well into the next century.

Good luck!

Multilingual SGML Documents

Before preparing multilingual SGML documents it is important to ensure:

- that the document's character set, as defined in the SGML declaration, contains all the characters (or accents) needed to set the required languages;
- that language attributes are assigned to those elements that may need to be processed in different ways for different languages (e.g. quoted text or speech); and
- that any short reference maps being used are not language dependent.

A.1 Multilingual character sets

The techniques needed to extend a document's character set are described in detail in Chapters 10 and 11. Two basic options are available:

(1) to extend the concrete syntax *and* the document character set, or
(2) to extend the document character set without extending the concrete reference syntax.

If the second technique is employed, element and entity names, and the replacement text of entities, cannot include characters defined in the extension to the document character set. For this reason, it is recommended that for multilingual documents the concrete syntax be extended to match the document's character set.

Where the techniques defined in ISO Standard 2022 are to be used to extend the range of characters allowed within the reference concrete syntax the multicode basic concrete syntax, defined in Annex D of ISO 8879 can be invoked by changing the syntax clause of the SGML declaration to read:

```
SYNTAX PUBLIC "ISO 8879-1986//SYNTAX Multicode Basic//EN"
```

When using this syntax, however, it should be noted that no markup delimiters can be entered while an alternative shift state is in force. Therefore, before entering a markup tag it will be necessary to use code 15 to return to the default shift state as all markup characters should be in the G0 character set.

NOTE: Many other techniques are available for expanding code sets, nearly all of which can be handled by SGML. Annex E of ISO 8879 details a number of techniques which go beyond the scope of this book.

A.2   Multilingual DTDs

Where a document consists of a number of subdocuments prepared in different languages, each subdocument can be marked up using a tag set appropriate to the language concerned. In this case, the SGML declaration of the main document defines the document character set to be used in all subdocuments, the syntax and syntax scope clauses determining the syntax needed to define the DTD at the start of each subdocument.

Where multilingual text is to be interspersed throughout a document rather than in discrete sections, a tag set that is suitable for all languages should be defined/selected. In most cases this tag set will be one that is specifically designed for the principal language of the book or its publisher. This basic tag set should then be modified to allow setting in more than one language. There are two ways in which this can be done:

(1)   by defining subelements whose specific purpose is to identify when a change of language has occurred, and

(2)   by adding a language attribute to each element that can contain text in more than one language.

If the first option is selected, the relevant subelements will need to be added to the model group of any element that contains data in a language other than the main language of the document. When this has been done a typical paragraph of multilingual text might take the form:

```
<p><en>When preparing French text the term
<fr>Éclaircissement<en> should precede all explanations.
```

Normally, however, multilingual documents will consist of parallel strings of text rather than small amounts of text embedded within a paragraph in another language (where the change of language will often not be significant). Such parallel text is best handled by associating a language attribute with a general-purpose element to indicate the language of the entered text. If such an attribute is defined for the paragraph element, for example, a typical section of parallel text might be entered as:

```
<p en>Without having a great experience of the world, I
do not allow myself to be taken in by the flatteries of
a pretty woman.
<p fr>Sans avoir une grande expérience du monde, je ne
me laisse pas prendre aux flatteries d'une jolie femme.
```

Where one language predominates, it should be defined as the default value for the language attribute, so that the attribute needs to be specified only when the element contains text in an alternative language. Where foreign language text occurs only in specific elements (e.g. quotations), the default values for the language attribute associated with these elements should be changed to that of the foreign language, rather than the main text language, to reduce the number of times the attribute value needs to be entered in a tag.

A.3   *Multilingual short reference maps* ————————————

Two major problems may be encountered when short references are used during the preparation of multilingual documents:

(1)   the same characters may be used for different purposes in different languages (or even within one language), and
(2)   different symbols may be used to indicate the same thing in different languages.

Both of these problems are particularly noticeable in short reference maps used to identify quoted sections of text. The first problem is illustrated in the following sentence:

```
"Whose idea was it to write 'Harold's False Eye' on the board?"
```

This sentence illustrates the two points about quoted text:

(1)   quotations can be nested (in certain languages), and

(2)   the end delimiter of a quotation may not be uniquely assigned to this
       role.

The second problem is illustrated in the Table A.1.

As far as SGML is concerned, the logical definition of a quote
should be the same in any language (e.g. ‹q›). To change the format of the
printed quotation marks from language to language, the program must
know which language is in use when it encounters each piece of quoted
text.

Before considering the problems of changing short reference maps
to suit the language being used, however, we need to consider how
different coding conventions can be catered for within a single language.
For example, in English documents two common conventions for nesting
quotes are encountered:

(1)   first level double quotes, with single quotes at the second level, and

(2)   first level single quotes, with double quotes at the second level.

To avoid being restricted to just one of these options, two sets of short
references are needed. For the first convention, the standard (ISO 646)
quotation mark symbol (") is the first link. In the second, however, the
ASCII single quote/apostrophe symbol (') cannot be used as the start
point, since this character serves two purposes. A single quote should
only be recognized as the start of a piece of quoted text where it is
preceded by a space, an opening bracket, a record start code or the end
delimiter of a tag.

Table A.1 Typical ways of quoting text.

Language	Start quotation mark	End quotation mark	Example
English	" or ‘	" or ’	He said "Hello" or ‘He said "Hello"’
French	«	»	Il dit «Bonjour»
German	» or › or „	« or ‹ or "	Er sagt »Gutten Tag« or »Er sagt ›Guten Tag‹.« or Er sagt „Guten Tag"
Finnish	» or „ or ’	» or " or ’	»Hän Sanoi ’Terve’»
Swedish	"	"	Han sade "Hej"

The initial map, which should be in force whenever elements that could contain quotes are being entered, could be either:

```
<!SHORTREF startqta '"'  quote-1a>
```

or:

```
<!SHORTREF startqtb " '"       quote-1b
                     "&#RS;'"  quote-1b
                     ">'"      quote-1b
                     "('"      quote-1c >
```

where the entities are defined as:

```
<!ENTITY quote-1a "<q><!USEMAP inquotea>" >
<!ENTITY quote-1b " <q><!USEMAP inquoteb>" >
<!ENTITY quote-1c "(<q><!USEMAP inquoteb>" >
```

To activate this initial short reference map, a declaration of the following form should be included in the document type definition:

```
<!USEMAP startqta textbook>
```

NOTES:

1)   *As the delimiter sequences used to identify quoted text using single quotes are not part of the set defined for the reference concrete syntax (see Table 3.3), they will need to be added to the list of valid short reference delimiters defined in the* SYNTAX *clause of the SGML declaration.*

2)   *Words beginning with an apostrophe, such as some Italian phrases and African names, need special treatment if* startqtb *is used. Normally, the apostrophe of such words will need to be entered as a* " *character reference or as* ', *where the entity is declared as character data in a declaration of the form:*

```
<!ENTITY apos CDATA "'">
```

3)   *The* quote-1b *entity definition shown above uses the unclosed start-tag option of SGML to delimit successive tags where a quote is identified immediately after another markup tag. If net-enabling start-tags are to be used in the document a fourth entity would be required to handle* /' *combinations.*

Once the first level of quotation has been recognized another map is required to:

- check for the end of the quote, and
- check for the start of an embedded quote.

As two alternative sets of short references could be used to identify embedded quotations within the ⟨q⟩ tag, the relevant short reference map must be associated with the tag by the addition of a short reference use declaration immediately after the start-tag for the element, rather than being permanently associated with the element through a ⟨!USEMAP...⟩ statement in the DTD. In this example, the map called inquotea is to be used when double quotation marks are being used at the outer level, while inquoteb will be used within quoted text surrounded by single quotes.

Where double quotes are used initially the new map is fairly straightforward – consisting of a double quote to identify the end of a quote together with the single quote entries used to identify the start of an embedded quote, giving it the form:

```
<!SHORTREF inquotea '"'       end-qt-a
                   " '"       start-2a
                   "&#RS;'"   start-2a
                   ">'"       start-2a
                   "('"       start-2b  >
```

where:

```
<!ENTITY end-qt-a ENDTAG   "q"              >
<!ENTITY start-2a " <q><!USEMAP inquot2a>" >
<!ENTITY start-2b "(<q><!USEMAP inquot2b>" >
```

Note that no short reference use map declaration needs to be associated with the end of a quoted element. This is because, as soon as an embedded subelement is completed, the map in force when the subelement started is automatically restored by the SGML parser.

Where single quotes are being used as the delimiters of the outer level of quoted text, however, a further set of potential problems needs to be allowed for in the specification of the inquoteb short reference map. Again, the problem arises because the use of a single ASCII code to represent either an apostrophe or the end of a quote is ambiguous. The distinguishing feature of an end quote is that it is followed by either:

- a space or record end code, or
- another punctuation symbol.

A suitable map for use after identifying the end of a single-quoted first level quotation might be:

```
<!SHORTREF inquoteb '"'       start-2b
                   "' "       eqt-b-sp
                   "'&#RE;"   eqt-b-sp
```

```
"!."       eqt-b-st
"!,"       eqt-b-cm
"!:"       eqt-b-co
"!;"       eqt-b-sc
"!?"       eqt-b-qu
"!!"       eqt-b-ex
"!)"       eqt-b-pa
"!]"       eqt-b-sb  >
```

NOTE: Again, the short reference delimiter sequences used in the above declaration will need to be added to the list of valid references in the document's SGML declaration.

The above list highlights one of the problems with the short references – SGML has no facility that allows entries of the same type to be grouped within a short reference mapping declaration in a way that is similar to that used for data tag template groups. (While data tags can be used where both characters are to be retained, they cannot be used if one of the characters is to be replaced by a tag, as is the case here.) This means that a separate entity needs to be defined for each combination of characters that could terminate the embedded piece of text, namely:

```
<!ENTITY eqt-b-sp  "</q> "  >
<!ENTITY eqt-b-st  "</q>."  >
<!ENTITY eqt-b-cm  "</q>,"  >
<!ENTITY eqt-b-co  "</q>:"  >
<!ENTITY eqt-b-sc  "</q>;"  >
<!ENTITY eqt-b-qu  "</q>?"  >
<!ENTITY eqt-b-ex  "</q>!"  >
<!ENTITY eqt-b-pa  "</q>)"  >
<!ENTITY eqt-b-sb  "</q>]"  >
```

while the entity used to activate the embedded quote can be defined as:

```
<!ENTITY start-2b "<q><!USEMAP inquot2b>" >
```

It should be noted, however, that the above list does not take into account quotes positioned immediately in front of a start- (or end-) tag or an entity open character, as such sequences cannot be resolved unambiguously. (It is presumed that tags and entity references will normally be separated from the end of quoted text by either a space or some form of punctuation.)

Once a second level of quotes has been encountered, a similar set of problems occur, with the further complication that the program needs to recognize where two quotes are closed at the same time. A suitable set of references for use where the first set of quotes are double quotes might be:

```
<!SHORTREF inquot2a '&#39;"'  eq-2a-1a
                "' "      eq-2a-sp
                "'&#RE;"  eq-2a-sp
                "'."      eq-2a-st
                "',"      eq-2a-cm
                "':"      eq-2a-co
                "';"      eq-2a-sc
                "'?"      eq-2a-qu
                "'!"      eq-2a-ex
                "')"      eq-2a-pa
                "']"      eq-2a-sb  >
```

where the various entity definitions are:

```
<!ENTITY  eq-2a-1a  "</q></q>"   >
<!ENTITY  eq-2a-sp  "</q> "      >
<!ENTITY  eq-2a-st  "</q>."      >
<!ENTITY  eq-2a-cm  "</q>,"      >
<!ENTITY  eq-2a-co  "</q>:"      >
<!ENTITY  eq-2a-sc  "</q>;"      >
<!ENTITY  eq-2a-qu  "</q>?"      >
<!ENTITY  eq-2a-ex  "</q>!"      >
<!ENTITY  eq-2a-pa  "</q>)"      >
<!ENTITY  eq-2a-sb  "</q>]"      >
```

Note especially the use of the ' character reference to define a single quote in the same string as a double quote in the first of the above short reference delimiter sets. (The same technique needs to be employed when adding the short reference string to the SYNTAX clause of the SGML declaration.) Alternatively, the string could have been enclosed in double quotes and the double quote replaced by a " character reference.

Where single quotes are used at the outer level, the second level map can be simplified to read:

```
<!SHORTREF inquot2b  '"&#39;'  eq-2b-1b
                '"'      eq-2b    >
```

where the associated entity declarations are:

```
<!ENTITY  eq-2b-1b  "</q></q>"     >
<!ENTITY  eq-2b     ENDTAG   "q"   >
```

but beware – in this case any single quotes preceding the double quote will be treated as apostrophes and will not close down the initial quote.

Similar techniques can be applied to other languages. French illustrates one of the simpler variants. When typed, quoted French text is normally treated in the same way as English. When prepared for output on a more sophisticated device, however, quoted text will normally be surrounded by *guillemets* or preceded by a long (em) dash. (Normally, the long dash only occurs at the start of a freestanding piece of quoted speech, with nothing to mark the end of the quote.) In certain circumstances, however, both a guillemet and a long dash can occur at the start of a piece of quoted text (e.g. when it is speech that is being quoted).

Where the guillemet symbol is available on the input keyboard, the only alteration needed is to change the double quotes in the startqta short reference map to the opening guillemet symbol (which can be entered as a character reference, e.g. «). In inquotea, however, the double quote needs to be replaced by the closing guillemet symbol (e.g. »), giving the definitions the form:

```
<!SHORTREF startqtf "&#171;"  quote-1f >
<!SHORTREF inquotef "&#187;"  end-qt-f
                     " '"      start-2f
                     "&#RS;'"  start-2f
                     ">'"      start-2f
                     "('"      start-fa  >
```

where:

```
<!ENTITY quote-1f "<q><!USEMAP inquotef>"  >
<!ENTITY end-qt-f ENDTAG    "q"            >
<!ENTITY start-2f " <q><!USEMAP inquot2f>" >
<!ENTITY start-fa "(<q><!USEMAP inquot2f>" >
```

French second level of quotations, where the text is surrounded by single angle brackets, pose special problems in SGML because few character sets assign special codes to these characters. There are two basic ways this type of quote can be generated on a French keyboard without using the single quote/apostophe key:

(1)   by use of the less-than and greater-than symbols, and
(2)   by assigning the otherwise unused 'quotation mark' (") symbol as the code used to mark the start and end of an embedded quote.

The first of these methods can only be applied if the delimiters for all SGML elements and declarations are changed in the concrete syntax so that they do not use the less-than or greater-than characters. While this is possible in SGML, this option will not be covered here as it requires a detailed knowledge of the SGML declaration structure, which is outside the scope of this book.

If the standard quotation mark symbol is assigned as the marker for embedded quotes, rather than the single quote/apostrophe, the second level short reference map can be simplified to:

```
<!SHORTREF inquotef '&#187;'  end-qt-f
                    '"'       start-2f  >
```

The only other map needed for French quotes is that to close the second level quotes, which becomes:

```
<!SHORTREF in-qt2-f '"'       end-qt-2  >
```

where end-qt-2 is defined as:

```
<!ENTITY end-qt-2 "</q>"   >
```

NOTE: The special case of speech within quoted text will be dealt with shortly, when the problems of outputting quotes are discussed.

For German, the situation is much the same as French, except that here the anführungzeichen (guillemets) point in the opposite directions, so » has to be used in startqtd and « in inquoted.

A.3.1   Mixing French, German and English quoted text

The techniques detailed above can be combined for use in a multilingual document. For this example, it will be presumed that both the French and German texts have been entered with guillemets delimiting the first level quotes, with double quote symbols used to delimit any embedded quotations. For the English text, however, the convention is for double quotes to delimit the first level of quotes and single quotes (apostrophes) to identify embedded quotes.

A map with three entries is needed to identify the three possibilities for the start of a quotation. This could take the form:

```
<!SHORTREF startqte '"'       quote-en
                    '&#171'   quote-fr
                    '&#187'   quote-de  >
```

where:

```
<!ENTITY  quote-en  "<q la=en lev=1><!USEMAP en1>"   >
<!ENTITY  quote-fr  "<q la=fr lev=1><!USEMAP fr1>"   >
<!ENTITY  quote-de  "<q la=de lev=1><!USEMAP de1>"   >
```

While only one element type is being used here, each entity is associated with different language and level attributes, as well as a specific short reference map. The appropriate element declaration might have the form:

```
<!ELEMENT q - - (#PCDATA|q|%phrases;|%refs;)+ >
<!ATTLIST q      la   (en|fr|de) en
                 lev  NUMBER     "1"          >
```

Short reference map en1 is similar to the English version of the inquotea map shown above, namely:

```
<!SHORTREF en1     '"'       end-qte
                   " '"      start-2e
                   "&#RS;'"  start-?e
                   ">'"      start-2e
                   "('"      start-ea  >
```

The French and German equivalents, fr1 and de1, would be declared as:

```
<!SHORTREF fr1     '&#187;'  end-qte
                   '"'       start-2f  >
```

and:

```
<!SHORTREF de1     '&#171;'  end-qte
                   '"'       start-2d  >
```

The declarations required for these entities are:

```
<!ENTITY  end-qte   "</q><!USEMAP startqte>"        >
<!ENTITY  start-2e  " <q la=en lev=2><!USEMAP en2>" >
<!ENTITY  start-ea  "(<q la=en lev=2><!USEMAP en2>" >
<!ENTITY  start-2f  "<q la=fr lev=2><!USEMAP fr2>"  >
<!ENTITY  start-2d  "<q la=de lev=2><!USEMAP de2>"  >
```

In this case, short reference map en2 is similar to in-qt2-a, having the relatively complicated form:

```
<!SHORTREF en2     '&#39;"'  eq-2e-1e
                   "' "      eq-2e-sp
                   "'&#RE"   eq-2e-sp
                   "'."      eq-2e-st
```

```
"," eq-2e-cm
":" eq-2e-co
";" eq-2e-sc
"?" eq-2e-qu
"!" eq-2e-ex
")" eq-2e-pa
"]" eq-2e-sb  >
```

associated with a new set of entity declarations reading:

```
<!ENTITY eq-2e-1e "</q></q><!USEMAP startqte>"    >
<!ENTITY eq-2e-sp "</q><!USEMAP en1> "            >
<!ENTITY eq-2e-st "</q><!USEMAP en1>."            >
<!ENTITY eq-2e-cm "</q><!USEMAP en1>,"            >
<!ENTITY eq-2e-co "</q><!USEMAP en1>:"            >
<!ENTITY eq-2e-sc "</q><!USEMAP en1>;"            >
<!ENTITY eq-2e-qu "</q><!USEMAP en1>?"            >
<!ENTITY eq-2e-ex "</q><!USEMAP en1>!"            >
<!ENTITY eq-2e-pa "</q><!USEMAP en1>)"            >
<!ENTITY eq-2e-sb "</q><!USEMAP en1>]"            >
```

The simpler French second level short reference map has the form:

```
<!SHORTREF fr2    '"'      endqt-2f  >
```

where the entity is defined as:

```
<!ENTITY endqt-2f "</q><!USEMAP fr1>" >
```

For German, the declarations take the form:

```
<!SHORTREF de2    '"'      endqt-2d  >
```

and:

```
<!ENTITY endqt-2d "</q><!USEMAP de1>" >
```

A.3.2   Controlling the output format of quotes

Where attributes have been used to identify the language or embedding level, the format of the quotes can be resolved prior to output by use of link set and link type declarations. Such declarations can be used to link each specific level and language to an element identifying the quote character required. For example, the following link type declaration could be defined for a document containing French, German and English text coded in the manner described above:

```
<!LINKTYPE output textbook polygot [
  <!ATTLIST    q if    CDATA    ""                                    >
  <!LINK quotes q [if="la=fr lev=1"] qt1 [start="&laquo;" end="&raquo;"]
           q [if="la=fr lev=2"] qt2 [start="&lang;" end="&rang;" ]
           q [if="la=de lev=1"] qt1 [start="&raquo;" end="&laquo;"]
           q [if="la=de lev=2"] qt2 [start="&rang;" end="&lang;" ]
           q [if="la=en lev=1"] qt1 [start="&ldquo;" end="&rdquo;"]
           q [if="la=en lev=2"] qt2 [start="&lsquo;" end="&rsquo;"] >
  <!USELINK quotes q > ]
>
```

NOTE: When using this type of link the order in which attributes appear in the start-tag may be critical. For this reason it is recommended that attributes are specified in a fixed order where more than one is likely to affect the appearance of the printed output.

The following element declarations need to be included in the DTD for the polygot concurrent document type if the above link is to be used:

```
<!ELEMENT qt1    - -    RCDATA >
<!ELEMENT qt2    - -    RCDATA >
<!ATTLIST qt1    start  '"'
                 end    '"'    >
<!ATTLIST qt2    start  "'"
                 end    "'"    >
```

The attribute lists associated with the two elements default to using the quote and apostrophe as the first and second level quote delimiters, these default values being automatically updated by the link set declaration.

NOTE: The names of the entities used in the above attributes are those in Annex D of ISO 8879. To invoke the entity declarations defined there for quotation symbols the following declarations are required at the start of the document:

```
<!ENTITY % ISOnum PUBLIC
 "ISO8879-1986//ENTITIES Numeric and Special Graphic//EN" >
<!ENTITY % ISOpub PUBLIC
 "ISO8879-1986//ENTITIES Publishing//EN" >
<!ENTITY % ISOtech PUBLIC
 "ISO8879-1986//ENTITIES General Technical//EN" >
%ISOnum; %ISOpub; %ISOtech;
```

Alternatively, the Addison-Wesley Numeric and Special Graphics set defined in Appendix B, which contains all three sets of quotes, can be invoked by entering:

```
<!ENTITY % AWnum PUBLIC
 "-//Addison-Wesley//ENTITIES Numeric and Special Graphic//EN" >
%AWnum;
```

Using the above techniques, all but one of the types of quotes mentioned above can be identified using short references. The exception is the French 'quoted quotation' – the one that requires a long dash at the start of the embedded quote. For this type of quote the second level French quotes declared in the link set declaration should be changed to:

```
q [if="la=fr lev=2"] qt2 [start="&mdash;" end=""]
```

A.4 Language-dependent character sets _____

The techniques shown above for dealing with multilingual quoted text can also be used to solve problems that occur where languages use different coding to represent the same characters.

For example, a typical word processing package may assign codes using the conventions laid down for a particular printer. In such cases, the French setting of an Epson-compatible printer may use code 93 to identify the section mark (§) and code 64 to identify the accented a-grave character (à). When the word processor is set up to drive a German version of the same printer, on the other hand, the code used for the section mark is 64, while code 93 identifies the u-umlaut (ü) character required in German text. How can these differences be resolved when short references are being used?

Firstly, the parser must be able to identify the language being used at any particular point in the document. Provided that specific tags, entities or short reference character strings are used to identify each change of language uniquely, a USEMAP declaration can be entered at each change of language.

Where specific elements are used to identify the language change, declarations of the form:

```
<!USEMAP lang-a elementx >
```

can be used in the document type declaration to call the relevant map at each language change.

Where short references and entities are used to identify the language change, the relevant entity declaration can contain a definition of the form:

```
<!ENTITY lang-b "<element><!USEMAP xyz>" >
```

Note that, in the document type declaration, the map name is followed by the name of the element to which it is to be applied (or a name list or parameter entity defining a number of elements that will activate the list). In the entity declaration, however, no such name is specified. In this case, the map only applies to the element currently in force.

NOTE: A consequence of this is that the element tag must precede the USEMAP *declaration.*

Typical language-related character set short reference maps might take the form:

```
<!SHORTREF  fr-map  '&#93;'   sect
                    '&#64;'   aacute
                      .
                      .
                      .               >
<!SHORTREF  de-map  '&#93;'   uuml
                    '&#64;'   sect
                      .
                      .
                      .               >
```

By combining this technique with those detailed above for quotes, composite maps capable of identifying all the short references applicable to a given language can be declared as part of the document definition, the appropriate definition being activated by the parser during text analysis.

B

Useful Publicly Declared Entities

This appendix lists six sets of publicly declared entities which can be used to request characters that are not directly available from your computer's keyboard. The six sets contain entity names that identify:

- accented characters used in Western European languages,
- a set of diacritical marks that can be used for building other accented characters,
- a full set of Greek characters,
- a set of commonly used numeric and other special graphic characters,
- a set of non-mathematical characters that frequently occur in published textbooks, and
- a set of mathematical symbols.

With the exception of the set of mathematical symbols, the entity names defined in this appendix can be used in any document prepared for Addison-Wesley that contains the relevant references to the entity set in its document type declaration subset.

The symbols listed in the maths entity set are basically a subset of the maths characters used by TEX. For completeness, the set includes a number of entity names that are also included in the set of special graphic characters, together with entity names for the basic mathematical signs. (It should be noted, however, that the enlarged versions of standard symbols are not included in the list as these are normally typeset by increasing the size of standard characters.) Before using characters in this set it is advisable to check that the characters required are available on the output system being used as not all typesetters will have these characters.

Where possible, the following entity names have been taken from the sets defined in Annex D of ISO 8879. Where no matching entity exists in these sets, the names suggested by the Americal Mathematical Society have been used providing they do not conflict with the eight character limit for entity names in the reference concrete syntax.

B.1   *Accented characters* —————————————————

To use any of the entities listed in this section in a document, include the following entity declaration and parameter entity reference in the document type declaration subset:

```
<!ENTITY % AWacc PUBLIC "-//Addison-Wesley//ENTITIES Accented Characters//EN">
%AWacc;
```

The following accented characters are useful for setting European languages:

á	&aacute;	Small a with acute accent
Á	&Aacute;	Capital A with acute accent
ă	&abreve;	Small a with breve accent
Ă	&Abreve;	Capital A with breve accent
â	&acirc;	Small a with circumflex accent
Â	&Acirc;	Capital A with circumflex accent
æ	&aelig;	Small ae dipthong (ligature)
Æ	&AElig;	Capital AE dipthong (ligature)
à	&agrave;	Small a with grave accent
À	&Agrave;	Capital A with grave accent
ā	&amacr;	Small a with macron accent
Ā	&Amacr;	Capital A with macron accent
å	&aring;	Small a with ring accent
Å	&Aring;	Capital A with ring accent (Angstrom)
ã	&atilde;	Small a with tilde accent
Ã	&Atilde;	Capital A with tilde accent
ä	&auml;	Small a with umlaut (diaeresis) accent
Ä	&Auml;	Capital A with umlaut (diaeresis) accent
č	&ccaron;	Small c with caron accent
Č	&Ccaron;	Capital C with caron accent

ç	&ccedil;	Small c with cedilla accent
Ç	&Ccedil;	Capital C with cedilla accent
ĉ	&ccirc;	Small c with circumflex accent
Ĉ	&Ccirc;	Capital C with circumflex accent
ď	&dcaron;	Small d with caron accent
Ď	&Dcaron;	Capital D with caron accent
ð	&eth;	Small eth (Icelandic character)
é	&eacute;	Small e with acute accent
É	&Eacute;	Capital E with acute accent
ě	&ecaron;	Small e with caron accent
Ě	&Ecaron;	Capital E with caron accent
ê	&ecirc;	Small e with circumflex accent
Ê	&Ecirc;	Capital E with circumflex accent
è	&egrave;	Small e with grave accent
È	&Egrave;	Capital E with grave accent
ē	&emacr;	Small e with macron accent
Ē	&Emacr;	Capital E with macron accent
ë	&euml;	Small e with umlaut (diaeresis) accent
Ë	&Euml;	Capital E with umlaut (diaeresis) accent
ĥ	&hcirc;	Small h with circumflex accent
Ĥ	&Hcirc;	Capital H with circumflex accent
í	&iacute;	Small i with acute accent
Í	&Iacute;	Capital I with acute accent
î	&icirc;	Small i with circumflex accent
Î	&Icirc;	Capital I with circumflex accent
ì	&igrave;	Small i with grave accent
Ì	&Igrave;	Capital I with grave accent
ī	&imacr;	Small i with macron accent
I	&Imacr;	Capital I with macron accent
ı	&inodot;	Small i without dot
ĩ	&itilde;	Small i with tilde accent
Ĩ	&Itilde;	Capital I with tilde accent
ï	&iuml;	Small i with umlaut (diaeresis)
Ï	&Iuml;	Capital I with umlaut (diaeresis) accent
ĵ	&jcirc;	Small j with circumflex accent
Ĵ	&Jcirc;	Capital J with circumflex accent
ĺ	&lacute;	Small l with acute accent
Ĺ	&Lacute;	Capital L with acute accent
ľ	&lcaron;	Small l with caron accent
Ľ	&Lcaron;	Capital L with caron accent
ń	&nacute;	Small n with acute accent
Ń	&Nacute;	Capital N with acute accent
ň	&ncaron;	Small n with caron accent
Ň	&Ncaron;	Capital N with caron accent
ñ	&ntilde;	Small n with tilde accent

Ñ	&Ntilde;	Capital N with tilde accent
ó	&oacute;	Small o with acute accent
Ó	&Oacute;	Capital O with acute accent
ô	&ocirc;	Small o with circumflex accent
Ô	&Ocirc;	Capital O with circumflex accent
œ	&oelig;	Small oe ligature
Œ	&OElig;	Capital OE ligature
ò	&ograve;	Small o with grave accent
Ò	&Ograve;	Capital O with grave accent
ō	&omacr;	Small o with macron accent
Ō	&Omacr;	Capital O with macron accent
ø	&oslash;	Small slashed o
Ø	&Oslash;	Capital slashed O
õ	&otilde;	Small o with tilde accent
Õ	&Otilde;	Capital O with tilde accent
ö	&ouml;	Small o with umlaut (diaeresis) accent
Ö	&Ouml;	Capital O with umlaut (diaeresis) accent
ŕ	&racute;	Small r with acute accent
Ŕ	&Racute;	Capital R with acute accent
ř	&rcaron;	Small r with caron accent
Ř	&Rcaron;	Capital R with caron accent
ś	&sacute;	Small s with acute accent
Ś	&Sacute;	Capital S with acute accent
š	&scaron;	Small s with caron accent
Š	&Scaron;	Capital S with caron accent
ŝ	&scirc;	Small s with circumflex accent
Ŝ	&Scirc;	Capital S with circumflex accent
ß	&szlig;	German sz ligature (sharp s)
ť	&tcaron;	Small t with caron accent
Ť	&Tcaron;	Capital T with caron accent
þ	&thorn;	Small thorn (Icelandic character)
Þ	&THORN;	Capital thorn (Icelandic character)
ú	&uacute;	Small u with acute accent
Ú	&Uacute;	Capital U with acute accent
ŭ	&ubreve;	Small u with breve accent
Ŭ	&Ubreve;	Capital U with breve accent
û	&ucirc;	Small u with circumflex accent
Û	&Ucirc;	Capital U with circumflex accent
ù	&ugrave;	Small u with grave accent
Ù	&Ugrave;	Capital U with grave accent
ū	&umacr;	Small u with macron accent
Ū	&Umacr;	Capital U with macron accent
ũ	&utilde;	Small u with tilde accent
Ũ	&Utilde;	Capital U with tilde accent
ü	&uuml;	Small u with umlaut (diaeresis) accent

Ü	`&Uuml;`	Capital U with umlaut (diaeresis) accent
ý	`&yacute;`	Small y with acute accent
Ý	`&Yacute;`	Capital Y with acute accent
ŷ	`&ycirc;`	Small y with circumflex accent
Ŷ	`&Ycirc;`	Capital Y with circumflex accent
ÿ	`&yuml;`	Small y with umlaut (diaeresis) accent
Ÿ	`&Yuml;`	Capital Y with umlaut (diaeresis) accent
ź	`&zacute;`	Small z with acute accent
Ź	`&Zacute;`	Capital Z with acute accent
ž	`&zcaron;`	Small z with caron accent
Ž	`&Zcaron;`	Capital Z with caron accent

B.2   Diacritical marks (accents)

To use any of the entities listed in this section in a document, include the
following entity declaration and parameter entity reference in the document type declaration subset:

```
<! ENTITY % AWdia PUBLIC "-//Addison-Wesley//ENTITIES Diacritical Marks//EN">
%AWdia;
```

The ten accents listed below are automatically added to the immediately preceding character:

´	`&acute;`	Acute accent
˘	`&breve;`	Breve
ˇ	`&caron;`	Caron
¸	`&cedil;`	Cedilla
^	`&circ;`	Circumflex accent
¨	`&die;`	Diaeresis
`	`&grave;`	Grave accent
¯	`&macr;`	Macron
~	`&tilde;`	Tilde
¨	`&uml;`	Umlaut mark

B.3   Greek alphabetic characters

To use any of the entities listed in this section in a document, include the
following entity declaration and parameter entity reference in the document type declaration subset:

```
<! ENTITY % AWgreek PUBLIC "-//Addison-Wesley//ENTITIES Greek Letters//EN">
%AWgreek;
```

The following entities can be used to request individual Greek characters within a document:

α	&alpha;	Small alpha, Greek
A	&Agr;	A, Greek capital alpha
β	&beta;	Small beta, Greek
B	&Bgr;	B, Greek capital beta
γ	&gamma;	Small gamma, Greek
Γ	&Gamma;	Capital gamma, Greek
δ	&delta;	Small delta, Greek
Δ	&Delta;	Capital delta, Greek
ϵ	&epsi;	Small epsilon, Greek
ε	&epsiv;	Small epsilon variant, Greek
E	&Egr;	E, Greek capital epsilon
ζ	&zeta;	Small zeta, Greek
Z	&Zgr;	Z, Greek capital zeta
η	&eta;	Small eta, Greek
H	&EEgr;	II, Greek capital eta
θ	&theta;	Small (straight) theta, Greek
ϑ	&thetav;	Small curly (open) theta variant, Greek
Θ	&Theta;	Capital theta, Greek
ι	&iota;	Small iota, Greek
I	&Igr;	I, Greek capital iota
κ	&kappa;	Small kappa, Greek
K	&Kgr;	K, Greek capital kappa
λ	&lambda;	Small lambda, Greek
Λ	&Lambda;	Capital lambda, Greek
μ	&mu;	Small mu, Greek
M	&Mgr;	M, Greek capital mu
ν	&nu;	Small nu, Greek
N	&Ngr;	N, Greek capital nu
ξ	&xi;	Small xi, Greek
Ξ	&Xi;	Capital xi, Greek
o	&ogr;	Small omicron, Greek
O	&Ogr;	O, Greek capital omicron
π	&pi;	Small pi, Greek
ϖ	&piv;	Small pi variant, Greek
Π	&Pi;	Capital pi, Greek
ρ	&rho;	Small rho, Greek
P	&Rgr;	P, Greek capital rho
σ	&sigma;	Small sigma, Greek
ς	&sigmav;	Small sigma variant, Greek
Σ	&Sigma;	Capital sigma, Greek
τ	&tau;	Small tau, Greek
T	&Tgr;	T, Greek capital tau

υ	&upsi;	Small upsilon, Greek
Υ	&Upsi;	Capital upsilon, Greek
φ	&phi;	Small (straight) phi, Greek
φ	&phiv;	Small curly (open) phi variant, Greek
Φ	&Phi;	Capital phi, Greek
χ	&chi;	Small chi, Greek
X	&KHgr;	X, Greek capital chi
ψ	&psi;	Small psi, Greek
Ψ	&Psi;	Capital psi, Greek
ω	&omega;	Small omega, Greek
Ω	&Omega;	Capital omega, Greek

B.4   Numeric and special graphic characters

To use any of the entities listed in this section in a document, include the following entity declaration and parameter entity reference in the document type declaration subset:

```
<! ENTITY % AWnum PUBLIC "-//Addison-Wesley/ENTITIES Numeric and Special Graphic//EN">
%AWnum;
```

The following entities can be used to request fractions and other symbols that may not be available on the keyboard or to request characters that might otherwise be treated as SGML markup or short references:

$\frac{1}{2}$	&half;	Fraction, one-half
½	&frac12;	Fraction, one-half, alternative notation
¼	&frac14;	Fraction, one-quarter
¾	&frac34;	Fraction, three-quarters
⅛	&frac18;	Fraction, one-eighth
⅜	&frac38;	Fraction, three-eighths
⅝	&frac58;	Fraction, five-eighths
⅞	&frac78;	Fraction, seven-eighths
⅓	&frac13;	Fraction, one-third
⅔	&frac23;	Fraction, two-thirds
⅕	&frac15;	Fraction, one-fifth
⅖	&frac25;	Fraction, two-fifths
⅗	&frac35;	Fraction, three-fifths
⅘	&frac45;	Fraction, four-fifths
⅙	&frac16;	Fraction, one-sixth
⅚	&frac56;	Fraction, five-sixths
^{1}	&sup1;	Superscript 1
^{2}	&sup2;	Superscript 2
^{3}	&sup3;	Superscript 3

-	&hyphen;	Hyphen
-	&shy;	Soft hyphen (only appears if at end of line)
—	&minus;	Minus sign
+	&plus;	Plus sign
±	&plusmn;	Plus-or-minus sign
<	&lt;	Less-than sign
=	&equals;	Equals sign
>	&gt;	Greater-than sign
÷	&divide;	Division sign
×	&times;	Multiplication sign
£	&pound;	Pound sign
$	&dollar;	Dollar sign
¢	&cent;	Cent sign
#	&num;	Number sign (hash)
%	&percnt;	Percent sign
&	&	Ampersand
*	&ast;	Asterisk
@	&commat;	Commercial at sign
[	&lsqb;	Left square bracket
]	&rsqb;	Right square bracket
{	&lcub;	Left curly brace
}	&rcub;	Right curly brace
\	&bsol;	Backslash = reverse solidus
_	&lowbar;	Lowline (baseline rule)
—	&horbar;	Horizontal bar
|	&verbar;	Vertical bar
¦	&brvbar;	Broken vertical bar
μ	&micro;	Micro sign
Ω	&ohm;	Ohm sign
°	&deg;	Degree sign
§	&sect;	Section sign
¶	&para;	Paragraph sign (pilcrow)
·	&middot;	Middle (decimal) dot
←	&larr;	Left pointing arrow
→	&rarr;	Right pointing arrow
↑	&uarr;	Upward arrow
↓	&darr;	Downward arrow
©	&copy;	Copyright sign
®	&reg;	Registered sign
™	&trade;	Trademark symbol
!	&excl;	Exclamation mark
¡	&iexcl;	Inverted exclamation mark
"	"	Quotation mark (double, straight)
'	'	Apostrophe
(	&lpar;	Left parenthesis (opening)

)	&rpar;	Right parenthesis (closing)
,	&comma;	Comma
.	&period;	Period (full stop)
/	&sol;	Solidus (shilling stroke)
:	&colon;	Colon
;	&semi;	Semicolon
?	&quest;	Question mark
¿	&iquest;	Inverted question mark
'	‘	Left (opening) single quotation mark
'	’	Right single quotation mark
"	“	Left (opening) double quotation mark
"	”	Right double quotation mark
,	&lsquor;	Rising single quote, left (low)
'	&rsquor;	Rising single quote, right (high)
,,	&ldquor;	Rising double quote, left (low)
"	&rdquor;	Rising double quote, right (high)
«	&laquo;	Left angle quotation mark (French opening guillemet)
»	&raquo;	Right angle quotation mark (French closing guillemet)
‹	&lsaquo;	Left single angle quotation mark (embedded guillemet)
›	&rsaquo;	Right single angle quotation mark (embedded guillemet)

B.5   Publishing characters

To use any of the entities listed in this section in a document, include the following entity declaration and parameter entity reference in the document type declaration subset:

```
<! ENTITY % AWpub PUBLIC "-//Addison-Wesley//ENTITIES Publishing Characters//EN">
%AWpub;
```

The following characters may be needed when a textbook is being prepared for typesetting:

	Em space
	En space (1/2 em)
	Digit space (width of number)
	1/3 em space (thick space)
	Punctuation space (width of comma)
	No break (required) space

—	`&mdash;`	Em dash
–	`&ndash;`	En dash
−	`&dash;`	Neutral dash/minus
...	`&hellip;`	Horizontal ellipsis (three dots)
...	`&mldr;`	Em leader (three dots)
..	`&nldr;`	En leader (double baseline dot)
○	`&cir;`	Circle, open
●	`&bull;`	Round bullet, filled
□	`&squ;`	Square, open
■	`&squf;`	Square bullet, filled
△	`&utri;`	Up pointing triangle, open
▽	`&dtri;`	Down pointing triangle, open
◁	`&ltri;`	Left pointing triangle, open
▷	`&rtri;`	Right pointing triangle, open
▲	`&utrif;`	Up pointing triangle, filled
▼	`&dtrif;`	Down pointing triangle, filled
◀	`&ltrif;`	Left pointing triangle, filled
▶	`&rtrif;`	Right pointing triangle, filled
◊	`&loz;`	Lozenge (total mark), open
◆	`&lozf;`	Lozenge, filled
☆	`&star;`	Star, open (big star)
★	`&starf;`	Star, filled (big star)
†	`&dag;`	Dagger
‡	`&Dag;`	Double dagger
√	`&check;`	Checkmark (tick)
♂	`&male;`	Male symbol
♀	`&female;`	Female symbol
☎	`&phone;`	Telephone symbol
ff	`&fflig;`	Small ff ligature
fi	`&filig;`	Small fi ligature
fl	`&fllig;`	Small fl ligature
ffi	`&ffilig;`	Small ffi ligature
ffl	`&ffllig;`	Small ffl ligature
⊕	`&target;`	Register mark or target

B.6   *Maths symbols*

To use any of the entities listed in this section in a document, include the
following entity declaration and parameter entity reference in the document type declaration subset:

```
<! ENTITY % AWmaths PUBLIC "-//Addison-Wesley//ENTITIES Maths Symbols//EN">
    %AWmaths;
```

The following symbols will allow simple mathematical expressions to be entered within a textbook without resorting to a special notation:

—	&minus;	Minus sign
+	&plus;	Plus sign
·	&middot;	Middle (decimal) dot
×	&times;	Multiplication sign
*	&ast;	Asterisk
÷	&divide;	Division sign
=	&equals;	Equals sign
◊	&loz;	Lozenge
<	&lt;	Less-than sign
>	&gt;	Greater-than sign
±	&plusmn;	Plus-or-minus sign
∓	&mnplus;	Minus-or-plus sign
⊕	&oplus;	Plus sign in circle
⊖	&ominus;	Minus sign in circle
⊗	&otimes;	Multiply sign in circle
⊘	&osol;	Solidus in circle
⊙	&odot;	Middle dot in circle
◯	&xcirc;	Large circle
○	&cir;	Circle
●	&bull;	Round bullet, filled
≍	&asymp;	Asymptotically equal to sign
≡	&equiv;	Equivalence sign
⊆	&sube;	Subset of, or equal to, sign
⊇	&supe;	Superset of, or equal to, sign
≤	&le;	Less-than-or-equals sign
≥	&ge;	Greater-than-or-equals sign
≼	&pre;	Precedes, or equals, sign
≽	&sce;	Succeeds, or equals, sign
~	&sim;	Similar-to sign
≈	&ap;	Approximation sign
⊂	&sub;	Subset sign
⊃	&sup;	Superset sign
≪	&Lt;	Double less-than sign
≫	&Gt;	Double greater-than sign
≺	&pr;	Precedes sign
≻	&sc;	Succeeds sign
←	&larr;	Left arrow
→	&rarr;	Right arrow
↑	&uarr;	Up arrow
↓	&darr;	Down arrow
↔	&lrarr;	Left-and-right pointing arrow
↗	&nearr;	NE pointing arrow

↘	`&searr;`	SE pointing arrow
≃	`&sime;`	Similar or equal to sign
⇐	`&lArr;`	Is implied by (left double arrow)
⇒	`&rArr;`	Implies (right double arrow)
⇑	`&uArr;`	Up double arrow
⇓	`&dArr;`	Down double arrow
⇔	`&lrArr;`	Left-and-right pointing double arrow
↖	`&nwarr;`	NW pointing arrow
↙	`&swarr;`	SW pointing arrow
∝	`&prop;`	Proportional to sign
╱	`&ssol;`	Short division sign
∞	`&infin;`	Infinity sign
∈	`&isin;`	Set membership sign
∋	`&ni;`	Not in, or owns, sign
△	`&utri;`	Up pointing triangle, open
▽	`&dtri;`	Down pointing triangle, open
╱	`&sol;`	Solidus (alternative division sign)
∀	`&forall;`	For all sign
∃	`&exist;`	At least one exists sign
¬	`&not;`	Not sign
⊥	`&bottom;`	Perpendicular sign
ℵ	`&aleph;`	Hebrew aleph
𝒜	`&mathsA;`	Maths swash A
ℬ	`&mathsB;`	Maths swash B
𝒞	`&mathsC;`	Maths swash C
𝒟	`&mathsD;`	Maths swash D
ℰ	`&mathsE;`	Maths swash E
ℱ	`&mathsF;`	Maths swash F
𝒢	`&mathsG;`	Maths swash G
ℋ	`&mathsH;`	Maths swash H
ℐ	`&mathsI;`	Maths swash I
𝒥	`&mathsJ;`	Maths swash J
𝒦	`&mathsK;`	Maths swash K
ℒ	`&mathsL;`	Maths swash L
ℳ	`&mathsM;`	Maths swash M
𝒩	`&mathsN;`	Maths swash N
𝒪	`&mathsO;`	Maths swash O
𝒫	`&mathsP;`	Maths swash P
𝒬	`&mathsQ;`	Maths swash Q
ℛ	`&mathsR;`	Maths swash R
𝒮	`&mathsS;`	Maths swash S
𝒯	`&mathsT;`	Maths swash T
𝒰	`&mathsU;`	Maths swash U
𝒱	`&mathsV;`	Maths swash V
𝒲	`&mathsW;`	Maths swash W

$\mathcal{X}$	`&mathsX;`	Maths swash X
$\mathcal{Y}$	`&mathsY;`	Maths swash Y
$\mathcal{Z}$	`&mathsZ;`	Maths swash Z
∪	`&cup;`	Union, or logical sum, sign
∩	`&cap;`	Intersection sign
∧	`&and;`	Logical and sign
∨	`&or;`	Logical or sign
⊢	`&vdash;`	Vertical and dash
⊣	`&dashv;`	Dash and vertical
⌊	`&lfloor;`	Left floor
⌋	`&rfloor;`	Right floor
⌈	`&lceil;`	Left ceiling
⌉	`&rceil;`	Right ceiling
{	`&lcub;`	Left curly brace
}	`&rcub;`	Right curly brace
⟨	`&lang;`	Left angle bracket
⟩	`&rang;`	Right angle bracket
|	`&verbar;`	Vertical bar
‖	`&par;`	Parallel line
\	`&bsol;`	Backslash (reverse solidus)
√	`&radic;`	Radical sign
⨿	`&coprod;`	Coproduct (amalgamation) operator
∏	`&prod;`	Product operator
∫	`&int;`	Integral operator
∮	`&conint;`	Integral operator with central o
Σ	`&sum;`	Summation operator
∇	`&nabla;`	Hamilton operator
⊔	`&sqcup;`	Square union sign
⊓	`&sqcap;`	Square intersection sign
⊑	`&sqsube;`	Square subset of, or equal to, sign
⊒	`&sqsupe;`	Square superset of, or equal to, sign
§	`&sect;`	Section sign
†	`&dag;`	Dagger
‡	`&Dag;`	Double dagger
¶	`&para;`	Paragraph sign (pilcrow)

Sample Document Type Declaration

This appendix contains a document type declaration (DTD) suitable for the production of textbooks. Though not designed to cover complex mathematical and technical work, the 99 elements declared in this DTD are suitable for coding Addison-Wesley's International Computer Science Series (ICSS) of textbooks, and will provide a good starting point for the design of book production DTDs. (In practice, 90% of any textbook can be marked up using just 25 of the codes described in this set. Another 25 of the tags only ever occur in the preliminary pages of books.)

The purpose of each of the elements declared in the DTD is described briefly below. Where practicable, an example showing the use of the element has been provided. Other examples of the use of the declared elements can be found in the main text. For ease of reference, elements have been described in the sequence in which they are declared in the DTD. An alphabetical list of the elements is provided at the end of the appendix.

C.1   The document type declaration

The document type declaration defined below will normally be added to the start of the document, immediately after the SGML declaration (see

Figure 3.1). Where the DTD is already known to the receiving system, the document type declaration can be simplified to read:

```
<!DOCTYPE textbook PUBLIC "-//Addison-Wesley//DTD SGML: An Author's Guide to
the Standard Generalized Markup Language//EN">
```

If the character sets defined in Appendix B are to be used within the document these should be added to the above declaration to give it the form:

```
<!DOCTYPE   textbook  PUBLIC "-//Addison-Wesley//DTD SGML: An Author's Guide to
the Standard Generalized Markup Language//EN"
 [ <!ENTITY % AWacc   PUBLIC
            "-//Addison-Wesley//ENTITIES Accented Characters//EN" >
   <!ENTITY % AWnum   PUBLIC
            "-//Addison-Wesley//ENTITIES Numeric and Special Characters//EN" >
   <!ENTITY % AWpub   PUBLIC
            "-//Addison-Wesley//ENTITIES Publishing Characters//EN" >
%AWacc; %AWnum; %AWpub; ]>
```

As far as possible, the names of elements in the following DTD match those of the equivalent entries in the DTD for a general class of documents defined in Annex E of ISO 8879. In the interest of clarity, however, the names of all parameter entities have been changed to reflect their role within this DTD.

```
<!DOCTYPE textbook
-- Known as "-//Addison-Wesley//DTD SGML: An Author's Guide to
the Standard Generalized Markup Language//EN"
   An SGML Application Conforming to International Standard ISO 8879 -
   Standard Generalized Markup Language --
   [ <!ENTITY % phrases  "hp0ihp1ihp2ihp3icit"    -- emphasized phrases -->
     <!ENTITY % lists    "liigliterms"                               >
     <!ENTITY % element  "xmpilqilipoemitableiadriartworkieqn"
                         -- elements of a paragraph starting on new line  -->
     <!ENTITY % topics   "top1itop2itop3"                            >
     <!ENTITY % refs     "hdrefifigrefitablerefifnrefiitreficitref"
                                                   -- references  -->
     <!ENTITY % copy     "pinotei%element;"                          >
     <!ENTITY % text     "%topics;i%copy;i%lists;"                   >
     <!ENTITY % floats   "figifn" -- items positioned relative to a page -->
     <!ENTITY % prelims  "prefaceiforewordiacknowlsiotherm"          >
     <!ENTITY % titles   "h0tih1tih2tih3tih4tih5t"                   >

                   <!-- Base document element -->
     <!ELEMENT textbook    - O (front, body, back?) +(%floats;iix)   >
```

```
<!ATTLIST textbook  version CDATA           "1"
                                            -- date or number, etc. --
                    status  CDATA           ""
                    security CDATA          #IMPLIED              >
<!ELEMENT (body|appendix) - O (h0|h1)+ -- body of text & appendices -->

            <!-- Highest division of body - e.g. Part -->
<!ELEMENT h0          - O (h0t, (%text;)*, h1+)                   >

            <!-- Main division of text - e.g. Chapter -->
<!ELEMENT (h1|%prelims;|glossary|bibliog)
                      - O (h1t, (%text;)*, h2*)                   >

            <!-- Sections within main division -->
<!ELEMENT h2          - O (h2t, (%text;)*, h3*)                   >

            <!-- Subsections within main division section -->
<!ELEMENT h3          - O (h3t, (%text;)*, h4*)                   >

        <!-- Sub-subsections within main division subsections -->
<!ELEMENT h4          - O (h4t, (%text;)*, h5*)                   >

            <!-- Lowest division of heading -->
<!ELEMENT h5          - O (h5t, (%text;)+)                        >
<!ATTLIST (h0|h1|h2|h3|h4|h5|%prelims;|appendix|glossary|bibliog)
                    number CDATA        ""     -- reference number --
                    id ID       #IMPLIED
                    stitle CDATA      #IMPLIED    -- short title -->

            <!-- Headings for divisions -->
<!ELEMENT (%titles;)   O O (#PCDATA|q|%phrases;)*                 >
<!ELEMENT hdref        - - (#PCDATA|%phrases;)*  -- reference to
                                                      heading --  >
<!ATTLIST hdref        refid IDREF        #REQUIRED
                       page (yes|no|y|n)  no                      >

            <!-- Topics within sections -->
<!ELEMENT top1        - O (th, (%copy;|%lists;|top2)+)
                                            -- first level topic --
<!ELEMENT top2        - O (th, (%copy;|%lists;|top3)+)
                                            -- second level topic --
<!ELEMENT top3        - O (th, (%copy;|%lists;)+)
                                            -- third level topic --
<!ELEMENT (th|hd)     - O (#PCDATA|q|%phrases;)*                  >
<!ATTLIST (top1|top2|top3|hd) id ID    #IMPLIED                   >

            <!-- Basic text elements -->
<!ELEMENT p           - O (#PCDATA|%phrases;|q|%element;|
                          %lists;|%refs;)+ -- paragraph of text -->
```

```
<!ELEMENT note       - - (#PCDATA|%phrases;|q|%element;|
                           %lists;|%refs;|p)+    -- note in text -->
<!ELEMENT (%phrases;)  - - (#PCDATA|%phrases;|q)+              >
<!ATTLIST cit          id ID          #IMPLIED                >

                <!-- Elements within a paragraph -->
<!ELEMENT l          0 0 (#PCDATA|q|%phrases;|%refs;)+
                                 -- freestanding line of text -->
<!ATTLIST l          position (left|right|centred|indented) #CURRENT >
<!ELEMENT q          - - (#PCDATA|q|%phrases;|%refs;)+
                                 -- quotation embedded in text -->
<!ELEMENT lq         - - (#PCDATA|%text;|h2|h3|h4|h5)+  -(fn)
                                           -- long quotation -->
<!ELEMENT poem       - 0 (pt, v+, cit?)                       >
<!ELEMENT pt         0 0 (#PCDATA|%phrases;|q|l)*
                                           -- title of poem -->
<!ELEMENT v          - 0 (l+)             --verse of poem -->
<!ATTLIST v          no CDATA       "1"                       >
<!ELEMENT adr        - 0 (l+)                  -- address -->

           <!-- Examples, illustrations and figures -->
<!ELEMENT xmp        - 0 (#PCDATA|%copy;|%lists;|%phrases;)* -(xmp)>
<!ATTLIST xmp        style CDATA        #IMPLIED
                     keep NMTOKEN       "all"
                     form (lines|runon)  lines               >
<!ELEMENT artwork    - 0 EMPTY                                >
<!ATTLIST artwork    sizex NMTOKEN      textsize
                                 -- defaults to text width --
                     sizey NUTOKEN      #REQUIRED
                     file ENTITY        #IMPLIED              >

        <!-- Figure = artwork/text + caption or other identifier -->
<!ELEMENT fig        - - (figbody, (figcap, figdesc?)?)  --figure-->
<!ATTLIST fig        id ID              #IMPLIED
                 number CDATA           ""
                  frame (box|rules|none)           none
               position (top|bottom|middle|asfound) asfound
                   type (column|page)              page
                  align (left|right|centred)       centred   >
<!ELEMENT figbody    0 0 (%copy;|%lists;)+  -- body of figure -- >
<!ATTLIST figbody    form (lines|runon)              lines    >
<!ELEMENT figcap     - 0 (#PCDATA|%phrases;)*  --caption of fig-- >
<!ELEMENT figdesc    - 0 (#PCDATA|%copy;|%lists;)*
                                 -- description of figure -->

                     <!-- Tables -->
<!ELEMENT table      - - (nt?, ht?, hc?, bt+, ft?)            >
<!ATTLIST table      id ID          #IMPLIED
                     cols NUMBER    #REQUIRED
                     tabs NUMBERS   "1 10 20 30 40 50 60 70"  >
```

```
<!ELEMENT nt           - O (#PCDATAι%phrases;)*
                           -- number or other identifier of table -->
<!ELEMENT ht           - O (#PCDATAιqι%phrases;ι%text;)*
                                              -- heading of table -->
<!ELEMENT hc           - O (r)+  -(bt,ft)    -- heading of columns -->
<!ATTLIST (hcιbtιft)   cols NUMBER      #IMPLIED              >
<!ELEMENT bt           - O (r)+                  -- body of table -->
<!ELEMENT ft           - O (r)+  -(hc,bt)        -- foot of table -->
<!ELEMENT r            O O (cιhcιbtιft)+         -- row in table -->
<!ELEMENT c            - O (#PCDATAιqι%phrases;ι%refs;ι
                           (hd?,(%text;)))* -- cell of table -->
<!ATTLIST c            straddle NUMBER      1                 >
<!ELEMENT (figrefιtablerefιcitref)         -- x-ref to fig/table --
                       - O (#PCDATAι%phrases;ιq)* -(cit)       >
<!ATTLIST (figrefιtablerefιcitref)
                       refid IDREF          #CONREF
                       page (yesιnoιnιy)    no                >


                       <!-- Lists -->
<!ELEMENT li           - - (it+)             -- list of items -->
<!ATTLIST li number (arabicιromanιalphaιdefaultιnone) default
           form  (compactιspaced)           spaced            >
<!ELEMENT it           O O (#PCDATAι%copy;ιliιqι%phrases;)*
                                              -- item in list -->
<!ATTLIST it           id ID            #IMPLIED              >
<!ELEMENT itref        - O EMPTY     -- generated item reference -->
<!ATTLIST itref   refid IDREF         #REQUIRED
                  page (yιn)          y                       >


                  <!-- Glossary style list -->
<!ELEMENT gl           - - (hd?, (gt, (gdιgdg))*) -- glossary list -->
<!ATTLIST gl           form (compactιspaced)   spaced
                       termhi NUMBER           2              >
<!ELEMENT gt           O O (#PCDATAιqι%phrases;)* -- glossary term -->
<!ATTLIST (gtιdt)      id ID            #IMPLIED              >
<!ELEMENT gdg          - O (gd+)   -- group of definitions for
                            glossary term (normally numbered) -->
<!ATTLIST gdg   number (arabicιromanιalphaιdefaultιnone)  default  >
<!ELEMENT gd           O O (#PCDATAι%copy;ιliιqι%phrases;ι%refs;)*
                            -- definition of glossary term -->
<!ATTLIST gd           source CDATA         ""
                       see IDREF            #IMPLIED
                       seealso IDREF        #IMPLIED          >


            <!-- List of term definitions, etc -->
<!ELEMENT terms        - - (dthd?, ddhd?)?, (dt, dd+)+)
                                             --list of terms-->
```

```
<!ATTLIST terms       style (columnsirunon)  runon                    >
<!ELEMENT (dthdiddhd)  - O (#PCDATA)     -- headings for columns -- >
<!ATTLIST (dthdiddhd)
                      style (romaniboldiitalicismallcap) roman        >
<!ELEMENT dt          O O (#PCDATAi%phrases;iq)* -- defined term -- >
<!ELEMENT dd          - O (#PCDATAiqi%phrases;i%refs;i%copy;)*
                                         -- definition description -->


                  <!-- Other elements of text -->
<!ELEMENT fn          - - (#PCDATAiqi%phrases;i%refs;i%copy;)*
                                   -(%floats;) -- footnote -->
<!ATTLIST fn          id ID            #IMPLIED                       >
<!ELEMENT fnref       - O EMPTY  --generated reference to footnote-->
<!ATTLIST fnref       refid IDREF      #REQUIRED
                      page (yesinoiyin)    no                         >
<!ELEMENT ix          - O (#PCDATA)    -(ix)  -- index entry -->
<!ATTLIST ix          id ID            #IMPLIED
                      print CDATA      #IMPLIED
                      linkwith NAMES   #IMPLIED
                      andwith NAMES    #IMPLIED
                      see CDATA        ""                             >
<!ELEMENT eqn         - - RCDATA                    -- equation -->
<!ATTLIST eqn         type NOTATION (a-witexisetm)   a-w             >
<!NOTATION a-w  PUBLIC "-//Addison-Wesley//NOTATION maths//EN"       >
<!NOTATION tex  PUBLIC "-//local//NOTATION TeX Formulae//EN"         >
<!NOTATION setm PUBLIC "-//BSI//NOTATION SETM coding//EN"            >


              <!-- Elements used in preliminary pages -->
<!ELEMENT front       O O (titlep & details* & toc? & figlist? &
                      (%prelims;)* )     -- preliminary pages -->
<!ELEMENT titlep      - O (title & (authorieditor)* & docnum? &
                          abstract? & publishr? & date? & (%text;)*)
                                          -- title page -->
<!ELEMENT title       - O ((#PCDATAiLiqi%phrases;)+i
                          (tline+ & subtitle*)) -- title of book -->
<!ATTLIST title       htitle CDATA     #IMPLIED    -- half title --
                      running CDATA    #IMPLIED
                      -- shorter title for running head/reference -->
<!ELEMENT tline       O O (#PCDATAiL+)          -- line of title -->
<!ELEMENT subtitle    - O (#PCDATAi%copy;)+                           >
<!ELEMENT (authorieditor)
                      - O (name, position*)                           >
<!ELEMENT name        O O (#PCDATAi%phrases;)*
                                        -- name to be printed -->
<!ELEMENT position    - O (#PCDATAiL+) -- one or more lines of text
                                   describing position(s) held
                                   or qualifications --      >
<!ELEMENT docnum      - O (#PCDATAiISBN)-- unique document number -->
<!ELEMENT ISBN        - - CDATA          -- ISBN (or ISSN) number -->
```

```
<!ATTLIST ISBN        type (book|serial)  book                   >
<!ELEMENT abstract    - O (#PCDATA|%copy;)+
                                      --abstract of paper, etc.-->
<!ELEMENT publishr    - O (name & (%text;))*  --publisher details-->
<!ELEMENT date        - O (#PCDATA|%copy;)+ -- publication date
                                            (freeform) -->
<!ELEMENT details     - O (copyrite? & publishr? & colophon* &
                           ISBN* & BLCIP? & LibCong? & dedicate* &
                           related*)    -- other details of book -->
<!ELEMENT copyrite    - O (#PCDATA|%copy;)+ -- copyright details -->
<!ELEMENT colophon    - O (#PCDATA|%copy;)+
                                      --details of printer, etc.-->
<!ELEMENT dedicate    - O (#PCDATA|%copy;)+ -- dedication of book -->
<!ELEMENT LibCong     - O (#PCDATA|%copy;)+
               -- Library of Congress Cataloguing in Publication Data -->
<!ELEMENT BLCIP       - O (#PCDATA|%copy;)+
                 -- British Library Cataloguing in Publication Data -->
<!ELEMENT related     - O (hd, (%text;)+)
                                    -- details of related titles -->
<!-- hd is automatically implied by <related>, but can be blank as
                           text within hd is optional -->
<!ELEMENT (toc|figlist|index)    -- items generated automatically --
                      - O EMPTY -- from contents of body and back -->
  <!ELEMENT back  - O ((appendix|glossary|bibliog|otherm)* & index?)
                      -- matter after main text -- >
<!-- Appendices can be treated as a top (h0) division of text (called
appendix) so that covering text can be entered to explain the purpose
of individual appendices. Individual appendices are then treated as
chapters (h1 divisions) within the main appendix division, the
appendix's title being treated as a chapter heading (h1t). Glossaries
and bibliographies are treated as separate chapters within the back
matter, and other matter can be added where necessary. The
automatically generated index is derived from the contents of the
index entry elements within the text.-->

                    <!-- Short reference maps -->
<!ENTITY    start-qt   STARTTAG   "q"   -- quoted phrase start-tag -- >
<!ENTITY    end-qte    ENDTAG     "q"   -- end of quoted text --      >
<!ENTITY    newcol     STARTTAG   "c"   -- start new column --        >
<!SHORTREF  quotes     '"'                  start-qt                  >
<!USEMAP    quotes     (p|note|%phrases;|%titles;|th|hd|pt|l|
                       it|gt|gd|dt|dd|fn|title)                       >
<!SHORTREF  endquote   '"'                  end-qte                   >
<!USEMAP    endquote   q                                              >
<!SHORTREF  tablemap   "&#TAB;"             newcol
                       '"'                  start-qt                  >
<!USEMAP    tablemap   table                                         >
<!USEMAP    #EMPTY     fig                                            >
]>
```

C.2   The parameter entities

Ten parameter entities are defined at the start of the DTD to simplify the format of the following declarations. These entities are:

(1)   %phrases;, which groups together the five types of highlighted phrases defined within the DTD;

(2)   %lists;, which groups together three types of list declared in the DTD;

(3)   %element;, which groups together eight elements commonly embedded within text (examples, long and short quotations, freestanding lines, poems, addresses, artwork and equations);

(4)   %topics;, which groups together the three levels of topic defined in the DTD;

(5)   %refs;, which groups together the six cross-reference elements declared in the DTD;

(6)   %copy;, which defines a commonly used set of elements suitable for entry of straightforward copy by combining the list defined by %element; with the paragraph and note elements;

(7)   %text;, which brings together all the elements used to define text, including topics, lists or straightforward copy;

(8)   %floats;, which defines elements whose position may be altered during pagination of the document;

(9)   %prelims;, which groups together four types of textual element that may occur before the main text; and

(10)   %titles;, which groups together the six types of section title provided for within the main text.

C.3   The base document element

The base document element for this DTD is <textbook>. A start-tag for this element must be entered, immediately after the DTD and any other declarations in the prolog, before any of the other tags defined in the DTD can be used. Optionally, the last tag entered in the document can be an end-tag for the base document element (e.g. </textbook>).

The three attributes associated with the base document element allow authors to indicate:

(1)   the version of the document being interchanged,

(2)   the current status of the document, and

(3)   any security classification associated with the document.

Each of these attributes can be defined using any character in the document's character set, but entity and character references cannot be used within the attributes. A typical document might be sent to the publisher with the following base document element start-tag:

```
<textbook version="3" status="final revision" security="confidential">
```

Alternatively, the version number could be entered in the form of a date, with or without the other optional attributes, for example:

```
<textbook version="25th December 1988">
```

The base document element has three components in its model definition:

(1)   `<front>` for the front matter preceding the main text,

(2)   `<body>` for the body of the text, and

(3)   `<back>` for those sections following the main text.

NOTE: The names used for the front matter and back matter elements of a textbook differ from those defined for the general document type described in Annex E of ISO 8879 because the definitions used within this DTD are more detailed than those provided by ISO 8879.

The `<back>` element is optional but the textbook must start with a `<front>` element since this element contains the compulsory title page. None of these basic subelements may occur more than once in a textbook file.

An inclusion group associated with the model of the base document element permits floating elements (such as figures, footnotes and index entries) to be entered at any point in the textbook, without their having to be specifically included in the model of the currently open element.

C.4   Elements in the body of the text —————————————

C.4.1   Headings

The elements permitted in the body of the text are basically the same as those defined in Annex E of ISO 8879. To allow for complex sets of appendices within textbooks the same model is used for both the body of the text and the structure of appendices.

The body of the text can either be split into a number of parts, indicated by a heading of level 0 (`<h0>`), or into a number of chapters, indicated by a heading of level 1 (`<h1>`). To allow for the situation where an introductory chapter may precede a series of parts or where a summary chapter follows the last part, these two elements may be used repeatedly in any order. At least one heading level must be defined at the start of the body of the text, though, as will be shown shortly, this heading need not contain any text.

Typically, the body of a textbook might start:

```
<body><h1>Introduction
<p>...
</h1><h0>Physics
<h1>Basic Forces
<p>...
```

The use of end-tags is optional for both the body of the text and any appendices, the end of the element being implied by the presence of another start-tag of the same or a higher level.

Within chapters four major divisions are recognized, each of which starts with a heading of the appropriate level:

(1)   sections (`<h2>`),
(2)   subsections (`<h3>`),
(3)   sub-subsections (`<h4>`), and
(4)   sub-sub-subsection (`<h5>`).

Each of these divisions has the same basic model, consisting of a title (e.g. `<h1t>`) followed by text and/or lower level headings.

Though this basic model indicates that each new level must start with a title, the general definition for titles shows that the textual components of this element (parsed character data, quoted text or highlighted phrases) are always optional, while the fact that both the start- and end-tag can be omitted means that the tags never need to be entered by the author, their presence being implied by the start of a new heading level and the start of the first text element within the section, respectively. This means that unheaded, numbered sections and subsections can be specified by use of entries such as:

```
<h4><p>This paragraph ....
```

While parts, chapters and, optionally, other section levels may be numbered in the printed book, these numbers should not be entered in the text as they will normally be generated automatically during pagination. As this may be confusing to authors, however, and as not all output systems will be able to generate the relevant section numbers automatically,

authors can optionally enter a heading number as an attribute to the
start-tag of a heading, for example:

```
<h2 number="3.5">
```

Two other attributes can be associated with each heading level to
provide:

(1)   a unique identifier (id) for the section, and

(2)   a shortened version of the title to be used in running headlines
       and/or cross-references.

If no attribute value is entered the program will imply values for both of
these attributes. In the case of id the implied attribute value will be Hn.n.n,
where n.n.n is a number indicating the relative position of the heading
within the book (e.g. H9.2.1 represents the first subsection heading in the
second section of Chapter 9). In the case of the stitle attribute, the implied
short title will be the heading of the element.

To see how these attributes are used in practice, consider the
following example:

```
<h1 id="rec1" stitle="Recognition">
Recognition as a Problem Solving Strategy
<p>...
```

In this case, the chapter will be numbered by the system using the
default style and sequence for chapter headings. The running headline for
the chapter will consist of the word Recognition on its own. When the chapter
is referred to elsewhere in the text, the cross-reference will use the id rec1
and the automatically generated text for the entry will use the short form of
the title, Recognition, instead of the full title of the chapter.

*NOTE: Numbers and short titles entered as attributes to headings will only appear in
the text where permitted by the house style. For example, short titles for sections and
subsections will not normally appear in the running headlines and, in the ICSS series
of textbooks, sub-subsections and lower are not numbered.*

The heading reference element (<hdref>) can be used to cross-refer to
any heading within the current document. Two attributes are associated
with this element:

(1)   refid allows the id of the heading being referred to to be specified, and

(2)   page allows authors to specify whether or not the relevant page number is
       to appear in the reference (overriding any default house style).

Normally, the reference will be entered in the form:

```
See <hdref refid="rec1">
```

to generate a reference such as 'See Chapter 9, Recognition' or as:

```
in <hdref refid="loads" page="yes">
```

to generate a reference such as 'in Section 4.6.5, page 123'.

C.4.2   Special topics

Where further subdivisions of the body of the text are required, up to three levels of topics (<top1>, <top2> and <top3>) can be embedded within any textual element. As with sections, topics are preceded by a topic heading (<th>) whose presence is automatically implied from the presence of the start-tag for the topic. This topic heading, as with general headings (<hd>), can be empty if the presence of topic is to be identified simply by the level of indent.

NOTE: In the ICSS house style, topic levels 1 and 2 will appear in the same format as heading levels 4 and 5 as both these headings are, like topics, unnumbered.

To prevent the accidental embedding of topics, the model for each topic allows for the entry of standard copy elements, such as paragraphs, notes and embedded text elements, lists and, where applicable, lower level topics. These elements may be repeated as required. At least one embedded element start-tag must follow the start-tag/heading of each topic, for example:

```
<top2><p>Text for topics is often indented...
```

or:

```
<top1>Elements of a topic
<li>Copy, including paragraphs, note, poems, addresses, etc.
<it>...
```

End-tags are optional for topics, their presence being impliable from the presence of a start-tag for the same, or a higher, level of topic or by entry of a new heading at any level. If followed by normal text, however, the presence of the end-tag is required to indicate that the normal text format is to be resumed.

As topics are unnumbered and never affect the running headline, the only attribute associated with them (and general headings within the text) is an id that provides a unique reference to any heading.

C.4.3   Basic text elements

The paragraph element (‹p›) forms the basic element of any textbook. As well as parsed character data (#PCDATA), paragraphs can contain the following embedded elements:

- highlighted phrases or citations (%phrases;);
- quoted text (‹q›);
- embedded elements, such as examples, separated long quotations, poems or individual lines of text, tables, addresses, artwork and equations (%elements;);
- lists, including lists of terms and glossary type definitions (%lists;); and
- references to footnotes, figures, tables, headings, etc. (%refs;).

The ‹/p› paragraph end-tag can be omitted whenever the paragraph is followed by a higher level of element (e.g. a heading or topic), by a note or by another paragraph.

Notes are the other major element found in the main text of textbooks. These are very similar to paragraphs, except that both the start- and end-tag must be present as a note can consist of more than one paragraph. The format of the printed note and the wording used to identify the note will depend on the house style. For example, in the ICSS textbooks, notes are preceded by the word NOTE: and are set in italic. A typical note might be entered as:

```
<note>For consistency major text elements in the front
and back elements are defined using the model for
chapters.
<p>Notes can contain more than one parargraph.</note>
```

Four types of highlighted phrase are allowed for within the DTD – ‹hp0›, ‹hp1›, ‹hp2› and ‹hp3›. The appearance of each of type of phrase will depend on the house style being used. For ICSS textbooks, as for the general DTD defined in ISO 8879, the default styles are:

- ‹hp1› set in italics,
- ‹hp2› set in bold,
- ‹hp3› set in bold italics, and
- ‹hp0› set in normal roman (within an otherwise highlighted element).

As the following example shows, phrases and quotations can be embedded within highlighted phrases:

```
... uttered the following verse: <hp1><q>Night shall
speak and give <hp0>thee</hp0> consel, night shall give
<hp0/thee/ victory.</q></hp1>
```

Both the start- and end-tag must be entered for each embedded highlighted phrase, though the amount of coding can be reduced by use of the net-enabling start-tag feature (see Chapter 7 and the last embedded phrase).

In practice, the quotation shown above would normally be set as an individual line. This can be achieved by the addition of a start-tag for the line element, for example:

```
... uttered the following verse:
<l><hp1><q>Night shall speak and give <hp0>thee</hp0>
consel, night shall give <hp0/thee/ victory.</q></hp1>
```

In this DTD only highlighted phrases, citations, short quotations and cross-references can be embedded within the parsed character data that normally forms the contents of the line element (`<l>`).

Since end-tags can be omitted for the line element, no end-tag is required if the line is immediately followed by another line element, or the start- or end-tag of a higher level element (e.g. a paragraph), but it would be required if the current paragraph continued after the separated line.

To allow authors to control the positioning of individual lines the line element has been assigned a `position` attribute. This attribute can have one of four values:

- `left` if the line is to be aligned with the left of the current measure,
- `right` if the line is to be aligned with the right of the current measure,
- `centred` if the line is to be centred on the measure, or
- `indented` if the line is to be indented by a predefined amount (the standard indent).

To reduce the amount of coding required for the line element, the default value for the `position` attribute has been defined by use of the `#CURRENT` keyword. This presence of this keyword means that a value must be specified the first time the line element occurs within the textbook but, after that, it need not be entered if the current line is to have the same attribute value as the last line.

One consequence of this rule is that the above example would be illegal if it represented the first occurrence of an individual line in the textbook because the program would look for the current value of the `position` attribute and, not finding one, declare the tag to be invalid. If it was the first occurrence of the line element in the textbook and the line was to be centred on the current measure, the example would need to be changed to read:

```
... uttered the following verse:
<l centred><hp1><q>Night shall speak and give <hp0>thee</hp0>
consel, night shall give <hp0/thee/ victory.</q></hp1>
```

To reduce the amount of coding required in line-oriented elements, such as addresses and verses of poems, the start-tag of a line can be omitted wherever ambiguity cannot arise.

Two types of quotations are provided for in the sample DTD – short quotations embedded in the current line of text (`<q>`) and long quotations which start on a new line of text (`<lq>`). The start- and end-tags of both these elements are compulsory since they mark the position at which quotation marks are to appear. The form of quotation mark used will depend on house style (and the language being used – see Appendix A).

Quotation marks (") entered in text will be treated as short references to short quotations (see Section C.7). Apostrophes (and grave accents) should never be used to bracket quotations. Your publisher will decide which type of quotation marks is to be used in the printed book. The relevant characters will be generated automatically during typesetting at the points indicated by the start- and end-tags of the quotation. (It should be remembered that in printed text there is a distinct difference in the appearance of the quotes used at the start and end of a quotation.)

While short quotations can only contain data characters, entities, character references, highlighted phrases and citations (or further embedded short quotations), long quotations can contain any type of text short of a complete chapter. The only restriction placed on long quotations is that they may not include footnotes (because they would almost certainly be numbered differently from the sequence within the textbook).

A typical long quotation might be entered as:

```
<p>The ISO definition for the steradian is:
<lq>The steradian is the solid angle which, having its vertex
in the centre of a sphere, cuts off an area of the surface of
the sphere equal to that of a square with sides of length
equal to the radius of the sphere<cit>ISO Recommendation
R 31, part 1, second edition, December 1965</cit></lq></p>
```

The above example also illustrates how citations of other documents can be made within text elements by use of the `<cit>` tag. The definition of this tag is the same as that for highlighted phrases, except that the tag can have an optional `id` attribute associated with it for cross-reference by the `<citref>` element.

Both the position and appearance of the citation will depend on the publisher's house style. Some publishers prefer citations to appear as footnotes to the page on which the citation occurs; others prefer separate lists at the end of the chapter or book. In some cases, different rules apply for citations within quotes, which may be printed as bracketed text. Irrespective of the required position, the same tag (`<cit>`) is used to identify the citation.

In this DTD no attempt has been made to control the sequence of the component parts of the citation because this can vary, though many publishers will insist on a fixed format. (If a fixed format is required, the model for the ‹cit› element will need to be decoupled from that of other highlighted phrases.)

Where the bibliographic references are collected in a separate bibliography at the end of the book or chapter, with textual cross-references in the text rather than straightforward reference numbers, the ‹citref› element should be used within the text at the point the citation would otherwise be entered. For example, Addison-Wesley have adopted the Harvard name and date system for bibliographic references so, within the text, the citation simply consists of the author's surname followed by the publication date, for example:

```
It has been shown (Roberts, 1980) that ...
```

or:

```
Roberts (1980) has demonstrated ...
```

In this case, the citation entered in the bibliography has the form:

```
<cit id="Roberts">Roberts, D. H. (1980). <q>LSI/VSI &ndash; What
does it signify?</q> IEE Conference on <q>The Impact of New
LSI Techniques on Communication Systems</q> <hp1>Colloquium
Digest</hp1> <hp2>41</hp2>, pp.1-4
```

Within the text, the citation reference is entered either as an attribute cross-reference of the form:

```
It has been shown <citref refid="Roberts"> that ...
```

if the output system is capable of generating the reference from the entered identifier, or as the contents of the ‹citref› element if the system cannot generate the contents automatically (or if a non-standard form of reference is required) for example:

```
Roberts <citref>1980</citref> has demonstrated ...
```

(If you have any doubts about the ability of your typesetter to generate citation cross-references or you have not yet decided on a publisher or printer, it is advisable to stick to the second form of the citation reference, entering the required text between the start- and end-tags for the ‹citref› element.)

When assigning identifiers to citations or other cross-referenced items, you should always remember that the standard name length (eight characters in the reference concrete syntax) may not be exceeded, and that the first character of each unique identifier must be alphabetic.

The inclusion of a ‹poem› element within the list of elements used in a scientific textbook may seem a bit strange but, as some authors like to quote poetry at the start of parts or chapters (or even elsewhere in the text), this element is a necessary part of any comprehensive DTD. To make the definition as useful as possible the model of a poem is defined as an optional title (‹pt›) followed by one or more verses (‹v›) followed, optionally, by a citation or other reference to the source of the poem (‹cit›).

As with other headings, the presence of the compulsory poem title can be implied by the program. As all the components of a poem title are optional, however, the title need not be present. Where a title is not present the ‹poem› tag should be followed immediately by the compulsory tag for the first verse, for example:

```
<poem><v>
```

To allow for multiple line poem titles, the line element (‹l›) has been declared as a subelement that can be embedded within ‹pt›, in addition to any parsed character data. In this case, it is advisable that the ‹pt› tag be specifically entered in front of the first ‹l› to make it clear that the line is part of the title, not a verse. The end-tags of both the line and poem title elements can, however, be omitted since their presence can be implied by the presence of the start-tag for the first verse, for example:

```
<poem><pt><l>Ode on Byzantium Beauties
<l><hp2>After Horace</hp2>
<v>Byzantium, home of fabled beauties,
<l indented>Unlike any other city,
...
```

Since some poems have numbered verses, a number attribute has been declared for the ‹v› element. To avoid confusion with the number attribute applied to headings or other features, the attribute name has been shortened to no. Though the default value for this attribute is "1", any string of data characters can be assigned as the attribute value, for example ‹v no="15:4"›.

Each verse of the poem is made up of a set of line elements. While the start of the first line can be implied from the start-tag for the verse the ‹l› start-tag should be present for other lines in the poem. The position attribute of the line element can be used to indent alternate lines if desired (see below).

NOTE: Books containing a number of poems will normally have their set of short references extended to allow the program to detect the start or end of lines automatically within poems.

If a citation is required at the end of a poem both its start- and end-tags must be present, but the end-tag for the last verse, like that of the poem, can be implied from the presence of a higher level of element, as the following example shows:

```
...as the following extract illustrates:
<lq><poem><pt><l centred>Fit The Seventh
<l left>THE BANKER'S FATE
<v>They sought it with thimbles, they sought it with care;
<l indented>They pursued it with forks and hope;
<l left>They threatened its life with a railway share;
<l indented>They charmed it with smiles and soap.
<v><l left>And the Banker, inspired with a courage so new
<l indented>It was a matter of general remark,
<l left>Rushed madly ahead and was lost to their view
<l indented>In his zeal to discover the Snark.
<cit>Lewis Carroll, <hp1>The Hunting of the Snark</hp1></cit></lq>
```

This example illustrates two important points about the use of the line element within poems. The addition of the centred attribute value to the first of the line start-tags reminds us that this attribute takes the last used value if not specifically entered. Therefore, to be sure of the position of a line, you should always specifically enter the required attribute value. Secondly, note how, at the start of the first verse, the presence of the line element has been implied from the model. This is only possible here because the current value for the line's position attribute is the correct one. Notice how, at the start of the second verse, the first line has had to be given a line start-tag so that the attribute value can be changed back to left from the previous indented value.

The address element (<adr>), like the verse element, consists of a series of lines. Again, the presence of the first line can be implied, so a typical address would be entered as:

```
<adr>Addison-Wesley Publishers Limited
<l>Finchampstead Road
<l>Wokingham
<l>Berkshire RG11 2NZ</adr>
```

The end-tag of the address element is not required if it is immediately followed by a higher level tag or another address.

C.4.4   Examples and other illustrations

Paragraphs may also require embedded examples (<xmp>), artwork or figures (<fig>). In addition, these elements may be required as freestanding textual elements between paragraphs of text. (Remember that figures are floating elements that can be included at any point in the textbook.)

Because examples may require a number of subelements, the `%copy;`, `%lists;` and `%phrases;` parameter literals have been used in the declaration for the `<xmp>` element to provide access to a suitable set, in addition to any parsed character data (`#PCDATA`) entered for the element. Because `%copy;` includes the `<xmp>` element as well as `<p>`, `<note>`, `<lq>`, `<l>`, `<poem>`, `<table>`, `<adr>`, `<artwork>` and `<eqn>`, the declaration for `<xpm>` also contains an exclusion clause forbidding the use of nested examples within an example.

Three attributes have been associated with the example element:

(1)   `style` allows the style required for the example to be specified in any form likely to be recognized by the text formatting system;

(2)   `keep` allows document preparers to specify the minimum number of lines that must be kept on the first page if the example needs to be split at a page/column boundary; and

(3)   `form` allows users to define whether or not line breaks entered within the example are to be retained in the printed example.

The default values for these attributes indicate that an implied style, as defined by the house style, is to be used, with lines breaks being honoured and all lines kept on the same page. The following example shows how these default values can be overridden to generate a typical lineprinter listing:

```
<xmp style="lineprinter listing" keep="4lines" lines>
Parameter listing as at 12-FEB-88
     Parameter            Value
     Line length          128
     Face                 Pica
     Size                 Normal
     Spacing              1
...
</xmp>
```

In this case, the first four lines of the entered example must be retained on the first page before a break is permitted.

Where the example consists of previously prepared artwork, without any accompanying text, the `<artwork>` element can replace it. (Alternatively, the `<artwork>` element can be a subelement within an example.) The empty artwork element has three attributes associated with it:

(1)   `sizex` to define the width of the artwork,

(2)   a compulsory `sizey` attribute to define its depth, and

(3)   an optional `file` attribute to define where it is stored if it has been prepared electronically.

By default, the horizontal width will be set to the standard text measure (`textsize`). The artwork depth must, however, be specified for each piece of artwork to ensure that sufficient space is left within the textbook.

Typical uses of the ⟨artwork⟩ example include:

```
<p>The following sign must be displayed at all times:
<artwork sizey=50mm file="danger1"></p>

<xmp>Press the key marked <artwork sizex=8mm sizey=4mm>. </xmp>
```

Here, the first piece of artwork (which is 50mm deep) is stored in a file identified by the external entity reference &danger1;. Typically, the declaration for this external entity will, in the DTD, take the form:

```
<!ENTITY danger1 SYSTEM "c:\figs\danger1" >
```

to indicate that, in this case, the relevant file is stored in the directory called `figs` on drive C of the local system.

Where artwork requires a caption or any other form of accompanying text, it should be treated as a figure (⟨fig⟩). A figure consists of a compulsory figure body (⟨figbody⟩) followed by an optional caption (⟨figcap⟩).

Because the figure body is compulsory its start- and end-tags can both be omitted, the start-tag being implied from the presence of the ⟨fig⟩ tag and the end-tag being implied either from the presence of a caption or from the end-tag of the figure itself (which cannot be implied). In contrast, the start-tag for the optional caption must be entered whenever this element is present.

The figure body can contain artwork or general copy elements (including lists) but not headings, topics or references to other figures or tables. Embedded subelements can be used in any order. At least one embedded element must be specified for each figure.

The figure caption can be supplemented by a description (⟨figdesc⟩) where required. When present, this optional subelement must always be entered immediately after the caption. Its presence can be used to imply the end of the ⟨figcap⟩ element, its own end-tag being impliable from the end-tag for the figure (⟨/fig⟩).

Six attributes are associated with the ⟨fig⟩ element:

(1)   `id` can be used to enter a unique identifier that allows cross-reference to the figure from elsewhere in the text,

(2)   `number` can be used for entry of a figure number (where preferred by the author for reference or required by output devices that are not able to generate their own numbers),

(3)   `frame` can be used to frame the figure with a box or top and bottom rules,

(4)   position allows authors to control the position of the figure on the printed page,

(5)   type allows the document designer to specify whether or not the figure is to occupy the whole width of a multicolumn page, and

(6)   align allows authors to specify how the figure is to be aligned with the text of the current column/page.

A further attribute is associated with the ‹figbody› element to allow users to specify whether or not line breaks are to be retained in text entered within the body of the text.

By default, the value of the id attribute will take the form Fa.b, where a is the number of the chapter in which the figure occurs and b is the number of the figure within that chapter (e.g. F9.5 for the fifth figure in Chapter 9). The default value for the frame attribute is none (no framing rules), the alternative values being box and rules. For position, the default value is asfound (i.e. may not be moved from entered position). Alternatively, the figure can be positioned at the top, bottom or middle of the page on which it falls. Figures are normally considered to be full-page illustrations, rather than being restricted to the width of the current text column, and will normally be centred on the text rather than left or right aligned. Any line breaks entered within the figure body will be retained unless the form attribute of the ‹figbody› element is given the value runon (it does not need the attribute name).

The following example shows how a typical figure might be coded:

```
<fig id="Karro" box bottom page centred>
<artwork sizex="140mm" sizey="110mm">
<figcap>The Karro Province (Lower Jurassic) in southern Africa
<figdesc>Black symbols show extent of existing lava remnants
</fig>
```

Here, the artwork (measuring 140 mm × 110 mm) is to be surrounded by a box when it is positioned at the foot of the page. (The page and center attribute values are, strictly speaking, unnecessary since they are the default values for their attributes but their entry does clarify the author's intentions.) Note that the only attribute name entered is that of the id attribute as the other names can be implied from the presence of the relevant value from the specified attribute value list. Also note that the figure has not been numbered by the author – the figure will automatically be numbered on output with the appropriate number for its position.

A figure containing text might be coded as:

```
<fig number="3" rules><figbody runon>
<p>[Refinement rules being applied ...]
<p>20) The number of pack-years of smoking: <l>** 17
```

```
<p>21) The number of years ago that the patient stopped
smoking: <l>** 0
<p>The degree of dyspnoea: <l>** NONE
<figcap>The application of refinement rules
</fig>
```

Here, the author has chosen to number the figures by way of identification (or because the output system being used cannot generate figure numbers). Because the line breaks in the printed text need not coincide with those created during text entry, the start-tag for the figure body element has been specifically entered, with the runon attribute specified. Individual line breaks required within paragraphs have, in this example, been indicated by use of the line element.

C.4.5   Tables

The declarations covering the coding of tables represent, not surprisingly, the most difficult part of the DTD to grasp. As the coding needed for tables can be fairly complex it will often need to be checked carefully before being typeset. For this reason, tables should be prepared as separate files, which can incorporated into the textbook as external entities. Typically, each table file will be identified in the prolog by an external entity declaration of the form:

```
<!ENTITY table1 SYSTEM "b:\figs\table1.ch5">
```

and referred to in the text by an entity reference, for example &table1;.

Figure C.1 illustrates a typical small table, which could be coded as:

```
<table id="results" cols=8>
<nt>5
<ht>Experimental Results
<hc><c>Distance of run (cm)
<hc cols=6><c straddle=6>Time of run (seconds)
<r><c straddle=5>Individual runs<c>Average Time</hc>
<c>The square of the average time (sec&sup2;)
<bt><c><c>1st<c>2nd<c>3rd<c>4th<c>5th
<r>
<r><c>90<c>3.0<c>2.9<c>2.9<c>3.0<c>2.8<c>2.9<c>8.4
<r><c>75<c>2.4<c>2.6<c>2.6<c>2.6<c>2.3<c>2.5<c>6.25
<r><c>60<c>2.3<c>2.4<c>2.2<c>2.2<c>2.3<c>2.3<c>5.3
<r><c>45<c>2.0<c>1.8<c>1.8<c>2.2<c>2.0<c>1.95<c>3.7
</table>
```

Table 5. Experimental results.

Distance of run (cm)	Time of run (seconds)						The square of the average time (sec^2)
	Individual runs					Average time	
	1st	2nd	3rd	4th	5th		
90	3.0	2.9	2.9	3.0	2.8	2.9	8.4
75	2.4	2.6	2.6	2.6	2.3	2.5	6.25
60	2.3	2.4	2.2	2.3	2.3	2.3	5.3
45	2.0	1.8	1.8	2.2	2.0	1.95	3.7

Figure C.1 Example of printed table.

Each table must start with a ‹table› start-tag and end with a matching ‹/table› end-tag. Three attributes can be associated with a table's start-tag:

(1) a unique identifier (id) to allow the table to be cross-referred to by a ‹tableref› element,

(2) a compulsory cols attribute defining the maximum number of columns across the table (including any embedded sub-columns), and

(3) an optional tabs attribute to define the tab points used when preparing the table (where the text is prepared using tabs).

In the absence of an explicit entry, the value for id will be presumed to be Ta.b, where a is the current chapter number and b is a number identifying the sequence of the table within that chapter. The default value for tabs will set the tab points at 10 character intervals.

In the above example the table has the unique identifier results. It has a maximum of eight columns but, because tab points have not been used to space out the entries, the tabs attribute has not been used.

NOTE: The entered tab positions should not represent how the text is to be printed, only how it has been prepared. The typesetter can use this information to reconstruct your table, irrespective of whether it has been prepared using spaces or tab codes to move from column to column.

The Addison-Wesley house style calls for tables to be numbered and captioned at the top of the table. The sequence of subelements within the ‹table› element has therefore been defined in this DTD as:

- optional number of table (‹nt›),
- optional heading for table (‹ht›),

- optional headings for columns (⟨hc⟩),
- body of table (⟨bt⟩>, and
- optional foot of table (⟨ft⟩).

The model for the ⟨nt⟩ element allows the table number to be entered either as straightforward parsed character data or as text containing highlighted phrases. (The Addison-Wesley house style requires the number to be printed in bold, i.e. ⟨hp2⟩.) The word Table will automatically be added to the front of the contents of the ⟨nt⟩ element, so this word does not need to be specified in the embedded text. The end of the table number can be implied from the presence of the following ⟨ht⟩ element, or from the beginning of the table itself.

As the heading for the table may consist of a number of sub-elements, the model for the ⟨ht⟩ element contains the %phrases; and %text; parameter entities, as well as parsed character data and short quotations. This means that table captions can contain multiple paragraphs, lists, notes and even headed topics if required, but not numbered headings. The end-tag for the heading can be omitted.

The ⟨hc⟩ element can be used to define headings for those columns that require them. Each heading is made up of a number of rows (⟨r⟩), the first of which is compulsory (and can, therefore, be implied by the program). While the general-purpose model for the ⟨r⟩ element allows rows to consist of a number of cells (columns), column headings, embedded bodies of table or foot of table elements, two of these elements, ⟨bt⟩ and ⟨ft⟩, should never appear within a heading. This is indicated by the exclusion clause at the end of the declaration for the ⟨hc⟩ element.

The ⟨hc⟩ element, along with the ⟨bt⟩ and ⟨ft⟩ elements, can have an optional cols attribute. This attribute defines the number of columns covered by the heading. By default, the implied value of this attribute is the number of columns yet to be completed in the current row or, if no row has been started, the number of columns in the table.

The coded version of Figure C.1 shows how subheadings can be created within the overall heading by embedding further ⟨hc⟩ elements. The first ⟨hc⟩ element, which contains no cols attribute, indicates that the main heading covers all columns of the table. The start-tag for this element is immediately followed by the start-tag for a cell (⟨c⟩) rather than a row, because the presence of the first ⟨r⟩ in any heading can be implied from the model for ⟨hc⟩. The start-tag for this first cell identifies the start of the heading for the first column of the table.

Once the heading for the first column has been defined, an embedded level of column headings is required to cope with the multiple levels of headings above columns 2 to 7. In this case, the embedded heading extends for only six of the seven columns remaining in the table, so the cols attribute must be used to restrict the width of the embedded heading. (If the subheadings had extended for all the remaining seven columns, the attribute value could have been omitted since it is implied to be the number of columns remaining in the table.)

As with the main ‹hc› element, the presence of the first of the row elements can be implied from the model, the ‹c› element being the first element that needs to be specifically entered. In this case, the first entry in the embedded heading is to straddle all six columns of the embedded heading. This is indicated by use of the optional straddle attribute of the cell tag, whose value indicates the number of consecutive columns the cell is to straddle.

The start of the second row of the embedded heading is indicated by entry of an ‹r› start-tag. The first cell in this row straddles five columns, the next cell heading the remaining column. The end of the embedded multiple level heading is indicated by the ‹/hc› end-tag. This returns the program to the original heading at the end of the seventh column, so the start of the heading for the final column needs to be signalled by another ‹c› start-tag.

Because each heading must be immediately followed by a tag indicating the start of the body of the text, an end-tag is never required for this element.

Like the column headings, the body of the table consists of a number of rows of data, each comprising a number of cells (normally one for each column). Again, the presence of the start-tag for the first of the embedded rows can be implied from the model of ‹bt›, and the end-tag of each row can be implied from the presence of a new row or the end of the body of the table. Within a row, the start of each cell must be identified but the end can be implied by the start of a new cell or row. From the entries for the first row of the above example, note that a blank cell requires a ‹c› tag only if it precedes filled cells. If the blank cell occurs at the end of the row, tags do not need to be entered since the start of a new row indicates that any remaining columns in the preceding row are blank.

No exclusions apply to the use of subelements in the rows entered in the body of the table, so it is possible to have headed subtables within the body of the text – provided your publisher will let you get away with this! Within each cell you can enter most kinds of text and you can even use a special ‹hd› element to define a heading for the entered text. Like the headings of topics, this optional heading can contain only parsed character data or highlighted phrases.

Normally, the foot of table cells either repeat the heading or contain totals for the columns. The model for the ‹ft› element excludes ‹hc› and ‹bt› as elements of an embedded row, but permits embedded ‹ft› elements and cells that straddle columns. As elsewhere in the table, cells in the foot of the table can contain parsed character data with embedded quoted text and highlighted phrases, or any of the main text elements, optionally preceded by a heading.

Where the data in a table does not contain entries that take up more than one line and the SGML parser can be set up to recognize positions within lines, the tabs attribute of the table element can be used to reduce the number of ‹c› elements that need to be entered by the typist. As shown in the following example, the list of numbers entered for this parameter can be used to imply the presence of the start-tags for columns and rows. (The first entry indicates where the ‹r›‹c› combination is required.)

```
<table cols=6 tabs="1 15 25 35 45 55">
<hc>
Product No.   1st Qtr.  2nd Qtr.  3rd Qtr.  4th Qtr.  Year
<bt>
1             14750     12250     14500     15500     57000
2              2000      1500      1750      2250      7500
3             12150     15200      9500     21750     58600
<ft>
Totals        28900     28950     25750     39500    123100
</table>
```

Note that, when this technique is being used, only the start of the first column in each section (heading, body and foot of table) needs to be identified by a specific tag. From its knowledge of the position of the start of each column, the program will be able to imply the following fully tagged version of this table:

```
<table cols=6>
<hc>
<r><c>Product No.<c>1st Qtr.<c>2nd Qtr.<c>3rd Qtr.<c>4th Qtr.<c>Year</r>
</hc><bt>
<r><c>1<c>14750<c>12250<c>14500<c>15500<c> 57000</r>
<r><c>2<c> 2000<c> 1500<c> 1750<c> 2250<c>  7500</r>
<r><c>3<c>12150<c>15200<c> 9500<c>21750<c> 58600</r>
</bt><ft>
<r><c>Totals<c>28900<c>28950<c>25750<c>39500<c>123100</r>
</ft></table>
```

Note how, in expanding the tagging, the program has discarded all spaces between the last character in a column and the start point of the next column, but it has retained spaces placed at the start of each column.

As will be shown shortly, a similar effect can be achieved by use of the tablemap short reference map, which allows the presence of ‹c› tags to be implied from the use of the tab key within a table.

C.4.6   *Cross-references to figures and tables*

The `<figref>` and `<tableref>` elements can be used to provide a cross-reference to figures or tables entered elsewhere in the same document/file, in a way similar to that used for the `<citref>` element. Two attributes are associated with these reference elements:

(1)   `refid` can be used to specify the unique identifier allocated to the figure or table, and

(2)   `page` can be used to request the inclusion of the number of the page on which the figure/table appears in the reference.

Because such references often cross subdocument boundaries (e.g. where the document is stored in a number of files), the default value for the `refid` attribute has been specified using the `#CONREF` keyword. This allows the reference to be specified either explicitly or implicity. If the attribute is present, the table/figure being referenced is in the same file and, therefore, the program can generate the necessary cross-references. Where it is not present, the author must enter the text for the cross-reference as the contents for the attribute. The following examples illustrate the difference between these two approaches:

```
as can be seen in <figref refid="Karro" y> ...
the figures shown in <tableref>Table 7.2</tableref> ...
```

In the first case, the presence of the `refid` attribute tells the program that it is to generate the relevant figure number, while the presence of the keyword `y` (short for yes) tells it that the relevant page number must be added to the reference to give an entry of the form:

```
as can be seen in Figure 4.4 on page 134 ...
```

Note that, when the `refid` attribute is present, no end-tag is permitted for the element since it cannot contain contents, the element automatically being treated as an `EMPTY` element when the `refid` attribute is present. For the table reference, however, the end-tag must be entered as, in this case, no `refid` entry has been specified. In such cases, the element itself must contain the required cross-reference, which can only consist of parsed character data, highlighted phrases and/or quoted text. (It should be noted that embedded citations have been specifically excluded from the list of highlighted phrases that can be embedded within these reference elements.)

C.4.7 Lists

Three types of list are provided for in the sample DTD:

(1)   ordinary lists (`<li>`),

(2)   glossary lists (`<gl>`), and

(3)   lists of terms (`<terms>`).

(The three basic types of list are illustrated in Figure 2.13.)
Ordinary lists can consist of any number of items (`<it>`). Each item can contain parsed character data (`#PCDATA`), optionally interspersed by highlighted phrases and short quotations, or one or more of the larger elements defined by the `%copy;` parameter entity (see Section C.2), including embedded paragraphs and notes. In addition, further levels of list can be requested to any required depth.
Two attributes are associated with the `<li>` element:

(1)   `number` can be used to control the way in which the individual items of the list are to be identified, and

(2)   `form` can be used to control whether or not spaces are to be left between the items in a list (`compact` or `spaced`).

Five options have been provided for the `number` attribute:

(1)   `arabic` to number the items in the list with arabic numbers,

(2)   `roman` to number the items in the list using roman numerals,

(3)   `alpha` to number the items in the list using alphabetic characters (up to a maximum of 26 items),

(4)   `default` to use the default method of marking list items, as defined by the house style being applied (e.g. hyphens, bullets, etc.), and

(5)   `none` to inhibit marking of the start of new items.

By default, items will be marked according to the rules laid down in the house style.
Within the list, each item can be given a unique identifier (`id`) that can be used within an item reference (`<itref>`) to cross-refer to the item. For example, if the fourth item in a list is defined as:

```
<it id="measure">the length of the line
```

the item can be cross-referred to by entering the tag:

```
<itref refid="measure">
```

to generate a reference of the form 'item d) on page 53', where d) is the alphabetic reference number allocated to the item within its list.

Where a page number is not required in an item cross-reference, the letter n can be used as an attribute of the ‹itref› tag to override the default setting of page=y. (The attribute name is not needed: the program can infer it because the attribute value is, by definition, unique to this attribute – see Chapter 6.)

As the following example shows, end-tags are not required for individual items, but must be entered at the end of each list (to ensure that the right level of list is closed down):

```
<p>Two attributes are associated with the list element
<li arabic><hp2>number</hp2> can be used to control the way in
which the individual items of the list are to be identified
<it id="form"><hp2>form</hp2> can be used to control whether
or not spaces are to be left between the items in a list
(<hp2>compact</hp2> or <hp2>spaced</hp2>).</li>
<p>...
```

In this example, the items in the list are to be numbered (1) and (2), respectively, and the second item in the list can be cross-referred to from another point in the book by use of an item reference of the form ‹itref id="form" no›. It should be noted that no start-tag was needed for the first item in the list as the presence of this tag can be implied from the model for ‹li›. (The tag would have to be present if the item required an identifier for cross-reference.)

Where the items in a list nccd hcadings, the glossary list element (‹gl›) should be used. The model for this element indicates that a glossary element consists of an optional heading (‹hd›) followed by any number of glossary terms (‹gt›) and their definitions (‹gd›). There must be at least one definition for each term. Where a number of definitions apply to a term, a glossary definition group can be specified by use of the ‹gdg› tag.

The two attributes associated with the ‹gl› element are:

(1)   form, which can be used to control whether or not spaces are to be left between items in the glossary list (compact or spaced), and

(2)   termhi, which defines the form of highlighting required for glossary terms.

The default value for termhi is 2, indicating that the default form of term highlighting should be the same as that used for highlighted phrases flagged by entry of an ‹hp2› tag.

Glossary terms normally consist of parsed character data (i.e. characters, character references and entity references), optionally including short quotations or highlighted phrases. A unique identifier can be added as an attribute to the ‹gt› tag to allow other definitions to cross-refer to the term. By default, the term itself is implied to be the required unique identifier.

Glossary definitions (‹gd›) can contain either parsed character data interspersed with highlighted phrases and short quotations, any of the larger elements defined by the %copy; parameter entity (paragraphs, notes, lines, examples, artwork, tables, etc.), simple lists (‹li›), references to figures or tables, or any combination of these elements.

Three attributes are associated with the ‹gd› element. The source attribute allows the source of the definition to be entered as a character data (CDATA) string. This attribute has no default value. Where a glossary definition simply cross-refers the reader to the definition entered for another term, the see attribute can be used (in place of the definition copy). Where the definition contains text as well as a cross-reference, the seealso attribute should be used. In both cases, the default value of the attribute is implied to be the last id attribute specifically entered for a glossary term, though this value should not be relied on as the output device may not be capable of remembering it.

The following examples show how attributes are normally used within glossary lists:

```
<gt>Face
<gd see="typeface">
<gt>Facsimile>
<gd seealso="scanner">An image produced at a receiving
station in response to signals sent from a scanner.
<gt>Factor
<gd source="Penguin Dictionary of Computers">
A data element which is one of the operands in an
arithmetical operation.
<gt>...
```

When printed these examples might appear as:

Face
See *typeface*.

Facsimile
An image produced at a receiving station in response to signals sent from a scanner.
See also *scanner*.

Factor
A data element which is one of the operands in an arithmetical operation. (*Penguin Dictionary of Computers*)

Where more than one definition exists for a term, the ‹gdg› element should be used to group the entered definitions. The number attribute

associated with this element can be used to number the entries. The values
that may be specified for this attribute are:

- `arabic` to number the definitions with arabic numbers,
- `roman` to number the definitions using roman numerals,
- `alpha` to number the definitions alphabetically,
- `default` to use the default house style for indicating the start of a new
  definition, and
- `none` to indicate that the start of each definition does not need to be
  specifically marked.

As with lists, the default value for this attribute is `default`, so unless
otherwise specified the house style rules will apply.

As at least one definition must occur in each group of definitions, the
first definition does not need to be preceded by a `<gd>` tag. End-tags are
optional for groups, providing they are followed by another glossary term
(`<gt>`) or by the compulsory end-tag for the list (`</gl>`). A typical glossary
definition group will, therefore, have the form:

```
<gt>Em
<gdg>A space whose width is equal to the current set
width and whose depth is the currently defined point
size
<gd>A unit of measurement equal to an em space. Often
incorrectly used in place of <hp1>pica</hp1> to
represent a space of 12 <hp1>points</hp1> wide. The term
<q>em of set</q> is often used in other books to
distinguish the correct definition when <q>em</q> is
being used for <q>pica</q>.
<gt>...
```

NOTE: The printed version of this entry is shown in Figure 2.13.

The principal difference between a list of terms and a glossary is
that, in the list of terms, the term being defined appears on the same line as
its definition. There are two basic types of list of terms – those with runon
entries of the type shown in Figure 2.13 and those where the term and its
definition appear in different columns, similar to a small table. The `style`
attribute of the `<terms>` element can be used to select which of these styles is
required for a particular list of terms. By default, the list will be set with the
definition(s) runon after the term(s).

Where the `columns` option is selected for the `style` attribute, optional
headings can be defined for the column containing the terms (`<dthd>`) and
that containing the definition descriptions (`<ddhd>`). The model for the `<terms>`

element allows either or both of these optional subelements to be entered immediately after the start-tag for the list.

A style attribute is associated with both of these heading elements to allow users to control whether the headings should be set using roman, bold, italic or roman small capitals (smallcap). The default value for this attribute is roman.

The list of terms consists of any number of defined terms (⟨dt⟩) followed by at least one definition description (⟨dd⟩). Where more than one definition applies to a term, separate descriptions can be used or more than one entry can be combined to form a single ⟨dd⟩ element, depending on the preferred house style. While the only subelements permitted in term names are those for highlighted phrases and quoted text, the definition description can also contain larger embedded copy elements, such as paragraphs and individual lines, as well as references to figures and so on.

Although none of the subelements within a list of terms requires an end-tag, the end of each list of terms must be indicated by entry of a ⟨/terms⟩ end-tag.

A typical list of terms might start:

```
<terms columns>
<dthd>Name<ddhd>Derivation
<dt>ALGOL<dd>Algorithmic Language
<dt>BASIC<dd>Beginner's All-purpose Symbolic Instruction Code
<dt>COBOL<dd>Common Business Oriented Language
<dt>FORTRAN<dd>Formula Translation
<dt>PL1<dd>Programming Language 1
 .
 .
 .
</terms>
```

When printed, the list might appear as:

Name	Derivation
ALGOL	Algorithmic Language
BASIC	Beginner's All-purpose Symbolic Instruction Code
COBOL	Common Business Oriented Language
FORTRAN	Formula Translation
PL1	Programming Language 1

If the definitions were to be run on immediately after the defined terms, the first *two* lines of the above example should be changed to ⟨terms runon⟩ (or just ⟨terms⟩) to produce a list of the form:

ALGOL: Algorithmic Language
BASIC: Beginner's All-purpose Symbolic Instruction Code
COBOL: Common Business Oriented Language
FORTRAN: Formula Translation
PL1: Programming Language 1

C.4.8   Footnotes and index entries

Footnotes should be entered into the text at the point at which they apply, rather than being created as part of a separate file. This ensures that the text of the footnote is always available at the point at which the reference occurs in the printed text.

NOTE: Footnotes are deprecated in the Addison-Wesley ICSS house style.

Typically, a footnote will be entered in the form:

... with a metallic finish⟨fn⟩Optional extra⟨/fn⟩ or ...

Note that no symbol or number has been entered with the footnote text. As the format and position of footnotes depends on house style, the relevant references are generated by the footnote handling program rather than the author/editor. It should also be noted that the ⟨/fn⟩ end-tag for the footnote must always be present (unless replaced by a null end-tag).

       Where a footnote is referred to elsewhere in the text, it can be given a unique identifier by use of the optional id attribute. At the point that the cross-reference is required, a footnote reference is generated by entry of a ⟨fnref⟩ tag with a refid attribute whose value matches the unique identifier of the footnote. As the text for the footnote reference is automatically generated by the program, ⟨fnref⟩ is declared as an EMPTY element and, therefore, requires no end-tag. If the reference should also contain details of the page on which the footnote occurred (e.g. because the footnote numbering sequence is reset at the start of each page/chapter), the attribute page=yes – or just yes – can be added to the tag to override the default value of no.

       As the following example shows, footnote references are perfectly valid within footnotes:

...where permitted⟨fn⟩By the Hague Convention. See also
⟨fnref="pirates" yes⟩⟨/fn⟩ and recognized ...

This example might generate a footnote of the form:

      † By the Hague Convention. See also footnote 1 on page 521

Where the output system being used is capable of automatically generating indexes from entries embedded within the text, such entries should be treated as separate index (`<ix>`) subelements. Index entries, which may only contain parsed character data, can occur at any point in a textbook because this element has been defined as an inclusion for the base document element (see Section C.3). Index entries cannot, however, be nested within other index entries (hence the exclusion at the end of the declaration for the index element).

The attributes which can be associated with the index entry (`<ix>`) element are:

- a unique identifier (`id`) that can be allocated to entries that are referred to by other entries,
- a `print` attribute that can be used to define the contents of an entry where the entry differs from the form used in the text,
- a `linkwith` attribute that allows the contents of the current entry to become a subentry of one or more identified entries,
- an `andwith` attribute that allows the contents of the entry to be output both as an individual entry and as a subentry of one or more identified entries, and
- a `see` attribute to link the current entry to another identified entry by means of a cross-reference containing the word *See*.

By default, the implied value for `id` is the first eight characters of the first word of the entry, while for the `print` attribute it is the index entry itself. The default value of the `linkwith`, `andwith` and `see` attributes is nothing (no links).

To see how these attributes interact, consider the following hypothetical entries in a book:

```
<h0><ix id="bord">Bordeaux</ix>
<p> ...
<h1><ix andwith="bord">Medoc</ix>
<p> ...
<h2><ix see="Appellation Controlee" andwith = "Medoc">
Pauillac</ix>
<p> ...
<h4><ix id="laf" print="Lafite-Rothschild, Ch." andwith="Bord Medoc">
Chateau Lafite-Rothschild
<p> ...
<p>The <ix linkwith="laf">1908</ix> vintage ...
```

Here, the main heading (Bordeaux) is to be referred to by other entries in the index as `bord`. The Medoc subheading is to be indexed both as an entry in its own right and as a subentry for the Bordeaux entry. As no identifier has been specified for this entry, its implied attribute is `id=Medoc`. (This implied identifier is used by the next two entries.)

The next entry shows how it is possible to use a single index entry in two ways. The entry itself is to take the form of a cross-reference, for example Pauillac, *see* Appellation Controlee, but the entry is also required as a subentry for the Medoc entry.

The Chateau Lafite-Rothschild entry, with the unique identifier of laf, appears at three points in the index:

- as a unique Lafite-Rothschild, Ch. entry,
- as a Chateau Lafite-Rothschild subentry to the Bordeaux entry, and
- as a Chateau Lafite-Rothschild subentry to the Medoc entry.

The last of the entries does not appear as an individual entry in the index. Instead, the linkwith attribute has been used to create a subentry for the Lafite-Rothschild, Ch. entry identified by the laf identifier.

It should be stressed, however, that many output systems will not be capable of cross-linking index entries automatically. Before using the linkwith and andwith attributes or implying any identifiers that will be referred to elsewhere, you should, therefore, check with your publisher/typesetter to ensure that they can handle these features during pagination.

C.4.9 Equations

The ‹eqn› element provides a simplified way of entering equations into textbooks. Because not all output devices are able to handle equations in the same way, no hard and fast rules have been laid down in the DTD. Instead, the ‹eqn› element has been defined using the RCDATA reserved word. This means that, as far as the parser is concerned, equations can contain only data characters, entity references and character references, with no embedded markup. This does not mean, however, that equations contain no embedded markup – it simply means that the form of the markup has not been declared within this DTD so the parser will suspend its SGML syntax rules until such time as it encounters the compulsory ‹/eqn› end-tag that closes the equation.

Within the equation element, one of three types of markup can be used:

(1) Addison-Wesley's standard mathematics coding scheme,
(2) Donald Knuth's TEX coding language, and
(3) the British Standard Method for Specifying Electronic Typographic Markup (SETM).

Each of these three options has been declared as a valid notation for use within the ‹eqn› element. Which of the three notations is to be used for a particular element can be controlled by means of the ‹type› attribute associated with ‹eqn›. The three values that this attribute can take are a-w, tex and setm. By default, the Addison-Wesley coding scheme (a-w) will apply so, for instance, to enter a TEX coded equation you must override this default value by adding tex to the ‹eqn› tag to give the embedded equation the form:

```
<eqn tex>\pi(\j_k\varphi_0) = \varphi(0)</eqn>
```

Using SETM notation the same equation would be entered as:

```
<eqn setm>&grp;([i]j[,k][ro]&grf;[,0] = &grf;(0)</eqn>
```

The coding of equations requires a textbook in its own right, so it is not possible to cover the whole subject in this appendix. For further details of the three coding schemes allowed for in this DTD you should, therefore, refer to:

- Addison-Wesley's Guide to Coding Mathematical Equations,
- Donald Knuth's *The TEXBook*, and
- British Standard *Method for Specifying Electronic Typographic Markup (SETM)* (in preparation).

C.5 Preliminary pages (front matter)

The front matter of a book consists of all those preliminary pages that precede the main text. Since the front matter comprises all the data entered between the start-tag for the base document element (‹textbook›) and the compulsory start-tag for the body of the text (‹body›), the presence of both the start- and end-tags for the ‹front› element is optional.

Because the order of the elements found in the front matter of textbooks can vary from book to book, the DTD uses SGML's **and** connector (&) to link the subelements listed in the model. When the %prelims; entity reference is expanded, the elements that make up the front matter element (‹front›) can be seen to be:

- a title page ‹titlep›,
- optionally, one or more pages of publisher's details (‹details›),
- an optional table of contents (‹toc›),
- an optional list of illustrations (‹figlist›),
- optional forewords, prefaces and acknowledgements (‹foreword›, ‹preface› and ‹acknowls›), and
- any other matter required before the main text (‹otherm›).

Between them, these elements (and their embedded subelements) provide a means of coding the preliminary pages of most books, despite the wide variety of forms found in such pages.

As the sequence of elements in a title page varies from book to book, the **and** connector has also been used to link the subelements of this page. The special subelements declared in the model for the title page are:

- ‹title› for the title of the book,
- ‹author› and ‹editor› for the name of the author(s) or editor(s) of the book,
- ‹docnum› for the optional ISBN or alternative document number,
- ‹abstract› (only used in those cases where the abstract appears on the title page itself),
- ‹publishr› for details of the book's publisher, and
- ‹date› for entry of an optional publication date.

In addition, most standard text elements can be used within the title page to enter details not catered for by the other elements of the ‹titlep› element. (Figure 2.11 illustrates why this set of elements has been added to the model for the title page.)

While the titles of many books can be entered in the form of parsed character data, optionally interspersed with quoted text or highlighted phrases, more complex titles may need to be split into a number of lines or into a main title followed (or even preceded) by one or more subtitles. In the case of complex headings, such as that shown in Figure 2.11, it will often be advisable to treat the title most commonly referred by the author/reader as the title line, with other parts of the title being treated as subtitles, for example:

```
<title><subtitle>The Life and Strange Surprizing
Adventures of <tline>Robinson Crusoe <subtitle>of York,
Mariner</title>
```

Two attributes have been associated with the ‹title› element:

(1) htitle to allow the format of the half-title to be defined where it differs from the full title, and

(2) running to allow the version of the title to be used in running head-lines throughout the book to be defined.

By default, both these elements are implied to contain the full version of the title, so any shortened versions must be explicitly entered. In the case illustrated above, the half title read Robinson Crusoe, and no running head was added to each page, so the start-tag for the title should read:

```
<title htitle="Robinson Crusoe" running="">
```

Within the title line element (‹tline›), any line breaks that are felt to be compulsory can be indicated by the presence of line element start-tags, for example:

```
<title><tline>INTRODUCTION <l>TO <l>EXPERT SYSTEMS
```

Note that, even though a subtitle is not required in this example, the ‹tline› element is compulsory here as ‹l› is not a valid element of a title, only of a title line. (This deliberate restriction prevents the use of subelements of the line element within titles that are not explicitly split into lines.) It should also be remembered that the first occurrence of a line element in any document must contain a value for the position attribute. Typically, this will result in the first line of the title being preceded by ‹l centred› rather than having an implied line break as shown above.

Within subtitles, a wider range of subelements has been permitted by use of the %copy; parameter entity within the declaration. This allows complex multiple line/paragraph entries to be defined where required.

The ‹author› and ‹editor› elements each contain two subelements, a compulsory ‹name› element and an optional ‹position› element. Because the ‹name› element is compulsory, neither its start- nor end-tag needs to be entered in the text. To allow the addition of qualifications, etc., the model for ‹name› permits the inclusion of highlighted phrases within the parsed character data of names.

By contrast, the details of the position of the author/editor must be preceded by a ‹position› start-tag. Where more than one position is held the entry can be split into a number of lines by use of the ‹l› element. (If highlighted phrases or quoted text are required in a single line ‹position› entry, the line should also be preceded by ‹l› as these subelements are not specifically included in the model for ‹position›.)

More than one author and/or editor can be specified for a book, as the following example shows:

```
<title>CLIMATES OF THE U.S.S.R.
<author>A. A. BORISOV
<editor>CYRIL A. HALSTEAD
<position>Lecturer in Geography,
<l>University of Glasgow
```

The ‹docnum› element can contain either a document number entered in the form of parsed character data or an ISBN or ISSN entered as character

data within an ‹ISBN› subelement. Because ISBN can contain only character data it must have an end-tag. In most instances, this will take the
form of a null end-tag, the start-tag ending in a matching slash to form a
net-enabling start-tag (refer to Chapter 7 for details of this SGML
feature). The type attribute of the ‹ISBN› element is used to define whether
the embedded number is an ISBN or an ISSN. This attribute defaults to
book to generate an International Standard Book Number but, if it is
changed to serial, an International Standard Serial Number will be
generated. For example:

```
<docnum><ISBN/0-201-17535-5/
```

will generate the sequence ISBN 0-201-17535-5, while:

```
<docnum><ISBN serial/0143-9472/
```

will generate the sequence ISSN 0143-9472.

Because a book may have two ISBN (e.g. for hardback and softback
versions) or an ISBN and an ISSN, the ‹ISBN› tag is repeatable.

Where an abstract is required on the title page, it can be entered
either in the form of parsed character data or with embedded copy
elements (paragraphs, notes, lines, artwork, poems, etc.).

The name of the book's publisher, where not added by the editorial
staff, can be supplemented by any element from the standard set of text
elements. These elements can occur in any order as the group is repeatable. For example, the publisher details shown in Figures 2.8 and 2.11 could
be entered as:

```
<publishr><name>ADDISON-WESLEY PUBLISHING COMPANY
<p>Wokingham, England &middot; Reading, Massachusetts &middot; Menlo Park,
California &middot; New York &middot; Don Mills, Ontario &middot; Amsterdam &middot;
Bonn &middot; Sydney &middot; Singapore &middot; Tokyo &middot; Madrid &middot; San Juan
```

or:

```
<publishr><adr>LONDON<name>The Folio Society
```

If you are entering the publisher details yourself please remember
that there is no letter 'e' in the tag name. (If it did contain the 'e' it would
be more than eight characters long and, therefore, be outside the limits set
for SGML's reference concrete syntax).

To allow for complex date forms, the model for the ‹date› element
allows standard copy elements (such as paragraphs, lines and highlighted
phrases) to be used in place of the normal parsed character date entry. In

most cases, however, the date will be entered exactly as it appears in the book, for example:

```
<date>1988
```

While a lot of options have been provided for use within the title page, it is not necessary to remember all of these as most books will only require a simple subset of these tags. The following example shows how the title page of the ICSS series textbook, illustrated in Figure 2.8, would be coded:

```
<titlep><title>LOCAL AREA NETWORK ARCHITECTURES
<author>David Hutchison
<position>University of Lancaster
<publishr><name>ADDISON-WESLEY PUBLISHING COMPANY
<p>Wokingham, England &middot; Reading, Massachusetts &middot; Menlo Park,
California &middot; New York &middot; Don Mills, Ontario &middot; Amsterdam &middot;
Bonn &middot; Sydney &middot; Singapore &middot; Tokyo &middot; Madrid &middot; San Juan
```

Figure 2.10 illustrated a typical page of publisher's details. Such pages can contain:

- copyright details (<copyrite>),
- one or more dedication (<dedicate>),
- details of the book's ISBN(s), Library of Congress and/or a British Library catalogue reference (<ISBN, <LibCong> or <BLCIP>),
- details about the publisher (<publishr>),
- a printer's colophon (<colophon>), and
- details of related books (<related>).

These elements, which may occur in any order, could be printed on one page or on a number of pages. For example, lists of related publications are often placed on the back of the half-title page, immediately in front of the title page, while dedications seem to occur almost at random in many books. Normally, however, most of these details are printed on the back of the title page.

With the exception of the <publishr> and <ISBN> elements (whose models have been described above) and the <related> element, the elements embedded within a <details> pages can contain parsed character data or one of the embedded subelements defined by the %copy; parameter entity (<p>, <n>, <xmp>, <lq>, <l>, <poem>, <adr>, <artwork> or <eqn>).

The <related> element differs from the other elements, however, in two respects. Firstly, it cannot consist just of parsed character data – one of the elements defined by the %text; parameter entity must precede any text.

Secondly, it is preceded by a heading (‹hd›). Though this heading is not an
optional subelement it does not need to be specifically entered for every list of
related publications because the program can automatically infer the
presence of the initial heading element, while the subelements of the heading
(parsed character data, quoted text or highlighted phrases) are all optional. It
is perfectly permissible, therefore, to start a list of related publications:

```
<related><li><it>Programming in Ada (2nd Edn.)
<it>Software Engineering (2nd Edn.)
...
```

rather than:

```
<related><hd>Selected Titles in the Series:
<li><it>Programming in Ada (2nd Edn.)
<it>Software Engineering (2nd Edn.)
...
```

The table of contents (‹toc›) and list of illustrations (‹figlist›) elements
are, like the ‹index› element, declared in the DTD using the keyword EMPTY for
the model to indicate that no text should be entered within these elements.
In each case, the program will automatically place the list it generates from
entries in the text at the point indicated by the relevant start-tag.

The other elements that optionally make up the preliminary pages of
a textbook – ‹foreword›, ‹preface›, ‹acknowls› and ‹otherm› – all share the declaration
for a chapter or other major text element (‹h1›). As mentioned above for
chapters, the presence of a heading (‹h1t›) is automatically implied for these
elements, though no contents need to be entered for such implied
headings. For forewords, prefaces and acknowledgements, the default
wording output as a heading in response to the relevant start-tag, as
defined for the house style being used, will normally be all that is needed.
Since there will not normally be any text associated with the ‹otherm› start-
tag, however, the relevant heading should be entered immediately after
the start-tag. The end of the hidden heading element will be implied by the
program when it encounters the first of the embedded text elements.
Similarly, the end of the foreword, preface or acknowledgements, etc., can
be implied from the presence of another tag at the same level or by the
presence of the ‹body› tag that identifies the start of the main text.

The number, stitle and id attributes defined for chapters can also, if
required, be associated with preliminary pages, though it is rarely necessary to cross-refer to these pages, and numbering and short titles are
unlikely to be a requirement for such sections.

Typically, a foreword would simply start:

```
<foreword>
<p>...
```

C.6   Ancillary text (back matter)

The back matter of a book consists of those sections that follow the main body of the text. The start of this optional subelement of the base document element (and the end of the main body of the text) should be indicated by entry of the ‹back› start-tag. No end-tag needs to be entered for the back matter, however, as its presence can be implied by the end of the book.

Back matter can consist of any number and combination of:

- appendices (‹appendix›),
- glossaries (‹glossary›),
- bibliographies (‹bibliog›), and
- sections of other matter (‹otherm›)

and a single ‹index› start-tag indicating the point at which the automatically generated index is to be output.

To allow for situations where appendices need to be grouped together, with or without an explanatory piece of text, the declaration for the ‹appendix› element is the same as that for the body of the text. This means that the ‹appendix› start-tag must be followed immediately by either an ‹h0› part heading or by an ‹h1› chapter heading. As with chapters, the headings embedded within the appendix element will be numbered automatically, using the house style laid down by the publisher, but in this case the word Appendix will precede the identifying number or letter, not Chapter. Any heading for the appendix should be entered before the first of the embedded text elements, the presence of the associated ‹h0t› or ‹h1t› heading tag being implied automatically by the program. Typically, a set of appendices will start:

```
<appendix><h1 number="A">Multilingual SGML Documents
<p>...
```

Glossaries and bibliographies are both treated in the same way as chapters, with a hidden title element, which can be blank, being followed by any of the text elements defined for the body of the text. Normally, glossaries will consist of one or more glossary lists (‹gl›), which may be headed, or preceded and/or followed by paragraphs of text. A typical glossary might start:

```
<glossary id="gloss"><p>This glossary ...
<gl><gt>Abstract syntax
<gd>Rules that define how markup is added to the data of
an SGML document, without regard to the specific
characters used to represent the markup
<gt>...
```

For bibliographies, the most commonly embedded element, after the hidden title element, will be the citation element (‹cit›). As citations normally run straight on from the text within which they are embedded, the ‹l› line element should be used within the bibliography to indicate that each citation is to start on a new line. (Alternatively, the bibliogrpahy can be treated as a list, with each citation forming an item in the list.) A typical bibliography might, therefore, start:

```
<bibliog stitle="Bibliography">Cited Publications
<l><cit id="Adams-1976">Adams, J. B. (1976), <q>A
probability model of medical reasoning and the MYCIN
model</q> <hp1>Mathematical Biosciences</hp1>,
<hp2>32</hp2>, 177-186.
<l><cit>...
```

It will be noted from the above examples that the three attributes associated with chapters (stitle‹/ix›, ‹![CDATA[number and id) also apply to ‹glossary› and ‹bibliog›. (Number, however, only needs to be used in those rare books with more than one bibliography or glossary.)

C.7 The short references

Only three short references have been defined in the sample DTD. These allow the start and end of quoted text to be identified from the presence of quotation marks within the relevant elements, and the start of a new column to be indicated by the presence of a tab code within a table.

The first short reference map (quotes) is used, within elements whose models permit embedded quotations, to associate the first quotation mark in the text with the entity &start-qt;. This entity contains the start-tag for the short quotation element (‹q›).

As soon as a quotation has been opened, the second of the short reference maps (endquote) comes into force. This map associates the next quotation mark encountered with the entity &end-qte;. This entity contains the end-tag for the short quotation.

One word of caution is necessary here. Though the model for short quotations permits further levels of embedded short quotations, these must have their start- and end-tags specifically entered, as the presence of embedded quotations cannot be implied from the presence of quotation marks. To see why this is so, consider the following illegally-coded piece of text:

```
... as Robert Burns said <q>And roars out "Weel done,
Cutty-sark"</q>.
```

When the program encounters the first of the above quotation marks the endquote short reference map will be in force because a short quotation has already been started. The endquote short reference map will treat the first quotation mark as the end of the first quotation, returning to the short reference map used for the main text element, quotes. When the second quotation mark is encountered, therefore, a new <q> tag will be generated, giving the fully expanded text the form:

```
... as Robert Burns said <q>And roars out </q>Weel done,
Cutty-sark<q></q>.
```

Obviously, this is incorrect as it will generate:

... as Robert Burns said 'And roars out' Weel done, Cutty-sark''.

One consequence of the general applicability of quote is that whenever a quotation mark (") is required as an element of the text other than a quotation delimiter, as in this sentence, it should be entered in the form of a " character reference to avoid accidentally opening an unwanted short quotation.

The third short reference map defined in this DTD, (tablemap) associates the entity &newcol; with the tab code (&#TAB;) and repeats the mapping of the quotation mark to the start-qt entity to ensure that quoted text is recognized within tables. The &newcol; entity contains the start-tag for a new cell of the table (<c>). The technique used here is very similar to that applied to the use of the tabs attribute of the <table> element; but there is one subtle difference. Where the short reference form of cell identification is used, only one tab code can occur between each cell *and at least one tab code must precede each cell*. To see the implications of this, consider the following table:

```
First Column    Second Column   Third Column</r>
Another entry   Another entry   Another entry</r>
```

If this table is to be coded correctly, the typist must remember to press the tab key before *every* entry. If, instead of pressing the tab key, the gap between columns is created by pressing the space bar, the program will not be able to generate the column tags, even though the screen representation of the table appears to be correct. In particular, it is important that a tab code is used at the start of each row, otherwise the initial <c> tag will not be present.

It should be noted that, in the above example, the start of each row has been implied from the model for the body of the table as this can only consist of a number of rows. Only the end of each row has been identified within the table by use of the ‹/r› end-tag. The only other tag needed in the table is the compulsory ‹bt› tag indicating the beginning of the body of the table.

Where a table containing tab codes has not been consistently coded (e.g. because spaces have been left between some columns or because more than one tab code has been used to move to the start of the next column), tablemap should be switched off by entry of the following declaration at the start of the table:

```
<!USEMAP #EMPTY>
```

This declaration should also be used in any table that uses the tabs attribute to determine the start position of its columns to avoid misinterpretation of any tab codes entered when the table was created.

It should also be noted that, unless the ‹!USEMAP #EMPTY› tag has been included in the table, entry of an unmatched quotation mark within the table will disable the recognition of subsequent tab codes, as a single quotation mark will cause the program to invoke the end-qte map until such time as the end of the quoted text has been identified.

The final short reference map use declaration ensures that, within figures, any short references currently in force are suspended until the end to the figure is detected. This prevents the program from accidentally misinterpreting data within figures.

C.8   Tag nesting ─────────────────────────

The following list shows how tags can be nested when using the sample DTD. All directly nestable tags have been specified in the list, including the floating and index items defined as inclusions to the base document type. Where tags can also contain text, the keywords #PCDATA, CDATA or RCDATA are included in the list as appropriate.

The list does *not* indicate the order in which the nested sub-elements can be used. While the order in which the subelements are listed gives some idea of the basic structure of the DTD, you will need to refer to the DTD to obtain accurate information on permitted nesting sequences.

‹abstract›	#PCDATA ‹p› ‹note› ‹xmp› ‹lq› ‹l› ‹poem› ‹table› ‹adr› ‹artwork› ‹eqn› ‹fig› ‹fn› ‹ix›
‹acknowls›	‹h1t› ‹top1› ‹top2› ‹top3› ‹p› ‹note› ‹xmp› ‹lq› ‹l› ‹poem› ‹table› ‹adr› ‹artwork› ‹eqn› ‹li› ‹gl› ‹terms› ‹h2› ‹fig› ‹fn› ‹ix›
‹adr›	‹l› ‹fig› ‹fn› ‹ix›

`<appendix>`	`<h0> <h1> <fig> <fn> <ix>`
`<artwork>`	`-`
`<author>`	`<name> <position> <fig> <fn> <ix>`
`<back>`	`<appendix> <glossary> <bibliog> <otherm> <index>`
`<bibliog>`	`<h1t> <top1> <top2> <top3> <p> <note> <xmp> <lq> <l> <poem> <table> <adr> <artwork> <eqn> <li> <gl> <terms> <h2> <fig> <fn> <ix>`
`<BLCIP>`	`#PCDATA <p> <note> <xmp> <lq> <l> <poem> <table> <adr> <artwork> <eqn> <fig> <fn> <ix>`
`<body>`	`<h0> <h1> <fig> <fn> <ix>`
`<bt>`	`<r> <fig> <fn> <ix>`
`<c>`	`#PCDATA <q> <hp0> <hp1> <hp2> <hp3> <cit> <hdref> <figref> <tableref> <fnref> <itref> <citref> <hd> <top1> <top2> <top3> <p> <note> <xmp> <lq> <l> <poem> <table> <adr> <artwork> <eqn> <li> <gl> <terms> <fig> <fn> <ix>`
`<cit>`	`#PCDATA <hp0> <hp1> <hp2> <hp3> <cit> <q> <fig> <fn> <ix>`
`<citref>`	`#PCDATA <hp0> <hp1> <hp2> <hp3> <fig> <fn> <ix>`
`<colophon>`	`#PCDATA <p> <note> <xmp> <lq> <l> <poem> <table> <adr> <artwork> <eqn> <fig> <fn> <ix>`
`<copyrite>`	`#PCDATA <p> <note> <xmp> <lq> <l> <poem> <table> <adr> <artwork> <eqn> <fig> <fn> <ix>`
`<date>`	`#PCDATA <p> <note> <xmp> <lq> <l> <poem> <table> <adr> <artwork> <eqn> <fig> <fn> <ix>`
`<dedicate>`	`#PCDATA <p> <note> <xmp> <lq> <l> <poem> <table> <adr> <artwork> <eqn> <fig> <fn> <ix>`
`<details>`	`<copyrite> <publishr> <colophon> <ISBN> <BLCIP> <LibCong> <dedicate> <related> <fig> <fn> <ix>`
`<dd>`	`#PCDATA <q> <hp0> <hp1> <hp2> <hp3> <cit> <hdref> <figref> <tableref> <fnref> <itref> <citref> <p> <note> <xmp> <lq> <l> <poem> <table> <adr> <artwork> <eqn> <fig> <fn> <ix>`
`<ddhd>`	`#PCDATA <fig> <fn> <ix>`
`<docnum>`	`#PCDATA <ISBN> <fig> <fn> <ix>`
`<dt>`	`#PCDATA <hp0> <hp1> <hp2> <hp3> <cit> <q> <fig> <fn> <ix>`
`<dthd>`	`#PCDATA <fig> <fn> <ix>`
`<editor>`	`<name> <position> <fig> <fn> <ix>`
`<eqn>`	`RCDATA`
`<fig>`	`<figbody> <figcap> <figdesc> <fig> <fn> <ix>`
`<figbody>`	`<p> <note> <xmp> <lq> <l> <poem> <table> <adr> <artwork> <eqn> <li> <gl> <terms>`

`<figcap>`	#PCDATA `<hp0>` `<hp1>` `<hp2>` `<hp3>` `<cit>` `<fig>` `<fn>` `<ix>`
`<figdesc>`	#PCDATA `<p>` `<note>` `<xmp>` `<lq>` `<l>` `<poem>` `<table>` `<adr>` `<artwork>` `<eqn>` `<li>` `<gl>` `<terms>` `<fig>` `<fn>` `<ix>`
`<figlist>`	–
`<figref>`	#PCDATA `<hp0>` `<hp1>` `<hp2>` `<hp3>` `<fig>` `<fn>` `<ix>`
`<fn>`	#PCDATA `<q>` `<hp0>` `<hp1>` `<hp2>` `<hp3>` `<cit>` `<hdref>` `<figref>` `<tableref>` `<fnref>` `<itref>` `<citref>` `<p>` `<note>` `<xmp>` `<lq>` `<l>` `<poem>` `<table>` `<adr>` `<artwork>` `<eqn>` `<li>` `<gl>` `<terms>` `<fig>` `<fn>` `<ix>`
`<fnref>`	–
`<foreword>`	`<h1t>` `<top1>` `<top2>` `<top3>` `<p>` `<note>` `<xmp>` `<lq>` `<l>` `<poem>` `<table>` `<adr>` `<artwork>` `<eqn>` `<li>` `<gl>` `<terms>` `<h2>` `<fig>` `<fn>` `<ix>`
`<front>`	`<titlep>` `<details>` `<toc>` `<figlist>` `<preface>` `<foreword>` `<acknowls>` `<otherm>` `<fig>` `<fn>` `<ix>`
`<ft>`	`<r>` `<fig>` `<fn>` `<ix>`
`<gd>`	#PCDATA `<p>` `<note>` `<xmp>` `<lq>` `<l>` `<poem>` `<table>` `<adr>` `<artwork>` `<eqn>` `<li>` `<q>` `<hp0>` `<hp1>` `<hp2>` `<hp3>` `<cit>` `<hdref>` `<figref>` `<tableref>` `<fnref>` `<itref>` `<citref>` `<fig>` `<fn>` `<ix>`
`<gdg>`	`<gd>` `<fig>` `<fn>` `<ix>`
`<gl>`	`<hd>` `<gt>` `<gd>` `<gdg>` `<fig>` `<fn>` `<ix>`
`<glossary>`	`<h1t>` `<top1>` `<top2>` `<top3>` `<p>` `<note>` `<xmp>` `<lq>` `<l>` `<poem>` `<table>` `<adr>` `<artwork>` `<eqn>` `<li>` `<gl>` `<terms>` `<h2>` `<fig>` `<fn>` `<ix>`
`<gt>`	#PCDATA `<q>` `<hp0>` `<hp1>` `<hp2>` `<hp3>` `<cit>` `<fig>` `<fn>` `<ix>`
`<h0>`	`<h0t>` `<top1>` `<top2>` `<top3>` `<p>` `<note>` `<xmp>` `<lq>` `<l>` `<poem>` `<table>` `<adr>` `<artwork>` `<eqn>` `<li>` `<gl>` `<terms>` `<h1>` `<fig>` `<fn>` `<ix>`
`<h0t>`	#PCDATA `<q>` `<hp0>` `<hp1>` `<hp2>` `<hp3>` `<cit>` `<fig>` `<fn>` `<ix>`
`<h1>`	`<h1t>` `<top1>` `<top2>` `<top3>` `<p>` `<note>` `<xmp>` `<lq>` `<l>` `<poem>` `<table>` `<adr>` `<artwork>` `<eqn>` `<li>` `<gl>` `<terms>` `<h2>` `<fig>` `<fn>` `<ix>`
`<h1t>`	#PCDATA `<q>` `<hp0>` `<hp1>` `<hp2>` `<hp3>` `<cit>`
`<h2>`	`<h2t>` `<top1>` `<top2>` `<top3>` `<p>` `<note>` `<xmp>` `<lq>` `<l>` `<poem>` `<table>` `<adr>` `<artwork>` `<eqn>` `<li>` `<gl>` `<terms>` `<h3>` `<fig>` `<fn>` `<ix>`
`<h2t>`	#PCDATA `<q>` `<hp0>` `<hp1>` `<hp2>` `<hp3>` `<cit>` `<fig>` `<fn>` `<ix>`
`<h3>`	`<h3t>` `<top1>` `<top2>` `<top3>` `<p>` `<note>` `<xmp>` `<lq>` `<l>` `<poem>` `<table>` `<adr>` `<artwork>` `<eqn>` `<li>` `<gl>` `<terms>` `<h4>` `<fig>` `<fn>` `<ix>`
`<h3t>`	#PCDATA `<q>` `<hp0>` `<hp1>` `<hp2>` `<hp3>` `<cit>` `<fig>` `<fn>` `<ix>`
`<h4>`	`<h4t>` `<top1>` `<top2>` `<top3>` `<p>` `<note>` `<xmp>` `<lq>` `<l>` `<poem>` `<table>` `<adr>` `<artwork>` `<eqn>` `<li>` `<gl>` `<terms>` `<h5>` `<fig>` `<fn>` `<ix>`
`<h4t>`	#PCDATA `<q>` `<hp0>` `<hp1>` `<hp2>` `<hp3>` `<cit>` `<fig>` `<fn>` `<ix>`
`<h5>`	`<h5t>` `<top1>` `<top2>` `<top3>` `<p>` `<note>` `<xmp>` `<lq>` `<l>` `<poem>` `<table>` `<adr>` `<artwork>` `<eqn>` `<li>` `<gl>` `<terms>` `<fig>` `<fn>` `<ix>`

`<h5t>`	`#PCDATA <q> <hp0> <hp1> <hp2> <hp3> <cit> <fig> <fn> <ix>`
`<hc>`	`<r> <fig> <fn> <ix>`
`<hd>`	`#PCDATA <q> <hp0> <hp1> <hp2> <hp3> <cit> <fig> <fn> <ix>`
`<hdref>`	`#PCDATA <hp0> <hp1> <hp2> <hp3> <cit> <fig> <fn> <ix>`
`<hp0>`	`#PCDATA <hp0> <hp1> <hp2> <hp3> <cit> <q> <fig> <fn> <ix>`
`<hp1>`	`#PCDATA <hp0> <hp1> <hp2> <hp3> <cit> <q> <fig> <fn> <ix>`
`<hp2>`	`#PCDATA <hp0> <hp1> <hp2> <hp3> <cit> <q> <fig> <fn> <ix>`
`<hp3>`	`#PCDATA <hp0> <hp1> <hp2> <hp3> <cit> <q> <fig> <fn> <ix>`
`<ht>`	`#PCDATA <q> <hp0> <hp1> <hp2> <hp3> <cit> <top1> <top2> <top3> <p> <note> <xmp> <lq> <l> <poem> <table> <adr> <artwork> <eqn> <li> <gl> <terms> <fig> <fn> <ix>`
`<index>`	`—`
`<ISBN>`	`CDATA`
`<it>`	`#PCDATA <p> <note> <xmp> <lq> <l> <poem> <table> <adr> <artwork> <eqn> <li> <q> <hp0> <hp1> <hp2> <hp3> <cit> <fig> <fn> <ix>`
`<itref>`	`—`
`<ix>`	`#PCDATA <fig> <fn> <ix>`
`<l>`	`#PCDATA <q> <hp0> <hp1> <hp2> <hp3> <cit> <hdref> <figref> <tableref> <fnref> <itref> <citref> <fig> <fn> <ix>`
`<li>`	`<it> <fig> <fn> <ix>`
`<LibCong>`	`#PCDATA <p> <note> <xmp> <lq> <l> <poem> <table> <adr> <artwork> <eqn> <fig> <fn> <ix>`
`<lq>`	`#PCDATA <top1> <top2> <top3> <p> <note> <xmp> <lq> <l> <poem> <table> <adr> <artwork> <eqn> <li> <gl> <terms> <h2> <h3> <h4> <h5> <fig> <fn> <ix>`
`<name>`	`#PCDATA <hp0> <hp1> <hp2> <hp3> <cit> <fig> <fn> <ix>`
`<note>`	`#PCDATA <hp0> <hp1> <hp2> <hp3> <cit> <q> <xmp> <lq> <l> <poem> <table> <adr> <artwork> <eqn> <li> <gl> <terms> <hdref> <figref> <tableref> <fnref> <itref> <citref> <p> <fig> <fn> <ix>`
`<nt>`	`#PCDATA <hp0> <hp1> <hp2> <hp3> <cit> <fig> <fn> <ix>`
`<otherm>`	`<h1t> <top1> <top2> <top3> <p> <note> <xmp> <lq> <l> <poem> <table> <adr> <artwork> <eqn> <li> <gl> <terms> <h2> <fig> <fn> <ix>`

<p>   #PCDATA <hp0> <hp1> <hp2> <hp3> <cit> <q> <xmp> <lq> <l> <poem> <table>
                          <adr> <artwork> <eqn> <li> <gl> <terms> <hdref> <figref> <tableref>
                          <fnref> <itref> <citref> <fig> <fn> <ix>

<poem>   <pt> <v> <cit> <fig> <fn> <ix>

<position>   #PCDATA <l> <fig> <fn> <ix>

<preface>   <h1t> <top1> <top2> <top3> <p> <note> <xmp> <lq> <l> <poem> <table>
                          <adr> <artwork> <eqn> <li> <gl> <terms> <h2> <fig> <fn> <ix>

<pt>   #PCDATA <hp0> <hp1> <hp2> <hp3> <cit> <q> <l> <fig> <fn> <ix>

<publishr>   <name> <top1> <top2> <top3> <p> <note> <xmp> <lq> <l> <poem> <table>
                          <adr> <artwork> <eqn> <li> <gl> <terms> <fig> <fn> <ix>

<q>   #PCDATA <q> <hp0> <hp1> <hp2> <hp3> <cit> <hdref> <figref> <tableref>
                          <fnref> <itref> <citref> <fig> <fn> <ix>

<r>   <c> <hc> <bt> <ft> <fig> <fn> <ix>

<related>   <hd> <p> <note> <xmp> <lq> <l> <poem> <table> <adr> <artwork> <eqn> <fig>
                          <fn> <ix>

<subtitle>   #PCDATA <p> <note> <xmp> <lq> <l> <poem> <table> <adr> <artwork> <eqn>
                          <fig> <fn> <ix>

<table>   <nt> <ht> <hc> <bt> <ft> <fig> <fn> <ix>

<tableref>   #PCDATA <hp0> <hp1> <hp2> <hp3> <fig> <fn> <ix>

<terms>   <dthd> <ddhd> <dt> <dd> <fig> <fn> <ix>

<textbook>   <front> <body> <back> <fig> <fn> <ix>

<th>   #PCDATA <q> <hp0> <hp1> <hp2> <hp3> <cit> <fig> <fn> <ix>

<title>   #PCDATA <l> <q> <hp0> <hp1> <hp2> <hp3> <cit> <fig> <fn> <ix>

<titlep>   <title> <author> <editor> <docnum> <date> <publishr> <top1>
                          <top2> <top3> <p> <note> <xmp> <lq> <l> <poem> <table> <adr> <artwork>
                          <eqn> <li> <gl> <terms> <fig> <fn> <ix>

<tline>   #PCDATA <l> <fig> <fn> <ix>

<toc>   —

<top1>   <th> <p> <note> <xmp> <lq> <l> <poem> <table> <adr> <artwork> <eqn> <li>
                          <gl> <terms> <top2> <fig> <fn> <ix>

<top2>   <th> <p> <note> <xmp> <lq> <l> <poem> <table> <adr> <artwork> <eqn> <li>
                          <gl> <terms> <top3> <fig> <fn> <ix>

<top3>   <th> <p> <note> <xmp> <lq> <l> <poem> <table> <adr> <artwork> <eqn> <li>
                          <gl> <terms> <fig> <fn> <ix>

<v>   <l> <fig> <fn> <ix>

<xmp>   #PCDATA <p> <note> <xmp> <lq> <l> <poem> <table> <adr> <artwork> <eqn>
                          <li> <gl> <terms> <fig> <fn> <ix> <hp0> <hp1> <hp2> <hp3> <hp3> <cit>

C.9 Alphabetical list of tags

The following table lists each element defined in this DTD in alphabetical order, together with the attributes that can be optionally associated with the element's start-tag:

`<abstract>`	Abstract of contents
`<acknowls>`	Acknowledgements
	`number` = number†
	`id` = unique identifier for cross-references†
	`stitle` = short version of title†
`<adr>`	Address
`<appendix>`	Appendices to main body of text
	`number` = number
	`id` = unique identifier for cross-references
	`stitle` = short version of title
`<artwork>`	Space for insertion of artwork
	`sizex` = width of artwork
	`sizey` = depth of artwork††
	`file` = name of file containing artwork
`<author>`	Author of publication
`<back>`	Matter at back of document (after body of text)
`<bibliog>`	Bibliography
	`number` = number†
	`id` = unique identifier for cross-references
	`stitle` = short version of title†
`<BLCIP>`	British Library Cataloguing in Publication data
`<body>`	Main body of text
`<bt>`	Body of table
	`cols` = number of columns
`<c>`	Cell of table row
	`straddle` = number of columns cell straddles
`<cit>`	Citation (reference to another publication)
	`id` = unique identifier for cross-references
`<citref>`	Citation references§
	`refid` = referred to unique identifier
	`page` = yes to add page number to reference
`<colophon>`	Printer's colophon
`<copyrite>`	Copyright details
`<date>`	Date of publication
`<dedicate>`	Dedication of book

‹details›   Publication details not on title page

‹dd›   Description of defined term

‹ddhd›   Heading for definition column
                    style = type style for heading

‹docnum›   Number or other unique identifier of document

‹dt›   Defined term
                    id = unique identifier for cross-references

‹dthd›   Heading for defined terms column
                    style = type style for heading

‹editor›   Editor of publication

‹eqn›   Equation
                    type = type of notation used to markup equation

lf30›fig›

                Figure
                    id ‑ unique identifier for cross-references
                    number = figure number (if not generated)
                    frame = type of frame for figure (box or rules)
                    position = position on page (top, bottom, etc.)
                    type = column if only to have single column width
                    align = type of alignment (left, right or centred)

‹figbody›   Body of figure
                    form = runon if entered lines to be run on

‹figcap›   Caption for figure

‹figdesc›   Description of figure

‹figlist›   Position of list of figures§

‹figref›   Cross-reference to figure§
                    refid = referred to unique identifier
                    page = yes to add page number to reference

‹fn›   Footnote
                    id = unique identifier for cross-references

‹fnref›   Cross-reference to footnote§
                    refid = referred to unique identifier††
                    page = yes to add page number to reference

‹foreword› Foreword
                    number = number†
                    id = unique identifier for cross-references
                    stitle = short version of title†

‹front›   Front matter of book

‹ft›   Foot of table
                    cols = number of columns covered

<gd>   Definition of glossary term
                 source = source of definition
                 see = cross-reference to other definition
                 seealso = link to further definition

<gdg>   Group of glossary definitions
                 number = form of numbering required

<gl>   Glossary list
                 form = compact if no space between entries
                 termhi = level of highlighting for terms

<glossary> Start of glossary
                 number = number†
                 id = unique identifier for cross-references
                 stitle = short version of title†

<gt>   Glossary term
                 id = unique identifier for cross-references

<h0>   Highest division of text (e.g. part of book)
                 number = number
                 id = unique identifier for cross-references
                 stitle = short version of title

<h0t>   Part title (compulsory, hidden tag)

<h1>   Main division of text (e.g. chapter of book)
                 number = number
                 id = unique identifier for cross-references
                 stitle = short version of title

<h1t>   Chapter title (compulsory, hidden tag)

<h2>   Section within main division
                 number = number
                 id = unique identifier for cross-references
                 stitle = short version of title

<h2t>   Section title (compulsory, hidden tag)

<h3>   Subsection within main section
                 number = number
                 id = unique identifier for cross-references
                 stitle = short version of title

<h3t>   Subsection title (compulsory, hidden tag)

<h4>   Sub-subsection within subsection
                 number = number
                 id = unique identifier for cross-references
                 stitle = short version of title

<h4t>   Sub-subsection title (compulsory, hidden tag)

\<h5\>	Lowest level of numbered heading
	number = number
	id = unique identifier for cross-references
	stitle = short version of title
\<h5t\>	Low level title (compulsory, hidden tag)
\<hc\>	Heading for table columns
	cols = number of columns covered (if less than the number remaining)
\<hd\>	Other type of heading
	id = unique identifier for cross-references
\<hdref\>	Cross-reference to heading§
	refid = referred to unique identifier††
	page = yes to add page number to reference
\<hp0\>	Highlighted phrase, style 0
\<hp1\>	Highlighted phrase, style 1
\<hp2\>	Highlighted phrase, style 2
\<hp3\>	Highlighted phrase, style 3
\<ht\>	Heading of table
\<index\>	Position of index§
\<ISBN\>	International Standard Book (or Serial) Number
	type = serial for ISSN number
\<it\>	Item in list
	id = unique identifier for cross-references
\<itref\>	Cross-reference to item in list§
	refid = referred to unique identifier††
	page = yes to add page number to reference
\<ix\>	Index entry
	id = unique identifier for cross-references
	print = printed form of entry
	linkwith = entry this entry is to be listed under
	andwith = entry this entry is also to be listed under
	see = cross-reference to other definition
\<l\>	Line of text
	position = position within measure
\<li\>	List
	number = type of numbering required
	form = compact if no space between items
\<LibCong\>	Library of Congress Cataloguing in Publication data
\<lq\>	Long quotation (indented, starting on new line)
\<name\>	Name of author/editor

<note>   Note

<nt>   Number of table

<otherm>   Other matter within preliminary pages
            number = number†
            id = unique identifier for cross-references
            stitle = short version of title†

<p>   Paragraph of text

<poem>   One or more verses of poetry

<position> Position held by author/editor

<preface> Preface
            number = number†
            id = unique identifier for cross-references
            stitle = short version of title†

<pt>   Poem title

<publishr> Publisher's details

<q>   Quotation within text

<r>   Row in table

<related>   Related publications

<subtitle> Subtitle of document

<table>   Table within text, etc.
            id = unique identifier for cross-references
            cols = maximum number of columns in table
            tabs = string defining tab positions used

<tableref> Cross-reference to table§
            refid = referred to unique identifier
            page = yes to add page number to reference

<terms>   List of term definitions
            style = columns if terms and definitions to be in different
            columns

<textbook> Name of main document type (used at start of document)
            version = version number or date
            status = status of document (e.g. draft or final)
            security = security classification

<th>   Topic heading

<title>   Title of document
            htitle = alternative form of half-title
            running = alternative form for running headline

<titlep>   Title page

<tline>   Line within document title

‹toc›   Position of table of contents§

‹top1›   First level topic
               id = unique identifier for cross-references

‹top2›   Second level topic
               id = unique identifier for cross-references

‹top3›   Third level topic
               id = unique identifier for cross-references

‹v›   Verse of poem
               no = number of verse

‹xmp›   Example
               style = agreed name of required format
               keep = number of lines to be kept on first page
               form = runon to ignore line endings in example

---

† Rarely used attribute
†† Compulsory attribute
§ Contents may be automatically generated by program

Index

In the index, references to sections are indicated by pairs of numbers linked by a dash (e.g. 101–113) and references to SGML terminology that are highlighted in the text are printed in bold (e.g. **234**).